Federal Banking Law and Regulations

A Handbook for Lawyers

Harding de C. Williams

ABA Section of
BUSINESS LAW

ABA
Defending Liberty
Pursuing Justice

The materials contained herein represent the opinions of the authors and editors and should not be construed to be the action of the American Bar Association or the Section of Business Law unless adopted pursuant to the bylaws of the Association.

Nothing contained in this book is to be considered as the rendering of legal advice for specific cases, and readers are responsible for obtaining such advice from their own legal counsel. This book is intended for educational and informational purposes only.

©2006 by the American Bar Association
All rights reserved.
Printed in the United States of America.
1-59031-473-5

Library of Congress Cataloging-in-Publication Data

De C. Williams, Harding.
    Federal banking law and regulations: a handbook for
      lawyers / Harding de C. Williams.
        p. cm.
    Includes index.
    ISBN-13: 978-1-59031-473-9 (pbk.: alk. paper)
    ISBN-10: 1-59031-473-5 (alk. paper)
  1. Banking law—United States. I. American Bar Association. Section of Business Law. II. Title.

KF969 2006
346.73'082—dc22

2006018115

Discounts are available for books ordered in bulk. Special consideration is given to state and local bars, CLE programs, and other bar-related organizations. Inquire at Book Publishing, American Bar Association, 321 North Clark Street, Chicago, IL 60610.

09 08 07 06 5 4 3 2 1

Contents

Acknowledgments ix
Introduction xi

> Chapter 1 **A Brief History of Banking Regulation** 1
> Introduction 1
> Early History 1
> Savings Institutions 4
> The 1930s 11
> Subsequent Developments 16
> Bank and S&L Holding Companies 21
> Preemption 27
>
> Chapter 2 **Deposit Insurance** 35
> Federal Deposit Insurance before the Reform Act 36
> Premium Disparity 37
> The "Free Ride" and Other Issues 39
> Basic Provisions of the Reform Act 41
> Basic Deposit Insurance Coverage 44
>
> Chapter 3 **Examinations, Enforcement, Conservatorships, and Receiverships** 49
> Conduct of Examinations 49
> Coordination of Examinations of State Institutions 59
> Examination of Holding Companies 65
> Receiverships and Conservatorships 73
> Resolution of Banks and Savings Associations during the Financial Crisis of 1980–1994 79
> Enforcement 82

iv Contents

Chapter 4	**Branches and Interstate Banking** 97	

Introduction 97
Bank Branching and Merger Laws Prior
   to Riegle-Neal I 98
Interstate Activity before 1994 102
Interstate Branching for Banks 103
Interstate Acquisitions by Bank Holding
   Companies 112
Non-Branch Facilities 114
Branching Laws Applicable to Savings Associations 117

Chapter 5	**Holding Companies** 121	

Early Holding Company Developments 121
Bank Holding Companies 122
Savings and Loan Holding Companies 127
S&L Holding Companies after GLBA 129
"Nonbank" Holding Companies 131
Financial Holding Companies 136
Mutual Holding Companies 141
Change in Control 142
Pre-GLBA Insurance Activities of National Banks 146
Post-GLBA Insurance Activities
   of National Banks 148
Insurance Activities of Savings Associations 149
Standards for Preemption of State
   Insurance Laws 149
The McCarran-Ferguson Act 150
Preemption of State Laws 151
State Anti-Affiliation Laws 151
State Laws Restricting Insurance Activities 152
Dispute Resolution 153
Other Provisions 154
"NARAB" 155
Post GLBA Developments 156

Chapter 6	**Four Policies Applicable to All Institutions** 159	

Introduction 159
Transactions with Affiliates 160
Exportation and Other Interest Rate Issues 172
Most Favored Lender Laws 173
Insider Loans 178
Tying Arrangements 184

Contents   v

Chapter 7 **Subsidiaries   193**
Introduction   193
Principal Kinds of Financial Institution
    Subsidiaries   194
Principal Subsidiaries of National Banks   195
Subsidiaries of State Banks   199
Financial Subsidiaries of National
    and State Banks   201
Subsidiaries of Savings Associations   208

Chapter 8 **Corporate Governance Rules   217**
Introduction   217
Federally Chartered Institutions   217
Directors' Qualifications and Duties   219
Notice of Change of Director or Senior Executive
    Officer   221
Director and Other Interlocks   222

Chapter 9 **Audits, Audit Committees,
and Financial Reporting   229**
Introduction   229
Audit Procedures and Standards   231
Application of the Sarbanes-Oxley Reporting
    and Auditing Rules to Listed Companies   233

Chapter 10 **Securities Activities of Banks   253**
Introduction   253
Financial Institutions as Issuers of Stock   253
Common Trust Funds   281
Securities Registration and Reporting
    under State Laws   287

Chapter 11 **Capital   291**
Background   291
Capital Standards for Banks and Savings
    Associations   295
Regulatory Capital for Holding Companies   302
Prompt Corrective Action   308
The Basel II Project   313
Structure of the Revised Basel Framework   319

Index   343

About the Author   361

List of Figures

Figure 1.1 Jurisdictions of Primary Federal Regulators and State Banking Departments   26

Figure 1.2 Chartering Agencies, Primary and Secondary Federal Regulators of Insured Depository Institutions   27

Figure 1.3 National Totals—Number of Institutions by Charter Class and Total Deposits June 20, 1995–June 30, 2005   28

Figure 1.4 Increase/Decrease in Number, Offices, and Deposits of Commercial Banks and Savings Institutions June 20, 1995–June 30, 2005   29

Figure 2.1 BIF and SAIF Assessment Schedules First Half of 2006   38

Figure 2.2 Assessment Base Distribution of Well-Capitalized Institutions by Percentage of Institutions and Percentage of Insured Funds As of December 31, 2004   41

Figure 3.1 Methods Used by the FDIC to Resolve Failing Banks during the Financial Crisis of 1980–1994   81

Figure 5.1 Bank and S&L Holding Companies Primary Federal Regulators and Applicable Regulations   126

Figure 7.1 Permissible Activities of Operating Subsidiaries of National Banks (12 CFR § 5.34)   197

List of Figures

Figure 8.1   Banking Laws Relating to Directors of National Banks, Federal Savings Associations, and Mutual S&L Holding Companies   218

Figure 8.2   Federal Reserve Board   226

Figure 8.3   Agency Guidance on Director's Duties   227

Figure 10.1   Agency Regulations Providing Registration Exemptions for Bank Securities   263

Figure 10.2   Administration of Exchange Act Sections   267

Figure 10.3   Section 12(i) Reporting for Institutions Subject to Registration under Sections 12(b) and 12(g) of the Securities Exchange Act of 1934   267

Figure 11.1   Risk-Based Capital Ratios   296

Figure 11.2   Basel II Transition Period   319

Figure 11.3   Calculation of Regulatory Capital for Banks   331

Figure 11.4   Calculation of Regulatory Capital for Savings Associations   339

Acknowledgments

The people listed below have provided invaluable assistance in many different ways to this project and they have my appreciation and thanks. It goes without saying that any errors and misinterpretations in this book are mine alone.

>Kate Anderson, Senior Editorial Consultant
>Charlotte M. Bahin, Partner, Lord Bissell & Brook LLP, Former Senior Regulatory Counsel, America's Community Bankers
>Christopher M. Cole, Regulatory Counsel, Independent Community Bankers of America
>Michael W. Hsu, Managing Editor of Legal and Regulatory Publications, America's Community Bankers
>Rebecca H. Laird, partner, Kirkpatrick & Lockhart Nicholson Graham LLP
>Tom Leahey, formerly in private practice in banking and securities law in Washington
>Sarah Miller, General Counsel, ABA Securities Association
>Richard J. Perry, Jr., Chief Operating Officer and General Counsel, Hovde Financial, Inc.
>Krista J. Shonk, Regulatory Counsel, America's Community Bankers
>Paul Smith, American Bankers Association
>Michael L. Stevens, Vice President and Director, Regulatory Affairs, Conference of State Bank Supervisors
>Jesse Stiller, OCC Historian (Special Advisor for Executive Communications)
>Mark J. Tenhundfeld, Director, Office of Regulatory Policy, American Bankers Association

Karen M. Thomas, Executive Vice President for Government Relations, Independent Community Bankers of America

Kathleen E. Topelius, Partner, Bryan Cave LLP

Rob Updegrove, Administrative Librarian, IS&MS/Library, Office of the Comptroller of the Currency

Introduction

The idea for this book occurred to me while I was writing and updating a book for bank directors several years ago. It was well received, and it seemed to me that there might be a wider audience for a book with less emphasis on governance and more on how institutions with different charters are regulated and how the bank regulatory structure came to be what it is today.

The book is designed to make some sense for readers unfamiliar with banking law of a regulatory system that involves institutions with at least eight different federal or state charters (not counting credit unions) and three kinds of holding companies, regulated by one of four federal agencies and, for state-chartered institutions, by one of 50 state banking agencies as well. It also covers some of the principal historic, political, and economic developments that have shaped the current system as it has evolved since the creation of the first contemporary federal banking agency, the Office of the Comptroller of the Currency, in 1863.

A book of this kind obviously omits more than it includes. It does not deal with how to run a bank, for example, but emphasizes the kinds of activities in which banks may, and may not, engage, either directly, or through subsidiaries and affiliates. In any case, I hope that what is included will be a useful guide for readers who are encountering the banking system for the first time.

CHAPTER **1**

A Brief History of Banking Regulation

Introduction

Federal bank regulation as it has evolved since the creation of the national banking system in 1863 is divided among several agencies in an overlapping and often confusing pattern that does not lend itself to neat divisions on an organization chart. This regulatory structure reflects the diversity and strength of the U.S. banking system and the way it has been shaped by political and market forces since colonial times.

This chapter is designed to give readers unfamiliar with federal banking law a sense of some of the events that shaped the history and current regulatory structure.

Early History

National Banks

The first contemporary federal banking agency, the Office of the Comptroller of the Currency (OCC) was created by legislation signed on February 23, 1863, generally referred to as the Currency Act of 1863. The OCC was created as an Office in the Treasury Department to charter and supervise national banks and to regulate the distribution of currency these banks were authorized to issue.[1] The first national bank, the First National Bank of Philadelphia, was chartered on June 30, 1863.[2] The Currency Act was replaced by the National Banking Act of 1864, which was signed on June 3, 1864.[3]

The authorization of national bank charters created a parallel scheme of state and federally chartered banks, which still is a cornerstone of our current banking system. This system adds lines of authority to the diagram of regulatory powers, but it is widely regarded not only as a principal source of strength for the banking industry but also as a source of innovation and experiment that many believe would not have been possible under a single federal bank regulator.

One of the bulwarks of the dual banking system is the U.S. Supreme Court's 1819 ruling in *McCulloch v. Maryland*,[4] in which the court considered both the constitutionality of the national bank charter and a tax imposed on the operations of the Second Bank of the United States. Maryland had enacted a measure in February 1818 that imposed a tax on banks not chartered in the state. The tax, which was assessed against the Baltimore branch of the Bank of the United States, consisted of either a tax on the notes issued by the bank (ranging from 10 cents for a $5 note to $20 for a $1,000 note) or a flat tax of $1,500 per year. The Bank refused to pay the tax, the state sued, and judgment was rendered against the branch's cashier, J.W. McCulloch.

On appeal by the Bank, a unanimous Supreme Court declared that the chartering of a national bank by the United States government was constitutional and that the Maryland tax was unconstitutional. In his opinion, Chief Justice Marshall cited the constitution's supremacy clause in Article VI, paragraph 2, which asserts that the constitution and the laws made under it "are the supreme law of the

---

1. Two attempts had been made since 1791 to create a bank with a national charter to issue currency and to perform certain central functions. Each was granted a 20-year charter by Congress, but both were controversial because of strong opposition by many to a U.S. central bank. Neither charter was renewed. These institutions were the Bank of the United States (1791–1811) and the Second Bank of the United States (1816–1836).
2. OCC, *Historical Milestones* http://www.occ.treas.gov/OCC140th/mile.htm.
3. This act is widely referred to as the National Banking Act of 1864. In 1874, Congress designated this Act "The National Bank Act" as a matter of law (12 USC 38).
4. 17 U.S. (4 Wheat.) 316 (1819).

land, and the judges in every state shall be bound thereby, [any provisions] of the constitution or laws of any state to the contrary notwithstanding."

"The states," Marshall wrote, in a frequently quoted passage, "have no power, by taxation or otherwise, to retard, impede, burden, or in any manner control, the operations of the constitutional laws enacted by congress to carry into execution the powers vested in the general government . . . this [case involves] a tax on the operations of the bank, and is, consequently, a tax on the operation of an instrument employed by the government of the Union to carry its powers into execution. Such a tax must be unconstitutional." [5]

Banking 1836–1863

Among the goals of the National Bank Act were the creation of a nationwide system of banks subject to uniform rules, the issuance of a national currency, and the financing of the Civil War.

At the time the Currency Act was enacted, and after the demise of the Second Bank of the U.S. in 1836, commercial banking was conducted exclusively by more than 1,500 state-chartered banks that had proliferated after 1838. According to the Columbia Encyclopedia:

> [Until] 1838, a bank charter could be obtained only by a specific legislative act, but in that year New York adopted the Free Banking Act, which permitted anyone to engage in banking, upon compliance with certain charter conditions. Free banking spread rapidly to other states, and from 1840 to 1863 all banking business was done by state-chartered institutions.[6]

These banks, many of which were loosely supervised, were authorized to issue their own currency, and by 1860 more than 10,000 kinds of bank notes were in circulation.[7] These notes were supposed to be redeemable on demand in gold or silver, but some banks, including many known as "wildcat banks" because of their remote location, did not always have the means to redeem their

---

5. *Id.*, p. 436.
6. The Columbia Electronic Encyclopedia, 6th ed. Copyright © 2001–2005, Columbia University Press http://www.bartleby.com/65/ba/banking.html.
7. Office of the Comptroller of the Currency, *About the OCC—Early Banking in the U.S.* http://www.occ.treas.gov/exhibits/hist2.htm.

currency. As a result of this profusion of notes and widespread counterfeiting, merchants and other note holders often had no idea whether the currency they held was genuine and if so, what it would be worth when presented at their local bank.

There were several efforts to solve these problems, including a state insurance system in New York in 1829, which reportedly worked well for 10 years and a system initiated by the Suffolk Bank in Boston, which began in the early 1820s, lasted until 1858. By 1825, most New England banks were members.

After early difficulties with the volatile notes of some rural banks, the Suffolk Bank became a kind of a miniature central bank for New England, redeeming at par the notes of an increasing number of rural banks that maintained reserves at Suffolk. As a result of this system, the money supply was more stable in New England during most of this period than it was in most other parts of the country.

Private clearinghouses also evolved after 1836 as lenders of last resort to perform some of the liquidity functions of the Second United States Bank and were able to increase the money supply by 2 to 4% during the financial panics of 1883 and 1907.[8]

As commercial banks were dealing with business loans and other commercial activities, other kinds of institutions were organized to provide loans to buy and build houses and to provide a safe place for wage earners and others to deposit their funds.

Savings Institutions

Savings institutions were organized in the early 1800s to provide banking services for ordinary citizens whose needs were not met by commercial banks. These institutions included mutual savings banks (MSBs), which were concentrated in the northeast, and building and loan associations.

---

8. Flaherty, Edward, *A Brief History of Central Banking in the United States*, http://www.freedomdomaine.com/banking/central01.html. See also Trivoli, George, *The Suffolk Bank—A Study of a Free-Enterprise Clearing System*, The Adam Smith Institute, 1979.

State-Chartered MSBs

MSBs, which were concentrated in the northeast, were organized on a philanthropic basis by public-spirited citizens to provide wage earners with a safe place to deposit funds and earn interest.

The initial concentration of MSBs in the northeast, and particularly in the large port cities, resulted from several factors. Many states, including Massachusetts, actively encouraged their organization. The large influx of immigrants in the port cities added to the demand for basic banking services. The names of the original New York savings banks reflect this market, for example, The Bowery, Dime, Emigrants and Seamen's Savings Banks. In Massachusetts, one of the largest MSBs was the former Boston Five Cent Savings Bank.

The first savings bank charter was issued to the Provident Institution for Savings in Boston in 1816, and the Philadelphia Savings Fund Society began operations on a voluntary basis the same year. Among the investments permitted for these institutions were first mortgages on real estate and high-grade industrial bonds and blue-chip common and preferred stock. MSBs, which were eventually supervised by state banking departments, were chartered in 19 states, but 95% were concentrated in eight states—Connecticut, Maine, Massachusetts, New Hampshire, New Jersey, New York, Pennsylvania, Rhode Island—and Washington, D.C. Between 1820 and 1910, the number of MSBs increased from 10 to 637 and assets from $1 million to more than $3 billion.[9]

MSBs were organized as trusts, run for the benefit of savers by a board of trustees supervised by state banking regulators. The boards of many MSBs are still referred to as boards of trustees.

Savings Associations

The first U.S. savings and loan association was the Oxford Provident Building Association of Philadelphia County founded in 1831. Patterned on British building societies, these early associations were organized to provide a way for members to pool their funds to provide loans to buy or build a home. Unlike MSBs, however, savings associations were owned by their members, who subscribed to

---

9. This discussion is based on FDIC, *History of the Eighties, op. cit.,* Ch. 6.

"shares" in the institution at the time of its organization. In Massachusetts these early building societies were called "cooperative banks"—a term they retain today.

In a 1997 OTS paper on this subject, the authors say that the "earliest mutual institutions were organized principally as stock organizations," but several characteristics distinguished them from stock institutions as we understand the term today.[10]

These characteristics include the fact that only shareholders were eligible to be borrowers, so that the success of the institution depended on the creditworthiness of its investors. "The order in which subscribers could take out loans was determined by an auction" in which the first loans went to the highest bidder.[11] Funds increased gradually as shareholders made monthly payments on their subscriptions and no new accounts were accepted after the initial subscription was solicited. Early associations terminated after a set number of years—10 in the case of Oxford Provident—and the remaining funds distributed to the shareholders. Shares were not traded as they are today in many stock corporations and depositors had no claim on the net worth of the institution except in rare case of dissolution of the association.

Later mutual associations evolved into conventional depository institutions. The distinguishing characteristics of the early associations disappeared.

By the turn of the century, the fundamental principle of the modern mutual was in place: the net worth of the association belonged to the depositors or shareholders as a whole, but they were unable individually to exercise the rights of equityholders. The principle was borne out in several late nineteenth century cases governing the rights of depositors in the event of dissolution.[12]

The National Banking Act of 1864

The Currency Act, and the subsequent National Banking Act of 1864, required national banks to buy U.S. bonds in an amount equal to one

---

10. This discussion is based on *Mutual Savings Associations and Conversion to Stock Form*, Dwight C. Smith and James H. Underwood, OTS, May, 1997.
11. *Id.*, p. 6.
12. *Id.*, p. 10.

third of their paid-in capital.[13] Banks would then issue uniform National Bank Notes, printed under the supervision of the OCC, equal to 90% of the market value of these bonds to create a uniform national currency. To counter the problem of discounting state bank notes, the National Bank Act required that these notes be redeemable on demand and at par at any national bank in the country.[14]

The tying of currency issuance to U.S. bond holdings had the following role in helping to finance the Civil War:

> If [a] bank wished to extend additional loans to generate more profits, then the bank had to increase its holdings of Treasury bonds. This provision. . . . was designed to create a more active secondary market for Treasury bonds and thus lower the cost of borrowing for the federal government.[15]

Many advocates of the National Bank Act hoped that the advantages of the new currency and other features of the Act would drive the currency issued by state banks out of existence and induce state banks to convert to national banks, thereby ensuring a single national currency and a single banking system.

This approach seemed to be working at first. Between 1863 and 1865, the number of state banks declined from 1,466 to 349—a decrease of 76%—and their assets declined by 86 percent. The number of national banks increased from 66 to 1,294 during this period, of which about 800 were converted state banks and the remainder *de novo* banks.[16]

To further the objective of putting state banks out of business, Congress adopted an amendment to the National Bank Act in 1866 that required every national and state bank to pay a tax of 10% "on the amount of notes of any person, State bank, or State banking association, used for circulation and paid out by them after [August 1, 1866]."[17]

---

13. Under the 1864 Act, the minimum capital requirement for national banks ranged from $50,000 for banks in places with a population of 6,000 or less, $100,000 for banks in cities with a population of 6,000 to 50,000, and $200,000 for banks in cities with populations exceeding 50,000.
14. National Banking Act of 1864, sections 22 & 23.
15. Flaherty, *op. cit.*
16. Flaherty, *op. cit.*
17. Act of June 13, 1866 (14 Stat. 98, 146).

The tax made state banking unprofitable and additional state banks converted to a national bank charter. During 1866 through the end of 1868, the first three years in which the tax was in effect, the number of state banks declined another 29% to 247—the lowest number they would reach after the creation of the national bank system.

Other state banks chose not to convert either because of the higher capital and reserve requirements for national banks or for other reasons. The remaining state banks survived by issuing demand deposits to holders of their notes. These checking accounts became so popular that by 1890 the Comptroller of the Currency estimated that only 10% of the nation's money supply was in the form of currency. Combined with lower capital and reserve requirements, as well as the ease with which states issued banking charters, state banks again became the dominant banking structure by the late 1880s.[18]

Between 1870 and 1890, the number of state banks increased from 325 to 4,016, compared to an increase in the number of national banks from 1,612 to 3,715. Assets of state banks as a percentage of national bank assets increased from 12.8% to 56.3% during this period.[19]

While checks were a significant factor in the revival of state banks, these banks also had lower capital requirements and more flexible lending powers than national banks. In addition, the supervision standards in some state were not as strict as those of the Comptroller.[20]

The Federal Reserve System

The National Banking Act was successful in producing a unified national currency and creating a network of banks subject to uniform regulations and examinations. It did not, however, put an end to financial panics, which occurred once in each of the four decades following its enactment, with a particularly severe crisis in 1907.

---

18. Flaherty, *op cit.*
19. Grossman, Richard. "US Banking History, Civil War to World War II," EH.Net Encyclopedia, edited by Robert Whaples. March 17, 2003. http://eh.net/encyclopedia/article/grossman.banking.history.us.civil.war.wwii.
20. These comments are based on information provided by Jesse Stiller, the OCC Historian, whose other title is Special Advisor for Executive Communications.

These panics were caused in part by two restrictions imposed on national banks by the National Bank Act. The first restricted the elasticity of the currency the bank could have in circulation. The Act limited the amount of notes a bank could have in circulation to a percentage of the market price of its government bonds. According to Flaherty:

> If prices in the Treasury bond market declined substantially, then the national banks had to reduce the amount of currency they had in circulation. This could be done be refusing new loans or, in a more draconian way, *by calling-in loans already outstanding*. . . . Consequently, the size of the money supply was tied more closely to the performance of the bond market rather than needs of the economy. (emphasis added) [21]

If loans were called and a critical number of borrowers declared bankruptcy because they could not repay their loans, the bank failed, and many depositors lost their funds.

The second restriction provided that a bank whose reserves fell below statutory requirements could be placed in receivership if it did not make up the shortfall with 30 days of being notified of the deficiency by the Comptroller. These shortfalls could occur as rural banks, in response to seasonal demand for farm credit, withdrew funds they had deposited with national banks in urban areas.

If too many urban banks tried to restore their reserves at the same time by selling securities or calling in outstanding loans, the securities market would collapse, runs on certain banks would begin (sparked by rumors of impending failure), and a crisis would result. "Anyone unable to withdraw their deposits before the bank's till ran dry lost their savings all together. Private deposit insurance was scant and unreliable. Federal deposit insurance was non-existent."[22]

Also contributing to these panics was the rise of demand deposits, referred to above, which were supported only fractionally by cash reserves. There was no outside source of liquidity for the banking system so that "any excess cash reserves in the banking system were quickly exhausted whenever much of the public sought to convert deposits into currency." [23]

---

21. Flaherty, *op cit.*
22. *Id.*
23. Spong, Kenneth, *Banking Regulation, Its Purpose, Implementation and Effect*, Fed. Res. Bank of Kansas City, 2000, p. 20.

These developments led Congress to create the National Monetary Commission in 1908 to investigate the causes of these disruptions and to recommend legislation.

The Commission's findings and recommendations led to the enactment of the Federal Reserve Act of 1913 (FRA).[24] The FRA created the Federal Reserve System (FRS), headed by a board of seven members (later named the Board of Governors of the Federal Reserve System). To counter the fears by many bankers, businessmen, and others about the centralized control of the banking system, FRS operations were place in 12 District Banks to be governed by nine directors, six of whom were elected by FRS member banks.

National banks were required to join the system and state-chartered banks were permitted to join voluntarily. State banks that have joined the System are referred to as "state member banks." The FRA addressed the problem of the inelasticity of currency by granting the Federal Reserve the power to "rediscount"—or make loans secured by—eligible paper of member banks. By borrowing against eligible assets, member banks could obtain funds to meet sizeable cash withdrawals or rapid increases in the demand for credit. The FRS was also authorized to hold reserves of member banks and to conduct monetary policy through open market operations.

The FRA granted the Federal Reserve the power to examine and supervise national banks in their capacity as FRS member banks. A resolution of the overlapping authority with the OCC was resolved in 1917: the OCC would retain its authority with respect to national banks and supply the Federal Reserve with reports of its examinations of these institutions.[25]

As authorized by the FRA, Federal Reserve District Banks issued Federal Reserve Bank Notes as legal currency in 1914 to begin to replace the Treasury notes, which had been the mainstay of U.S. currency until then.

The FRA granted the Federal Reserve the power to examine and supervise state member banks, requiring that these banks comply with the Board's capital and reserve requirements. This authority made the Federal Reserve the first contemporary federal agency to examine and supervise state-chartered banks.

---

24. Act of Dec. 23, 1913, ch. 6 (38 Stat. 260).
25. This discussion is based on Spong, *op. cit.*, p. 21.

Amendments to the FRA in 1917 provided that a state bank that joined the system could "retain its full charter and statutory rights as a state bank or trust company, and may continue to exercise all the corporate powers granted it by the State in which it was created."[26] The FRA does, however, subject state member banks to two restrictions that are imposed on national banks by the National Bank Act. State banks are treated as though they were national banks for purposes of the branching restrictions of the McFadden Act,[27] which is discussed in Chapter 4, and section 16 of the Glass-Steagall Act,[28] which is discussed in Chapter 10.

The 1930s

Congressional response to the financial crisis of the Depression included an intense period of legislative activity during 1932–34, which was designed to restore confidence in the banking system.[29]

This period saw the enactment of laws providing federal deposit insurance for accounts in banks and savings associations, federal charters and a federal liquidity facility for savings associations, and extensive amendments the National Bank and Federal Reserves Acts.

The Banking Act of 1933[30] created the FDIC, prohibited member banks from paying interest on demand deposits, authorized the Federal Reserve to set interest rate ceilings on time deposits, and added section 23A, relating to transactions with affiliates, to the Federal Reserve Act. The Act also adopted the four sections known as the Glass-Steagall Act, which prohibited banks from engaging in certain securities activities.[31]

Although Congress imposed restrictions on securities activities of banks, in Glass-Steagall, it excluded securities of banks and savings associations from the registration requirements of the Securities Act

---

26. 12 USC 330.
27. 12 USC 36.
28. 12 USC 24 (seventh).
29. This period also saw the enactment of the acts that imposed federal regulation on the securities industry, the Securities Act of 1933 and the Securities Exchange Act of 1934, which are discussed in Chapter 10.
30. June 16, 1933, ch. 89, 48 Stat. 163.
31. This Act, which was partially repealed in 1999, is discussed further in Chapter 10.

of 1933. There were several reasons for this exclusion according to one analyst, including the fact that the securities activities of national banks were regarded as having been well regulated by the Comptroller of the Currency for the preceding 70 years. In addition, the Roosevelt Administration needed the support of the banking industry which was regarded as vital to the economic recovery.[32]

Federal Deposit Insurance for Commercial Banks

Perhaps the most far-reaching legislation relating to the banking system was the authorization in 1933 of federal insurance for deposits of banks.[33] This program, which was enacted as section 12B of the Federal Reserve Act by section 8 of the National Bank Act of 1933 became law on June 16, 1933.[34]

This legislation initially offered deposit insurance of accounts in commercial and savings banks for up to $2,500. This insurance program was to be administered by the FDIC, an independent agency headed by a three-person board of directors, which was required to begin a temporary insurance program on January 1, 1934.

The establishment of the FDIC was funded by capital contributions of $150 million by the Treasury Department and subscriptions to Class B stock by each Federal Reserve Bank of one-half of its surplus as of January 1, 1933. The initial annual insurance premium assessment was one half of one percent of insurable deposits. One half of this amount was payable immediately and the remained payable on call by the FDIC.

National banks and state member banks were required to obtain deposit insurance. State nonmember banks could join the fund upon certification of solvency by their state regulator and after examination and approval by the FDIC. Because of the short time between the signing of the 1933 Banking Act and the starting date of January 1, 1934, the FDIC had to examine almost 8,000 state nonmember

---

32. These comments are based on a conversation with Jesse Stiller, *Supra.*
33. Proposals for some form of federal deposit insurance had been introduced in Congress since 1886 and insurance programs had been adopted by several states during 1829–1866 and 1908–1930. (FDIC, *History, op. cit.,* Ch. 2.)
34. June 16, 1933, ch. 89, 48 Stat. 163.

banks in three months. These banks had been examined and supervised by state banking agencies, but the quality varied greatly. In addition to restoring public confidence in the banking system by insuring individual accounts, deposit insurance was viewed as a way to bring state banks under uniform federal supervision as the "price" for these benefits.[35]

Deposit insurance was voluntary for state nonmember banks during the agency's early years, but the initial legislation required these banks to join the Federal Reserve System within two years as a condition of retaining their insurance. This deadline was never applied. It was extended twice and then repealed in 1939 before it was scheduled to take effect.[36]

In any case, the FDIC, with its powers of examination and supervision, became the primary federal regulator of state nonmember banks and the secondary federal regulator of national banks and state member banks.

After its initial examinations to determine minimal acceptability for deposit insurance, and later examinations to determine capital adequacy, the agency shifted its attention to developing standards for safety and soundness examinations, which would be the foundation of the examinations the agency performs today. These examinations were designed to:

- appraise assets to determine net worth;
- assess asset quality;
- identify practices that could lead to financial difficulties;
- evaluate bank management; and
- assess compliance with law and regulations.

The FDIC was given supervisory powers at that time, including the authority to approve branch applications and capital reductions by insured nonmember banks and to approve mergers of all insured banks with uninsured institutions. The insurance of an insured bank could be terminated for failure to correct unsafe and unsound practices.

---

35. Stiller, *supra*.
36. This discussion is based on *A Brief History of Deposit Insurance in the United States*, FDIC, 1998, ch. 4.

The Banking Act of 1935[37] provided that all institutions that were insured under the temporary program, which ended on September 1, 1935, would be admitted to the permanent program unless they decided to withdraw. At that time, 34 banks withdrew and 14,219 banks were admitted to deposit insurance.[38]

Federal Deposit Insurance for Savings Banks

Federal supervision of MSBs began, as it did with state nonmember banks, with the authorization of federal deposit insurance in 1933. Deposit insurance was voluntary for MSBs, and many savings banks were opposed to the program. Only 56 savings banks, less than 12% of all MSBs, were admitted to the permanent program on September 1, 1935.[39] One of the reasons for this lower participation was that MSBs had not been subject to the kinds of "runs" that had affected commercial banks. MSBs had no demand deposits and could restrict early withdrawal of their savings accounts. As a result, many savings banks believed they did not need deposit insurance. Others regarded themselves as "preferred risks" and objected to being assessed for deposit insurance at the rates applied to commercial banks. A third factor was political: some were simply opposed to deposit insurance because it was a Roosevelt "New Deal" program.[40]

Under the permanent program, individual accounts were insured from one half of 1% of insured deposits to $5,000. The deposit insurance premium (or assessment) was reduced to 1/12 of 1% of *total* deposits. This formula achieved two of the FDIC's goals: it reduced insurance assessments of smaller banks, which generally held a higher percentage of insured deposits to total deposits than larger banks, and, by spreading the cost of the program over the assets of the entire banking system, it maintained an adequate level of assessment income for the FDIC.[41]

---

37. August 23, 1935, ch. 619 (49 Stat. 209).
38. In 1950, the federal deposit insurance program, which had been enacted in 1933 as 12B of the Federal Reserve Act, was removed from that Act by the Federal Deposit Insurance Act of 1950; Sept. 21, 1950, 64 Stat. 873 and codified separately in the U.S. Code at 12 USC 1811 *et seq.*
39. FDIC, *History, op. cit.*, p. 37.
40. *Id.*, pps. 29–30.
41. FDIC, History, *op. cit.*, pps. 36–37.

By 1975, however, 70% of all MSBs were federally insured and the remainder, primarily cooperative banks in Massachusetts, were privately insured. These banks applied for federal deposit insurance in 1985 as a result of private insurance crises in Ohio and Maryland. About 95% of these choose the FDIC and the remainder elected to be insured by the Federal Savings and Loan Insurance Corporation (FSLIC), the deposit insurance fund for savings associations, created in 1934, which is discussed below.[42]

Federal Charters and Deposit Insurance for Savings Associations

Federal involvement in the savings association industry began with the enactment of the Federal Home Loan Bank Act of 1932 (FHLBank Act),[43] which established the Federal Home Loan Bank System under the administration of a new agency, the Federal Home Loan Bank Board (FHLBB). The Bank System was designed to reduce foreclosures and to encourage home ownership by providing an alternative source of funds for savings associations in the form of low-cost advances.

The System consists of 12 regional Home Loan Banks, which are government sponsored but owned by their members who are required to purchase stock as a condition of membership. Commercial banks and credit unions became eligible for membership in the Bank System in 1989.

The Home Owners' Loan Act of 1933 (HOLA)[44] ushered in the dual system for savings associations by authorizing the FHLBB to approve federal mutual charters for *de novo* savings associations and for those converting from a state charter.

Federal supervisory authority over state-chartered savings associations began in 1934 with the creation of the Federal Savings and Loan Insurance Corporation (FSLIC)[45] to insure deposits of federal and state savings associations. The FHLBB was designated as the board of

---

42. An Examination of the Banking Crisis of the 1980s and Early 1990s, FDIC, Ch. 6., p. 213.
43. July 22, 1932, ch. 522, 47 Stat. 725, 12 USC 1422, *et seq.*
44. June 13, 1933, ch. 64, 48 Stat. 128, 12 USC 1461 *et seq.*
45. Title IV of the National Housing Act of 1934, June 27, 1934, 48 Stat. 1246 (12 USC §1724 et seq.). Title IV was repealed by section 407 of Public Law 101–73 (Aug. 9, 1989, 103 Stat. 183) (FIRREA) in connection with the creation of the Savings Association Insurance Fund (see discussion in main text).

directors of the FSLIC, thereby combining the deposit insurance and chartering function (for federal associations) in a single agency.

Subsequent Developments

As banking institutions began offering new products and expanding geographically in the post-World War II period, many MSBs and savings associations wanted to raise additional capital by converting to a stock charter.

Mutual institutions are not able to raise funds in the capital markets and, as a result, their capital consists primarily of retained earnings. This restriction limits their ability to grow by engaging in new activities or by expanding geographically. In addition, these institutions were often unable to retain or hire valuable employees because they were not able to provide the higher income typically offered by stock institutions, or offer incentives such as stock option plans.

Conversion would also enable institutions to organize a holding company, which would, among other things (as noted in Chapter 5), permit them to diversify their activities and to offer their depositors and the general public products and services that they could not offer directly.

Mutual to Stock Conversions— Savings Associations

In 1948, section 5(i) of HOLA[46] was amended to permit a federal mutual savings associations to convert to a "savings and loan type of institution" organized under the law of the state where the association is located and then, with the approval of the FHLBB and FSLIC, to convert to a state stock charter in states that authorized these conversions. The House report on this amendment noted that section 5(i) in the original version of HOLA permitted any member of an FHLBank to convert to a federal association, and the "reciprocal arrangement for the conversion of a Federal association to a State

---

46. 12 USC 1464(i).

institution would seem equitable and sound."[47] At this time, only three states permitted stock charters for savings associations.[48]

Since federal savings associations, which were all mutual at that time, the 1948 amendments provided a way for federal associations located in states that permitted mutual-to-stock conversions to convert to a stock charter if they wished to do so. Conversion by mutual associations was controversial, but opposition was not strong enough to cause Congress to ban conversions of state associations. Congress apparently didn't want to preempt state law on this issue at that time.

Part of the opposition to conversions was related to the principle that institutions devoted to housing finance should remain in mutual form and had no business converting to a stock charter. Another consideration was the fact that historically, and under current law, the net worth of mutual institution belonged to the savers and borrowers in the unlikely event of a liquidation of the institution's assets—not to investors.[49]

By the late 1950s, the organization of stock savings and loan associations was permitted in 20 states.[50]

In 1955, concerned that "the rules governing such transactions varied from state to state and, in a number of cases, appeared to favor management at the expense of depositors," the FHLBB imposed a moratorium on all association conversion until 1961 and adopted another in 1963, which was scheduled to expire in 1974. Congress extended this moratorium until June 30, 1976 but permitted the agency to process a limited number of pending applications and a certain number of additional test cases. The legislation also permitted federal associations to retain their federal charter after conversion if they were located in state that permitted state stock charters.[51]

---

47. Sen. Rept. 1393 (May 25, 1948) to Public Law 895, July 3, 1948, ch. 825, 62 Stat. 1239. Report at U.S. CONG. & ADMIN. NEWS, 80th Cong. 2nd sess, p. 2315.

48. OTS, *Mutual Savings, op. cit.*, p. 24, footnote 40.

49. OTS conversion regulations, as they evolved, placed net worth of a converting association into a "liquidation account," which is currently codified at 12 CFR 563b.450–485.

50. OTS, Historical Framework for Regulation of Activities of Unitary Savings and Loan Holding Companies, p. 3.

51. Pub. Law 93–495, Oct. 28, 1974, 88 Stat. 1500, amending section 203(d) of the National Housing Act. Current OTS conversion regulations, at 12 CFR Part 563b, were subject to a comprehensive revision published Aug. 9, 2002 (67 FR 52010).

Mutual to Stock Conversions—MSBs

Beginning in 1969, MSBs in New England were permitted to convert to a stock form of ownership. New Hampshire was the first state to grant this authority and by 1985, mutual-to-stock conversions by savings banks were permitted in all of the New England states. The rate of conversions increased in 1986 following the authorization of conversions by Massachusetts in 1985. Seventy two MSBs converted during this period, with 48 conversions in 1986 alone.[52]

Federal Charters for MSBs

In 1978, Congress amended HOLA to permit the FHLBB to grant a federal mutual charter to state-chartered savings banks that had retained their mutual form of ownership under state law. This legislation, which brought dual banking to the savings bank industry, was later modified to a permit a state mutual savings bank to convert to a federal stock charter and to permit state-chartered stock savings banks to convert directly to a federal stock charter.

The new federal savings bank charters were similar to their corresponding federal savings association charter with some modifications, and currently, there are no substantive differences between the two charters. As these differences disappeared, many savings institutions with a federal savings and loan association or savings bank charter believed that having "bank" in their corporate name was a valuable marketing asset. As a result, the FHLBB adopted regulations permitting institutions with a federal savings and loan association charter to "indicate" that they are a federal savings bank and institutions with a savings bank charter to indicate that they are a federal savings and loan association.[53]

In addition, HOLA was amended in 1982 to provide that "any Federal association can designate itself as a Federal savings bank or the reverse."[54]

As stated by the OTS in the section-by-section analysis of its 1996 final rules on corporate governance: "Today, charters for both

---

52. *Understanding the Experience of Converted New England Savings Banks*, Jennifer L. Eccles and John P. O'Keefe, FDIC BANKING REVIEW, Vol. 8, No. 1, 1995, p. 3.
53. 12 CFR 543.1.
54. Section 5(i)(2)(C), 12 USC 1464(i)(2)(C).

types of institutions are identical, except for a possible difference in corporate title."[55]

Accordingly, OTS regulations on charters for federal mutual associations provide that organizers who prefer a mutual savings bank charter may simply substitute "federal savings bank" for "federal savings association" in the charter form and, at their discretion, substitute "trustee" for "director."[56] The same provision is in the regulations for charters of federal stock associations, except for the reference to the term "trustee." [57]

"NOW Accounts" for Banks and Savings Institutions

In 1973, Congress enacted legislation[58] to permit banks and savings institutions in Massachusetts and New Hampshire to allow customers to write check-like instruments called NOWs (negotiable orders of withdrawal) on interest-bearing accounts. MSBs in these two states had been offering NOW accounts, which had been approved under state law.

NOW accounts had originated in Massachusetts in 1970. Although they were a small percentage of total MSB deposits at the time,[59] they raised questions of competitive equality among depository institutions in those states.

The Senate Report on the 1973 legislation pointed out that "At the present time, the legality of NOW accounts is determined by the laws, banking regulations, and judicial decisions of the individual states."[60] Prior to the use of these accounts, depositors in most savings institutions could not "write a check" to pay bills. Some institutions, however, had offered a means of withdrawal of funds by nonnegotiable instruments.[61]

---

55. OTS, *Corporate Governance*, final rule, 61 FR 64007, 64009. (Dec. 3, 1996).
56. 12 CFR 544.1.
57. 12 CFR 552.3.
58. Pub. Law 93–100, Aug. 16, 1973, 87 Stat. 342. codified at 12 UC 1832.
59. As of March 1, 1973, NOW accounts represented only 3/4 of 1% of all MSB deposits in Massachusetts and 1/7 of 1% of MSB deposits in New Hampshire. Sen. Rpt. 93–149, p. 2015, U.S. CONG. & ADMIN NEWS, 82nd Cong., 1st sess.
60. *Id.*, p. 2016.
61. Some savings institutions had permitted these withdraws by means of "payable through" drafts, which were nonnegotiable instruments payable though a commercial bank. Credit unions had used these instruments, which were called "share drafts," for many years.

These accounts were extended to the other New England states in 1976, to New York and New Jersey in 1978 and 1979, respectively, and were extended nationwide in 1980, as noted below. They are limited to deposits held by individuals and nonprofit organizations.

The NOW accounts in Massachusetts and New Hampshire also caused concerns because they, in effect, "jumped the gun" on ongoing debates within the banking industry and in Congress about whether depository institutions should be able to pay interest on demand deposits (basically, "checking accounts"), and whether savings institutions should be able to offer demand deposits at all (with or without interest) to enable them to compete more effectively with banks.[62]

Efforts were underway in other states to permit MSBs to offer NOW accounts, and Congress considered whether to impose a blanket prohibition on these accounts pending resolution of the these issues or to carve out an exception for these two states. The final law opted for the latter course, with the Senate Banking Committee concluding that, because of the small size of these accounts, federal intervention was not required at that time. The Committee noted that it would be considering the extension of these accounts to all institutions when it began its deliberations on the recommendations of a major Presidential commission that had filed a report in late 1971.[63]

These issues were also bound up in debates over the timing of phasing out of controls on interest rates depository institutions could pay on saving accounts. These controls were imposed in 1966 based on "a finding by Congress that interest rate competition was putting an enormous upward pressure in savings rates paid by thrift institutions beyond their ability to pay. . . ."[64] To encourage the flow of funds into housing finance, savings associations were permitted to pay 25 basis points more on savings accounts than banks.

In legislation enacted in 1980, (1980 Act),[65] Congress directed the agencies, working through a new Depository Institutions Deregulation Committee (DIDC), to phase out these controls by March 31, 1986.

---

62. The Federal Reserve's Reg Q prohibited, and still does, the payment of interest by member banks on demand deposits. This prohibition is also applies to state nonmember banks by section 18(g) of the FDIA (12 USC 1828(g)), and to federal savings associations by section 5(b)(1)(B) of HOLA (12 USC 1464(b)(1)(B)).

63. This was the Hunt Commission, formally called the President's Commission on Financial Structure and Regulation.

64. Sen. Rpt. 93–149, *op cit.*, p. 2014.

65. The Depository Institutions Deregulation and Monetary Control Act of 1980, Pub. Law 96–221, March 31, 1980, 94 Stat. 132.

The Garn-St Germain Act of 1982 directed the DIDC to eliminate the interest rate differential by Jan. 1, 1984, and develop "a money market deposit account" with no interest rate ceilings to enable institutions to compete with nonbank money market accounts. The Act also authorized federal associations to offer demand accounts for business customers, and, after 1989, to all customers.

The evolution of NOW accounts from operations under the laws of two states conducted by state-chartered institutions to accounts authorized for all institutions under federal law is often cited as a prime example of the ability of the dual system to permit "experiments"—to permit evaluation of the feasibility of new activities on a small scale.

Bank and S&L Holding Companies

Between 1956 and 1970, Congress enacted legislation to deal with the expansion of bank and S&L holding companies.

Bank Holding Companies (BHCs)

The Bank Holding Company Act (BHCA) of 1956[66] was enacted to curb the interstate expansion multi-bank holding companies into interstate networks of banking and nonbanking activities and to restrict their circumvention of state branching restrictions. This Act included the "Douglas Amendment,"[67] which prohibited bank holding companies from acquiring banks in other states unless the law of that state specifically permitted such acquisitions. The Act also restricted nonbanking activities of multi-bank BHCs.

As discussed in greater detail in Chapter 5, Congress was concerned that unlimited expansion of multi-bank holding companies could enable them to acquire as many banks as needed to monopolize a particular market.

The BHCA Amendments of 1970[68] gave the Federal Reserve the authority to regulate the formation and operation of one-bank

---

66. May 9, 1956, ch. 240, 70 Stat. 133.
67. Formerly codified in section 3(d) (12 USC 1842(d)) and repealed by the 1994 interstate branching legislation discussed in Chapter 4.
68. Pub. Law 91–607, Dec. 31, 1970, 84 Stat. 1760, codified at 12 USC 1841 *et seq.*

holding companies. It limited the nonbanking activities of all BHCs (subject to narrow exemptive authority) to "those that are so closely related to banking as to be a proper incident thereto."[69]

As discussed in Chapter 5, the Gramm Leach Bliley Act (GLBA),[70] enacted in 1999, permits BHCs that elect to become financial holding companies to engage in a wider set of financially related activities.

Savings and Loan Holding Companies (S&LHCs)

At the time of the enactment of the S&L Holding Company Act (S&LHCA) of 1959 (the Spence Act),[71] the only stock associations were state-chartered. Congressional concerns included the possibility of the holding company diverting the financial resources of the S&L subsidiary to the parent. The activities of associations at that time were limited primarily to residential mortgage lending in limited geographic areas, but there was some concern about multiple S&LHCs.

To allow time for study of S&L holding companies, the Spence Act imposed a moratorium on the acquisition of additional associations by existing S&LHCs and limited new holding companies to the acquisition of a single association. The S&L Holding Company Act Amendments of 1967[72] imposed activity restrictions on multiple S&LHCs but permitted any company engaged in a lawful business to acquire a single association.

Today, one-S&L (unitary) holding companies organized after May 4, 1999, are limited, with some exceptions, to activities that are permissible for the financial holding companies authorized by GLBA.

Holding companies are discussed in greater detail in Chapter 5.

Abolition of the FHLBB and FSLIC

In 1989, the Financial Institutions Reform, Recovery and Enforcement Act of 1989 (FIRREA)[73] made extensive changes in the way savings associations were regulated and insured. FIRREA rewrote

---

69. 12 USC 1843(c)(8). The Federal Reserve was permitted to exempt certain BHCs in existence before July 1, 1968 from these restrictions.
70. Pub. Law 106–102, Nov. 12, 1999, 113 Stat. 1338.
71. Pub. Law 86–374, Sept. 23, 1959, 78 Stat. 691.
72. Pub. Law 90–255, Feb. 14, 1967, 82 Stat. 5, codified at 12 USC 1467a.
73. Pub. Law 101–73, Aug. 9, 1989, 103 Stat. 183.

HOLA to abolish the FHLBB, repeal title IV of the National Housing Act (NHA), and to make the following additional changes in the way savings associations are regulated:

- the authority to charter and supervise federal savings associations and federal savings banks was transferred to the Office of Thrift Supervision (OTS), a new office in the Treasury Department;
- the FSLIC was abolished and its deposit insurance functions were transferred to a new Savings Association Insurance Fund (SAIF) to be administered by the FDIC;
- the former FDIC insurance fund was redesignated the Bank Insurance Fund (BIF); BIF and SAIF were to be funded and administered separately by the FDIC;[74]
- the Federal Home Loan Bank System was transferred to a new independent agency—the Federal Housing Finance Board;
- several provisions of former title IV of the NHA, including the S&L Holding Company Act and certain other powers of the former FSLIC with respect to state-chartered savings associations, were added into HOLA; and
- the FHLMC was made a separate government sponsored enterprise under the supervision of the Department of Housing and Urban Development.

FIRREA's amendments of the FDIA, HOLA, and other banking laws included a single definition of "depository institutions," which divided them into two mutually exclusive categories: "banks" and "savings associations." These definitions are located in section 3 of the FDIA.

A Subset of "Banks"

One set of exceptions to this "universal" definition of "bank" in the FDIA is found in the BHCA. The definition of "bank" in section 2(c)(1)(A) of the BHCA references the definition in section 3(h) of the FDIA ("any bank,. . . . the deposits of which are

---

74. BIF and SAIF were merged on March 31, 2006, in accordance with the terms of the FDIC Reform Act of 2005, Pub. Law 109–171, Title II, Subtitle B, Feb. 8, 2006, 120 Stat. 9. This legislation is discussed in Chapter 2.

insured in accordance with the provisions of [the FDIA]"). Section 2(c)(2) then carves out several exclusions from the definition of "bank" *for purposes of the BHCA only.* These exclusions include certain trust companies, industrial loan companies, and credit card banks, which are discussed in Chapter 5.

FDIA Definitions

The definitions of depository institutions in section 3 of the FDIA can be summarized as follows:

Banks

National banks	banks chartered by the OCC
State banks	state-chartered banks, which include trust companies. savings banks, industrial banks (or similar institution that the FDIC finds to be operating in the same manner as an industrial bank), or other banking institutions that are "engaged in the business of receiving deposits, other than trust funds" and any cooperative bank or other unincorporated bank the deposits of which were insured by the FDIC on August 8, 1989 (the day before FIRREA was enacted).

Savings Associations

Federal associations	insured institutions with a federal savings association or federal savings bank charter granted by the OTS or the former FHLBB.
State associations	these are insured state-chartered savings and loan associations and other savings institutions that are not banks whose state charter reflects their historic designations (e.g., building and loan and homestead associations), any corporation (other than a bank) that the FDIC and OTS jointly determine to be operating in substantially the same manner as a savings association, and cooperative banks that were insured by FSLIC on Aug. 8, 1989.

Primary Federal Regulators

FIRREA also adopted section 3(q) of the FDIA to revise the definition of the federal agencies that have the primary authority to examine and supervise insured banks and savings associations. Section 3(q) defines these agencies as the "appropriate federal banking agency." These agencies are referred to in many publications, and in this book, as **primary federal regulators (PFRs)**. Responsibilities of the PFRs include:

- conducting examinations
- initiating supervisory and enforcement actions
- assigning composite CAMELS ratings
- approving branch and other supplications
- reviewing change of control applications
- approving mergers (if it is the PFR of the resulting institution)

Two PFRs, the OCC and OTS, are also chartering agencies—for national banks and federal savings associations, respectively. Figure 1.1 shows the jurisdiction of PFRs relating to depository institutions and their holding companies.

Secondary Federal Regulators

This term is not defined in the FDIA. It has been used in several charts on the authority of federal banking agencies to distinguish the authority the agencies exercise as PFRs and the authority the FDIC and Federal Reserve Board exercises in their respective capacities as insurers of deposits and supervisors of institutions in the Federal Reserve System.

Figure 1.2 shows the jurisdiction of the federal agencies in their roles as PFRs, as secondary federal regulators, and the roles of the federal and state agencies as grantors of charters.

Other Regulators

The charts in Figures 1.1 and 1.2 are starting points in outlining agency responsibilities. As noted throughout this book, however, there are not only other lines of authority within these four agencies (the FDIC, for example, has authority to approve certain activities of state banks and their subsidiaries), but there are also nonbanking agencies that have rulemaking authority affecting depository

Jurisdiction of Primary Federal Regulators and State Banking Departments
(Saving associations are referred to as "S&Ls")

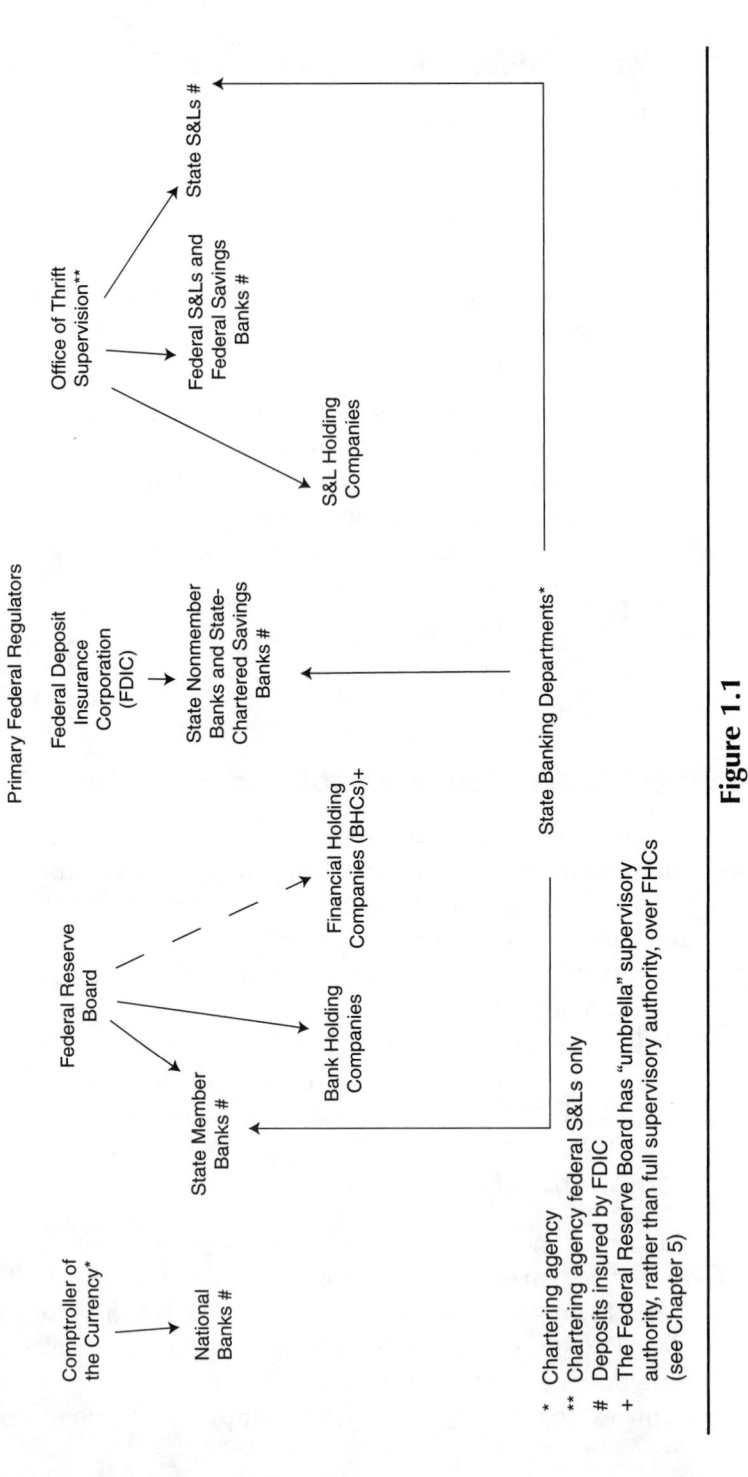

Primary Federal Regulators

Comptroller of the Currency* → National Banks #

Federal Reserve Board → State Member Banks #
Federal Reserve Board → Bank Holding Companies
Federal Reserve Board ⇢ Financial Holding Companies (BHCs)+

Federal Deposit Insurance Corporation (FDIC) → State Nonmember Banks and State-Chartered Savings Banks #

Office of Thrift Supervision** → State S&Ls #
Office of Thrift Supervision** → Federal S&Ls and Federal Savings Banks #
Office of Thrift Supervision** → S&L Holding Companies

State Banking Departments* → State Member Banks #
State Banking Departments* → State Nonmember Banks and State-Chartered Savings Banks #
State Banking Departments* → State S&Ls #

* Chartering agency
** Chartering agency federal S&Ls only
\# Deposits insured by FDIC
\+ The Federal Reserve Board has "umbrella" supervisory authority, rather than full supervisory authority, over FHCs (see Chapter 5)

Figure 1.1

Figure 1.2
Chartering Agencies, Primary and Secondary
Federal Regulators of Insured Depository Institutions

Institution	Chartering Agency	Primary Federal Regulator*	Secondary Federal Regulator
National Bank	OCC	OCC	Fed, FDIC
State Nonmember Bank	State agency	FDIC	FDIC
State Member Bank	State agency	Fed	Fed, FDIC
State Savings Bank	State Agency	FDIC	FDIC
Federal Savings Association	OTS	OTS	FDIC
Federal Savings Bank	OTS	OTS	FDIC
State Savings Association	State agency	OTS	FDIC

*These agencies are defined as the "appropriate federal banking agency" in section 3(q) of the FDIA.

institutions. Offices in the Treasury Department enforce money laundering and currency transactions regulations.

The Regulators' Universe

Figure 1.3 shows the distribution of deposits and offices by charter class as of June 30, 1995 and June 30, 2005. Figure 1.4 shows the amount and percentage increases and decreases in these numbers between these two dates. This 10-year period shows several dramatic changes in the data relating to commercial banks, including a 98% increase in deposits, an increase in the number of commercial bank offices by almost 20%, and a decrease in the total number of banks by over 25%. The number of savings institutions shows a decrease of over 37% and an increase in deposits of more than 38%.

Preemption

The preemption of state banking laws by federal banking laws and policies is discussed in several chapters in this book, including Chapter 4 (interstate branching), Chapter 5 (insurance activities), Chapter 6 (exportation of interest rates), and Chapter 10 (securities activities).

Figure 1.3
National Totals—Number of Institutions by Charter Class and Total Deposits
June 20, 1995–June 30, 2005

	Number of Institutions 1995	Number of Institutions 2005	Offices 1995	Offices 2005	Deposits (in billions) 1995	Deposits (in billions) 2005
Commercial Banks	**10,166**	**7,549**	**65,321**	**78,030**	**2,472.6**	**4,904.2**
National	2,941	1,864	30,633	38,110	1,337.1	2,946.5
State	7,225	5,685	34,688	39,920	1,135.5	1,957.6
State Member	995	906	10,206	14,074	439.4	765.6
State Nonmember	6,230	4,779	24,482	25,846	696.1	1,191.9
Savings Institution	**2,082**	**1,294**	**15,637**	**14,004**	**738.8**	**1,023.6**
Federal Savings Associations & Federal Savings Banks	1,185	749	10,479	9,525	512.3	784.2
State Savings Institutions	897	545	5,158	4,479	226.4	239.5
State Savings Bank	604	449	4,046	4,034	188.5	233.8
State Savings Association	293	96	1,102	445	37.9	15.7
U.S. Branches of Foreign Banks	**41**	**13**	**41**	**13**	**5.9**	**3.1**
Total	**12,289**	**8,856**	**80,999**	**92,047**	**3,214.6**	**5,993.7**

Source: FDIC, Summary of Deposits, Summary Tables Report.
* Includes deposits in domestic offices (50 states and DC) Puerto Rico and U.S. Territories

Figure 1.4
Increase/Decrease in Number, Offices, and Deposits of Commercial Banks and Savings Institutions
June 20, 1995–June 30, 2005

Commercial Banks	1995	2005	Differences	
number	10,166	7,749	– 2,617	– 25.7%
offices	65,321	78,030	+ 12,709	+ 19.5%
deposits*	$ 2,472.6	4,904.2	+ 2,431.6	+ 98.3%
Savings Institutions	**1995**	**2005**	**Differences**	
number	2,082	1,294	– 788	– 37.8%
offices	15,637	14,004	– 1,633	– 10.4%
deposits*	$ 738.8	1,023.6	+ 284.8	+ 38.5%

Source: FDIC, Summary of Deposits, Summary Tables Report.
*in billions

Federal courts have historically upheld the assertions of the OCC and OTS that Congress, in creating the national bank system and authorizing the creation of federally chartered savings associations, intended that these institutions be able to exercise the powers granted to them by federal law on a nationwide basis without interference from the laws of the state or states in which they operate.

These assertions grounded in the history of the U.S. banking system beginning at least with *McCulloch v. Maryland*, with its application of the Supremacy Clause and the legislative history of the National Bank Act, both of which are discussed above.

The OCC asserts that it is the principles of preemption and findings that national banks are not subject to state supervision and regulation that "make the system 'dual.'"[75]

National Banks

A recent case that outlined the grounds for declaring a federal law preemptive of a state law is *Barnett Bank of Marion County, N.A. v. Nelson*.[76] These grounds are characterized by the OCC as follows:

> First, Congress can adopt express language setting forth the existence and scope of preemption. Second, Congress can adopt a framework for

---

75. OCC, "National Banks and the Dual System," September, 2003, p. 2.
76. 517 U.S. 25 (1996).

regulation that "occupies the field" and leaves no room for states to adopt supplemental laws. Third, preemption may be found when state law actually conflicts with Federal law. Conflict will be found when either: (i) compliance with both laws is a "physical impossibility;" or (ii) when the state law stands "as an obstacle to the accomplishment and execution of the full purposes and objectives of Congress." (citations omitted).[77]

Barnett itself provided an instance of a state law that was an obstacle to an authorized activity of national bank. In 1974, Florida adopted a law prohibiting insurance agents affiliated with financial institutions to sell insurance. Financial institutions included banks other than banks that were not in a holding company and that were located in towns with a population of less than 5,000. This law was diametrically opposed to the authority enacted in 1916 (at 12 USC 92) allowing national banks to sell insurance as agents in towns of the same size. Barnett Bank, a subsidiary of a bank holding company, was prohibited by Florida law from acting as an agent and selling insurance in a town with a population of less than 5,000 people. The court held that the Florida law constituted an obstacle to Barnett's exercise of its authorized powers and held that the state law was preempted.

The court, however, was faced with another issue. Bill Nelson, who was the Florida Insurance Commissioner, argued that preemption was prohibited by the McCarran Ferguson Act,[78] a statute designed to prevent federal regulation of the insurance industry. That Act, at 15 USC § 1012(b), provides that state insurance laws could not be preempted by a federal law unless that law "specifically relates to the business of insurance."

The Supreme Court rejected rulings in the lower court and arguments by insurance industry representatives that the 1916 law did not "specifically relate" to the insurance business, and reversed the lower courts and held in favor of the Bank.

The Court summed up the "many formulations" of conflicts standards defined by the courts in analyzing preemption cases and stated:

> In defining the pre-emptive scope of statutes and regulations granting a power to national banks, these cases take the view that normally Con-

---

77. Preamble to OCC, "Bank Activities and Operations; Real Estate Lending and Appraisals," Final rule, 69 FR 1904 (Jan. 13, 2004) at p. 1910.
78. March 9, 1945, 59 Stat. 33 (15 U.S.C. 1011 *et seq.*).

gress would not want States to forbid, or impair significantly, the exercise of a power that Congress explicitly granted. To say this is not to deprive States of the power to regulate national banks, where (unlike here) doing so does not prevent or significantly interfere with the national bank's exercise of its powers.[79]

As noted in Chapter 5, GLBA incorporates the McCarran Ferguson Act and *Barnett* into its provisions on insurance activities of banks into section 104 of the Act, "Operation of State Law."

Section 104(a) provides in part that:

> The Act entitled "An Act to express the intent of Congress with reference to the regulation of the business of insurance" and approved March 9, 1945 (15 U.S.C. 1011 et seq.) (commonly referred to as the "McCarran-Ferguson Act") remains the law of the United States."

Section 104(d)(2)(A), provides in part:

> (2) Insurance sales.—
> (A) In general.—In accordance with the legal standards for preemption set forth in the decision of the Supreme Court of the United States in Barnett Bank of Marion County N.A. v. Nelson, 517 U.S. 25 (1996), no State may, by statute, regulation, order, interpretation, or other action, prevent or significantly interfere with the ability of a depository institution, or an affiliate thereof, to engage, directly or indirectly, either by itself or in conjunction with an affiliate or any other person, in any insurance sales, solicitation, or cross-marketing activity.

On January 13, 2004,[80] the OCC adopted final regulations incorporating many of the principles the courts have developed in preemption cases over the years involving national banks and covering other matters, such as predatory lending. These actions adopted three new regulations in 12 CFR Part 7, Bank Activities and Operations, and amendments to 12 CFR Part 34, Real Estate Lending and Appraisals.

Federal Savings Associations

Federal savings associations, like national banks, have a long history of favorable court cases involving state laws that interfere with their operations.

---

79. Preamble *op. cit.*, p. 1910, quoting 517 U.S. 25, 33.
80. "Bank Activities and Operations; Real Estate Lending and Appraisals," 69 FR 1904.

In 1982, in *Fidelity Federal Savings Loan Assn. v. de la Cuesta*,[81] the U.S. Supreme Court upheld a rule by the Federal Home Loan Bank Board (Board) that preempted a California law prohibiting the enforcement of "due on sale" clauses in mortgage loans made by federal associations. These clauses declare a mortgage loan due and payable at the time the underlying property is sold or otherwise conveyed.

The Court held that the Board acted within its statutory authority in issuing the regulation.

> The Board, an independent federal regulatory agency, was formed in 1932 and thereafter was vested with plenary authority to administer the Home Owners' Loan Act of 1933. . . . Section 5(a) of the HOLA, 12 U.S.C. 1464(a) (1976 ed., Supp. IV), empowers the Board, [458 U.S. 141, 145] "under such rules and regulations as it may prescribe, to provide for the organization, incorporation, examination, operation, and regulation of associations to be known as 'Federal Savings and Loan Associations.'" Pursuant to this authorization, the Board has promulgated regulations governing "the powers and operations of every Federal savings and loan association from its cradle to its corporate grave." *People v. Coast Federal Savings & Loan Assn.*, 98 F. Supp. 311, 316 (SD Cal. 1951).[82]

With respect to an intentional preemption of state law by an agency, the Court said:

> When the administrator promulgates regulations intended to pre-empt state law, the court's inquiry [is the following]:
>
> "If [h]is choice represents a reasonable accommodation of conflicting policies that were committed to the agency's care by the statute, we should not disturb it unless it appears from the statute or its legislative history that the accommodation is not one that Congress would have sanctioned."[83]

The Court found that the preemption of the California due on sale prohibition was beneficial to the residential mortgage market and housing finance in several ways, including the maintenance of a healthy secondary market for these loans, and upheld the Board's preemption.

---

81. 458 U.S. 141 (1982).
82. *Id.*, at p. 144
83. *Id.*, at 154, quoting *United States v. Shimer*, 367 U.S. 374, 381, 383 (1961).

Conclusions

The survival and vitality of the dual banking system is remarkable considering the fact that state governments and the federal government each tried at different times to tax the other's banking system out of existence. These efforts were a result of "the dynamic tension between centralization and decentralization in U.S. banking [that] is as old as the debate between Thomas Jefferson and Alexander Hamilton over the First Bank of the United States."[84]

Not only did both tax strategies fail, but the tax imposed by the federal government, as noted above, had exactly opposite result of that intended: state banks prospered as a result of demand deposits they adopted to avoid the federal tax on their notes.

Federal Reserve Board Governor Mark W. Olson has remarked that these conflicts have been worked out over time "in typically American fashion," which is "to have it both ways. We have nationally chartered banks supervised by the federal government and state-chartered banks supervised by both state and federal regulators."[85]

Another example of having it both ways is the fact that organizers of banks and savings associations can choose from a variety of charters—state or federal, stock or mutual, commercial bank or savings institution—and, by organizing holding companies, still be able, as discussed in Chapter 5, to engage, if they wish to do so, in all of the financial services permissible for financial holding companies.

Many of the events and major banking acts that are alluded to or not covered in this chapter are discussed throughout this book. These include the development of federal deposit insurance, additional background on bank and savings and loan holding companies, the expansion of financial services permitted for financial holding companies, and the auditing and other requirements of the Sarbanes-Oxley Act.

---

84. Federal Reserve Governor Mark W. Olson, "Dual Banking System and the Current Condition of the Banking Industry," remarks at the annual meeting of the Conference of State Bank Supervisors, Salt Lake City, Utah, May 31, 2002.

85. *Id.*

CHAPTER 2

Deposit Insurance

The federal deposit insurance program is one of the cornerstones of the U.S. banking system and one of the principal components of the federal safety net, which is referenced below. As discussed in Chapter 1, the Banking Act of 1933[1] added a section to the Federal Reserve Act to create the Federal Deposit Insurance Corporation (FDIC) and the insurance system, which is one of the Depression-era programs that revitalized the U.S. banking system. The insurance program is now administered under the Federal Deposit Insurance Act, which was enacted as a free-standing statute in 1950.[2]

Deposit insurance is a key element in the "safety net," which is a term given by regulators and others to programs that underlie the stability and efficiency of the banking system. The safety net also includes: critical elements of the federal payments system (which involves the clearance and settlement of checks and other items), and the Federal Reserve Board's emergency and other "discount window" loans.[3] The "protection of the safety net" is a key priority of federal banking laws, regulations, and supervision, and the safety net itself

---

1. June 16, 1933, ch. 89, 48 Stat. 163.
2. Federal Deposit Insurance Act of 1950, ch. 967 (Sept. 21, 1950), 64 Stat. 873, codified at 12 USC 1811 *et seq.*
3. The federal payments system and discount window loans, which are not covered in this book, are implemented by the Federal Reserve Board's Regulation J (12 CFR Part 210) and Regulation A (12 CFR Part 2001), respectively.

has been characterized as having "[provided] depository institutions and financial market participants with safety, liquidity, and solvency unheard of in previous years."[4]

As this book went to press in July, 2006, the federal deposit insurance system was undergoing changes brought about by legislation signed in February, 2006, The "Federal Deposit Insurance Reform Act of 2005" (Reform Act), discussed below,[5] which made several changes in the federal deposit insurance program, including a merger of the deposit insurance funds, indexing insurance coverage to inflation, and revising the way insurance assessments are determined.

Following is a brief summary of the federal deposit insurance system as it operated before the changes mandated by the Reform Act took place.

Federal Deposit Insurance before the Reform Act

Deposits in banks and savings associations before the Reform Act were insured by two insurance funds, the Bank Insurance Fund (BIF) and the Savings Association Insurance Fund (SAIF).

These funds were created in the aftermath of the S&L crisis by the Financial Institutions Reform, Recovery and Enforcement Act of 1989 (FIRREA),[6] which amended the FDIA to:

- rename FDIC's Federal Deposit Insurance Fund as the Bank Insurance Fund (BIF); and
- require the FDIC to assume responsibility for the new SAIF, which was created to replace the former Federal Savings and Loan Insurance Corporation (FSLIC)—the agency that had insured accounts of savings associations (see Chapter 1).

FIRREA required BIF and SAIF to be administered and funded separately and prohibited commingling of their assets. On August 9, 1989, the date of enactment of FIRREA, institutions that were members of the FDIC, predominantly commercial and FDIC-supervised

---

4. Remarks by Alan Greenspan, Chairman of the Federal Reserve Board, "The Financial Safety Net," at the 37th Annual Conference on Bank Structure and Competition of the Federal Reserve Bank of Chicago, Chicago, Illinois, May 10, 2001.

5. The Federal Deposit Insurance Reform Act of 2005 (Reform Act) Pub. Law 109-171, Title II, Subtitle B (Feb. 8, 2006), 120 Stat. 9.

6. Pub. Law 101-73 (Aug. 9, 1989), 103 Stat. 183.

savings banks, became members of BIF, and institutions whose accounts were insured by the FSLIC, primarily state and federal savings associations, became SAIF members.

Premium Disparity

1989

FIRREA set a designated reserve ratio (DRR) for each fund of 1.25% (125 basis points) of estimated insured deposits, which could be increased to 150 basis points for either fund if the FDIC determined that the higher percentage was justified by higher risks of default by the fund's members.

1991

A new premium methodology was imposed by the FDIC Improvement Act of 1991 (FDICIA),[7] which required the FDIC to develop a risk-based assessment system in which better-capitalized and financially healthy institutions would pay lower deposit insurance premiums than those that pose greater risk to their insurance fund.

The FDIC was required to set these premiums twice a year for each fund for semiannual periods beginning January 1 and July 1. In setting these rates, the FDIC was required to consider several factors, including each fund's reserve ratio and earnings, the financial condition of the industry and potential future losses to the funds from institutions insolvencies.

To meet these requirements, the FDIC developed the matrix format shown in Figure 2.1, in which premiums are plotted by supervisory status and capital adequacy and set an initial premium range of 23 to 31 basis points for BIF and SAIF.

1996

BIF reached its DRR in May, 1996, and qualified effective January 1, 1999, for the zero-27 basis-point schedule that the FDIC had adopted for members of either fund when their fund reached its DRR.

---

7. The Federal Deposit Insurance Company Improvement Act of 1991, Pub. Law 102-242 (Dec. 19, 1991), (FDICIA), 105 Stat. 2236, section 302 amending sec. 7(b) of the FDI Act (12 USC 1817(b)).

Figure 2.1
BIF and SAIF Assessment Schedules
First Half of 2006

Supervisory Subgroups
(Assessments are in basis points)

Capitalization	A	B	C
Well capitalized	0	3	17/1/
Adequately capitalized	3	10	24
Less than adequately capitalized	10	24	27

/1/ Premiums are a percentage of insured deposits expressed in basis points (each basis point equals one one-hundredth of one %).

Capitalization standards
   Well capitalized: Minimum total risk-based capital: 10%; Tier 1 capital: 6%; and Tier 1 leverage ratio: 5%.
   Adequately capitalized: Minimum total risk-based capital: 8%; Tier 1 capital: 4%; and Tier 1 leverage ratio: 4%.
   Less than adequately capitalized: Institutions that do not qualify as adequately capitalized.

Supervisory subgroups
   Subgroup A: Financially sound institutions with only a few minor weaknesses.
   Subgroup B: Institutions with weaknesses that, if not corrected, could lead to significant deterioration of the institution and increased risk of loss to BIF or SAIF.
   Subgroup C: Institutions that pose a substantial probability of loss to BIF or SAIF unless effective corrective action is taken.

It had become clear much earlier, however, that SAIF, for several reasons,[8] would not reach its DRR for a few more years if at all thereby prolonging a premium disparity that would place SAIF members at a long-term competitive disadvantage. This disparity could have also led to further diversion of insured deposits from

---

8. These reasons included the fact that SAIF at its inception, had a lower reserve ratio than BIF and the fact that a substantial portion of SAIF premiums were diverted to pay the interest on 30-year "FICO bonds" issued to pay the costs of the resolution of savings association failures that had occurred before 1987. FICO is the Financing Corporation, a mixed-ownership government corporation created in 1987 by CEBA. FICO bond premiums were about 1.26 basis points of insured deposits for the third quarter of 2006.

SAIF to BIF, which happened briefly in 1995, thereby making it more difficult, if not impossible, for SAIF to reach its DRR. These developments led to the eventual recapitalization of SAIF by means of a special assessment on SAIF members.

Sept. 30, 1996

Congress approved the "Deposit Insurance Funds Act of 1996" (Funds Act),[9] which imposed a special assessment on SAIF members and on certain BIF member banks that held SAIF-insured deposits (Oakar banks) to recapitalize SAIF. The basic assessment was 65.7 basis points of SAIF-assessable deposits, with discounts for Oakar and certain other institutions. This assessment brought in $4.5 billion[10] and resulted in the SAIF reaching its DRR on Oct. 1, 1996, which also became the effective date of the zero-27 basis point deposit insurance assessment schedule for SAIF members. As noted above, this assessment schedule remained in effect through the enactment of the Reform Act.

The "Free Ride" and Other Issues

The BIF-SAIF premium disparity that ended with the recapitalization of SAIF in 1996 was replaced by another kind of disparity that was one of the major contributors to deposit insurance reform in 2006.

The "Free Ride"

This disparity was between institutions that had paid deposit premiums under the pre-1996 schedules and that qualified for the zero percent premium assessment after it had been adopted, and institutions that were organized and became members of BIF or SAIF after

---

9. The Funds Act is set out in Division A, Title II, Subtitle G, of the Omnibus Consolidated Appropriations Act, 1997, Public Law 104-863 (Sept. 30, 1996) 110 Stat. 3009 *et seq.* (The Funds Act can be found at 110 Stat. 3009-479, and p. 480 of the pdf version of Pub. Law 104-863.)

10. FDIC, *A Brief History of Deposit Insurance in the United States*, September, 1998, p. 58.

1996. These institutions enjoyed the full benefits of deposit insurance coverage without paying any insurance premiums because they were well capitalized and had qualified for the zero percent premium rate from the time they were organized.

The FDIC was unable to impose premiums on these or any other well-capitalized institutions because of the "assessment ceiling" provisions in FDICIA providing that once either fund reaches its DRR, the FDIC may not assess further premiums against institutions in the lowest risk category in that fund except as required to maintain the fund at its DRR.

The agency could set higher assessments only for institutions that had financial, operational, or compliance problems or that were undercapitalized as shown in Figure 2.1. The principle was that *some* premiums should be assessed against institutions with higher risk profiles not only to serve as an incentive to solve their supervisory problems but also to compensate their insurance fund for the greater risk of insolvency they presented to the fund.

As a result of the increasing prosperity of the banking industry in recent years, increasing numbers of pre-1996 institutions qualified for the zero basis point premium rate, and the post-1996 institutions remained well-capitalized. By the end of 2004, as shown in Figure 2.2, over 93% of insured institutions holding over 98% of the deposit insurance assessment base qualified were in the zero percent premium category.

At the House hearings on an early version of the proposed Reform Act, FDIC Chairman Donald E. Powell testified as follows:

> The current statute governing deposit insurance premiums . . . also permits banks and thrifts to bring new deposits into the system without paying any premiums. Essentially, the banks that were in existence before 1997 endowed the funds and newcomers have not been required to contribute to the ongoing cost of the deposit insurance system. Since 1996, almost 1,100 new banks and thrifts, which hold $262 billion in assessable deposits, have joined the system and never paid for insurance. Other institutions have grown significantly without paying additional premiums. *Through premiums paid up to 1996, in effect, older and more slowly growing institutions are subsidizing these new and fast-growing institutions.*[11] (emphasis added)

---

11. Before the Subcommittee on Financial Institutions and Consumer Credit of the House Committee on Financial Services, March 17, 2005.

Figure 2.2
Assessment Base Distribution of Well-Capitalized Institutions by Percentage of Institutions and Percentage of Insured Funds As of December 31, 2004[*]

BIF Assessments	Supervisory Category		
	A	B	C
percentage of institutions	93.3%	5.0	0.8
percentage of assessment base	98.2%	1.1	0.4
SAIF Assessments	Supervisory Category		
	A	B	C
percentage of institutions	93.1%	5.7	0.8
percentage of assessment base	98.8%	1.1	0.1

[*] "BIF Assessment Ratio for the Second Semiannual Assessment Period of 2005," and "SAIF Assessment Ratio for the Second Semiannual Assessment Period of 2005," staff memoranda to the FDIC Board of Directors, May 10, 2005.

Basic Provisions of the Reform Act

Merger of BIF and SAIF

The Reform Act[12] merges the two deposit insurance funds, BIF and SAIF, into a new Deposit insurance Fund (DIF). The merger occurred on March 31, 2006.

Premiums

The Reform Act ended the "free ride" by requiring all institutions to be assessed a premium based on a revised risk-based system. The FDIC is granted greater flexibility in setting premium schedules and is no longer required to set premiums and re-evaluate the premium schedule every six months.

Reserve Ratio

FDIC can set the designated reserve ratio of the fund to insured deposits at levels between 1.15 and 1.50% of insured deposits. If the

---

12. The discussion of the provisions of the Reform Act is based on the Conference Report on the Reform Act, H. Rept. 109-171, and "Reg/Ops," March, 2006, America's Community Bankers.

ratio falls below 1.15%, the FDIC must develop a plan to restore the Fund to that level within 5 years. The restoration plan can include limits on use of the transitional assessment credit, which is discussed below, until the reserve ratio is restored to 1.15%.

Dividends

The free ride is ended by a requirement that all institutions be assessed at least minimum premiums. The FDIC is required to provide a dividend or rebate to insured institutions of 100% of its premium income in excess of that required to maintain the Fund's DRR at 1.50% of insured deposits. When the Fund's DRR reaches 1.35%, the FDIC is required to pay a premium dividend equal to 50% of premium income in excess of that required to maintain the reserve ratio at 1.35%.

Allocation Factors

The amount of the dividend that each eligible institution will receive will be determined by FDIC regulations based on each eligible institution's relative contribution to the DIF and the former BIF and SAIF, taking into account such factors as:

1. Their share of the total assessment base as of December 31, 1996;
2. The total assessments paid by the institution or its predecessor after that date to the DIF or its predecessors: BIF and SAIF;
3. The portion of assessments paid that reflect any "higher levels of risk" assumed by the institution; and
4. Such other factors that the FDIC deems appropriate.

Transitional Credit

A transitional deposit insurance premium credit of $4.7 billion, approximately the size of the 1996 special assessment that recapitalized SAIF, is made available to eligible institutions based on their respective percentage of total industry assessable deposits on December 31, 1996 and other factors to be considered by the FDIC.

To be eligible for the credit, the institution must have been in existence on December 31, 1996, or be a successor to an institution in existence on that date, and must have paid at least one insurance assessment before that date.

These credits may be used to offset future insurance assessments—100% of such assessments in 2006–2007, 90% in 2008–2010, and 100% thereafter. For institutions that exhibit financial, operational, or compliance weaknesses at the beginning of an assessment period, the credit will be reduced to an amount equal to the average assessment rate on all institutions for that period.

Deposit Insurance Coverage

Inflation Index

The basic deposit insurance maximum of $100,000 per account is defined for technical purposes as the "standard maximum deposit insurance amount" (SMDIA) and can be indexed to inflation each year for five years beginning April 1, 2010, upon approval by the FDIC and the National Credit Union Administration (NCUA). The adjustment, calculated on an index published by the Department of Commerce, will be adjusted to the nearest $10,000.

Retirement Accounts

Deposit insurance coverage of certain retirement accounts are increased from $100,000 to $250,000, subject to the same inflation adjustments as those for regular accounts.

Employee Benefit Plans

Pass through coverage for employee benefit plans is permitted even if the institution is not authorized to accept such plans because of inadequate capital. Supervisory action may be taken against the institution but the insurance coverage of the accounts will not be affected.

An interim rule with request for comment to implement these provisions, effective April 1, 2006, was published March 23, 2006.[13]

---

13. FDIC, "Deposit Insurance Regulations; Inflation Index; Certain Retirement Accounts and Employee Benefit Plan Accounts," Interim rule with request for comments, 71 FR 14629 (March 23, 2006).

Basic Deposit Insurance Coverage

Basic Accounts

Until indexed for inflation, as provided for in the Reform Act, the principal and interest on individually owned accounts are insured for up to $100,000. The rules for these "plain vanilla" accounts in the examples below are straightforward, but determining deposit insurance coverage on other insured accounts, several examples of which are listed below, is sometimes more difficult.

The FDIC regulations provide that insurance coverage is based on "the ownership rights" in the deposit accounts a depositor has at the same bank, rather than the number of accounts the depositor has at that bank.[14]

Examples

- Depositor A is the sole owner of a checking account with a balance of $80,000 at Bank X. *Coverage:* The balance in A's checking account is fully insured.
- A deposits $50,000 in a savings account at Bank X. *Coverage:* The savings account is not insured separately because the "ownership rights" in the two accounts are the same. *Coverage:* A is insured for $100,000 of the combined balance of $130,000 in the two accounts.
- A then opens a joint checking account of $100,000 with B at Bank X. *Coverage:* The joint account is insured separately for up to $100,000 because A's ownership interest in the joint account is different from A's individual ownership accounts in his or her checking and savings accounts.
- A opens an Individual Retirement Account at Bank X for $100,000. *Coverage:* The IRA is insured for $100,000 because FDIC regulations provide for separate insurance for these and certain other employee benefit accounts.
- A opens a checking account at Bank Y for $100,000. *Coverage:* A's account at Bank Y is insured for $100,000 if Bank Y is separately chartered and insured in relation to Bank X, even if Bank X is a subsidiary of a holding company that also controls Bank Y.

---

14. 12 CFR §330.3.

Revocable Trusts

These are testamentiary accounts in which the grantor or grantors are able to provide deposit insurance protection for funds payable to qualified beneficiaries in the event the institution fails before the death of the grantor.

POD Accounts

The most common type of revocable trust is the payable-on-death (POD) account. These are revocable trusts in which the grantor deposits funds into a revocable trust account, names the beneficiaries, and enters the amount they are to receive on a signature card at the institution. The grantor "owns" the funds for deposit insurance purposes and can revoke the trust at any time. The trust becomes irrevocable upon the grantor's death. If the bank fails before the grantor's death, the interests of "qualified beneficiaries"—basically the grantor's spouse, parents, children, grandchildren, and siblings—are insured up to $100,000 each.

The coverage of beneficiaries on these accounts is separate from that afforded to any single-ownership accounts held by grantor or by any beneficiary at the same institution. If a POD is established by two or more grantors, including a husband and wife, the interests of each qualified beneficiary are insured separately for $100,000 for each grantor.

Example

Husband and wife, H and W (grantors) each create an individually owned POD account and a joint POD account at Bank A. There is $300,000 in each of these accounts. Each account provides for a distribution of $100,000 each to the grantors' two children upon the death of the grantor of each individual account and the same distribution from the joint account upon the death of the surviving grantor.

Bank A fails before the death of the grantors or the children. The total insurance coverage for these accounts is $900,000:

$100,000 for each of the grantor's individual accounts	=	$200,000
$100,000 for the grantors from their joint account	=	100,000
$100,000 for each child from each of the three POD accounts		
($100,000 per child from each account = $200,000		
× three accounts	= 600,000	600,000
Total insurance		$900,000

In addition, any individually owned accounts held by the children at Bank A would be insured for up to $100,000 each.

More complex arrangements, generally called "family trusts" or "living trusts" by the FDIC, can be created by grantors for estate and tax planning purposes. The FDIC says

> . . . living trust coverage is based on the interests of qualifying beneficiaries who would become entitled to receive trust assets when the trust owner dies (or if the trust is jointly owned, when the last owner dies). This means that, when determining coverage, the FDIC will ignore any trust beneficiary who would have an interest in the trust assets only after another living beneficiary dies.[15]

Other Accounts

Other accounts that are eligible for deposit insurance include the following:

- Accounts held by an agent, nominee, guardian, custodian, or conservator;
- Annuity contract accounts;
- Revocable trust accounts;
- Accounts of a corporation, partnership, or unincorporated association;
- Accounts held by a depository institution as the trustee of an irrevocable trust;
- Irrevocable trust accounts;
- Funds of the U.S. deposited by official custodians of such funds;
- Accounts of a state, county, municipality, or political subdivision; and
- Funds underlying stored value, payroll, and other kinds of access cards (regulations re-proposed at 70 FR 45571 (Aug. 8, 2005)).

BIF-SAIF Merger

On March 31, 2006, the FDIC merged BIF and SAIF into the Deposit Insurance Fund. Conforming amendments to the agency's regulations were published April 21, 2006.[16]

---

15. FDIC, "Insuring Your Deposits."
16. FDIC, "Revisions to Reflect the Merger of the Bank Insurance Fund and the Savings and Loan Insurance Fund," Final rule 71 FR 20524 (April 21, 2006).

Conclusion

The federal deposit insurance program is the key element of the federal safety net discussed above, and the goal of "protection of the insurance funds"—now the insurance fund after the BIF-SAIF merger—is one of the foundations of banking laws and regulations affecting the activities of banks and savings associations as well as those of their subsidiaries and affiliates.

The program was responsible for restoring public confidence in the banking system during the Depression and it has obviously worked since then. No depositor has lost any money from an FDIC-insured account since the program's inception.

One of the reasons agencies take their responsibility so seriously is that the solvency of the fund is implicitly guaranteed by the ultimate safety net—the U.S. taxpayer. This is a not a guarantee that anyone expects to call upon in the future. There has been only one insolvency of a federal deposit insurance fund since the program began—that of the former Federal Savings and Loan Insurance Corporation (FSLIC)—and that cost the taxpayers an estimated $125 billion.[17]

---

17. Timothy Curry and Lynn Shibut, *The Cost of the Savings and Loan Crisis: Truth and Consequences,* FDIC BANKING REVIEW, Vol. 13, No. 2 (2000).

CHAPTER **3**

Examinations, Enforcement, Conservatorships, and Receiverships

Conduct of Examinations

Introduction

Examinations are the means by which bank regulators determine the financial health of the institutions they supervise. A short definition might be that an examination is the means for an agency to assess the likelihood that an institution could become insolvent. The Federal Reserve Board (Board) provides a more formal definition:

The essential objectives of an examination are to:

1. provide an objective evaluation of a bank's soundness and compliance with banking laws and regulations;
2. permit the Federal Reserve to appraise the quality of management and directors; and
3. identify those areas where corrective action is required to strengthen the bank, improve the quality of its performance, and enable it to comply with applicable laws, rulings, and regulations.[1]

---

1. Federal Reserve Board Commercial Bank Supervision Manual, Preface.

In 2005, Julie L. Williams, Acting Comptroller of the Currency, described the examination process as follows:

> Bank examiners have access to all aspects of a bank's affairs and the flow of communications between a bank and the supervisory agency is open and continuous. Not only the quality and classification of assets. . . . but also the bank's lending and investment practices, consumer disclosures, adequacy of security systems and internal controls, quality of management, and future financial prospects, among other things, are of concern to bank examiners.
>
> Bank management is expected to be open and forthcoming with bank examiners. *Examiners expect to get the information they need when they ask for it, and they expect to be told important things without having to ask.* And examiners are expected to be direct and frank in expressing their concerns about the bank and the corrective actions they expect. Because of this extraordinary flow of sensitive and confidential information between banks and their supervisors, the bank supervisory process in this country has always been and remains a predominantly confidential process between the bank and its supervisor.[2] (emphasis added)

Types of Examinations

The banking agencies conduct three basic types of examinations:

- *Safety and Soundness.* Sometimes referred to as "full-scope" examinations, these are the examinations that determine the fundamental financial health of a bank or savings association.
- *Compliance.* These examinations cover consumer compliance and fair lending issues.
- *Specialty.* These are also referred to as "targeted" examinations and cover areas such as trust activities and information technology.

Scoring

Safety and soundness examinations are scored on the basis of a "CAMELS" composite rating, of 1 to 5. A rating of 1 indicates superior condition and 5 shows a strong likelihood of failure. CAMELS is the acronym for the six components on which the composite rating

---

2. Julie L. Williams, Acting Comptroller of the Currency, remarks before the New York Bankers Association, Washington, D.C., July 19, 2005.

is based: Capital adequacy, Asset quality, Management, Earnings, Liquidity, and Sensitivity to market risk. CAMELS ratings are discussed in more detail below.

Most compliance and specialty examinations are also scored on a similar 1-to-5 composite rating of applicable components.

Safety and Soundness Examinations

The conduct of safety and soundness examinations of banks, savings associations, and their affiliates is the responsibility of an institution's primary federal regulator. Requirements relating to the frequency of these examinations are found in Sections 10(d)(1) and (3) of the Federal Deposit Insurance Act (FDIA),[3] which were enacted in 1991.

Examination Frequency

A safety and soundness examination of each institution with assets of $250 million or more must generally be conducted every 12 or 18 months, depending on the size and financial condition of the institution.

The examination frequency for institutions with total assets of less than $250 million is once every 18 months if the institution:

- has a CAMELS rating of 1 or 2;
- is well-capitalized, which is defined as:
  - total risk-based capital of 10% or more,
  - a tier 1 capital ratio of 6% or more,
- is not subject to a formal enforcement proceeding or order by its primary or secondary federal regulator; and
- has not undergone a change in control for a period of 12 months since its last examination.[4]

The Board, FDIC, and OTS have entered into arrangements with all state banking agencies to conduct safety and soundness examinations of state-chartered institutions during alternate examination cycles.

---

3. 12 USC 1820(d)(1)&(3).
4. Agency rules on frequency of examinations are found in the following sections of 12 CFR: OCC § 4.6; Federal Reserve § 208.64; FDIC § 337.12; and OTS § 563.171.

Compliance Examinations

These examinations measure an institution's compliance with civil rights, consumer protection, and other public interest laws including those relating community reinvestment, equal credit opportunity, fair landing, truth in lending, truth in savings, and fair credit reporting.

Frequency

Compliance examinations are generally conducted concurrently with safety and soundness examinations and a separate compliance rating, which is also a based on a descending scale of 1 to 5, is assigned to the institution. (The OTS adopted a formal policy in April, 2002 to combine safety and soundness and compliance examinations into a single comprehensive examination.)

Performance Ratings

Institutions' ratings for most compliance examinations are scored in accordance with the Interagency Consumer Compliance Rating System, which provides a scale of 1 to 5, with 1 representing the highest level of performance and 5 the lowest. Three of the most relevant factors evaluated in this system are:

- the nature and extent of present compliance with consumer protection and civil rights laws and regulations;
- the commitment of management to compliance and its ability and willingness to ensure continuing compliance; and
- the adequacy of operating systems, including internal procedures, controls, and audit activities designed to ensure compliance on a routine and consistent basis.[5]

There are four ratings for examinations under the Community Reinvestment Act (CRA), which assess the institution's performance in helping to meet the credit needs of its community. These are: Outstanding, Satisfactory, Needs to Improve, and Substantial Noncompliance.

---

5. The discussion of compliance examinations is based on: OCC, Consumer Compliance Examination - Overview, August 1996, FDIC, Compliance Examination Manual; and OTS RB 37-8, Nov. 20, 2004.

Specialty Examinations

Specialty examinations evaluate activities relating to information technology and other activities listed below plus others not listed, including acting as registered transfer agents and as broker/dealers of government and municipal securities. The FDIC suggests that specialty examinations, like compliance examinations, should, if possible, be conducted concurrently with safety and soundness examinations, unless the size or arrangement of the department makes it impractical or inefficient to do so. In any case, specialty exams are generally subject to the same frequency as safety and soundness examinations.[6]

Among the principal specialty examinations are the following.

Trust Activities

Examinations of trust activities are conducted and scored on the basis of the Uniform Interagency Trust Rating System (UITRS) adopted by the FFIEC in 1998.[7]

These examinations determine if an institution's policies or the way it administers accounts has resulted in a contingent liability or estimated loss that could impair the institution's capital and damage its reputation. A financial institution's failure to perform its fiduciary duties and meet its responsibilities with appropriate care, skill, and prudence, and in accordance with fiduciary principles and applicable laws and regulations, could harm trust customers and expose the institution to possible loss or surcharge.[8]

These examinations are assigned a composite rating of 1 to 5 with the most favorable rating being 1. This rating embodies the composite ratings of the following components:

- Management
- Operations, Internal Controls, and Auditing
- Earnings
- Compliance
- Asset Management

---

6. FDIC, S&S Manual *op. cit.,* Sec 1.1.
7. FFIEC, Uniform Interagency Trust Rating System, Notice, 63 FR 54704 (Oct. 13, 1998).
8. FDIC, Trust Examination Manual, Overview.

Information Technology (IT)

A primary objective of the IT examination is to determine the validity and reliability of the records produced by the automated system; therefore, the emphasis is on an evaluation of internal controls.

IT operations are evaluated on the basis of the FFIEC Information Technology (IT) Examination Handbook, which is a series of 12 booklets on this subject developed between January, 2003 and August 2004. Subjects in this handbook include:

- Audit
- Information security
- Supervision of technical service providers
- Retail payments systems

Money Laundering

Examinations relating to compliance with federal money laundering laws are more formally referred to as Bank Secrecy Act/Anti-Money Laundering examinations. These examinations have no fixed schedule and are, according to the FDIC:

> generally subject to the same examination intervals. . . . as safety and soundness examinations. . . . [findings] from BSA examinations are generally included within the safety and soundness report. However, a separate BSA examination may be conducted in some instances . . . Although a separate rating system for BSA does not exist, the BSA findings can affect both the management ratings and the overall composite [CAMELS] rating of the institution.[9]

A new BSA examination manual, the *Bank Secrecy Act/Anti-Money Laundering Examination Manual*, was released by the FFIEC and adopted by the banking agencies in June, 2005.[10] Examiners began using the new manual on July 1, 2005.

CAMELS Ratings

The CAMELS rating is the score given an institution after a Safety and Soundness examination. As noted above, the score is a compos-

---

9. FDIC, Risk Management Manual of Examination Policies, section 1.1.
10. FFIEC Release NR 2005-64, June 30, 2005.

ite rating based on the ratings of the institution in each of six areas for which CAMELS is an acronym:

- Capital adequacy,
- Asset quality,
- Management,
- Earnings,
- Liquidity, and
- Sensitivity to market risk.

Both the composite rating and the ratings of each of the six components are made on a scale of 1 (indicating the strongest performance) to 5 (a critically deficient level of performance). The formal name for the CAMELS system is the Uniform Financial Institutions Rating System (UFIRS). The following summary descriptions of the CAMELS components and ratings are derived from the Federal Register Notice in which the FFIEC adopted the current version of UFIRS in 1996.[11]

Capital Adequacy—A financial institution is expected to maintain capital commensurate with the nature and extent of risks to the institution and the ability of management to identify, measure, monitor, and control these risks. The effect of credit, market, and other risks on the institution's financial condition should be considered when evaluating this component.

Asset Quality—This rating reflects the quantity of existing and potential credit risk associated with the loan and investment portfolios, other real estate owned (generally, real estate acquired through foreclosure), and other assets, as well as off-balance sheet transactions. The ability of management to identify, measure, monitor, and control credit risk also is reflected here.

Management—The capability of the board of directors and management, in their respective roles, to identify, measure, monitor, and control the risks of an institution's activities, and to ensure a financial institution's safe, sound, and efficient operation in compliance with applicable laws and regulations is reflected in this rating. Generally, directors need not be actively involved

---

11. Federal Financial Institutions Examination Council, Uniform Financial Institutions Rating System (UFIRS), Notice, 61 FR 67021 (December 19, 1996).

in day-to-day operations; however, they must provide clear guidance regarding acceptable risk exposure levels and ensure that appropriate policies, procedures, and practices have been established. Senior management is responsible for developing and implementing policies, procedures, and practices that translate the board's goals, objectives, and risk limits into prudent operating standards.

Earnings—This rating reflects not only the quantity and trend of earnings but also factors that may affect the sustainability or quality of earnings. The quantity as well as the quality of earnings can be affected by excessive or inadequately managed credit risk, which could result in excessive loan losses. In addition, the assumption of high levels of market risk by the institution could result in undue exposure of its earnings to volatility in interest rates.

Liquidity—Consideration should be given to the current level and prospective sources of liquidity compared to funding needs, as well as to the adequacy of funds management practices relative to the institution's size, complexity, and risk profile. In general, funds management practices should ensure that an institution is able to maintain a level of liquidity sufficient to meet its financial obligations in a timely manner and to fulfill the legitimate banking needs of its community.

Sensitivity to Market Risk—This component reflects the degree to which changes in interest rates, foreign exchange rates, commodity prices, or equity prices can adversely affect a financial institution's earnings or economic capital. When evaluating this component, consideration should be given to: management's ability to identify, measure, monitor, and control market risk; the institution's size; the nature and complexity of its activities; and the adequacy of its capital and earnings in relation to its level of market risk exposure. For many institutions, the primary source of market risk arises from nontrading positions and their sensitivity to changes in interest rates. For others, trading activities are a major source of market risk.

Under the UFIRS, as noted above, each financial institution is assigned a composite of 1 to 5 based on the evaluation and rating of the six CAMELS components. Following is a summary of these ratings:

Composite 1—Sound in every respect and generally have components rated 1 or 2. Any weaknesses are minor and can be handled in a routine manner by the board of directors and management. These institutions are the most capable of withstanding the vagaries of business conditions and are resistant to outside influences such as economic instability in their trade area.

Composite 2—Fundamentally sound. For an institution to receive this rating, generally no component rating should be more severe than 3. Only moderate weaknesses are present and are well within the board of directors' and management's capabilities and willingness to correct. They are stable and are capable of withstanding business fluctuations and are in substantial compliance with laws and regulations. There are no material supervisory concerns and, as a result, the supervisory response is informal and limited.

Composite 3—These institutions exhibit a combination of weaknesses that may range from moderate to severe and require more than normal supervision, which may include formal or informal enforcement actions. Management may lack the ability or willingness to effectively address weaknesses within appropriate time frames. Institutions in this group generally are less capable of withstanding business fluctuations than those institutions rated a composite 1 or 2. Additionally, these financial institutions may be in significant noncompliance with laws and regulations. Risk management practices may be less than satisfactory relative to the institution's size, complexity, and risk profile. Failure appears unlikely.

Composite 4—For these institutions, failure is a distinct possibility if the problems and weaknesses are not satisfactorily addressed and resolved. There are serious financial or managerial deficiencies that result in unsatisfactory performance. Weaknesses and problems are not being satisfactorily addressed or resolved by the board of directors and management. Institutions in this group generally are not capable of withstanding business fluctuations and there may be significant noncompliance with laws and regulations. Risk management practices are generally unacceptable relative to the institution's size, complexity, and risk profile. Close supervisory attention is required, which means, in most cases, formal enforcement action is necessary to address the problems.

Composite 5—These institutions exhibit extremely unsafe and unsound practices or conditions; exhibit a critically deficient performance; often contain inadequate risk management practices relative to the institution's size, complexity, and risk profile. The volume and severity of problems are beyond management's ability or willingness to control or correct. Immediate outside financial or other assistance is needed in order for the financial institution to be viable. Failure is highly probable.

Determining the CAMELS Ratings[12]

The agencies instruct examiners not to "derive the composite rating merely by computing an arithmetic average of the component ratings," since that approach "will not reflect the true condition of the . . . association."

Some components may be given more weight than others depending on the association's size, complexity of operations, and risk profile. The management component, for example, may be given "special consideration" in determining a composite rating because the ability of management to address the risks posed by changing business conditions and the initiation of new activities are important factors in evaluating an association's overall risk profile.

The institution's overall composite rating, and particularly its management component, must reflect its scores on compliance and specialty examinations. The OTS, for example, says that an association's management rating cannot be higher than 2 if its compliance rating is 3, and should be no higher than 3, if the compliance rating is 4 or 5. The management rating also must reflect findings on the association's technology risk controls.

---

12. The discussion in this section is based on OTS, RB 37-4, Ratings: Developing, Assigning and Presenting, Nov. 30, 2004.

Coordination of Examinations of State Institutions

Background

The Federal Financial Examinations Council (FFIEC) has noted that the three federal banking agencies that supervise state-chartered banks and savings associations[13]

> "have a long history of coordinating with the State banking departments[14] in fulfilling a mutual goal of promoting a safe and sound banking system [and that this cooperation] promotes efficiency in the examination process, reduces the regulatory burden on state-chartered, insured depository institutions, and improves the supervisory process"[15]

For their part, the state banking departments have coordinated their activities through the Conference of State Bank Supervisors (CSBS), not only in working with the federal agencies on state-federal cooperation but also working among themselves on coordinating examination and supervision of state-chartered institutions with branches in more than one state.

The development of coordination procedures accelerated during the late 1980s and early 1990s as additional states entered into interstate branching compacts and as Congress adopted measures requiring federal agencies to work with state agencies to coordinate examinations of state banks and savings associations.

In 1992, CSBS entered into an agreement with the FDIC and the Board, individually to encourage the negotiation and formation of working agreements between these agencies and state banking departments. This Agreement was followed by another in 1995 and finally by two "nationwide agreements" adopted in 1996, which are discussed below.

---

13. The FDIC, the Federal Reserve Board, and the OTS.
14. The FFIEC points out that that "state banking department "includes any separate thrift (i.e., savings association) department or division of a State."
15. FFIEC, Guidelines for Relying on State Examinations, Notice and final guidelines, 60 FR 33206, 33207 (June 27, 1995).

Federal Statutory Requirements Relating to Coordination of Examinations

Meanwhile, in 1991, Congress had adopted section 10(d) of the FDIA, which prescribed the 12- and 18-month safety and soundness examination intervals discussed above, and encouraged federal banking agencies to alternate their examinations of state institutions with state banking departments whose examination reports meet federal standards.[16] This section was amended in 1994 to provide additional requirements relating to coordination of bank examinations and directed the FFIEC to develop standards for reliance by federal agencies on examination reports by state banking departments in connection with, among other things, the alternating federal-state examinations of state institutions.[17]

In addition, section 10(d)(3) of the FDIA requires the federal banking agencies to:

1. Coordinate their own examinations of federally chartered institutions and affiliates;
2. Coordinate their examinations of individual institutions with examinations conducted institution by other agencies;
3. Work with state supervisors to coordinate both the conduct of examinations of state institutions and the number, types, and frequency and contents of required reports; and
4. Eliminate duplicate requests for information about an institution by using reports of other agencies that have examined the institution.

This subsection also required the federal banking agencies to develop a system by September, 1996, for determining which federal or state banking agency "will be the lead agency responsible for managing a unified examination of each insured depository institution and its affiliates, as required by this subsection."

---

16. Section 111 of the FDIC Improvement Act (FDICIA), Pub. Law 102-242 (Dec. 19, 1991), 105 Stat. 2236, adding new subsection (d) to section 10 of the FDIA (12 USC 1820(d)).

17. Sections 305, 306 and 349 of the Riegle Community Development and Regulatory Improvement Act (CDRIA), Pub. Law 103-325 (Sept. 23, 1994), 108 Stat. 2160, adding paragraphs (6)–(9) to section 10(d) of the FDIA (12 USC 1820(d)).

CSBS Nationwide Agreements

As noted above, the CSBS had entered into agreements with the federal banking agencies to coordinate examination of state banks several years before the adoption of 10(d) of the FDIA in 1994 and the enactment of the 1994 Riegle-Neal interstate branching legislation, sometimes referred to as "Riegle-Neal I."[18]

After these developments, CSBS entered into an Interstate Banking and Branching Supervisory Protocol on April 20, 1995 (the Protocol) with the FDIC and Board to coordinate the examination of state-chartered, multi-state banks, and to allocate responsibilities between "home states"—those in which a bank is chartered—and "host states"—states into which a bank branches.

The 1995 Protocol evolved into two more detailed nationwide agreements relating to multi-state banks. The first was a Nationwide Cooperative Agreement (Cooperative Agreement) signed on Nov. 13, 1996 and revised Dec. 9, 1997. This agreement was followed on Nov. 14, 1996 by the execution of a Nationwide Federal/State Supervisory Agreement (Supervisory Agreement) among state bank regulators, the FDIC, and the Board.

The Cooperative Agreement

This Agreement outlines the roles of home states and host states in the examination and supervision of state banks that branch across state lines. It provides that the home state supervisor is responsible for conducting safety and soundness examinations of multi-state banks, including branches of home state banks located in host states. The home state agency, however, may use host state examiners to examine for safety and soundness, trust operations, and electronic data processing in host state branches and should use those examiners to examine for compliance with host state laws relating to community reinvestment, consumer protection, and fair lending.

The home state supervisor is responsible for bringing enforcement actions against a multi-state bank and must notify all host state supervisors immediately when a formal or informal enforcement action is brought.

---

18. The Riegle-Neal Interstate Banking and Branching Efficiency Act of 1994, Pub. Law 103-328 (Sept. 28, 1994), 108 Stat. 2315.

The Supervisory Agreement

This document is designed to provide a "seamless supervisory process" of multi-state banks by state banking departments and the federal agencies. Safety and soundness examinations are generally to be conducted on a joint basis with a single examination report. These exam schedules should conform to preexisting arrangements for separate examinations in alternating examination cycles. The Board notes that joint examinations will normally be used for the larger, more complex organizations; alternate examinations are generally reserved for smaller organizations.[19]

This Agreement also applies to federal-state coordination of examinations of banks located in a single state, thereby fulfilling the 1994 Congressional mandate to develop a unified examination system.

The state agency and appropriate federal agency must each designate a primary contact person to coordinate the supervisory and examination responsibilities of their respective agencies for banks to be examined. They are responsible for, among other things, setting examination schedules and developing off-site monitoring plans. To further minimize duplication, the federal agencies will alternate with state agencies each year in the appointment of a single Examiner in Charge for each bank to be examined.

The Agreement also provides flexibility for state and federal agencies to conduct independent or special examinations in exceptional circumstances. The regulator initiating the independent or special examination will make every effort to provide appropriate notice to the other regulators prior to commencing the examination.

Enforcement actions arising from joint examinations are usually initiated by the federal or state agency whose representative is the examiner in charge.

In May 2004, the State-Federal Working Group, comprised of representatives of CSBS, the Board, and the FDIC, reaffirmed and expanded the Supervisory Agreement to reemphasize the need for cooperation and communication among the parties in view of the increasing complexity and variety of banking organization activities and the involvement of nonbank agencies in the examination and supervision of banking organizations, which is discussed below.

---

19. SR Letter 96-33, Nov. 22, 1996, footnote 1.

Standards for Reliance on Examinations by State Agencies

In 1995, the FFIEC published its guidelines for reliance on state examinations of banks and savings associations.[20] These guidelines provide that the following criteria may be considered, in whole or in part, by a federal banking agency when determining the acceptability of a state report of examination under section 10(d) of the FDIA:

1. The completeness of the state examination report.
2. The adequacy of documentation maintained to support observations made in examination reports.
3. Adequacy of the department's budgeting, examiner staffing and training, and whether it is accredited by CSBS.
4. Adequacy of the working agreement between the state banking department and the federal banking agency.

The federal banking agencies retain the option to conduct a follow-up examination in cases in which a state examination report appears insufficient or the condition of an insured institution, as indicated in the examination report or other sources, appears to be seriously deteriorating.

Currently, all 50 states, Puerto Rico, and the Virgin Islands have entered into working agreements with the FDIC and the Federal Reserve Board to conduct joint or alternating examinations of state-chartered banks.

Subsequent Developments

Many bank affiliates are subject to regulation by nonbanking agencies, such as the Securities and Exchange Commission and state insurance regulators. The role of these "functional regulators" has received increased attention since banking organizations were permitted in 1999 to offer new financial services through financial holding companies (FHCs) (discussed in Chapter 5).

In response to these developments, CSBS entered into several new cooperative agreements including a Model Cooperative Agreement with the National Association of State Insurance Commissioners (NAIC), a Nationwide Cooperative Agreement for Multi-State Trust Institutions in 1999, and, in 1998, agreements to coordinate the supervision of multi-state foreign banks that are supervised by state banking agencies.

---

20. Guidelines for Relying on State Examinations, *op. cit.*

FDIC Special Examinations—2002

On January 29, 2002, the FDIC executed an agreement with the other three banking agencies called the Coordination of Expanded Supervisory Information Sharing and Special Examinations (Interagency Agreement). The agreement enables the FDIC to conduct special examinations of any institution that represents a "heightened risk" to the deposit insurance funds or exhibits deteriorating conditions or other adverse developments regardless of current rating or capital level.

Associations subject to these joint examinations are generally those that have a CAMELS composite rating of 3, 4, or 5; or are "undercapitalized" under prompt corrective action standards.[21] The agency said it would pay particular attention to larger institutions and assign a full time examiner to each of the eight largest banking organizations.

FDIC Special Examinations—2005

On January 18, 2005, the FDIC amended the 2002 *Interagency Agreement* to permit it to examine organizations that are deemed to pose a heightened risk to the insurance funds, even though they are not in a deteriorating condition.

A background memorandum[22] to the FDIC Board of Directors pointed out, in effect, that while the 2002 agreement works well with institutions using conventional regulatory risk-based (Basel I) capital standards[23] and conventional risk measurement methods, it is not

---

21. Defined as: total risk-based capital ratio of less than 8%; tier 1 risk-based capital ratio of less than 4%; or a leverage ratio that is less than 4% (or less than 3.0% for associations with a CAMELS composite rating of 1).

22. The discussion and quotes in this section are excerpted from a background memorandum to the FDIC Board from FDIC staff on the open meeting agenda item for this amendment, which was captioned "Examination Activities for Insurance Purposes."

23. Basel I and Basel II, which are discussed in detail in Chapter 11, are capital frameworks developed by an international committee of central bank representatives located in Basel, Switzerland. The purpose of these standards is to align capital requirements more closely to the economic risk posed by various classes of assets and activities of financial institutions. The regulatory risk-based capital standards that currently apply to all FDIC-insured U.S. banks and savings associations, and to bank holding companies, are based on the Basel I framework, which was developed in the late 1980s. The U.S. banking agencies are in the preliminary stages of preparing a proposed Basel II framework for publication, public comment, and ultimate adoption. When adopted, Basel II is expected to apply only to a relatively small number (approximately 12–15) of the largest U.S. banking organizations.

useful for larger and more complex banking organizations. These entities (most of which are preparing for Basel II capital standards) are "using their own risk estimates of credit and operational risk [that] are more subjective and can sometimes be subject to an 'optimistic bias' based on more complex methodologies that involve more subjective assumptions."

The agency says:

> Institutions holding 41 percent of the assets of FDIC-insured institutions now use *their own estimates of risk* to determine their capital requirements for market risk. Moreover, a number of large insured institutions may soon be able to calculate their regulatory capital requirements based on their own-estimates of credit risk and operational risk. (emphasis added)

This subjectivity means even those large banking organizations that are well capitalized under these standards and have a CAMELS rating of 1 or 2 may be basing their capital requirements and risk analysis on faulty assumptions that could distort their deposit insurance premiums and conceal unstable financial conditions. The risks posed by organizations using these methods are characterized as "assumption risk" or "model risk," that magnifies the potential for unexpectedly bad financial outcomes." In the FDIC's view, these assumptions and models themselves are part of the risk analysis problem.

The FDIC says that the new agreement will not cause it to "embark on a [new] program of regular periodic examinations of non-FDIC supervised institutions." If it needs additional information, the agency says that in most cases, it would either review information from the institution's previous examination reports or obtain the information it needs from the institution's primary federal regulator.

This agreement generated some controversy among members of the FDIC Board of Directors and was adopted by a 3–2 vote.

Examination of Holding Companies

Bank Holding Companies

Section 5(c)(2) of the BHCA[24] authorizes the Federal Reserve Board to examine bank holding companies and their subsidiaries to determine

---

24. 12 USC 1844(c)(2).

the nature of their operations and financial condition and to assess the risks the holding company may pose to its subsidiary banks and savings associations (if any).

This section, however, provides that the Board may conduct examinations of functionally regulated subsidiaries only if it has reasonable cause to believe the subsidiary is engaged in activities that pose a material risk to a subsidiary bank or association.

In addition, the Board in conducting examinations of bank holding companies must, "to the fullest extent possible,"

- rely on examination reports of the holding company's subsidiary banks and savings associations that were conducted by these institutions' federal or state supervisory agency; and
- defer to examination reports of the primary regulators of the holding company's functionally regulated subsidiaries, including SEC examinations of securities broker-dealers, SEC, or state examinations of registered investment advisers, and state examinations of insurance companies.

BHC Composite Rating

On December 6, 2004, the Board published a notice that a new system for providing composite ratings for bank holding companies, which had been published for comment in June, 2005, would become effective on January 1, 2005.[25] The new rating system replaces the former "BOPEC" rating.[26]

The Board says the new system is consistent with the increased emphasis of the banking agencies on risk management. The former system provided a more static analysis of the financial condition of the "discrete legal entities" within the holding company. The new system is a shift away from historical analysis to a more forward looking assessment of risks management and provides a framework for the assessment of the risk posed by the nondepository entities of the holding company to its depository institution subsidiaries.

The new composite rating is referred to by the Board as **RFI/C(D)**.

---

25. Bank Holding Company Rating System, Notice, 69 FR 70444, (Dec. 6, 2004). The request for comment was published at 69 FR 43996 (July 23, 2004).

26. "BOPEC" is an acronym for: Bank subsidiary; Other nonbank subsidiaries; Parent company; Earnings (consolidated); and Capital.

This designation is made up of a composite rating, four components and several subcomponents, each of which is assigned a rating based on a 1 to 5 numeric scale, with 1 being the highest rating and 5 the lowest. The elements of this new rating system are:

Composite rating:

C—is the composite rating of the holding company, which is based on an evaluation and rating of its managerial and financial condition and an assessment of future potential risk to its subsidiary depository institution(s).

The Board says

> the composite rating encompasses both a forward-looking and static assessment of the consolidated organization, as well as an assessment of the relationship between the depository and nondepository entities. . . . the C rating is not derived as a simple numeric average of the R, F, and I components; rather, it reflects examiner judgment with respect to the relative importance of each component to the safe and sound operation of the BHC.[27]

Components and subcomponents:

R—indicates the quality of the holding company's risk management and is supported by the following subcomponents:

- Board and Senior Management Oversight;
- Policies, Procedures, and Limits;
- Risk Monitoring and Management Information Systems; and
- Internal Controls

F—rates the financial condition of the company and has the following subcomponents:

- Board and Senior Management Oversight;
- Policies, Procedures, and Limits;
- Risk Monitoring and Management Information Systems; and
- Internal Controls

I—is the potential impact of the parent company and nondepository subsidiaries (nondepository entities) on the subsidiary depository institutions.

---

27. *Id.*, p. 79446.

D—is the rating for the depository institution subsidiaries and will generally reflect the primary regulator's assessment of these institutions. The Board points out that:

> For BHCs with only one subsidiary depository institution, the (D) component rating generally will mirror the CAMELS composite rating for that [institution] . . . for BHCs with multiple subsidiary [institutions], the CAMELS composite ratings for each of the depository institutions should be weighted, giving consideration to [their] asset size and the relative importance . . . within the overall structure of the organization. In general, it is expected that the resulting (D) component rating will reflect the lead depository institution's CAMELS composite rating.[28]

Significant risk management and financial condition considerations relating to the institution will be factored in to the consolidated R and F ratings, which are then factored into the composite C rating. In cases in which a difference of opinion on the safety and soundness of the institution arises between the Board and the institution's primary regulator, the opinion of the Board "consistent with current practice" will reflected in the institution's rating.

The fact that the C rating is not an average of the ratings of each component in the standard implies that more weight might be given one component than another. As to weighting the Board says:

> [the] weight afforded to each subcomponent in the overall component rating will depend on the severity of the condition of that subcomponent and the relative importance of that subcomponent to the consolidated organization. Similarly, some components may be given more weight than others in determining the composite rating, depending on the situation of the BHC.[29]

A simplified version of this rating system requires only the assignment of the risk management component rating and composite rating to noncomplex bank holding companies with assets of $1 billion or less.

---

28. BHC Rating System, op. cit., p 70448.
29. *Id.*, p. 79450.

With respect to implementation of the new rating system, the Board says the new system:

> incorporates factors that have been routinely considered by examiners for years in evaluating a BHC's condition, the [new] system should not have a significant effect on the conduct on inspections [of BHCs] or on the regulatory burden of supervised institutions.[30]

S&L Holding Companies[31]

The OTS has exclusive authority to examine registered S&L holding companies, under section 10(b)(4) of the S&L Holding Company Act[32] subject to two exceptions.

- The first exception, as noted in Chapter Five, is that a company with both a bank and a savings association subsidiary is a bank holding company and is not an S&L holding company. Examinations of these companies are therefore carried out by the Federal Reserve as primary federal regulator of BHCs. The OTS remains the primary federal regulator (and examiner) of the company's savings association subsidiary.
- The second exception involves S&L holding companies with functionally regulated subsidiaries (or with a functionally regulated parent company). In these cases, the OTS will coordinate examinations and information gathering with the entity's primary regulator. Functionally regulated entities are defined in the handbook as: registered broker-dealers, investment companies and investment advisers, insurance companies (including agencies), and entities regulated by the Commodities Futures Trading Commission.

---

30. *Id.*, p. 70446.
31. The discussion in this section is based on the OTS Holding Company Handbook.
32. 12 USC 1467a(b)(4).

Risk Classifications

The OTS emphasizes that the principal purpose of these examinations is to evaluate the current and prospective effect the holding company has on its savings association subsidiary. The agency divides S&L holding companies into two risk categories:

> Category I—Noncomplex, or relatively low-risk, "shell" holding company with no significant activities other than controlling the association.
>
> Category II—Complex or higher-risk holding company enterprises. These include companies owned by retail companies, insurance underwriters and agents, securities broker-dealers, and manufacturing companies. One of the things an examiner must determine is how familiar holding company management is with savings association laws, regulations, and accounting practices.

The OTS points out that its examination procedures for Category II companies are sufficiently flexible to accommodate the wide range of asset sizes of these companies and the variety of activities in which they engage.

While examiners should focus on the entire company, they should determine the areas in the company that pose the greatest risk to the association and concentrate their resources on those areas.

Components of the Composite Examination Rating

The final examination rating for a Category II holding company is a composite rating based on the ratings of the following four "CORE" components, which are rated on a scale of 1 to 3:

- *Capital*—level of consolidated capital and composition.
- *Organizational structure*—risks of the activities conducted by each entity within the enterprise.
- *Relationship*—assessing how the holding company's management and board of directors oversees and monitors the relationship between the holding company and the association.

- *Earnings*—assessment of the financial performance and liquidity of the holding company enterprise as a consolidated entity, and whether earnings show any trends that might lead it to require the association to provide funds through dividends or other means.

The CORE analysis for Category I companies is much simpler than that for Category II companies and in many of these Category I companies, the analysis would primarily reflect the financial condition of the association subsidiary.

Composite Rating

This rating should reflect how the present and prospective risks and conditions of the holding company affect the association and is comprised of the following three grades:

- *A—above average.* The holding company is financially strong and can be called upon to provide financial and managerial resources to the association if necessary.
- *S—satisfactory.* The effect of the holding company on the association is neutral and exhibits financial conditions or operations that pose only a remote threat to the association and may have some reliance on the association for dividends or other funds to service the holding company's debt service.
- *U—unsatisfactory.* This rating, equivalent to a CAMELS rating of 4 or 5, should be given only in the most severe circumstances, and carries the presumption that an enforcement action is necessary. A "U" would be given in situations in which the holding company exhibits an inordinate reliance on the association for dividends or other financial support or in which the association is inordinately reliant on the parent for critical operating systems.

Closing Meetings of Examiners with Management and the Boards of Directors

The banking agencies encourage examiners to meet with the board of directors of an institution or holding company at the conclusion of an examination and require examiners to hold these meetings under certain circumstances.

Meetings with management. Before conducting closing interviews with management, examiners should have determined a composite rating with the concurrence of the OTS regional office so that they "are final or subject to revisions only in rare instances."[33] Examiners should explain to management the criteria used in reaching their conclusions and that these conclusions are based in a careful consideration of the association's managerial, operational, and financial performance and compliance with relevant laws and regulations.

Meeting with boards of institutions. The FDIC says examiners should meet with the board of directors of a institution after an examination if the examiners propose to give the institution a composite CAMELS rating of 3, 4, or 5; propose an informal or formal enforcement action; or propose to give the institution a CRA rating of "needs to improve" or "substantial noncompliance."[34]

These meetings provide an opportunity for the board to learn of other problems that may have been revealed during the examination and to discuss steps that the board and management should take to remedy them. These meetings also provide examiners with an opportunity to assess the willingness and ability of the board to resolve these problems.

The Board suggests that to the extent possible, meetings with the boards of directors of state member banks should included representatives of the relevant state banking departments.

Meetings with management and boards of holding companies. The Board's examination guidance provides that when appropriate, meetings of examiners with the boards of BHCs may be held jointly with the board of directors of the lead bank subsidiary of the holding company and the bank's primary federal or state supervisor.[35]

The OTS says examiners should hold a meeting with representatives of the holding company after the examination report is completed to ensure that all issues raised by the examination are understood, and resolved, if possible. These meetings are not necessarily held with the board of directors unless:

> the holding company presents a recurring material adverse effect on the subsidiary [association], there is an ongoing significant violation of law and regulations, or the holding company will be rated unsatisfactory . . . the meeting would include . . . examination findings and conclusions [and] possible enforcement remedies.[36]

---

33. OTS Examination Handbook, Section 070.
34. FDIC, Compliance Examination Manual, Part V.
35. BHC Supervision Manual, Section 5000.0.9.2.
36. OTS Holding Company Examination Handbook, Section 200.

Receiverships and Conservatorships

If the financial condition of an institution deteriorates to the point at which its survival is questionable, its chartering agency may take one of two actions. If the agency believes there is a chance that the institution can be saved, it will place the institution into a conservatorship, appointing a conservator to preserve its value as a going concern. If the agency believes an institution's survival is not possible (or, if the institution already is in a conservatorship and believes its survival is no longer possible), the agency will place the institution in receivership for the purpose of liquidation or otherwise disposing of the institution's assets.

Under current law, state and federal chartering agencies (the OCC and OTS) that place an institution into conservatorship may oversee that activity. When these agencies decide to place an institution they have chartered into receivership (whether it is in a conservatorship or not at the time the receivership decision is made), they must appoint the FDIC as receiver to wind up its affairs. The OTS, which also has the power to place state savings associations into receivership or conservatorship, must appoint the FDIC receiver of these institutions as well.[37]

The process of winding up the affairs of an institution is generally referred to as a "resolution" of the institution, which, according the FDIC, includes:

> . . . a disposition plan for a failed or failing institution . . . designed to (1) protect insured depositors, and (2) minimize the costs to the relevant insurance fund that are expected from covering insured deposits and disposing of the institution's assets. Resolution methods include purchase and assumption transactions, insured deposit transfer transactions and straight deposit payoffs. A resolution can also refer to an open bank assistance plan provided to an institution to help prevent it from failing.[38]

Following is a summary of the current law on these appointments as it has evolved since the 1930s.

---

37. Section 5(d)(2)(A) & (d)(2)(E)(ii) of the Home Owners' Loan Act (12 USC 1464(d)(2)(A) & (d)(2)(E)(ii)).

38. FDIC, Managing the Crisis: The FDIC and RTC Experience 1980–1994, p. 3, note 1.

Developments in the 1930s

When Congress first created the FDIC as a temporary agency in the National Bank Act of 1933, it provided that the FDIC be appointed receiver of all national banks. In the same year, Congress also enacted the Home Owner's Loan Act of 1933, creating the Federal Home Loan Bank Board (FHLBB—now the OTS) to charter, supervise, liquidate, or appoint a receiver for the newly authorized federal savings associations.

The FHLBB's power to appoint receivers for federal institutions was transferred to the FDIC by the Home Owner's Loan Act of 1934 (HOLA). The FDIC was also authorized to accept appointment as receiver for state banks placed into receiverships by state banking agencies. While many states often did not make these appointments during the 1930s, "most states now require the FDIC to be appointed as receiver."[39]

Congress approved these receivership laws against a background of 1,200 bank failures between 1921 and 1930, in which depositors were treated as unsecured creditors of the bank, and generally had to wait several years to receive a portion of their deposits. With the advent of deposit insurance,

> Congress believed that the appointment of the FDIC [as receiver for national banks, and for state banks at the request of state agencies] simplified procedures, eliminated duplication of records, and vested responsibility for liquidation in the largest creditor (the FDIC in its corporate capacity, as subrogee for the insured deposits it had paid), whose interest was to obtain the maximum possible recovery.[40]

1991 Amendments to the FDIA

In 1991, the FDIC Improvement Act (FDICIA) added four provisions to the FDIA, plus conforming amendments, relating to conservatorships and receiverships. Three of these relate to the Prompt Corrective Action (PCA) program enacted by FDICIA in new section 38 of the FDIA,[41] which requires the primary federal bank regulators to impose increasingly severe sanctions on institutions whose regulatory capital falls below minimum levels (PCA is also discussed in Chapter 11).

---

39. FDIC, Resolutions Handbook, Ch. 7, p. 69.
40. *Idid.* p. 69.
41. Section 38 is codified as 12 USC 1831o.

The three PCA amendments and the fourth, non-PCA amendment, provide as follows.

Appointments under section 38(f). Section 38(f) of the FDIA requires the primary federal regulators to place an institution in receivership (or conservatorship with the concurrence of the FDIC) within 90 days of its becoming critically undercapitalized (tangible equity of less than 2% of total assets) unless the agency believes an alternative procedure would better accomplish the purposes of the PCA program.

The agency may make two additional 90-day extensions after which time it must appoint a conservator or receiver unless the agency, in consultation with the FDIC, determines that the institution, because of positive net worth, positive earnings, and other favorable indicators, is not likely to fail.

Appointment under section 11(c)(9).[42] This section permits an institution's primary federal regulator, after consultation with the appropriate state regulator, to appoint the FDIC as conservator[43] or receiver for a state bank or savings association that is critically undercapitalized or fails certain other PCA requirements.

Appointment under section 11(c)(5). FDICIA amended the pre-1991 "general grounds" for appointment of conservators and receivers in section 11(c)(5), which are discussed below, to add two PCA-related grounds for these appointments.

FDIC "Self-appointment." The fourth FDICIA amendment[44] permits the FDIC to appoint itself conservator or receiver for any state or federal institution if it finds that one or more of the "general grounds," listed below, for the appointment of a conservator or receiver exist and that the appointment is necessary to reduce the risk to the deposit insurance funds. At the time the FDIC Resolutions Handbook was published in 1998, the FDIC had used this authority only once and has not done so since.[45]

---

42. Section 11 is codified as 12 USC 1821.
43. The appointment as conservator under this section is subject to a requirement in section 11(c)(11) that a federal regulator may not appoint a conservator for a state or federal institution under the PCA grounds of section 11(c)(5) without the consent of the FDIC, unless the agency has given the FDIC 48 hours notice of its intention to make the appointment.
44. Section 11(c)(10), (12 USC 1821(c)(10)).
45. Resolution Handbook, *op. cit.* p. 70.

"General Grounds" for Appointment of a Conservator or Receiver

Section 11(c)(5) lists general grounds for placing a bank or savings association in conservatorship or receivership. These grounds include conditions in which the institution:

- is insolvent or is otherwise unlikely to be able to pay its creditors on a timely basis or meet its obligations to depositors, including their ability to withdraw funds;
- has experienced a substantial dissipation of assets due to violations of laws or regulations or engaging in unsafe or unsound practices;
- has concealed books and records, or has refused to submit its books, papers, records, or affairs for inspection to any examiner or to any lawful agent of an appropriate supervisor;
- has incurred losses that have depleted most or all of its capital so that there is no reasonable prospect for it to become "adequately capitalized" as defined in the PCA standards;
- has committed a violation of laws or regulations that is likely to cause insolvency or otherwise damage the institution;
- has violated laws or had engaged in unsafe and unsound practices that have resulted in a substantial dissipation of the institution's assets and earnings;
- has been found guilty of one or more criminal offenses relating to money laundering;[46]
- has, by resolution of its board of directors, its shareholders (or its members, if it is a mutual savings association) consented to the appointment of a conservator or receiver; or
- under PCA standards,:
  - is undercapitalized, has no reasonable prospect of becoming adequately capitalized, or has failed to submit or implement an acceptable capital restoration plan under section 38; or
  - is critically under capitalized or has substantially insufficient capital.

---

46. These provisions are 31 USC §§ 5322 (reporting and recordkeeping requirements generally) and 5324 (structuring transactions to avoid reporting); 18 USC§§ 1956 (laundering to conceal illegal source of funds), 1957 (transaction involving funds obtained illegally), and 1960 (operation of unlicensed money transmittal businesses).

State Institutions

Section 11(c)(4) authorizes the FDIC to appoint itself sole conservator or receiver of a state bank or savings association that has been closed under state law, if "general grounds" for these appointments existed at or after the time it was closed or if depositors are unable to withdraw funds after it has been closed for 15 days or more.[47]

FDIC as Conservator

A federal or state agency that places an institution into conservatorship is also authorized to appoint the FDIC as conservator, and the FDIC may, but is not required to, accept the appointment. As of the end of 1997, the OTS had made one such appointment. Neither the OCC nor any state agency had done so.[48]

Powers of Conservators and Receivers

There are certain actions that must be taken whether an institution is in a conservatorship or receivership. As a result, there is considerable overlap in the statutory powers conferred on conservators and receivers, with added powers for receivers to affect a resolution of the affairs of the institution. These common powers, which are summarized below, are designed to ensure that conservators and receivers have the flexibility to accomplish their respective purposes.

The FDIC points out that a conservatorship is designed to keep the institution open and operating "for a period of time to return [it] to a sound and solvent operation [and to] preserve the 'going concern' value of the institution." Once the institution has been placed in a receivership, the FDIC staff, working with employees of the institution,

> bring all accounts forward to the closing date and post all applicable entries to the general ledger, making sure that everything is in balance. The FDIC then creates two complete sets of inventory books containing an explanation of the disposition of the failed institution's assets and liabilities, one set for the assuming institution (if there is one) and one for the receivership.[49]

A receivership, or "receivership estate," is a legal entity separate from the FDIC itself, i.e., separate from the FDIC in its "corporate" capacity.

---

47. 12 USC 11(c)(4). This provision dates back to at least 1989.
48. Resolution Handbook, *op. cit.*, p. 69, footnote 1.
49. *Id.* pps. 70–71.

In addition, the FDIA requires that when the FDIC has been appointed conservator of a federal or state institution, the institution remains under the supervision of its appropriate federal or state regulator until the FDIC determines that the institution is solvent and ready to resume normal operations, or determines to place it into receivership.[50]

FDIC and OTS Powers as Conservator

The FDIC as conservator is authorized to take such action as may be:

- necessary to put the insured depository institution in a sound and solvent condition; and
- appropriate to carry on the business of the institution and preserve and conserve the assets and property of the institution.[51]

HOLA provides that the OTS as conservator:

> shall have all the powers of the members, the stockholders, the directors, and the officers of the association and shall be authorized to operate the association in its own name or assets in the manner and to the extent authorized by the [OTS] Director.[52]

General Powers and Duties of the FDIC as Conservator or Receiver.[53]

As conservator or receiver, the FDIC is granted broad powers to manage the institution as a going concern or to dispose of its assets and wind up its affairs. Among these powers are those that require or permit the FDIC as conservator or receiver to:

- succeed to all rights, titles, and powers of the institution, and its officers, directors, shareholders, or members, and to its books, records, and assets;
- operate and manage the institution, collect all obligations and money due it, and preserve the institution's assets and property;
- merge the institution with another insured depository institution, including purchase and assumption (P&A) transactions

---

50. Section 11(c)(2)(D) and (c)(3)(D), respectively, (12 USC 1821(c)(2)(D) & (c)(3)(D)).
51. Section 11(d)(2)(D), (12 USC 1821(d)(2)(D)).
52. Section 5(d)(2)(E)(i), (12 USC 1464 (d)(2)(E)(i)).
53. Unless otherwise noted, the powers discussed in this section are found in section 11(d) of the FDIA (12 USC 1821(d)).

or other dispositions of the institution's assets and liabilities as the receiver deems advisable;
- determine the validity of claims against the institution, disallow claims determined to be invalid, and pay valid claims in accordance with the priorities in the depositor preference provisions discussed below;
- repudiate contracts the receiver deems to be burdensome or a hindrance to orderly administration of the institution's affairs[54]; and
- suspend legal actions pending against the institution for up to 90 days for a receiver and 45 days for a conservator to enable it to evaluate the case and determine how to proceed.

Additional Powers and Obligations of the FDIC as Receiver

These include the power or the obligation of the FDIC to:
- place the institution in liquidation and dispose of its assets;
- make prompt payment of insured accounts to depositors as soon as possible after closing an institution either by payment of cash or transfer of the insured amount to another insured institution;
- pay other claims, including payments to holders of uninsured depositors, in accordance with the depositor preference provisions of the FDIA, which are summarized in the next section; and
- charter new national banks, including "bridge banks," and, with the approval of the OTS, new federal associations to receive such assets and liabilities of the failed bank or association as the receiver deems appropriate.

Resolution of Banks and Savings Associations during the Financial Crisis of 1980–1994

Many of the FDIC's procedures for dealing with failed institutions were developed during the thrift and banking industry crises of 1980–1994, during which 1,617 banks and 1,295 savings associations failed or required financial assistance.[55]

---

54. Section 11(e)(1) ,(12 USC 1221(e)(1)).
55. FDIC, Resolutions Handbook, p. 2.

The FDIC has conducted several studies of this period. The information in this section is based primarily on three of these publications: *The Resolution Handbook, An Examination of the Banking Crisis of the 1980s and Early 1990s*, December, 1997, and *Managing the Crisis: The FDIC and RTC Experience 1980–1994*, August, 1998.

Resolution of Banks by the FDIC

At the beginning of the crisis, the FDIC relied on two principal methods of resolving failing banks: A P&A transactions and direct deposit payouts. A purchase and assumption transaction is one in which "a healthy institution . . . purchases some or all of the assets of a failed bank or thrift and assumes some or all of the liabilities, including all insured deposits and may assume all of the deposit liabilities of the failed bank or association."[56]

In a direct deposit payout, the FDIC writes checks to depositors for their insured deposits plus any interest accrued through the day of closing. Until the enactment of the depositor preference provisions of the FDIA in 1993, holders of uninsured deposits in failed institutions in effect became unsecured creditors of the institution, whose rights were determined under state law. Depositor preference, which applies to all institutions that closed after August 10, 1993, provides that a failed institution's depositors, including the FDIC subrogated to the claims of insured depositors it has already paid, have priority over general creditors.[57]

New resolution techniques evolved during the crisis as a result of the increasing number of failed institutions, including several large and complex ones, and because of a requirement in FDICIA that the agency resolve failed institutions on a least cost basis. In 1983, the FDIC had introduced the insured deposit transfer (IDT) transaction, which involves the transfer of insured deposits and secured liabilities of a failed bank to a healthy institution that acts as agent for the

---

56. FDIC, Managing the Crisis: The FDIC and RTC Experience 1980–1994, August, 1998, Chapter 2, p. 56.

57. An Examination of the Banking Crisis of the 1980s and Early 1990s (Examination), December, 1997, Chapter 2, p 126. These provisions, which were enacted in the Omnibus Budget Reconciliation Act of 1993, and codified at section 11(d)(11), (12 USC 1821(d)(11)), require the receiver (having already paid claims of insured depositors) to pay in the following order: (a) administrative expenses of the receiver; (b) deposit liability claims (basically uninsured depositors); (c) other general or senior liabilities; (d) subordinated obligations; and (c) shareholder claims.

Figure 3.1
Methods Used by the FDIC to Resolve Failing Banks during the Financial Crisis of 1980–1994

Purchase and Assumptions	1,188	73.5%
Insured Deposit Transfers	176	10.9%
Open Bank Assistance	133	8.2%
Straight Deposit Payoffs	120	7.4%

Source: FDIC, *Managing the Crisis: The FDIC and RTC Experience 1980–1994*, Chapter 3, Chart L3-1.

FDIC. The accounts of depositors of the failed bank are, in effect, transferred intact to the new bank.[58] These transactions lowered FDIC overhead thereby satisfying least cost requirements.

Another resolution procedure used during the first three years of the crisis was open bank assistance (OBA), which was authorized in 1950, and used through 1992. (See Chapter 2.) OBA was designed to prevent a bank from closing by authorizing the FDIC to provide assistance by making loans and purchasing assets to prevent the bank from closing. The types of resolution methods used by the FDIC during the crisis are shown in Figure 3.1 above.

Resolution of Savings Associations by the RTC

Savings associations during this period were resolved by the Resolution Trust Corporation (RTC), an independent agency created by FIRREA and charged with resolving failed savings associations that met two qualifications:

- they must have been insured by the former Federal Savings and Loan Insurance Corporation (FSLIC) before August 9, 1989, (the date the FSLIC was abolished); and
- they must have been placed in conservatorship or receivership between December 31, 1988 and December 31, 1995, the date on which the RTC ceased operations.

The RTC inherited 262 institutions from FSLIC with assets of $115 billion and ultimately resolved 747 institutions, of which 497, or 66.5%, were handled by P&A transactions.[59]

---

58. Managing the Crisis, *op. cit.*, Chapter 9, p. 226.
59. Crisis, *op. cit.*, pps. 14–15. RTC statutory authority is still on the books as section 21A of the Federal Home Loan Bank Act (12 USC 1441a).

Recent Data

Institution failures declined dramatically after 1994 with eight in 1995, six in 1996, and one in 1997. There were 29 failures during 2000–2004, 22 of which were resolved by P&A transactions. The end of the first quarter of 2006 marked the seventh consecutive quarter without a failure of an insured bank or savings association with 2005 being the first calendar year in the history of the FDIC in which there had not been a failure of an insured bank or savings association. This result is due in large measure to the increasing income and earnings posted by insured institutions in recent years.[60]

Enforcement

Introduction

The exit meetings of examiners with management and the board of directors, as noted above, provide an opportunity for a discussion of problems that examiners have found at the bank and an opportunity for a discussion of actions that should be taken to correct them.

The OCC points out that:

> Good faith discussions between the board and the OCC generally are successful in bringing about a speedy and mutually acceptable resolution of differences. . . . Failure to correct cited problems promptly and decisively can result in more severe OCC action.[61]

The banking agencies have a variety of increasingly severe enforcement actions they can employ against institutions and individuals, ranging from a relatively mild board resolution to civil money penalties of up to $1 million per day and referral to the Justice Department for criminal prosecution.

Enforcement actions can be brought against individual institutions, their subsidiaries, and their holding companies and against individual officers, directors, and other "institution-affiliated parties" (IAPs). IAPs are defined in the FDIA as including officers, direc-

---

60. FDIC, Quarterly Banking Report, 4th Quarter, 2005, FDIC Annual Report, 2005.
61. OCC, The Director's Book, 1997, p. 96.

tors, controlling stockholders, and other persons associated with the institution. IAPs also include the institution's independent contractors, including attorneys, accountants, and appraisers, who have knowingly or recklessly participated in:

- any violation of any law or regulation;
- any breach of fiduciary duty; or
- any unsafe or unsound practice that has caused or is likely to cause more than a minimal financial loss to, or a significant adverse effect on, the insured institution.[62]

Following are the three least serious supervisory actions involving the boards of directors of institutions that are used by the agencies to deal with problems discovered during examinations.

Informal Enforcement Actions

Board Resolution and Commitment Letter

This is usually a resolution drafted by an institution's primary federal regulator and signed by the institution's board of directors addressing deficiencies at the bank and setting a timetable for correcting them.

Memorandum of Understanding (MOU)

An MOU is a more formal version of the commitment letter that is used to specify a time period for correcting violations of law or unsafe or unsound banking practices. The OCC says it uses an MOU "only when problems do not pose a serious threat to the bank and when the agency expects that the bank will cooperate in correcting the problem so the legal enforcement will not be required to achieve compliance." It also points out that an MOU, like a commitment letter, is not administratively or judicially enforceable.

The following are more formal—and enforceable—actions that may be brought against a bank, savings association, or IAP.

---

62. Section 3(u) (12 USC 1813(u)).

Formal Enforcement Actions

Formal Agreement

These agreements, which the OTS calls supervisory agreements, are similar to an MOU except that the institution's primary federal regulator may enforce the order by seeking a cease and desist (C&D) order or an assessment of civil money penalties (CMP) on an institution or IAP.

Cease & Desist Order

The agency may use a cease and desist order (C&D) order to compel the bank or one or more IAPs to take positive actions to correct deficiencies or violations of law or to stop certain practices. The OCC says "C&Ds are issued most often when the agency is not confident that bank management has the ability and willingness to take the necessary corrective action or when the problems are so severe that a lesser action cannot be justified."[63]

These actions are generally brought when the agency has cause to believe that the institution or an IAP is:

- engaging or is about to engage, in an unsafe or unsound practice in conducting the business of the institution, or
- violating, has violated, or is about to violate:
  - any law, rule, or regulation or
  - any condition imposed in writing by the agency in connection with the granting of any application or
  - any written agreement entered into with the agency.

Temporary C&D Orders

These orders are imposed in cases in which a notice is served on either a bank or an IAP and the agency believes immediate action is needed to prevent dissipation of assets or insolvency of the bank. These orders take effect immediately but can be appealed by the bank to federal district court within 10 days of issuance.

---

63. OCC, The Director's Book, 1997, p. 99.

Scope of C&D orders

The agencies' C&D authority permits them to effect a broad range of remedies to correct or remedy the effects of violations of laws and regulations, including the power to:

- require a party to take affirmative action to correct or remedy any conditions resulting from the violation;
- require IAPs to make restitution for losses caused to the institution or for unjust financial gain;
- restrict the growth and activities of the institution;
- rescind agreements or contracts;
- require the institution to employ qualified officers or employees; and
- "take such other action as the banking agency determines to be appropriate."

Enforcement of C&D Orders

If the order is against a bank, it is generally presented to the bank's board of directors and will be binding on the bank if it is signed by a majority of the board members. If the board consents to the order, it is binding on all of the directors and remains in effect until terminated by the OCC.

If the bank's board of directors does not consent to the order, the agency may bring a formal C&D proceeding under the Administrative Procedures Act. An adverse ruling by the agency (after a hearing and recommendation by an administrative law judge) may be appealed by the bank to the appropriate U.S. Court of Appeals.

If the agency prevails in the case and the bank or the IAP fails to comply with the order, the agency may impose civil money penalties (CMPs) against the party, or seek an injunction in federal district court to compel compliance with the orders. The OCC points out that CMPs against institutions are used principally in situations in which the bank files late or erroneous financial reports with the agency. Further provisions of agency CMP authority are summarized below.

Civil Money Penalties

The FDIC points out that the failure of a bank to comply with any final cease and desist order can be the basis of a civil money penalty imposed against the bank, any officer, director, or other IAP,[64] or for subsequent action (discussed below) to terminate the institution's deposit insurance.

Basis of CMPs

The FDIA authorizes increasingly severe civil money penalties for institutions and IAPs that violate final agency orders or commit other violations. These offenses include:

- violations of the following:
  - temporary or final agency orders relating to regular and temporary cease and desist proceedings,
  - removal or prohibition orders relating to IAPs,
  - capital directives or capital restoration plans, and
  - regulations on recordkeeping and reporting of monetary transactions;
- violations of any law or regulation, including those relating to
  - loans to insiders,
  - transactions with affiliates,
  - tying arrangements, and
  - change in control;
- violations of any written condition imposed by a federal banking agency in connection with the grant of an application; or
- violation of any written agreement between an institution and the agency.

These are referred to as "civil offenses" in the following summary of the three tiers of civil money penalties.

Three-tiers of Civil Money Penalties

The FDIA authorizes the federal banking agencies to impose civil money penalties on institutions or IAPs (parties) in accordance a three-tier system as follows:

First tier: Up to $5,000 for each day during which any "civil offenses" described above continues.

Second tier: Up to $25,000 for each day during which the civil offense continues by a party that also
- recklessly engages in an unsafe or unsound practice or breaches any fiduciary duty; and

---

64. FDIC, Risk Management Manual of Examination Policies, section 15.1.

- such conduct causes or is likely to cause a more than minimal loss to the institution; or
- has resulted in a monetary gain or other benefit to the IAP.

Third tier: Up to $1 million per day in the case of an individual and the lesser of $1 million, 1% of total assets per day for an institution, if the party's conduct meets the criteria of a second tier violation and the party:

- knowingly commits a civil offense;
- engages in any unsafe or unsound practice in conducting the affairs of such depository institution; or
- breaches any fiduciary duty; and
- knowingly or recklessly causes a substantial loss to the institution or results in a substantial pecuniary gain or other benefit to such party.

Enforcement and Judicial Review of CMPs

CMP orders are enforceable in federal district court. In these actions, the courts have jurisdiction to enforce payment of the penalty mandated by the orders, but may not modify, suspend, set aside, or enjoin the enforcement of the order itself.

The person or institution subject to the penalty may obtain an agency hearing on the penalty by submitting a request within 20 days after the notice of assessment.

Agency orders under section 8 (except those involving criminal matters) may be appealed to an appropriate U.S. Court of Appeals. Decisions of these courts may be appealed to the U.S. Supreme Court.

Safety and Soundness Directives

The federal banking agencies are required by the FDIA[65] to develop standards to ensure safe and sound operations by banks and savings associations in several areas including internal controls, information systems, internal audits, loan documentation, credit underwriting; interest rate exposure; asset growth; compensation, and benefits, asset quality, compensation standards, and other items the agency deems advisable.

---

65. Section 39 (12 USC 1831p-1).

Institutions that are found to be deficient in one or more of these areas may be subject to a requirement by its primary federal regulator that develop a compliance plan showing how and when the institution will correct the deficiencies. Agency orders and directives on safety and soundness issues can be enforced in federal district court.

Prompt Corrective Action (PCA)

Institutions whose regulatory capital falls below certain statutory levels specified in section 38 of the FDIA[66] are subject to the imposition of capital restoration plans by their primary federal regulator and to increasingly severe restrictions of their activities. The enforcement powers conferred by these PCA provisions, which were adopted in 1991, include placing an institution into conservatorship or receivership, as discussed above, ordering the removal of directors and officers and other IAPs and requiring the election of a new board of directors. (PCA is discussed more fully in Chapter 11 and above in the discussion of receiverships.)

Capital restoration plans are enforceable in federal district court. Noncompliance with a plan can subject the institution to civil money penalties.

Capital Directives

The 1991 PCA authority was preceded by legislation enacted in 1983,[67] which grants the three banking agencies the power to establish minimum capital standards and to issue directives requiring banks to remedy deficiencies in these levels. This authority, which was a precursor to the Basel I capital standards activity in the U.S. and which is still on the books, has not apparently been used since the early 1990s.

Removal and Prohibition Orders

Serious misconduct by an IAP can result in an agency order removing that person from office and prohibiting that person from participating in the affairs of any insured bank or savings association and certain other institutions.

---

66. 12 USC 1831o.
67. Sec. 908 of the International Lending Supervision Act of 1983, Pub. Law. No. 98-181 (Nov. 30, 1983) (12 U.S.C. 3907).

Section 8(e) of the FDIA[68] provides that the director, officer, or other IAP of a bank or savings association may be removed from office and prohibited from service with any insured institution on the basis of agency findings of serious violations of banking laws or regulations generally or findings that the IAP violated specific laws listed in the statute.

General Violations of Laws, Orders, or Written Conditions

An agency may initiate a "three-stage" proceeding based on its findings relating to an IAP's "conduct, effect, and culpability"[69] as follows:

First: The agency must determine that the IAP has:
- violated
  - any law or regulation;
  - any final C&D order; or
  - any written condition imposed by the agency in connection with an application by the institution or any written agreement between the institution and the agency;
- engaged or participated in any unsafe or unsound practice in connection with any insured depository institution or business institution; or
- committed a breach of his or her fiduciary duty that has caused or is likely to cause a financial loss or other damage to the institution.

Second: The agency must find that this conduct has resulted in:
- financial or other damage to the institution;
- prejudice to the interests of depositors; or
- financial gain to the IAP.

Third: The agency must find that the above violations:
- involved personal dishonesty on the part of such party; or
- demonstrated willful disregard by such party for the safety or soundness of the institution.

On the basis of these findings the agency may issue a notice to the IAP of its intention to issue a removal and prohibition order against that person.

---

68. 12 USC 1818(e).
69. Director's Book, *op. cit.*, p. 105.

Specific Violations

A banking agency may also initiate removal and prohibition proceedings against the following persons:

- an IAP that has violated the civil or criminal provisions of federal laws on reporting and recordkeeping of certain monetary transactions (other than an inadvertent violation);[70]
- an officer or director who knew that an IAP had violated certain criminal laws relating to reporting and recordkeeping of monetary transactions and money laundering[71] (and the agency finds that the officer or director did not take appropriate action to stop or prevent the recurrence of the violation); or
- an officer or director of an insured depository institution has committed any violation of the Depository Institution Management Interlocks Act[72] (discussed in Chapter 8).

Enforcement

As in the procedure for issuing a C&D order, the hearing for a removal case is heard by an administrative law judge (ALJ) of the institution's primary federal agency. In removal actions brought by the OCC, however, the ALJ's decision is certified to the Federal Reserve Board for a final decision. Final orders in these procedures remain in effect until stayed or set aside by the agency or a reviewing court.

Temporary Suspension Orders

After serving notice in the above actions, and before the administrative procedures begin, an agency can issue an immediate suspension or prohibition order against an IAP if the agency determines that such action is necessary for the protection of the institution or its depositors. These orders are effective upon service but can be challenged in federal district court within 10 days of service. The order remains in effect until it is stayed by the court, dismissed by the agency, or supplanted by a permanent order.

---

70. 31 USC §§ 5311–5332.

71. These provisions are 31 USC §§ 5322 (reporting and recordkeeping requirements generally) and 5324 (structuring transactions to avoid reporting); 18 USC§§ 1956 (laundering to conceal illegal source of funds), 1957 (transaction involving funds obtained illegally), and 1960 (operation of unlicensed money transmittal businesses).

72. 12 U.S.C. 3201 et seq.

Criminal Violations

Indictment

If an IAP is indicted for a crime involving dishonesty or breach of trust that is punishable by imprisonment for a term exceeding one year under state or federal law, (general crime) or a criminal violation of the federal money laundering laws (see footnote 71), the agency may suspend the IAP from office or prohibit that person from further participation in the conduct of the affairs of the institution if it determines that the IAP's continued service would harm depositors or damage public confidence in the institution.

Duration of Order after Indictment

These orders are effective until the information, indictment, or complaint is finally disposed of or until the order is terminated by the agency.

Conviction

If a "judgment or conviction or an agreement to enter a pretrial diversion or similar program"[73] relating to a general crime is entered against an IAP, the agency, if it finds that continued service by that person would harm depositors or impair public confidence in the institution, may issue an order to remove the IAP from office or prohibit the IAP from further participation in the affairs of the institution.

In case of a conviction or an agreement relating to a money laundering crime, the agency is required to issue an order of removal or prohibition.

Duration of Notice or Order after Conviction

Orders relating to criminal conviction remain effective until the completion of any hearing or appeal of the case or until the agency terminates the order.

Effect of Acquittal

A finding of not guilty or other disposition of the criminal charge does not preclude the agency from initiating a removal, prohibition, or suspension action under its civil authority, which is discussed above.

---

73. Section 8(g)(1)(C)(i), (12 USC 8(g)(1)(C)(i)).

Scope of Orders—Industrywide Prohibition

Although some of the statutory language in section 8(e) refers to orders that suspend an IAP from office and from participating in the affairs of his or her institution, section 8(e)(6) imposes a broader prohibition. It provides that any person subject to a removal order for civil or criminal violations is permanently prohibited, unless written consent is subsequently granted by the agency issuing the order, and the institution's primary federal regulator, from participating in the affairs of all depository institutions, their primary federal regulator, and several other agencies, including:

- credit unions and the National Credit Union Administration;
- the Farm Credit Administration and any institutions chartered by that agency, which include Federal Land Banks and Farm Credit Banks;
- any Federal Home Loan Bank; and
- the Federal Housing Finance Board.[74]

The prohibition on participation in the affairs of these entities includes bans on soliciting or voting proxies or voting for directors.

Judicial Review

After any hearing in section 8, except a hearing in connection with the temporary suspension, the agency shall make its decision and issue its order. Unless or until an appeal has been filed, the issuing agency may modify or terminate the order before a petition for review has been filed with the appellate court and may do so after the filing with the court's permission.

Agency orders, except those issued in connection with criminal proceedings, may be appealed to the U.S. Court of Appeals in the circuit in which the institution is located or in the U.S. Court of Appeals for the District of Columbia. These decisions may be appealed to the U.S. Supreme Court. Unless specifically ordered by the court, the filing of an appeal will not operate as a stay of the order.

---

74. Section 8(e)(7)(D)(iv) (12 USC 1818(e)(7)(D)(iv)) lists the "Secretary of the Treasury" as the appropriate federal regulator of these entities.

Enforcement of Agency Orders

The appropriate agency may enforce its orders under section 8 and orders issued in connection with prompt corrective action and safety and soundness enforcement actions in federal district court. The district courts in these cases, with certain exceptions, do not have the power to enjoin, modify, or terminate the agency order.

The imposition of civil money penalties is governed by the three-tier set of penalties discussed above.

Additional Enforcement Powers of the FDIC

Termination of Insurance

The FDIC may initiate a proceeding for termination of an institution's deposit insurance if it finds that:

- the institution or its directors or trustees have engaged or are engaging in unsafe or unsound practices in conducting the business of the institution;
- the institution is in an unsafe or unsound condition to continue operations as an insured institution; or
- the institution or its directors or trustees have violated any law, regulation, order, or condition imposed in writing by the FDIC in connection with the approval of any application or other request by the institution, or written agreement entered into between the institution and the agency.[75]

At least 30 days before commencing administrative proceedings, the FDIC must notify the institution's primary federal regulator, if that agency is not the FDIC, and the appropriate state authority (if the FDIC is the institution's primary federal regulatory) of the basis for its action. This notice is issued for the purpose of obtaining the correction of the practices that are the basis for the FDIC's proposed termination of insurance.

If, after the notice is given, the FDIC finds that the conditions at issue have not been corrected, it may begin an administrative proceeding with notice and hearing. The agency's final order may be appealed under the procedures outlined under "Judicial Review," above. Provisions are included in these orders to make certain that

---

75. FDIA, section 8(a) (12 USC 1818(a)).

the institution's depositors do not lose their deposit insurance on their accounts in existence at the time of the order.

Money Laundering Violations

The FDIC is empowered, under certain circumstances, to revoke the deposit insurance of state banks and savings associations that have been convicted of a criminal offense under the federal money laundering statutes[76] (which are cited in footnote 40).

In making its decision, the agency must consider the following factors with respect to the institution:

- the involvement or knowledge of its board of directors or trustees and senior management relating to the offense;
- the extent to which the offense or offenses occurred despite existence of policies and internal controls to prevent their occurrence;
- the degree of cooperation by the institution;
- the extent to which the institution has implemented additional internal controls; and
- the extent to which the revocation would have on the need of the local community for banking services.

Enforcement Action against Non-FDIC Supervised Institutions and IAPs

The FDIC was granted the power in 1989 to bring certain enforcement actions against institutions for which it is not the primary federal regulator if the institutions' primary federal regulator fails to take action after a request in writing from the FDIC.

This request may be based on an examination of an institution by the FDIC or its primary federal regulator or on other information, and is limited to proposed enforcement actions relating to change in control and transactions with affiliates.[77]

If the other agency, within 60 days of receiving the request, does not take the recommended enforcement action or provide a proposal

---

76. The statutes relating to the activities are found at 31 USC §§ 5322 (reporting and record keeping requirements generally) and 5324 (structuring transactions to avoid reporting), and 18 USC§§ 1956 (laundering to conceal source of funds), 1957 (transactions involving funds obtained illegally), and 1960 (operation of unlicensed money transmittal businesses).

77. This authority is found in sections 7(j) and 18(j) of the FDIA (12 USC 1817(j) and 1828(j)), respectively.

that is responsive to its concerns, the FDIC may initiate the recommended enforcement action if its Board of Directors determines that:

- the institution is in an unsafe or unsound condition;
- the institution or IAP is engaging in unsafe or unsound practices, and the recommended enforcement action will prevent the institution or the IAP from continuing such practices; or
- the conduct or threatened conduct (including any acts or omissions) poses a risk to the deposit insurance fund or may prejudice the interests of the institution's depositors.

Conclusion

This chapter is not about governance, but it illustrates one of the principal responsibilities of an institution's board of directors—reviewing examination reports and ensuring that management is taking action to solve problems raised in the report. Failure to do so can, obviously, lead to lower composite ratings, more formal enforcement actions, and, in extreme cases, insolvency. CAMELS ratings of 4 or 5 indicate serious trouble, and falling to a CAMELS 3 rating should be a wake up call.

The detail of the composite ratings of the safety and soundness, specialty, and compliance examinations, coupled with reviews by the examiner in charge and the backup of regional office review, is designed to ensure that the CAMELS score is not derived from superficial analysis.

Regulators frequently point out that some institutions with CAMELS ratings of 1 may have flaws in their risk analysis or procedures that are not apparent during periods of high net income. These flaws could cause problems during economic downturns.

The seamless range of supervisory and enforcement actions available to the agencies is geared to provide boards of directors with the opportunity to cooperate with supervisors to correct problems without the necessity for more formal procedures. The flaws mentioned above for highly rated institutions would likely be handled by a board resolution or similar informal supervisory action.

The cooperation between state and federal agencies in examinations of state institutions, including alternate examinations by state and federal agencies and the standards for acceptance by federal agencies of state examination reports are an answer to the charge of "competition in laxity" that has been leveled by some against the dual system.

CHAPTER **4**

Branches and Interstate Banking

Introduction

The current ability of state and national banks to branch across state lines is a relatively recent development. Historically, states not only prohibited branching across state lines but also imposed limits on the ability of state-chartered banks to branch within the state.

As recently as 1965, 17 states prohibited their banks from establishing any branches, 17 permitted limited intrastate branching, and 16 states permitted statewide branching. National banks could not branch at all until Congress enacted the McFadden Act[1] in 1927, which permitted them to open branches in cities or towns in which they were located to the extent state banks could do so. In 1933, this restriction was eased to permit national banks to branch within their state in the same manner as state banks.

From 1956 to 1994, bank holding companies were prohibited by the Douglas Amendment to the Bank Holding Company Act[2] from acquiring a bank in another state unless the acquisition was permitted by the law of that state.

By the early 1990s, state restrictions on intrastate branching had eased. At the end of 1992, the number of states that permitted some form of statewide branching had risen to 39, while 11 states retained stricter limits on branching within the state.

As state restrictions on in-state branching were being reduced, pressures for interstate branching were building. Maine enacted a bill

---

1. Feb. 25, 1927, 44 Stat. 1228, 12 USC 36.
2. Formerly codified in section 3(d) (12 USC 1842(d)).

permitting nationwide interstate banking in 1978. By mid-1994, as Congress was considering interstate branching legislation, 34 states permitted nationwide interstate banking, 15 were members of regional interstate banking compacts, and one state, Montana, banned interstate banking.[3]

In 1994, Congress approved the Riegle-Neal Interstate Branching and Banking Efficiency Act of 1994 (Riegle-Neal I)[4] which provided a comprehensive framework for interstate branching by national and state banks. In the best tradition of the dual banking system, Congress, as it drafted the bill, was able to draw on the experience of 49 states that had already approved some form of interstate branching.

Mergers are the principal means by which individual banks can acquire a branch in another state under Riegle-Neal I. Banks are able to develop *de novo* branches[5] only in states that permit this activity. At year-end 2005, only 17 states permitted entry by *de novo* branching. Following is a summary of the federal laws relating to bank branching and mergers that were in effect when Riegle-Neal I was enacted.

Bank Branching and Merger Laws Prior to Riegle-Neal I

Definition of Branch

When Riegle-Neal I was signed in 1994, the McFadden Act defined a branch of a national bank as an office of the bank "at which deposits are received, or checks paid, or money lent." The definition of "domestic branch" in the FDIA[6] for both state member and nonmember banks was identical in all material respects to the McFadden Act definition.

---

3. The discussion of developments in branching law is from H. Rept. 103-448 on the 1994 interstate legislation (see footnote 4, below), pps. 19–21.

4. The Riegle-Neal Interstate Banking and Branching Efficiency Act of 1994 (Interstate Branching Act), Pub. Law 103-328, Sept. 29, 1994, 108 Stat. 2315.

5. A *de novo* branch is one that is started "from scratch" by the acquiror rather than being acquired in a merger or purchased from another institution.

6. Section 3(o), FDIA, 12 USC 1813(o).

Geographic Limits

The McFadden Act provided, with certain narrow exceptions, that a national bank could establish and operate new branches only "within the limits of the city, town or village in which [it] is situated," and at any point in the state in which it was located, to the extent permitted for state banks by the law of that state. As noted below, state banks that are members of the Federal Reserve System (state member banks) are subject to the same geographic restrictions on branching as national banks.

Branching Regulations

Following are the principal agency regulations relating to branch applications and approvals:

OCC	12 CFR §5.30
Federal Reserve Board (Board)	12 CFR §208.6
FDIC	12 CFR Part 303, Subpart C: §§303.40–303.45
OTS	Branches of federal associations: 12 CFR §§545.92, 545.93, and 545.95.

These regulations, while not identical, have several requirements in common. Applicants must provide the public with an opportunity to comment on the proposal by publishing a notice of the application in a newspaper in the community affected by the proposed branch. Among the factors considered by the agencies is the adequacy of the applicant's CRA compliance record, its capital adequacy, and managerial competence.

Capital Requirements

Applicants, with certain exceptions, must meet the minimum capital ratios prescribed for "adequately capitalized" under the FDIC's prompt corrective action regulations,[7] which are:

- total regulatory capital to risk-weighted assets of 8% or more (eligible Tier 2 capital may not exceed Tier 1 capital)[8];

---

7. 12 CFR Part 325, Subpart B.

8. "Tiers" are measures of the "quality" of capital components instruments for regulatory purposes, based in part on the predictability of their value in case of an institution's insolvency. Components of Tier 1, the highest category, include common and certain preferred stock. Tier 2 is comprised of less reliable components, such as subordinated debt and an allowance for losses on loans and leases (ALLL). These components are discussed in detail in Chapter 11.

- Tier 1 capital to risk-weighted assets of 4% or more;
- a leverage ratio: Tier 1 capital to total assets of 4% or more (3% if institution has CAMELS (see discussion of CAMELS in Chapter 3) rating of "1" and is not experiencing or planning rapid growth); and
- an added requirement for savings associations is that tangible capital must equal 1.5% of adjusted total assets. (Capital is discussed in Chapter 11.)[9]

Branching of State Member Banks

The first three paragraphs of section 9 of the Federal Reserve Act (FRA),[10] after imposing certain restrictions on the ability of a state member bank to retain branches after it becomes a Federal Reserve System member, provides in effect that branching by sate member banks is subject to McFadden Act limits.

> . . . . nothing [in this section] shall prevent any State member bank from establishing and operating branches in the United States. . . . subject to the same limitations and restrictions as are applicable to the establishment of branches by national banks [subject to the approval of the Board rather than the OCC].

Branching of State Nonmember Banks

Section 18(d) of the Federal Deposit Insurance Act (FDIA)[11] provides as follows:

> No State nonmember insured bank. . . . shall establish and operate any new domestic branch unless it shall have the prior written consent of the [FDIC], and no State nonmember insured bank. . . . shall move its main office or any such branch from one location to another without such consent. The factors to be considered in granting or withholding the [approval of these actions] shall be those enumerated in section 1816 of this title [relating to factors to be considered in an application for deposit insurance].

---

9. Undercapitalized institutions with capital restoration plans that have been accepted by their primary federal regulator pursuant to PCA requirements under 12 USC 1831o may file applications to establish a branch and to engage in certain other activities under 12 CFR §303.204.

10. 12 USC 321.

11. 12 USC 1828(d).

The Bank Merger Act (BMA)

Mergers between depository institutions are governed by the terms of the Bank Merger Act (BMA),[12] which provides, among other things, that mergers are subject to final approval by the primary federal regulator of the resulting institution (which the BMA defines as the "responsible agency").

This means that no insured depository institution shall merge with another unless the transaction has been approved by the "the responsible agency," which is

- the OCC if the resulting institution is a national bank;
- the Board if the resulting institution is a state member bank;
- the FDIC if the resulting institution is a state nonmember bank (or a savings bank supervised by the OTS);[13] or
- the OTS if the resulting institution is a savings association.

The responsible agency, among other things, must request reports from the Attorney General and other federal banking agencies on competitive effect of the transaction and may not approve the transaction if the proposed merger would result in a monopoly, or restraint of trade, unless it finds that the anticompetitive effects of the transaction are outweighed by the benefits to the community.

The agency must also evaluate the:

- financial and managerial resources of the participants;
- future prospects of the existing and proposed institutions,
- convenience and needs of the community to be served; and
- effectiveness of the parties in combating money laundering.

Mergers under the National Bank Consolidation and Merger Act

This Act, which was adopted Nov. 7, 1918,[14] permits national banks to combine with other depository institutions in the same state. Prior to the enactment of Riegle-Neal I, this Act permitted a national bank to acquire another national bank or state bank with its main

---

12. Sec. 8(c), FDIA, 12 USC 1828(c).
13. This is this likely a reference to "section 10(*l*))" savings banks, which are discussed in Chapter 5.
14. Nov. 7, 1918, ch. 209.

office in another state. The target institutions in these transactions usually had their main offices in a state in which the acquiring national bank already operated branches.[15]

Interstate Activity before 1994

The pre-1994 branching restrictions discussed above did not serve as a total bar to interstate activities of financial institutions.

Federal savings associations, which are discussed in the next section, historically have been able to branch across state lines, and bank holding companies were able to acquire banks in other states in transactions that were not barred by the Douglas Amendment. Federal savings associations have been able to branch across state lines since their creation in 1933. With their narrow focus on housing finance, associations were not perceived as having the economic impact of a commercial bank, and Congress never saw fit to impose the kinds of branching restrictions on federal associations that it imposed on national banks in the McFadden Act.

Failing Bank Acquisitions

In 1992, Congress amended the Federal Deposit Insurance Act (FDIA) to authorize the FDIC to approve emergency acquisitions of failing institutions by banks, bank holding companies, and savings associations, with banks being able to acquire failing savings associations and vice versa. These "failing institution acquisition" provisions also include acquisitions across state lines and (in keeping with the S&L Holding Company Act as it was then) permit "any company" to acquire a failing savings association.[16]

Relocation of a National Bank's Main Office

National banks, upon approval of two-thirds of its shareholders (and a certificate of approval by the OCC), may move their main office to

---

15. *Business Combinations,* COMPTROLLER'S LICENSING MANUAL, January, 2004.
16. The Garn -St Germain Act Depository Institution Act. Pub. Law 87-320, Oct. 15, 1982, 96 Stat. 469, section 116, adding new subsection (f) to section 13 of the FDIA, codified at 12 USC 1823(f).

"any . . . location" that is not more than 30 miles from the limits of the "city, town or village" where the office was originally located.

This authority (12 USC 30), which was enacted in 1886,[17] was interpreted by the OCC prior to Riegle-Neal I as permitting a national bank that relocates its mains office to retain the former office as a branch even if the bank could not have opened a branch at the old location under the McFadden Act. The agency also permitted national banks to move its main office to another state so long as the 30-mile limit was observed and to retain the office in the former state as a branch—thereby permitting the bank to operate on an interstate basis.

Not surprisingly, these policies gave rise to considerable litigation with the OCC prevailing in virtually all of these cases.[18] The OCC successfully argued, among other things, that there was nothing in section 30 that imposed a geographic limit on the location of the new office, and nothing that conferred McFadden Act jurisdiction over the use of the former main office.

Interstate Branching for Banks

As noted above, by the time Riegle-Neal I was signed on September 29, 1994, all but one state permitted some form of interstate branching by banks. Riegle-Neal I was designed to provide uniform legal standards for interstate branching laws, while providing states until June 1, 1997 with an opportunity to "opt out" of interstate branching by merger. All states have now "opted-in" to this procedure.

Statutory Structure

Riegle-Neal I's provisions relating to interstate transactions fall into three groups.

The first provides the basic authority for banks to engage in interstate transactions. These rules are in a new section 44 of the FDIA,[19]

---

17. May 1, 1886, ch. 73, 24 Stat. 18, 12 USC 30.
18. See, *e.g.,* Ramapo Bank v. Camp, 425 F.2d 333, 344 (3d Cir. 1970), *cert. denied,* 400 U.S. 828 (1970), and Interpretations—Corporate Decision #96-58, September 30, 1996, Published in Interpretations and Actions October 1996.
19. 12 USC 1831u.

which expands the kind of merger transactions the banking agencies may approve under the BMA and

- provides a uniform legal framework for these transactions;
- preempts state laws that are inconsistent with this framework; and
- imposes uniform standards on post-merger branch retention, national and state concentration limits, and application of host state laws to branches of out-of-state banks.

The second group of sections makes technical and conforming amendments to the FDIA and the National Bank Act, including the McFadden Act.

The third group amends the Bank Holding Company Act to permit the Federal Reserve to approve acquisitions of out-of-state banks bank holding companies.

Basic Transaction Authority

Mergers

Section 44 expands the power of the banking agencies to approve mergers under the Bank Merger Act to include approval of interstate mergers between banks with the same and different charters. These transactions may be approved without regard to the interstate merger laws of either the "home state"—the state in which the acquiring bank is headquartered (if a national bank) or chartered (if a state bank) located, or the laws of the "host state"—the state in which the target bank is located.

Interstate Merger Involving Acquisition of Branches Only

If permitted by the laws of the host state, a bank may acquire one or more branches of a bank in a host state without acquiring the bank. In these cases, the branches are treated as a bank whose home state is the state in which the branches are located.

Establishing New Branches

Riegle-Neal I amends the McFadden Act and section 18(d) of the FDIA to permit the agencies to approve applications by banks to establish *de novo* branches in another state. These are free-standing branches established in a host state by an out-of-state bank without the acquisition of a host state bank or purchase of existing branches of a host state bank.

The laws of the host state must explicitly permit these branches and that law must apply equally to all categories of banks. These applications are subject to most of the requirements applicable to applications for interstate mergers, including evaluations of CRA performance, and capital adequacy. As of the end of 2004, 17 states had enacted laws to permit *de novo* branching by out-of-state banks.

Post-Merger Branch Retention and Continuing Operations

Additional Branches

Following an interstate merger, the resulting bank can branch in any location where any bank involved in the transaction could have branched under federal or state law if that bank had not been a party to the merger.

Continuing Operations

The bank resulting from an interstate merger may, subject to the approval of the responsible agency, retain and operate, as a main office or a branch, any office that any bank involved in the merger was operating as a main office or a branch immediately before the merger.

Example. Bank A merges with bank B in another state to form resulting bank C. C can retain the branches of former banks A and B, can choose either A's or B's former main office as its man office, and can branch wherever A and B could have branched before the merger.

Limitations on Interstate Activity

Age Laws

A state may adopt a law or regulation requiring that a bank chartered in that state must have been in existence for up to five years before it may be acquired by an out-of-state bank. These age limits may not be circumvented by the creation of "shell banks." These are banks chartered solely for the purpose of acquiring a target bank and do not open for business until they acquire all or substantially all of the assets of the target bank. Shell banks are deemed to have the age of the target bank for purposes of acquisitions by out-of-state banks. Otherwise, the shell bank, by acquiring an in-state bank that has been in business for 20 years, for example, could claim that the age of the newly acquired bank is measured, for purposes of Riegle-Neal I, from the date of the acquisition.

Concentration Limits

An interstate merger may not be approved if the resulting bank and its savings association affiliates:

- control more than 10% of the total amount of deposits of insured depository institutions in the United States; or
- other than its first time entry into the state, control more than 30% of the deposits of all insured banks and savings associations in any state in which both banks participating in the merger had a branch prior to the merger.

Example:

- Bank X, headquartered in state A, has branches in states B, C, and D
- Bank Y, headquartered in state B, has branches in states A, C, and D
- Bank X and Y propose to merge with Bank X as the resulting institution.

The merger would not be approved under this provision if, after the merger, Bank X would control more than 30% of the deposits of all insured banks and savings associations in *any one* of the following states: A, B, C, or D.

A state may, by law or policy, set a concentration limit higher than 30% of deposits so long as the law or policy does not discriminate against out-of-state banks, bank holding companies, or their subsidiaries. These concentration limits do not apply to mergers between affiliated banks.

Mergers Primarily for Deposit Production

In keeping with the principle that banks should serve the credit needs of their communities, Riegle-Neal I prohibits the use of interstate branching primarily for deposit production, that is, gathering deposits in a host state branch that is located primarily for the purpose of making loans in the bank's home state or in a third state.

The banking agency regulations relating to this practice require each agency to determine whether the loan-to-deposit ratio of each branch established under Riegle-Neal I in a host state is at least 50% of the statewide ratio for all banks in that state. If a interstate branch's ratio is below the 50% level, the responsible agency, after pursuing certain administrative proceedings and analyzing mitigating circumstances, may prohibit the bank from opening additional branches. It could also order the bank to close one or more branches, unless the bank provides an acceptable plan to meet the credit needs of the communities it serves in the host state.[20]

State Law Issues

Preservation of State Laws

Riegle-Neal I provides that the interstate mergers and bank holding company acquisitions authorized by its amendments to the relevant banking acts do not interfere with state tax and antitrust laws. States also retain the right to:

- administer their branching laws;
- supervise banks chartered in the state; and
- impose notice and reporting requirements on branches of out-of-state banks so long as these requirements do not discriminate against out-of-state banks and are not preempted by federal law.

CRA Compliance and Capital Requirements

In considering a Riegle-Neal application, the primary federal regulator must take into account the federal CRA compliance record of the applicant and banks that would be an affiliate of the resulting bank, and the compliance of the applicant with state CRA laws. An unsatisfactory CRA compliance rating can be grounds for disapproval of the application. The applicant must also be adequately capitalized.

Application of Host State Laws to Branches of Out-of-State, State Banks

The provisions on this subject in Riegle-Neal I set out in section 24(j) of the FDIA.[21] Section 24(j) was amended in 1997 by the Riegle-Neal Amendments Act of 1997 (Riegle-Neal II),[22] to remedy deficiencies

---

20. Agency regulations on this subject are found at (12 CFR): OCC-Part 25, subpart E; FDIC-Part 369; Board §208.28.
21. 12 USC 1831u(j)(1).
22. Pub. Law 105-24 (July 3, 1997), 111 Stat. 238.

in the original version The amended section provides that the laws of a host state, including laws relating to community investment, consumer protection, fair lending, and the establishment of intrastate braches, apply to host state branches of out-of-state, state banks to the same extent that host state laws apply to a branch of an out-of-state *national* bank located in the host state.

To the extent that host state law is inapplicable to a branch in that state of an out-of-state, state bank (because that law is not applicable to a branch of an out-of-state national bank (as the result of federal preemption of the state law, or otherwise)), the law of the home state of the out-of state bank will apply to its branch in the host state.

Some host state laws apply to a branch of an out-of-state national bank because the state law is not preempted by federal law. These include state laws relating to contracts, collection of debts, acquisition and transfer of property, taxation, zoning, crimes, torts, and homestead rights.[23] These are state laws that the OCC has determined are not preempted under its general preemptive powers derived from the Constitution's Supremacy Clause.

In other instances, federal law "specifically incorporates state law standards, such as the fiduciary [trust] powers statute at 12 U.S.C. 92a(a)."[24]

In these cases, section 24(j)(1) provides that as to matters covered by these "non-preempted" host state laws, host state branches of out-of-state, state banks are governed by the laws of that state bank's home state.

Example: Bank X, headquartered in state A, has a branch in state B. The activities of the branch in state B with respect to trust activities, debt collection, and the other "non-preempted" host state laws referred to above, will be governed by the laws of state A (Bank X's home state) rather than by the laws of host state B.

Activities of Branches of Out-Of-State, State Banks

Section 24(j)(2)[25] provides that an out-of-state, state bank can conduct any activities at its host state branch that are permissible under the bank's home state "to the extent" such activity is permissible:

---

23. 12 CFR §§7.4007 – 7.4009.
24. OCC, "Bank Activities and Operations; Real Estate Lending and Appraisals," Final rule, 69 F 1904 (Jan, 13, 2004), p. 1905.
25. 12 USC 1831a(j)(2).

- for a bank chartered in the host state, or
- for a branch in the host state of an out-of-state national bank.

Many in the banking industry believed that even after the Riegle-Neal II amendment, section 24 still did not achieve the stated Congressional goal of providing parity between national banks and state banks with respect to interstate activities. As a result, the Financial Services Roundtable filed a petition with the FDIC requesting rulemaking to clarify certain laws relating to interstate activities of insured state banks and their subsidiaries, including section 24.[26]

Proposed Amendment

In response to the petition, the FDIC published a notice of proposed rulemaking (NPR) on October 14, 2005[27] that would, among other things, create a new Subpart F, "Preemption," to its branching rules at 12 CFR Part 362.

The proposal would define "activity conducted at a branch" to mean an activity "of, by, through, in, from, or substantially involving, a branch." In the preamble to the proposal the FDIC says:

> Since a national bank branch gets the benefit of preemption whether or not the entire activity is performed in its branch, and since Congress intended to grant state banks full parity with national banks in this area, the definition in the proposed rule is designed to clarify that a branch of an out-of-state state bank gets the benefit of preemption whether or not the entire activity is performed in the branch.[28]

The NPR would define "activities conducted at a branch" to mean" an activity of, by, through, in, from, or substantially involving a branch."[29] The full parity that this definition is designed to provide can be illustrated by the following example:

> National bank N and state bank S are both headquartered in state A. Both banks have a branch in state B but not in state C. Each bank proposes to

---

26. "Petition for FDIC Rulemaking Providing Interstate Banking Parity for Insured State Banks," filed March 4, 2005 and published at 70 FR 13413 (March 21, 2005).
27. FDIC, "Interstate Banking; Federal Interest Rate Authority," Notice of proposed rulemaking (NPR), 70 FR 60019 (Oct. 14, 2005).
28. *Id.*, p. 60027.
29. *Id.*, p. 60030.

open an automated teller machine (ATM) in state C, which has a law that prohibits out-of-state banks with no branches in state C to open an ATM in that state.

Federal law (as discussed in more detail below under "Non-Branch Facilities") provides that ATMs are not "branches" for purposes of the FDIA or the National Bank Act. Section 24(j)(2), therefore would not apply to the ATM Bank N proposes to open in state C because the ATM is not a branch under the interstate branching provisions of the FDIA.

- *Result:* N can open the ATM in state C. It is not clear under Riegle-Neal II whether S can open an ATM in state C.[30]
- *Reason*-National banks: ATMs are not branches and there are no geographic limits on establishment of ATMs and related facilities by national banks.
- *Reason*-State banks: ATMs are not branches for state banks, but there is no federal law, other than Riegle-Neal II, as interpreted by the FDIC that would permit the law of one state to preempt the law of another state with respect to opening a non-branch facility (and with respect to many other banking activities).

The proposed definition of "activities conducted at a branch" in the NPR is designed to permit activities such as opening the ATM by Bank S, since a branch (whether in the state bank's home state or in a host state) must fund the withdrawals and accept the deposits made at an ATM—clearly activities "by, through, in, and from a branch."

As of the end of April, 2006, the FDIC had not taken further action on the NPR.

Conforming and Technical Amendments

Amendments to the McFadden Act

Riegle-Neal I makes two amendments to the McFadden Act relating to retention of branches by national banks that merge or move across state lines. The first provides that a national bank may not acquire a branch in a state in which it has no branches except

---

30. The FDIC points out that there were neither committee reports nor a conference report on Riegle-Neal II. The agency's proposed definition of "activities at a branch" relies on statements by the bill's proponents during consideration of the bill by the House and Senate. These statements provide ample evidence of congressional intent to provide "full parity" but little to provide a history of the scope Congress intended to provide for branches of state banks. NPR, *op. cit.*, pp. 60023–60025.

under the provisions of section 44, or by means of an emergency acquisition under the FDIA.

The second amendment imposes limits on branches a national bank may retain after it relocates its main office to another state after May 31, 1977—the effective date of the amendment. The amendment provides in effect, that a national bank that relocates its main office from State A to State B may retain branches in State A only under the terms of Riegle-Neal I. The amendment means that after the relocation, the bank will have to "re-acquire" its branches in State A (if possible) under the terms of Riegle-Neal I as if it were a bank located in State B with no branches in State A.

The amendment was designed to replace the branch retention policies that the OCC had applied prior to Sept. 29, 1994, the date of enactment of Riegle-Neal I (and continued to apply until the effective date of the amendment) to national banks that had relocated their main office under the 30-mile rule of 12 USC 30. These policies are discussed in the prior section.[31]

While the amendment ended the independence of 12 USC 30 from the McFadden Act, national banks can still relocate their main office to another state within the 30-mile rule (12 USC 30 was not repealed) with a minimum of red tape. This relocation provides the bank with a *de novo* facility in State B, thereby enabling it to branch in State B under the McFadden Act and to recover its branches in State A under the normal procedures of Riegle-Neal I. Riegle-Neal I also applies these branch retention restrictions to state banks that relocate their main office across a state line after May 31, 1997.

National Bank Branches in Host States

A third amendment to the McFadden Act provides that a branch of a national bank in a host state is subject to the host state laws on community investment, fair lending, consumer protection, and intrastate branching to the same extent these laws apply to a branch of a bank chartered in that state unless:

- the application of the law to the branch is preempted by federal law; or

---

31. In its decisions in 12 USC 30 applications after the date of enactment and before May 31, 1997, the OCC argued that Congress had implicitly approved of its application of the law in its pre- Riegle-Neal I rulings on 12 USC 30 by not making the amendment to the McFadden Act effective immediately on the date of enactment of Riegle-Neal I.

- the Comptroller finds that it is discriminatory in its application to the branch as compared its application to the branch of a bank chartered in that state.

The power to enforce any state law applicable to a branch of a national bank is vested in the OCC.

State laws, other than those listed above and certain tax laws, apply to a branch of a national bank in a host state in the same manner as they apply to a branch of a national bank headquartered in the host state

Other provisions in this section:

- amend 12 USC 30 (the 30-mile main office relocation provision) to provide that a national bank's ability to retain a former main office as a branch is determined by the provisions added to the McFadden Act by Riegle-Neal I, as discussed above; and
- change the name of the Act of Nov. 7, 1918, referenced above, to the "National Bank Consolidation and Merger Act," and add provisions to permit a national bank to engage in a merger or consolidation transaction with a national bank in another state.

Interstate Acquisitions by Bank Holding Companies

Acquisitions by a BHC

Acquisitions of an out-of-state bank by a bank holding company must be approved by the Federal Reserve under the BHC Act. As under section 44, the Board is authorized to approve the acquisition by a bank holding company of a bank in another state (the target bank) without regard to whether the acquisition is prohibited by the laws of any state.

These transactions are subject to many of the same procedures and limits as those applicable to transactions under section 44.

Concentration Limits

An acquisition by a bank holding company of a bank in another state may not be approved by the Board if:

- the bank holding company and its affiliated depository institutions either before the acquisition controls, or after the acquisition would control, more than 10% of the total amount of deposits of insured depository institutions in the United States; or
- other than its first-time entry into the state, immediately before the acquisition, the bank holding company, including any of its affiliated depository institutions, controlled any depository institution or any branch in the home state of the target bank or in any other state in which in the target bank maintained a branch; and
- upon completion of the acquisition, the applicant and its depository institution affiliates would control 30% or more of the deposits of insured depositories in the host state of the target bank; or in any other state in which the target bank maintained a branch.

Concentration Limits

A state may set a limit by law or policy that is higher than 30% of deposits within the state that may be controlled by a bank or bank holding company (and its depository institution affiliates) and may impose that limit on interstate mergers or acquisitions so long as the law or policy that sets this standard does not discriminate against out-of-state banks, bank holding companies, or their subsidiaries.

Age Laws and Shell Banks

A state may adopt a law or policy requiring that a bank must have been in existence for up to five years before it may be acquired by a BHC. As is the case with transactions by individual banks under section 44, a bank that is chartered solely for the purpose of acquiring another bank and does not open for business until it acquires all or substantially all of the assets of the other bank is deemed to have the age of the acquired bank for purposes of acquisitions by out-of-state bank holding companies.

Other Branching Issues

Agency

Any bank subsidiary of a bank holding company may act as agent for a depository institution affiliate of the holding company and the agency will not be considered a branch. Agency activities include closing, servicing, and receiving payments on loans, receiving deposits, and renewing certificates of deposits and other time deposits.

Interagency Policy on Branch Closings

Section 42 of the FDIA[32] requires all insured depositories to file a notice with their primary federal regulator 90 days before closing a branch. The institution must also mail a notice of the planned closing to customers of the branch and post a notice in the branch at least 30 days before the closing.[33]

These communications must tell customers that they may send comments on the closing to the institution's primary regulator and provide that agency's address. The agency in its discretion may hold a meeting of interested parties to discuss, among other things, alternative ways to replace the branch. The agencies do not have the authority to approve or disapprove the closing. This procedure ensures that the bank receives public comment on the planned closing, but the final decision is left to the business judgment of the bank

A "branch" for purposes of this policy excludes ATMs, RSUs, and loan production offices. A closing does not include the relocation of a branch to another site in the same neighborhood or a closing of a branch of a failing institution.

Non-Branch Facilities

Laws Relating to Non-Branch Facilities and Activities

In 1996, the definitions of "branch" for national and state banks were amended to clarify that ATMs and other remote facilities are excluded from the definition.[34]

---

32. 12 USC 1831r-1.
33. Branch Closings (Joint Policy Statement), 64 FR 34844 (June 29, 1999).
34. The Economic Growth and Paperwork Reduction Act of 1996 (EGRPRA), Pub. Law 104-208 (Sept. 30, 1996), 110 Stat. 3009-394, section 2205, amending section 5155(j) of the Revised Statutes (12 USC 36(j)) and section 3(o) of the FDIA (12 USC 1813(o)).

The definition of "branch" for national banks in the McFadden Act, with the new language in italics, now provides:

> The term "branch" as used in this section shall be held to include any branch bank . . . [or] additional office . . . at which deposits are received, or checks paid, or money lent. *The term "branch" as used in this section, does not include an automated teller machine or a remote service unit."*[35]

As noted above, this definition is identical in all material respects to the definition of "domestic branch" in section 3(o) of the FDIA for both state member and state nonmember banks.[36]

The 1996 amendment was designed to resolve persistent questions about the kinds of off-premises services that banks could offer in remote facilities for the convenience of customers without going to great lengths to avoid having the facility considered to be a branch. With this amendment, banks could operate their own ATMs and other remote facilities without McFadden or FDIA definitional issues.

In 1999, the OCC adopted new regulations[37] relating to remote service units (RSUs), deposit production offices (DPOs), and facilities that combined these services with a loan production office (LPO), asserting that as long as the services performed at these facilities met the regulatory standards they were not branches.

Remote Service Unit (RSU)—§ 7.4003

This is an automated facility, as noted above, that performs core branching services but is not a branch. It is defined as a facility operated by a customer of the bank that:

> conducts banking functions, such as receiving deposits, paying withdrawals, or lending money. . . . . An RSU includes an automated teller machine, automated loan machine, and automated device for receiving deposits. An RSU may be equipped with a telephone or televideo device that allows contact with bank personnel. An RSU is not a "branch" within the meaning of [the McFadden Act] and is not subject to state geographic or operational restrictions or licensing laws.

---

35. 12 USC 36(j).
36. 12 USC 1813(o).
37. *Investment Securities; Rules, Policies, and Procedures for Corporate Activities; Bank Activities and Operations,* Final rule, 64 FR 60092 (Nov. 4, 1999).

Deposit Production Office (DPO)—§ 7.4004

DPOs are offices that can be operated by the bank or an operating subsidiary at a site other than the main office or a branch of the bank. Bank employees at these offices may solicit deposits, provide customers with forms necessary for opening an account, and assist them in completing these forms, but may not accept the customer's deposit. That would be a "receipt" of a deposit, which is prohibited in a facility that is not a branch. The rule provides:

> All deposit and withdrawal transactions of a bank customer using a DPO must be performed by the customer, either in person at the main office or a branch office of the bank, or by mail, electronic transfer, or a similar method of transfer.

Deposits can be made by the customer at an ATM located on the premises of the DPO.

In contrast to its DPO policy, OCC interpretations permit loan production offices to engage in virtually all aspects of making a "loan" without the facility being characterized as a branch.

Loan Production Offices (LPOs)

The OCC's policies with respect to permissible activities of LPOs have evolved through Interpretive Letters rather than by regulation. A 2001 Interpretive Letter held that an LPO could do the following without being a "branch" under federal law:

- accept loan applications;
- underwrite the loan using credit standards developed by the bank;
- have a loan officer at the LPO approve or deny the loan based on these criteria (with certain authority to make exceptions based upon personal judgment); and
- give the loan proceeds to the borrower.

These activities were performed by an LPO in State A operated by an out-of-state national bank that had no branches in State A. State A asserted that the LPO was a branch under the laws of State A. Since State A had not adopted laws permitting out-of-state institutions to organize *de novo* branches in the state, the state claimed that the LPO was an impermissible *de novo* branch of the national bank.

In its response, the OCC said "while [State A] may define a 'branch' for purposes of state law, the definition of a national bank 'branch' is governed by federal law. *First National Bank in Plant City v.*

Dickinson, 396 U.S. 122 (1969)." The OCC then provided its analysis of the "make loans" element of the McFadden definition, citing cases and earlier Interpretive Letters, holding that the activities of the LPO in question did not fall within this definition The OCC asserted, for example, that its regulation at 12 USC §7.1004, providing that an LPO will not be regarded as a branch if its loans are approved at the bank's main office or at a branch is not a legal requirement that approvals must be made at these locations, but was merely a "safe harbor." The agency asserted that

> [m]oreover, the core branching function that is required under the McFadden Act is "making" loans. It is apparent that neither loan origination nor the technical act of loan approval, taken separately, constitutes the making of a loan.[38]

Combination of Loan Production Office, Deposit Production Office, and Remote Service Unit—§7.4005

This section provides that since a loan production office, a deposit production office, and a remote service unit are not branches, the combining of these facilities at a single site does not create a branch.

Messenger Services—§7.1012

The use of messenger or courier services by national banks to pick up and deliver items related to transactions between a bank and its customer is not a "branching" activity.

Branching Laws Applicable to Savings Associations

Federal Savings Associations

Federal Associations

As noted above, federal savings associations historically have been able to branch across state lines. This authority is found in section 5(r) of the Home Owners' Loan Act (HOLA),[39] which conditions

---

38. OCC Interpretive Letter # 902, Jan., 2001.
39. 12 USC 1461 *et seq.*

this authority on the association's meeting CRA and capital standards, as well as one of two asset composition tests: the qualified thrift lender (QTL) test at 12 USC 1467a(m) or the "tax test" in the tax code at 26 USC 7701(a)(19), both of which are discussed in Chapter 5.

There are no "McFadden" branching restrictions for federal savings associations in the Home Owners' Loan Act (HOLA) or in OTS regulations. In its rules on branching of federal associations, the OTS says that federal associations:

> may branch in any State or States of the United States and its territories . . . This exercise of OTS authority is preemptive of any State law purporting to address the subject of branching by a Federal savings association.[40]

RSUs

For federal savings associations, a branch does not include electronic facilities. A "branch" is defined as "any office *other than* its home office, agency office, administrative office, data processing office, or an electronic means or facility under part 555 of this chapter [relating to Electronic Operations]." (emphasis added)

HOLA provides that a federal association may establish remote service units for the purpose of crediting savings or demand accounts, debiting such accounts, crediting payments on loans, and the disposition of related financial transactions, as provided in regulations developed by the OTS.[41]

Electronic Operations

OTS rules, at 12 CFR Part 550, Electronic Operations, are more general than those for national banks. Section 555.200, for example, provides that

> A Federal savings association. . . . may use, or participate with others to use, electronic means or facilities to perform any function, or provide any product or service, as part of an authorized activity. Electronic means or facilities include, but are not limited to, automated teller machines, automated loan machines, personal computers, the Internet, the World Wide Web, telephones, and other similar electronic devices.

---

40. 12 CFR §545.92(c).
41. 12 CFR §545.92(a) and Sec. 5(b)(1)(F) of HOLA (12 USC 1464(b)(1)(F)).

Neither federal nor state associations are required to notify the OTS before engaging in an electronic activity unless they are planning to establish a transactional website.

State Savings Associations

The ability of state savings associations to branch across state lines depends on state law. A state association that is prevented from interstate branching by state law may convert to a federal association and branch in accordance with section 5(r) of HOLA. The OTS Examination Manual states as follows:

> A state-chartered thrift institution is not required to file an application or notice . . . with the OTS in connection with the establishment or relocation of a branch office. In addition, the installation of an automated teller machine (ATM) does not require the filing of an application or notice with the OTS.[42]

This policy also is reflected in the preamble to OTS interim final branching rules, adopted in 2004:

> Currently, State-chartered savings associations are not required to file any application or notice with OTS regarding changes to their home or branch offices. This has not raised any significant safety and soundness concerns for State-chartered savings associations. Accordingly, OTS has decided to modify its branch and home office application and notice requirements for Federal savings associations [only] to ease regulatory burden to the extent feasible.[43]

Conclusion

The expansion of interstate branching of state banks through state compacts and unilateral action that began in 1978 is frequently cited as a prime example of the ability of the dual system to test the feasibility of new approaches to emerging issues before Congress considers the issue. Another example is the use of NOW accounts by saving institutions in Massachusetts and New Hampshire in the early 1970s, which is discussed in Chapters 1 and 5.

---

42. Section 100 *Branching Activities*, p. 100.1.
43. 69 FR 68239, 68240 (Nov. 24, 2004).

The development of an interstate branching law applicable to all 50 states and to both national banks and state banks has proven more difficult than many had expected. One of the remaining difficulties—the issue of parity between national banks and state banks—is addressed by the FDIC's October 2005 notice of proposed rulemaking, which is discussed in this chapter. The proposal appears to solve the problem of parity, but whether it will eventually do so remains to be seen.

CHAPTER 5

Holding Companies

A depository institution holding company is a corporation, joint venture, partnership, trust, or other legal entity whose ownership interest in a depository institution meets the definition of "control" in the Bank Holding Company Act (BHCA) or the Savings and Loan Holding Company Act (S&LHCA).[1]

The primary federal regulators of bank holding companies (BHCs) and S&L holding companies (S&LHCs) are the Federal Reserve Board (Board) and the Office of Thrift Supervision (OTS), respectively. There are several variations of these two kinds of holding companies, which are discussed below and listed in Figure 5.1 on page 126.

Early Holding Company Developments

Early bank holding companies, which generally involved control of two or more banks by an individual or group of individuals, date back to at least the 1890s.[2] These "chain banks," which originated in the Northwest and the South, were organized primarily to overcome intrastate, and in some cases, interstate, branching restrictions. They grew rapidly between 1900 and 1920, and by 1931, 176 chain banking organizations were operating 908 banks with assets of $927 million.

---

1. The BHCA and S&LHCA are codified respectively at 12 USC 1841 *et seq.*, and 12 USC 1467a.

2. The discussion in this section is based on ROBERT T. CLAIR and PAULA K. TUCKER, *Interstate Banking and the Federal Reserve: A Historical Perspective,* Federal Reserve Bank of Dallas, ECONOMIC REVIEW, Nov., 1989.

By the end of 1945, there were 115 chain organizations operating 522 banks with combined assets of $4.62 billion.

A variation of chain banks that arose prior to the 1920s were "group banks," which were essentially bank holding companies as we know them today. The group consisted of two or more banks controlled by a corporation, which held controlling stock in each of its subsidiary banks.

The principal advantage of group banks was their ability, as corporations, to finance their growth by raising capital in the financial markets. The growth of chain banks, by contrast, was limited by the financial resources of the individual or individuals who formed the chain.[3]

Group banks experienced rapid growth during the 1920s, fueled in part by the stock market boom. By 1931, there were 97 group banking organizations operating 978 banks with an addition 1,219 additional branch offices. In 1930, the Board reported that 10 of the largest 34 largest operated in more than one state, one of which controlled banks in eight states.

Bank Holding Companies

The Banking Act of 1933

In 1933, Congress granted the Board limited authority to supervise BHCs that controlled at least one bank that was a member of the Federal Reserve System (FRS). The parent company, then called a "holding company affiliate," included a company that owned or controlled a majority of the capital stock of a member bank or more than 50% of the number of shares voted for election of directors in the preceding election.

The Board was not given the extensive powers over BHCs that it has today. It was given the power to examine and supervise BHCs only when the parent company had to make a decision that required a formal vote of the shares of the subsidiary bank (most likely including cases in which state or federal law required approval of the decision by a majority of the bank's shareholders). In these cases, the BHC had to acquire a "voting permit" from the Board. The granting of this permit entitled the Board to examine and supervise the BHC, and to implement certain restrictions on the BHC's activities.

---

3. *Ibid.*, p. 5.

Several bills relating to BHCs were introduced in Congress after 1933 to strengthen the agency's authority to regulate BHCs, but it was not until the enactment of the Bank Holding Company Act of 1956[4] that Congress subjected BHCs to broader federal regulation. The 1956 Act strengthened the Board's authority with respect to BHCs that controlled more than one bank (multi-bank holding companies).

During its consideration of the proposed holding company legislation, the Senate Banking Committee observed that by December 31, 1954, 18 BHCs had obtained voting permits from the Board in accordance with the 1933 Act. The agency estimated that at least 46 holding companies would be covered by the terms of the pending bill, which applied to companies that controlled more than 25% of the stock of each of two or more banks.

The principal concerns relating to multi-bank holding companies were their potential to acquire as many banks as needed to create a monopoly in a particular geographic area and using bank funds to finance their own nonbank business activities.

The Senate committee report on the 1956 bill cited testimony of then-Board Chairman William McChesney Martin, Jr., stating that the two principal concerns posed by multi-bank holding companies were:

1. the unrestricted activity of a holding company group to add to the number of its banking units, making possible the concentration of commercial bank facilities in a particular [geographic] area under a single control and management; and
2. the combination under single control of both banking and nonbanking enterprises, permitting departure from the principle that banking institutions should not engage in business wholly unrelated to banking. Such a combination involves the lending of depositors' money, whereas other types of [businesses], not connected with banking, do not involve this element of trusteeship.[5]

Other concerns included:

- the possibility that the parent company would either force the bank to make loans to finance speculative business projects, or force it to compensate the parent for losses incurred in business ventures; and

---

4. May 9, 1956, ch. 240, 70 Stat. 133.
5. S. Rept No. 1095 July 25, 1958, p. 2483, U.S. CONG. AND ADMN. NEWS, 85th Cong., 2nd sess.

- the potential for the parent company to use the deposits of the bank as "capital" to fund businesses of the parent, for the parent to use its market power to discriminate against persons that were not depositors, and charging holding company competitors higher interest rates on commercial loans than it charged noncompetitors.

The 1956 Act required holding companies to register with the Board before acquiring control of a second bank, and gave the agency the power to regulate and supervise the operation of multi-bank holding companies. The Act restricted certain BHC activities but did not prohibit permitting the company from acquiring shares:

> of any company all the activities of which are of a financial, fiduciary or insurance nature and which the [Federal Reserve] Board by order has determined to be so closely related to the business of banking or of managing or controlling banks as to be a proper incident thereto.[6]

In 1956, Congress did not believe that coverage of one-bank holding companies under the Act was warranted.

This issue was revisited in 1966, with the Senate Committee concluding that after reviewing all of the testimony presented at hearings on the bill, "there was no substantial evidence of abuses occurring in one-bank holding companies."[7] The Committee further concluded that repeal of the one-bank holding company exemption would make it more difficult for individuals to hold or form small independent banks. In order to minimize potential conflicts, however, the Committee voted to extend the provisions of section 23A of the Federal Reserve Act, relating to transactions of FRS banks with their affiliates, to state nonmember banks supervised by the FDIC.

The 1956 Act also repealed the exemption in the BHCA for long-term trusts, with the Senate Committee Report noting that the Alfred I. duPont Trust controlled 30 banks in Florida and other nonbank businesses.[8] This Trust was further evidence of the anticompetitive potential of multi-bank holding companies. Although trusts may have been subject to restrictions under state trust laws with respect to

---

6. 1956 Act, *op cit.*, section 5(c)(6), 70 Stat. 173.
7. S. Rept. No. 1179, June 7, 1966, p. 2385, U.S. CONG. AND ADMN. NEWS, 89th Cong., 2nd sess. on the bill that became *An Act to amend the BHCA of 1956*, Pub. Law 89-485, July 1, 1966, 80 Stat. 236.
8. *Id.*, p. 2388.

aggressive business strategies, that did not apply to other BHCs, the sheer size of an entity controlling 30 banks in a single state—with no apparent limit to the number of banks it *could* eventually control—prompted the Committee to repeal the long-term trust exemption.

In 1967, however, the Senate Banking Committee found that 23 banks with more than $1 billion in assets were subsidiaries of one-bank holding companies. These included the six largest banks in the country, which held more than 20% of the deposits of the country's entire banking system. The Committee also found that the percentage of deposits held by all banks in one-bank holding companies had increased from 10% in early 1967 to more than 40% in 1970.[9]

Because of their exemption from the BHCA of 1956, one-bank holding companies were not prevented by the federal banking laws from engaging in any business subject only to the restrictions of the antitrust laws. At hearings held by the Senate Banking Committee in 1969, Chairman Martin reiterated his concerns about the potential for anticompetitive practices arising from the combination of banking and commerce:

> If a holding company combines a bank with a typical business firm, there is a strong possibility that the bank might deny credit to competing firms or grant credit to other borrowers only on the condition that they agree to do business with the affiliated firm. If we allow the line between banking and commerce to be eased, we run the risk of cartelizing our economy [and] we could later see country's business firms clustering about banks in holding company systems in the belief that such an affiliation would be advantageous or even necessary to their survival.[10]

The BHCA Amendments of 1970[11] retained the 1956 activities restrictions quoted above virtually unchanged and applied them to one-bank holding companies. These restrictions are now found at section 4(c)(8) of the BHCA,[12] which provides in relevant part that a BHC generally may control the shares of any company:

> the activities of which had been determined by the Board by regulation or order under this paragraph as of the day before November 12, 1999, to be so closely related to banking as to be a proper incident thereto (subject to such terms and conditions contained in such regulation or order, unless modified by the Board); . . .

---

9. S. Rpt. No. 91-1084, Aug. 10, 1970, p. 5521, U.S. CONG. & ADMN. NEWS, 91st CONG., 2nd sess.
10. *Id.,* p. 5521–5522.
11. Pub. Law 91-607, Dec. 31, 1970, 84 Stat. 1760.
12. 12 USC 1843(c)(8).

November 12, 1999 is the day before the signing of the Gramm Leach Bliley Act (GLBA, or GLB Act),[13] which authorizes BHCs that elect to become financial holding companies (FHCs) to engage in an expanded list of permissible financial activities.(FHCs are discussed below.)

Nonbank activities that are permissible for BHCs under section 4(c)(8) of the BHCA include consumer, mortgage, and commercial lending; limited insurance sales; securities brokerage and certain securities activities (including a limited amount of underwriting of corporate equity securities); credit card operations; and ownership of a savings association.

Examination and Supervision

While the Board is the primary federal regulator of the BHC, the holding company's depository institution subsidiaries continue to be regulated by their primary federal regulator. Activities of regulated

Figure 5.1
Bank and S&L Holding Companies Primary Federal Regulators and Applicable Regulations

Primary Federal Regulator	Federal Reserve Board	Office of Thrift Supervision
Statute	Bank Holding Company Act[14]	S&L Holding Company Act[15]
Holding Companies	Bank Holding Company Financial Holding Company Mutual Bank Holding Company	S&L Holding Company Mutual S&L Holding Company
Regulations	12 CFR Part 225 (Regulation Y)	12 CFR Parts 574, 575, & 583
Regulatory Capital Rules*	Regulation Y, Appendices A, B, D & E	None

*Capital rules for bank holding companies are discussed in Chapter 11.

---

13. Public Law 106-102, Nov. 12, 1999, 113 Stat. 1338.
14. 12 USC 1841 *et sec.*
15. 12 USC 1467a.

nonbank subsidiaries of both BHCs and FHCs are supervised by their "functional regulators" (for example, the Securities and Exchange Commission (SEC) and state insurance regulators), with "umbrella" supervisory authority vested in the Board.

Savings and Loan Holding Companies

Legislation involving S&L holding companies evolved on a separate track from BHCA legislation.

The first federal banking law relating to S&LHCs, the "Spence Act,"[16] which was enacted in 1959, imposed a two-year moratorium on the acquisition of additional savings associations by S&LHCs that already controlled one association. The Federal Home Loan Bank Board (FHLBB) was directed to conduct a survey of the implications of holding company control of stock savings associations and submit a report to the House and Senate Banking Committees along with any draft legislation it deemed advisable.

Congressional concerns with S&LHCs were similar to those it had with BHCs in 1956, but the Senate Report on the Spence Act acknowledged that the situation with S&LHCs was different from those involving holding companies "both because of the nature of the [S&L] industry and because of differences in stage of development which savings and loan holding companies have reached, as compared with public utility holding companies or bank holding companies."[17]

While the Report alluded to possible anticompetitive effects of increasing holding company ownership of savings associations, there was less emphasis on the harmful effects of combining banking and commerce (savings associations could not make commercial loans at that time, for example). There was concern, however, about: absentee ownership in an industry that is closely tied to the local community, "financial manipulation and intercorporate dealings," and entanglement of associations in schemes designed to promote interests unrelated to homeownership.[18]

---

16. Pub. Law 86-374, Sept. 23, 1959, 73 Stat. 691.
17. S. Rpt. No. 810, Aug. 25, 1959, p. 2888, U.S. Cong. and Admn. News, 86th Cong., 1st sess.
18. *Id.,* p. 2887.

This activity culminated in the Savings and Loan Act Amendments of 1967,[19] which imposed limits on nonbanking activities of multiple S&LHCs but not on otherwise lawful activities of S&LHCs that controlled one savings association (unitary S&LHCs).

This ability to conduct unrestricted activities continued until the enactment of the Competitive Equality Banking Act of 1987 (CEBA).[20] This Act provided that unitary S&LHCs could no longer engage in unrestricted activities unless their savings association subsidiaries became "qualified thrift lenders" (QTLs). To meet this test, the savings association was required to hold at least 60% of its assets in residential mortgages and other housing-related investments.

Multiple S&LHCS, which were otherwise restricted to engaging in a limited set of activities approved by OTS regulations, were free of activities restrictions after CEBA if all, or all but one, of their savings association subsidiaries had been acquired in supervisory acquisitions and all of the subsidiaries met the QTL test (QTL-qualified multiples).

The QTL test was a response to Congressional concerns that savings associations were becoming more "bank-like" as a result of legislation in the early1980s that had expanded their investment powers beyond mortgage lending to include, among other things, limited authority to make commercial and consumer loans. Congress devised the test to keep associations focused on housing finance and to make this focus the "price" for their unlimited unitary holding company powers.

The QTL test has since been raised to 65% of portfolio assets, but the categories of assets that qualify for the test have been expanded to include consumer and education loans, loans to small businesses, and credit card loans.

In 1996, Congress added an alternative test to the QTL test that would enable an association to be a qualified thrift lender. This test, which qualifies an association as a "domestic building and loan association" under the Internal Revenue Code,[21] originated in the early 1950s in connection with favorable tax treatment that was accorded savings associations at that time. It was added as an alternative to the QTL test to provide associations with greater flexibility in maintaining their qualified thrift lender status.

---

19. Pub. Law 90-255, Feb. 14, 1967, 82 Stat. 5.
20. Pub. Law 100-86, Aug. 10, 1987, 101 Stat. 552.
21. Section 7701(a)(19), (26 USC 7701(a)(19).

S&L Holding Companies after GLBA

The GLB Act, signed Nov. 12, 1999, ended unrestricted activities of S&LHCs that were organized after May 4, 1999 and that did not have on or before that date, an application pending at the OTS to organize a unitary holding company.

Grandfathered S&L Holding Companies

Unitary and QTL-qualified multiple S&LHCs that were in existence on May 4, 1999, may continue to engage in activities in which they were engaged on that date and in any activities in which *they could have engaged* under the S&LHCA on that date so long as:

1. they control at least one association that they controlled on that date (or that they acquired pursuant to an application filed on or before that date); and
2. the association or associations under their control are qualified thrift lenders.

Non-grandfathered S&L Holding Companies

S&LHCs that were organized after May 4, 1999, and those that were organized before that date that lose their grandfathered status, are limited to engaging in the "post-GLBA" activities listed below.[22] Grandfathered S&LHCs lose that status if they are acquired by a company or other entity that is engaged in activities other than "post-GLBA" activities. These post-GLBA activities are:

1. "Section 4(k)" activities permissible for financial holding companies, which are discussed below;
2. "Section 4(c)(8)" activities permissible for BHCs; and
3. the following permissible activities for non-QTL-qualified multiples:
   a. furnishing or performing management services for a savings association subsidiary of such company;

---

22. In November, 2001, the OTS published a notice of proposed rulemaking (NPR) on activities of non-grandfathered S&LHCs, which it withdrew on Jan. 9, 2002 (press release OTS 02-03). In the release, OTS said that after meeting with industry representatives and reviewing comments on the proposal, it concluded that it could "deal with any new issues in this area through guidance or case-by-case determinations." The NPR was published at 66 FR 56488 (Nov. 8, 2001).

b. conducting an insurance agency or escrow business;
   c. holding, managing, or liquidating assets owned or acquired from a savings association subsidiary of such company;
   d. holding or managing properties used or occupied by a savings association subsidiary of such company;
   e. acting as trustee under deed of trust; and
   f. activities permissible for multiples by regulation on March 5, 1987.[23]

Examination and Supervision

The OTS regulation of S&LHCs is confined primarily to ensuring that the holding company is not engaging in transactions that are detrimental to the safety and soundness of the association subsidiary and monitoring holding company activities that may adversely affect the association's customers.

The S&LHCA was amended in 1996 to provide in effect that a BHC that controls a savings association is not an S&LHC. The OTS therefore has no authority to examine or supervise the BHC but remains the primary federal regulator of the saving association subsidiary or subsidiaries of the BHC.

Interstate Acquisitions

The S&LHCA has a provision similar to the former Douglas amendment in the BHCA (which is discussed in Chapter 4) that prohibits a company, including an S&LHC, from engaging in a transaction directly or through one or more subsidiaries in which it would become a multiple S&LHC that controls an association in more than one state unless:

1. the transaction involves a failing association;
2. the acquiring company controlled an association in the other state on or before March 5, 1987; or
3. the laws of the other state specifically approve acquisitions of in-state associations by out-of-state S&LHCs or out-of-state associations.[24]

---

23. These activities, at 12 USC§ 584.2-1(b), include acquisition of unimproved real estate for development, data processing, storage, and other services for affiliates and development and administration of employee benefit plans.

24. Sec. 10(e)(3) of HOLA (12 USC 1427a(e)(3)).

Other Provisions

State-chartered savings banks and FDIC-supervised cooperative banks may elect to be treated as a savings association for purposes of the S&LHCA so long as they meet the qualified thrift lender requirements discussed above. This provision, which was added to the former National Housing Act in 1987, provided these institutions with the opportunity to take advantage of the unrestricted activities enjoyed by S&L holding companies organized before the enactment of GLBA.[25]

This section is still on the books, but it appears to provide little advantage to these institutions after the enactment of GLBA.

"Nonbank" Holding Companies

As noted in Chapter 1, some specialized banks, such as credit card banks and industrial loan companies (ILCs) are excluded from the definition of "bank" for purposes of the BHCA. Companies that control these banks are therefore not BHCs and are not subject to the section 4(c)(8) activity restrictions of the BHCA, or to the section 4(k) restrictions for FHCs.

Prior to CEBA, the BHCA defined a bank as an institution that offered demand deposits or made commercial loans, and restricted BHCA activities, as noted above, to those that are closely related to banking. In the late 1970s, several commercial companies that wanted the advantages of bank affiliation acquired banks and avoided coverage under the BHCA by declaring that the bank would offer either commercial loans or demand deposits, but not both. The acquisition of these "nonbank banks" breached the wall between banking and commerce that Congress had intended to build in 1970.

Because the BHCA definition referred to "demand deposits," some of these companies were able to make commercial loans *and* offer their customers check-like instruments drawn on time deposits rather than demand deposits. As discussed in Chapter 1, these instruments were generally referred to as negotiable orders of withdrawal, or NOWs, and this "NOW account loophole" effectively erased any

---

25. This authority is found in section 10(l) of the Home Owners' Loan Act (12 USC 1467a(l)).

distinction between banks that conformed to the BHC definition and those that did not.[26]

Congress addressed this issue in CEBA, which redefined "bank" in the BHCA to close the loophole. The new definition included all banks that are FDIC insured, or institutions that made both commercial loans and offered deposit accounts from which the customer could pay third parties by check "or similar means for payment to third parties."[27]

Grandfathering of Nonbank Banks

CEBA provided that companies that had acquired nonbank banks prior to March 5, 1897, and were not bank holding companies on that date, would not be treated as bank holding companies after that date so long as they and their bank subsidiary adhered to growth and activities limits specified in new section 4(f) of the BHCA.[28] Under current law, these companies may not acquire control of another insured institution, or, with certain exceptions, acquire more than 5% of the stock of such institutions.

These companies' subsidiary banks are, among other things, limited to activities in which they were engaged on March 5, 1987, and may not permit affiliates to incur overdrafts on their accounts at the bank or to incur overdrafts, including intraday overdrafts at their Federal Reserve District Bank on behalf of an affiliate. These prohibitions do not apply to inadvertent overdrafts beyond the bank's control and overdrafts in connection with activities of primary gov-

---

26. In 1986 (before the enactment of CEBA), the Supreme Court held that the reference to "demand deposits" in section 2(c) of the BHCA means, literally, deposits withdrawable on demand, and does not include NOW accounts. In an attempt to stop nonbank banks from evading BHCA coverage by offering NOW accounts, the Federal Reserve had amended Regulation Y to change the definition of "demand deposit" to cover NOW accounts by defining these accounts to include deposits that are payable on demand "as a matter of practice." The court noted that NOW accounts, although functioning like traditional checking accounts, are (as time deposits) subject to "a seldom but nevertheless absolute right to require prior notice of withdrawal," are not, therefore, withdrawable "on demand" and therefore are not, under the plain language of the statute, demand deposits. Board of Governors, FRS v. Dimension Financial Corp., *et al.,* 474 U.S. 361, 368 (1986).

27. Section 101 of CEBA adopting new section 2(c)(1) of the BHC (12 USC 1841(c)(1)).

28. 12 USC 1843(f).

ernment securities dealers and with activities permissible for financial holding companies.

These CEBA provisions exempted 57 companies that were operating nonbank banks. By May 2006, according to the Board, this number had declined to six companies.

CEBA also carved out several exceptions from the definition of "bank" in the BHCA, including certain trust companies, and two types of limited-purpose institutions: "credit card banks," and industrial loan companies (ILCs).[29]

The FDIC has reported that there were approximately 56 ILCs, and 40 credit card banks in operation at the end of 2003.

Credit Card Banks

Credit card banks are institutions with a state or national bank charter that limit their activities exclusively to credit card operations. To qualify for the BHCA exclusion, these banks may accept collateral to secure consumer credit card loans, but may not:

1. accept demand deposits or other deposits on which the customer may write checks or similar instruments;
2. accept time or savings deposits of less than $100,000;
3. have more than one branch where deposits are accepted; and
4. issue commercial credit cards or otherwise make commercial loans.

There are no prohibitions on the creation of new credit card banks. Organizers of these banks generally secure a regular national or state bank charter and voluntarily limit its activities to conform to the BHCA exclusion. Delaware, however, does have a special charter for credit card institutions that conforms to the BHCA requirements.[30] As insured institutions, credit card banks are subject to virtually all of the rules and regulations of the FDIC and their chartering agency, including those pertaining to transactions with affiliates, tying arrangements, and others that are cited below for ILCs.

---

29. Credit card banks and ILCs are excluded from the definition of "bank" in sections 2(c)(2)(F) & (H), respectively, of the BHCA (12 USC 1841(c)(2)(F) & (H)).
30. Del. Code, Title 5, Ch. 15.

Industrial Loan Companies

ILCs are state-chartered FDIC-insured institutions that originated in the early 1900s as finance companies for lower-income borrowers. It took some time, however, before these institutions were insured:

> These early ILCs offered relatively high interest unsecured loans to factory workers who could not otherwise obtain credit. Instead of receiving deposits, these companies typically raised funds by issuing "certificates of investment" or "certificates of indebtedness." However, Colorado and Rhode Island began to authorize ILCs to receive deposits, sometimes denoted as "thrift certificates," and the FDIC began to issue federal deposit insurance in these states as early as 1958. However, most ILCs were not qualified to become federally insured until the Garn-St Germain Act of 1982 authorized FDIC insurance for ILCs meeting regulatory standards.[31] (footnotes omitted)

Several ILCs applied for FDIC insurance before 1982, and at least six became federally insured from 1958 through 1979. Several states also required ILCs to obtain federal deposit insurance as a condition of keeping their charters. After 1982, federally insured ILCs, particularly in Utah, became a favorite "nonbank-bank" charter for companies that were not eligible to become a BHC.

CEBA limited the exclusion of ILCs from coverage under the BHCA to those that had been chartered in a state that had a law in effect or under consideration on March 5, 1987, that required, or would require, ILCs to obtain federal deposit insurance. ILCs chartered in these states are then excluded from coverage under the BHCA if they meet any one of the following conditions:

1. The asset of the ILC must be less than $100 million.
2. The ILC does not accept "demand deposits that the depositor may withdraw by check or similar means for payment to third parties."[32]
3. Control of the ILC has not been acquired by any company after August 10, 1987.

---

31. Raymond Natter, Barnett, Sivon & Natter, P.C., "The Industrial Loan Company Controversy," *eNewsletter,* Aug., 2005, ABA Banking Law Committee, Section on Business Law.

32. Section 2(c)(2)(H) of the BHCA (12 USC 1841(c)(2)(H)). The General Accountability Office (GAO) points out that this language permits ILCs that wish to do so to offer NOW accounts to its customers. ("Industrial Loan Companies—Recent Asset Growth and Commercial Interest Highlight Differences in Regulatory Authority" GAO-05-621, Sept., 2005, p. 6). See also summary of *Dimension* case in footnote 25.

CEBA also provided that uninsured ILCs would be grandfathered as long as they refrained from engaging directly or through an affiliate, in any activity in which they were not lawfully engaged on March 7, 1987.

The exclusion of any grandfathered ILC will be defeated if the institution permits any overdraft on its account at a Federal Reserve Bank including intraday overdrafts, on behalf of an affiliate. There are several exceptions to this restriction, however, including overdrafts caused by inadvertent errors, overdrafts in connection with primary government securities dealers and in connection with activities permissible for financial holding companies.

ILCs were chartered in seven states as of mid-2004: California, Colorado, Hawaii, Indiana, Minnesota, Nevada, and Utah. As of March 31, 2006, there were 38 ILCs operating in Utah, including several controlled by automobile companies, investment banks, and other commercial and financial companies. The banking departments of the other six states listed a total of approximately 70 ILCs operating in their states at year-end 2005, including 21 nondepository financial services loan companies in Hawaii and 29 industrial loan and thrift companies in Minnesota. Few of the ILCs operating in these states appeared to be controlled by commercial companies.

ILCs remain controversial in some quarters, primarily because they permit the ownership by commercial companies of institutions that provide most banking services. The FDIC pointed out, however, that it, along with the Utah Department of Financial Institutions, has extensive authority to examine not only ILCs, but also their affiliates and their nonbank holding companies.[33] In addition, ILCs are subject to virtually all of the regulations applicable to commercial banks, including prompt corrective action, insider lending, money laundering, transactions with affiliates (which include transactions with the parent company), CRA, anti-tying, interstate branching, and consumer protection regulations, such as truth in lending and fair credit practices.

---

33. *Supervision of Industrial Loan Companies: A Historical Perspective*, FDIC SUPERVISORY INSIGHTS, Summer, 2004. See also GAO ILC Report, *op. cit.* As this book went to press in July, 2006, one of the principal ILC controversies related to an application for deposit insurance filed with the FDIC by Wal-Mart in July, 2005 in connection with the application to the Utah Department of Financial Institutions to charter a Utah ILC. The size of the company has reinforced concerns in many quarters about the anticompetitive effects of combining banking and commerce.

Financial Holding Companies

In GLBA, Congress amended the BHCA to permit qualifying BHCs to engage in a broader range of financial service activities by becoming "financial holding companies." (FHCs). New section 4(k) of the BHCA permits FHCs to engage in activities that are "financial in nature," incidental to such activities and activities that are "complementary" to financial activities.

"Pre-approved" Financial Activities

New section 4(k)(4) defines the following activities as being financial in nature:

1. Lending, exchanging, transferring, investing for others, or safeguarding money or securities.
2. Providing life, health, property, and casualty insurance; issuing annuities; and acting as principal, agent, or broker for purposes of the foregoing, in any State.
3. Providing financial, investment, or economic advisory services, including advising an investment company.
4. Issuing or selling instruments representing interests in pools of assets permissible for a bank to hold directly.
5. Underwriting, dealing in, or making a market in securities.
6. Engaging in the United States in certain activities in which a bank holding company may engage outside U.S.
7. Merchant banking (see below).
8. Portfolio investments by insurance affiliates (see below).
9. Activities that were permissible for BHCs under section 4(c)(8) of the BHCA on November 12, 1999.

Merchant Banking[34]

FHC affiliates, other than depository institutions or their subsidiaries, may acquire up to 100% of the shares in a company engaged in com-

---

34. The discussion of merchant banking and portfolio investments is based in part on *A Summary of Gramm-Leach-Bliley Act*, Kirkpatrick & Lockhart Nicholson Graham LLP, Nov., 1999.

mercial or other activities that are not permissible for the FHC so long as the shares are held in connection with a "bona fide underwriting or merchant or investment banking activity, including investment activities engaged in for the purpose of appreciation and ultimate resale or disposition of the investment."

The shares may be held for as long as required to enable the affiliate to sell or otherwise dispose of the company "on a reasonable basis." The holding company may not actively manage the company as though it were a normal affiliate, but can manage it to the extent necessary to obtain a reasonable return on its sale or other disposition.

Portfolio Investments by Insurance Affiliates

These are investments—in shares, assets, or ownership interests—made in the ordinary course of business and in accordance with state law, by insurance companies that are predominantly engaged in underwriting life, accident, and health, or property and casualty insurance (other than credit-related insurance) or providing and issuing annuities.

During the period such shares, assets, or ownership interests are held, the bank holding company may not routinely manage or operate such company except as may be necessary or required to obtain a reasonable return on investment.

"Designated Activities"

The Act directs the Federal Reserve to adopt regulations authorizing FHCs to engage in the following:

1. Lending, trust, and other activities
2. Transfers of money or other financial assets by any device or instrumentality
3. Arranging or facilitating financial transfers for third parties

New FHC Activities

The Board, in consultation with, and subject to the veto of, the Treasury Department, may approve additional financially related (or complementary) activities for FHCs.

Becoming an FHC

To become an FHC, BHCs must submit an application to their appropriate Federal Reserve Bank certifying, among other things, that all depository institutions controlled by the company are well capitalized and well managed, as those terms are defined in agency regulations, as of the date the company files its election. All depository institutions in the company must also be rated satisfactory or better under the Community Reinvestment Act.[35]

An FHC can lose its status as an FHC if one or more of its depository institutions becomes less than "well capitalized" or if it is rated as less than "well managed." If the FHC does not correct these deficiencies within 180 days after notice from the Federal Reserve, or a longer period as prescribed by the agency, the FHC must either:

1. divest its depository institutions; or
2. stop engaging in activities other than the "4(c)(8) activities" that are permissible for a BHC. This cessation requirement does not apply to activities conducted by the institutions themselves or by their subsidiaries, including financial subsidiaries.

FHCs may not engage in new financial activities or acquire a company engaged in such activities so long as the CRA rating of any of its depository institution subsidiaries is less than "satisfactory."

Examination and Supervision of FHCs

The Federal Reserve is not the primary federal regulator of an FHC as it is for a BHC. FHCs are subject to "functional regulation"—a procedure in which functionally regulated FHC subsidiaries continue to be supervised by their functional regulators. The SEC and state insurance regulators, for example, will continue to supervise companies in the FHC that are engaged in securities and insurance activities.

The Federal Reserve retains an "umbrella" supervisory authority over FHCs. It can examine and require reports from functionally reg-

---

35. FRB, SR Letter 00-1(SUP), *Procedures to Become a Financial Holding Company,* Feb. 8, 2000.

ulated subsidiaries but can take action against these nonbank companies only if their activities endanger the safety and soundness of the bank or banks in the FHC and if it concludes that action against the bank itself would not be effective.

Rulemaking

The authority to determine whether an activity is financial in nature or incidental to a financial activity is shared by the Board and the Treasury Department. The Board may not determine that an activity has either of these characteristics if the Treasury objects to the determination. The Treasury may also make recommendations to the Board, which also may decline to take further actions.

In deciding whether a service is financial in nature, the Board must consider:

1. the purposes of the BHCA and the GLB Act;
2. changes or reasonably expected changes in the marketplace in which financial holding companies compete;
3. changes or reasonably expected changes in the technology for delivering financial services; and
4. whether such activity is necessary or appropriate to allow an FHC and its affiliates to—
    a. compete effectively with other financial services companies in the U.S.;
    b. efficiently use technology to deliver financial information and services that are financial; and
    c. offer customers any available or emerging technological means for using financial services or for the document imaging of data.

Notice

An FHC and its subsidiaries (other than depository institutions and their subsidiaries) can generally engage in financial activities either *de novo* or by acquisition of companies engaged exclusively in permissible financial activities without providing prior notice to the Board or obtaining approval of the Board. Conduct of activities that are "complementary" to financial activities must be approved in advance by the Board.

Other Companies

An FHC may acquire up to 5% of the shares of a company that is "substantially engaged" in activities permissible for an FHC without prior notice to the Board (other than for acquisitions of a savings association or its holding company) if the acquired company divests the impermissible activities within two years of the acquisition. A company is "substantially engaged" in permissible activities when at least 85% of its gross income is attributable to, and at least 85% of its consolidated total annual gross revenues is derived from, the conduct of permissible activities.[36] Failure of the acquired company to divest its impermissible activities would result in divestiture proceedings by the Board.

Grandfathered Companies

A company that is not a BHC and becomes an FHC after the date of enactment of GLBA may continue to engage in any activity and retain direct or indirect ownership or control of shares of a company engaged in any activity if the holding company:

1. was lawfully engaged in the activity on September 30, 1999;
2. is predominantly engaged in financial activities (meaning that its annual gross revenues from FHC activities—except revenue from subsidiary depository institutions—is at least 85% of the annual gross revenues of the company);
3. refrains from prohibited cross-marketing activities;
4. does not, subject to narrow exceptions, expand its grandfathered activities; and
5. ceases such activities, by divestiture if necessary, within 10 years after the date of enactment of GLBA unless extended for an additional five years by the Board.

---

36. 12 CFR § 225.85.

Mutual Holding Companies

Mutual S&L Holding Companies

This holding company structure, enacted by CEBA,[37] is designed to permit a mutual savings association to enjoy the advantages of being in a holding company structure, including issuance of stock and other access to capital markets, while preserving the advantages of mutual ownership, including insulation from hostile takeovers and proxy fights.[38]

To reorganize into a mutual holding company (MHC), a mutual savings association organizes a mutual savings and loan holding company (MHC), which is a mutual entity chartered and supervised by the OTS. The mutual institution then converts to a stock charter and transfers 100% of its voting stock to the MHC.

The MHC, which is controlled by the depositors of the subsidiary association, retains control of a majority of the voting stock, but may raise capital by issuing up to 49.9% of that stock, and any nonvoting stock the association may have issued, to the public.

"Mid-tier" Stock Holding Company

In 1998, OTS issued regulations[39] to permit MHCs to create an "intermediate" stock holding company (SHC), commonly called a "mid-tier" stock holding company. In this structure, 100% of the stock of the savings association is held by the SHC, which can issue up to 49.9% of its own stock to the public. The parent mutual holding company owns at least 50.1% of the stock of the SHC.

This structure is designed, among other things, to make the securities of the mutual holding company more competitive in the capital markets because shares of a stock company—the SHC—are understood in these markets as opposed to shares issued by a mutual company (which is an unfamiliar entity to these markets) on behalf of a subsidiary stock institution.

---

37. Section 107(a), adding a subsection to the National Housing Act, which, upon the enactment of FIRREA, became section 10(o) of the S&LHCA (12 USC 1467a(o)).

38. OTS MHC regulations are at 12 CFR Part 575.

39. OTS, "Mutual Holding Companies, Final rule, 63 FR 11361 (March 9, 1998).

Permissible Activities of MHCs

MHCs and SHCs may engage in activities permissible for the following:

- financial holding companies, which are discussed above;
- multiple savings and loan holding companies, which are discussed above;
- service corporations and operating subsidiaries of federal savings associations which are discussed in Chapter 7; and
- service corporations of state-chartered associations in a state where the MHC has its home office.

Mutual Bank Holding Companies

CEBA also authorized mutual savings banks and cooperative banks to reorganize to form a mutual bank holding company, which is to be regulated on the same terms and subject to the same limitations "as any other bank holding company."[40] Bank MHCs, unlike savings associations MHCs, are organized under state law.[41]

Change in Control

The "Change in Bank Control Act"[42] provides that the acquisition of control of any insured depository institution by any person "acting directly or indirectly or through or in concert with one or more other persons" must be approved by the primary federal regulator (PFR) of the institution to be acquired. An "insured depository institution" includes a company that controls a bank or saving association irrespective of whether it is a "company" for purposes of the bank or S&L holding company acts.[43]

---

40. Section 107(b) of CEBA, adding subsection (g) to section 3 of the BHHCA, (12 USC 1842(g)).

41. See, for example, *Mutual Holding Companies,* ch. 167H, title XXII, Part I., Mass. Gen. Laws.

42. Codified in section 7(j) of the Federal Deposit Insurance Act (12 USC 1817(j)). This legislation is a combination of the Change in Bank Control Act and the Change in S&L Control Act, which were originally enacted by titles VI and VII, respectively, of the "Financial Institutions Regulatory and Interest Rate Control Act of 1978," Public Law 95-630, Nov. 10, 1978, 92 Stat. 3641.

43. FDIA, Section 7(j)(18)(12 USC 1817(j)(18)).

The idea here is to enable the agencies to have some control over individuals and other prospective bank and savings association acquirers that do not fall within the definition of a "company" for purposes of these holding company acts.

"Control"

The basic definitions of control of a bank, savings institution (or other company), which are substantially the same in the regulations of both the Fed and the OTS,[44] provide that control is deemed to exist when a person or entity, acting alone or in concert with others, meets any one of the following tests with respect to a bank, savings association, or other company:

- controls, or has the power to vote, 25% or more of the outstanding shares of any class of voting stock;
- has the power to control the election of a majority of the board of directors;
- has the power to exercise a controlling influence over its management or policies; or
- is a person who is a general partner of, or has contributed more than 25% of the capital to, a company.[45]

Change in Control Notice

Prospective acquirers must provide detailed information about themselves in the change in control notice filed with the PFR, including the following:

- personal history, business background, and experience and affiliations during the past five years;
- a description of any pending civil or criminal proceedings;
- information on any criminal indictments or convictions by a state or federal court;
- a statement of the assets and liabilities and related statements of income and sources and application of funds for each of the preceding five fiscal years; and
- the terms and conditions of the proposed acquisition and the manner in which the acquisition is to be made.

---

44. 12 CFR 225.2(e), and 12 CFR 583.7(a) respectively.
45. This test is in the OTS rules only.

When the agency receives a change of control notice, it is required to conduct a thorough investigation of the prospective acquirers including the "competence, experience, integrity, and financial ability" of each person named in the notice as potential acquirer. The agency must then:

- publish the name of the institution proposed to be acquired and the names of those involved in the application;
- solicit public comment on the proposal, particularly from persons in the geographic area where the institution proposed to be acquired is located;
- conduct a thorough investigation of the background, character, including any record of criminal activity, financial resources, and other relevant information about the persons involved in the application; and
- if the institution to be acquired is state-chartered, solicit the views of the banking department of the chartering state.

If the application is not approved, the prospective acquirers may request an agency hearing on the proposed acquisition. If the agency reaffirms its denial of the acquisition, the prospective acquirers may appeal the decision to an appropriate U.S. court of appeals.

The findings of the appropriate Federal banking agency shall be set aside if found to be arbitrary or capricious or if found to violate procedures established by the Act.

The Board says that after reviewing the submitted information it, and by implication, the other agencies, "may initiate name checks with certain other U.S. government agencies (including law enforcement) on some or all of the individuals related to the proposal."[46]

Definitions

Acting in Concert

The Federal Reserve defines the term as including "knowing participation in a joint activity or parallel action toward a common goal of acquiring control of a state member bank or bank holding company whether or not pursuant to an express agreement."[47]

---

46. FRB, Supervisory Letter SR 03-19 on guidance on change in bank control procedures, November 19, 2003.
47. 12 CFR 225.41(b)(2).

The OCC defines acting in concert as:

(i) knowing participation in a joint activity or parallel action toward a common goal of acquiring control whether or not pursuant to an express agreement; or

(ii) a combination or pooling of voting or other interests in the securities of an issuer for a common purpose pursuant to any contract, understanding, relationship, agreement, or other arrangement, whether written or otherwise.[48]

Person

A person is "an individual or a corporation, partnership, trust, association, joint venture, pool, syndicate, sole proprietorship, unincorporated organization, or any other form of entity not specifically listed herein."

Control

Control means the power, directly or indirectly, to direct the management or policies of an insured depository institution or to vote 25% or more of any class of voting securities of an insured depository institution.

Insured Depository Institution

As noted above, this term includes a bank or S&L holding company and any other company that controls an insured depository institution that is not a bank or S&L holding company. This means that persons seeking control of a company that controls an institution such as an ILC or credit card bank that is excluded from the definition of "bank" in the BHCA are also covered.

Exceptions

The Change in Control Act does not apply to transactions that are covered by the Bank Holding Company Act, the Bank Merger Act, or the Savings and Loan Holding Company Act.

---

48. 12 CFR 5.50(d).

Compliance

Some persons may inadvertently violate the Change in Control Act by inadvertently acquiring control of an institution or by misinterpretation of Act's filing requirements. Persons who intend to purchase shares in an institution in an amount that falls short of control may inadvertently acquire control as a result of a miscalculation of the number of shares that would create a presumption of control. Others, for example, may unexpectedly inherit shares in an amount that creates this presumption.

The Board advises persons in these situations to contact their district Federal Reserve Bank, if the Board has jurisdiction over the transaction. All four federal banking agencies have procedures for persons who wish to rebut the presumption of control by, among other things, providing evidence to the agency that they do not intend to manage, or exercise control over, the institution or holding company in question.[49]

The Board says that "the complexity of an ownership position [as defined in the statute] sometimes does not lend itself to easy interpretation of the requirements to file a notice."[50] It advises prospective acquirers and persons who believe they may have inadvertently acquired control of a depository institution, as a result, for example, of inheriting shares in an institution or controlling company, to check with their district Federal Reserve Bank, if the Board has jurisdiction, or, presumably, with the PFR of the institution involved. After the fact notice procedures are available in these instances.

Pre-GLBA Insurance Activities of National Banks

Incidental Powers

Under the "incidental powers" authority in the National Banking Act,[51] national banks could sell directly as agent, and without geographic limit of the office, fixed and variable rate annuities. The OCC

---

49. Agency regulations relating to rebuttal of a presumption of control are found as follows (all at 12 CFR): OCC, §5.50(f)(2)(v); Board: §225.41(g); FDIC: §303.82(e); and OTS: §574.100.
50. FRB Sup Let, *op. cit.*
51. 12 USC 24 (Seventh).

had permitted national banks to sell, "and in some cases to underwrite," credit related and title insurance without geographic limitation.[52]

Sales from Towns of under 5,000

A historic source of insurance powers for national banks is a 1916 statute that authorizes banks to sell insurance as an agent from towns with populations of less than 5,000. This provision originated with a letter written by the Comptroller of the Currency on June 8, 1916 to a member of the Senate Banking Committee expressing concern about the difficulties of running a profitable national bank in a small town. This section provides in part as follows:

> [a national bank] located and doing business in any place the population of which does not exceed five thousand inhabitants. . . . may [under rules adopted by the Comptroller] act as the agent for any fire, life, or other insurance company [licensed by the state in which the bank is located] by soliciting and selling insurance and collecting premiums on policies issued by such companies . . . [53]

The OCC, backed by several court cases, has interpreted this section as permitting insurance sales to be made nationwide from a national bank located in a place of 5,000 inhabitants or from a branch or other office of a national bank located outside such place so long as that branch or office is located in a place with a population of 5,000.

An agent in the bank can do the same things a state-licensed nonbank agent can do, including meeting prospects outside a community of 5,000 so long as bank's agents are managed and paid through a bona fide agency, which among other things, accepts premiums, processes applications for insurance, and maintains records, and so long as the agents use the agency as their place of business for state licensing purposes.[54]

---

52. *Comparison of Powers of Federal Savings Associations to the Powers of National Banks,* OCC and OTS, Jan. 17, 1997.

53. 12 USC 92.

54. The discussion of the place of 5,000 provision is derived primarily from OCC Interpretive Letter # 753, Nov. 4, 1996.

Post-GLBA Insurance Activities of National Banks

Sales from Towns of under 5,000

Congress left this authority intact.

Authorized Products

Under GLBA's authority, national banks may not underwrite insurance products unless:

- the insurance product was authorized by OCC in writing as of Jan. 1, 1999, or was lawfully provided by national banks as principal;
- the OCC authorization has not been not overturned by a court; and
- the product is not title insurance or an annuity.

Title Insurance

National banks may:

- sell title insurance as an agent in states in which state banks are authorized by state law (other than by a state "wildcard statute") to sell title insurance as agent; and
- continue to sell and underwrite title insurance if they were actively and lawfully engaged in these activities before Nov. 12, 1999—except that the bank must "push out" any title insurance underwriting "first to an insurance affiliate, or if no insurance affiliate exists, to any subsidiary providing insurance as principal."[55]

Definition of Insurance

Insurance products eligible to be authorized products are those that:

- were regulated as insurance under the law of the state in question as of Jan. 1, 1999; and

---

[55]. H. Rept. 106–74, Part 3, on H.R. 10, the "Financial Services Act of 1999" (the House version of the bill that was enacted as GLBA), p. 190.

- were first offered after Jan. 1, 1999 and were classified as insurance by the state insurance regulator, and include the following kinds of insurance: life, health, title, property and casualty (including auto, fire, theft, and malpractice), malpractice, fire, title, auto, etc.) and annuity contracts that are qualified contracts under section 72 of the Internal Revenue Code.

The definition of an insurance product does not include a bank product or service of a bank that is a:

- loan, letter of credit, or other extension of credit;
- trust or other fiduciary service;
- deposit product;
- qualified financial contract (QFC), as defined in section 11 of the FDIA;[56] or
- financial guaranty that does not have insurance component.

Insurance Activities of Savings Associations

Federals savings associations may sell credit-related insurance and fixed annuities on an agency basis. Service corporations of federal savings associations can sell title, life, casualty, and other kinds on insurance on an agency basis subject to any state laws that prohibit depository institutions from engaging in such sales. (See Chapter 7 for a discussion of activities of savings association subsidiaries.)

Standards for Preemption of State Insurance Laws

In drafting the insurance provisions of GLBA, Congress was faced with the challenge of balancing competing claims of the states and the OCC, with the states claiming that recent OCC preemption policies

---

56. Sections 11(e)(8)-(10) of the FDIA (12 USC 1821(e)(8)-(10)) provide special treatment for QFCs when the FDIC is appointed receiver or conservator of a depository institution, and authorize the FDIC to define additional contracts that qualify as QFCs (see also 12 CFR 360.5). A QFC includes "any securities contract, commodity contract, forward contract, repurchase agreement, swap agreement, and any similar agreement that the FDIC determines by regulation to be a qualified financial contract. . . ." (FDIA, sec. 11(e)(8)(D)(i))

were overreaching and the OCC claiming that several these laws imposed illegal restraints on the exercise by national banks of insurance powers authorized by federal law. (See the discussion of preemption of state laws by the OCC and OTS in Chapter 1.)

Preemption issues are dealt with in section 104 of the Act,[57] which attempts to strike a balance between federal and state interests and provides new mechanisms to resolve disputes and to encourage uniform licensing laws among the states. The final version of section 104:

- reaffirmed the states' exclusive rights to regulate the insurance business as provided in the McCarran-Ferguson Act,[58] which "remains the law of the United States"[59];
- provided that the standards for evaluating the validity of state laws that purportedly interfere with the lawful conduct of insurance activities by depository institutions shall be governed by the principles enunciated in *Barnett Bank of Marion County, N.A. v Nelson*,[60] the 1996 Supreme Court case that held that a state may not by law, regulation, order, or other action "prevent or significantly interfere" with the conduct of insurance activity by an insured depository institution (this case is also discussed in Chapter 1);
- created an expedited procedure in the U.S. Courts of Appeals for resolution of disputes about "insurance issues," including whether a state law is preempted by a federal law; and
- created a mechanism to encourage states to adopt uniform or reciprocal licensing standards or face imposition of federal standards.

The McCarran-Ferguson Act

As noted above, GLBA makes it clear that the states remain in control of insurance regulation. The Act explicitly states that the McCarran-Ferguson Act remains the law of the land. Section 2 of the Act provides in part as follows:

---

57. 12 USC 6701.
58. March 9, 1945, ch. 20, 59 Stat. 33, 15 USC 1011, *et seq.*
59. Sec. 104(a), 12 USC 104(a).
60. 517 U.S. 25 (1996).

> The business of insurance, and every person engaged therein, shall be subject to the laws of the several States which relate to the regulation or taxation of such business. No Act of Congress shall be construed to invalidate, impair, or supersede any law enacted by any State for the purpose of regulating the business of insurance . . . unless such Act specifically relates to the business of insurance . . . [61]

Section 104 also makes it clear that everyone who engages in the insurance business in any state as principal or agent must be licensed under the laws of the state in which these activities are conducted.

Preemption of State Laws

GLBA provides a multi-layered set of standards designed to the preempt state laws that interfere with the conduct of insurance activities by national banks and other depository institutions and their affiliates without disturbing state laws that do not apply to these activities. After asserting the primacy of the McCarran-Ferguson Act and state licensing laws, section 104 outlines standards for preempting two sets of state laws:

- laws that prevent or restrict affiliations of depository institutions; and
- laws that restrict the ability of depository institutions to engage in any activities authorized by GLBA.

State Anti-Affiliation Laws

GLBA provides a "blanket" preemption of state anti-affiliation laws other than those relating to insurance activities. Section 401(c)(1) provides that this preemption standard invalidates any state law that would prevent or restrict a national or state bank, a federal or state savings association or its affiliate from affiliating with "any person" as authorized not only by GLBA but also by "*any other provision of federal law.*" (emphasis added) This section would apply, for example, to state laws that would restrict affiliations of banks and securities firms.

---

61. 15 USC 1012.

This provision clarifies that it is not intended to interfere with states' exercise of their regulatory powers including the processing of licensing and merger applications, approval of affiliations between insurers and depository institutions, and enforcing consumer protection rules, so long as the states' actions in these matters do not discriminate against banks.

State Laws Restricting Insurance Activities

"Blanket" Standard

As in the affiliation section discussed above, GLBA provides a "blanket" preemption relating to insurance activities. Section 104(d)(1) provides that with certain exceptions, that no state law or regulation shall prevent or restrict a bank or savings associations or their affiliates from engaging directly or indirectly in *any activity* permitted by GLBA and the amendments made by GLBA.

State Laws Relating to Sales, Solicitations, and Cross-Marketing of Insurance

These insurance sales activities are singled out in section 104(d)(2) for a separate preemption standard as follows:

- *The Barnett Standard.* In accordance with the legal standards of preemption enunciated in the Barnett case, no state laws and regulations may "prevent or significantly interfere" with the ability of a depository institution or its affiliate to sell, solicit, or cross-market insurance products;
- *Safe Harbors.* The Act lists 13 categories of state laws relating to insurance sales that are shielded from preemption by the banking agencies under any of the preemption standards in section 104. Most of these rules are similar to consumer protection laws already applicable to depository institutions. Among these safe harbors are laws that would prohibit tying arrangements and coercion, protect customer privacy, and require certain consumer disclosures.

Anti-Discrimination Standard

Section 104(e) provides that, except for the safe harbors summarized above, no state law, regulation, interpretation, or order may "regulate the insurance activities authorized or permitted under this Act or any other provision of federal law" for a depository institution if the law or regulation:

- is by its terms or in its effect, more adverse to the bank than to nonbank entities engaging in the insurance business;
- prevents a bank from engaging in authorized insurance activities; or
- conflicts with the purpose of the Act to permit affiliations between depository institutions and others engaged in the insurance business.

These standards do not apply to state laws, rules, or other actions relating to insurance sales, solicitations, or cross-marketing that were issued or adopted before Sept. 3, 1998, except for laws that are subject to safe harbor protection. In other words, the anti-discrimination rules *do* apply to state safe harbor laws enacted before Sept. 3, 1998.

Dispute Resolution

An expedited procedure for review is provided for disputes that may arise between a federal and state regulator including whether a state law, regulation, order, or interpretation regarding any insurance sales or solicitation activity is properly treated as preempted under federal law.

In such disputes, the federal or state regulator may seek expedited judicial review of the question in the U.S. Court of Appeals for the circuit in which the state is located or in the District of Columbia Circuit. The court is directed to render a decision within 60 days unless the parties agree to an extension. In these cases, the court is directed to decide the case with "equal deference" to each side in the dispute. This means that the OCC, for example, or other federal agency involved in the dispute, will not be accorded the traditional deference that the federal appeals courts have traditionally granted to an agency's interpretation of the laws it administers.

The equal deference rule will *not* apply to disputes involving state insurance sales laws enacted before Sept. 3, 1998, unless the laws in question fall within the Act's safe harbor protections, which are summarized above.

Barnett

For disputes relating to state laws other than those subject to safe harbor protections, the preemption standard of the *Barnett* case (i.e., a state may not prevent or significantly interfere with the ability of a bank to engage in any insurance sales, solicitation, or cross-marketing activities) will apply irrespective of whether the laws in dispute were enacted before or after Sept. 3, 1998.

Other Provisions

State Laws Not Affected by Blanket Preemption

Among the state laws and regulations that are not preempted by the general activities preemption in GLBA are those that:

- relate to the McCarran Ferguson Act;
- apply only to entities other than banks that are engaged in insurance;
- do not apply to or regulate insurance sales, solicitations, or cross-marketing activities; and
- relate to the securities, antitrust, and general corporation laws, and other state laws of general applicability if such laws are not inconsistent with the general purposes of GLBA.

Insurance Customer Protections

Section 46 of the FDIA, added by GLBA[62], directs the federal banking agencies to develop customer protection regulations relating to sales of insurance by banks and their subsidiaries. Each agency must also develop a consumer complaint procedure for receiving and resolving complaints alleging a violation of the consumer protection rules. The agencies' first final rules on this subject were published Dec. 4, 2000.[63]

---

62. 12 USC 1831x.
63. "Consumer Protections for Depository Institution Sales of Insurance," Final Rule, 65 FR 75821, (Dec. 4, 2000).

These rules apply to retail sales practices, solicitations, advertising, or offers of insurance and require that the bank or savings association's practices and solicitations relating to insurance sales:

- ensure that the institution policies include antitying and anticoercion provisions:
- make it clear that the institution's insurance products are not covered by deposit insurance;
- provide physical segregation of banking and insurance product activity;
- provide that if the institution permits employees who accept deposits to refer a potential customer to a qualified salesperson, the person making the referral receives no more than a one-time nominal fee of a fixed dollar amount for each referral that does not depend on whether the referral results in a transaction;
- ensure that all persons who sell or offer for sale insurance products are appropriately qualified and licensed; and
- ensure that institution's eligibility rules for life and health insurance do not discriminate against persons subject to domestic violence.

"NARAB"

GLBA provided for the imposition of federal uniform licensing standards on the insurance industry within three years of enactment (Nov. 11, 2002) unless a majority of the states by that date had established uniform licensing laws or a system of reciprocity to recognize licenses of nonresidents to sell insurance in their state.[64] "NARAB" is the acronym for the National Association of Registered Agents and Brokers that would have been established if the states did meet the deadline.

As it happened, the states met the deadline and the Association was not organized.[65]

---

64. Section 321.

65. The effect of the NARAB proposal as a stimulus to state action and the benefits of the goals achieved by the states were discussed at hearings before the Senate banking in 2004. "Examination of [GLBA] Five Years After Its Passage," Senate Banking Committee, July, 13, 2004.

Post GLBA Developments

In 2001 and 2002, the OCC published preemption determinations in the Federal Register declaring that certain provisions of the West Virginia Insurance Sales Consumer Protection Act and the Massachusetts Consumer Protection Act were preempted by the GLBA Barnet standards.

West Virginia

The OCC concluded that the following parts of the West Virginia law were preempted and therefore not applicable to national banks:

- provisions requiring financial institutions to use separate employees for insurance sales;
- provisions prohibiting bank employees from making referrals or solicitation to customers about insurance products until after the bank has approved the loan or credit;
- restrictions on banks' use of information acquired in the course of making a loan to solicit or offer insurance to the customer, unless the bank first obtains written consent from the customer; and
- a requirement that financial institutions segregate locations used for insurance sales from deposit-taking and lending areas.

The OCC concluded that the following provisions of the law would not be preempted and thus would apply to national banks:

- a prohibition against requiring or implying that the purchase of insurance from a financial institution is required as a condition of approving a loan;
- a provision prohibiting a financial institution from offering an insurance product in combination with other products unless all of the products are available separately; and
- the requirement that the commitment to purchase insurance occurs when the loan is approved and that the actual sale of the insurance must be completed independently and through separate documents.

The OCC found that although none of these provisions were protected by the GLBA safe harbor provisions, the first two comported generally with tying restrictions applicable to national banks[66] and the third would not substantially affect the bank's insurance activities.

---

66. 12 USC 1972. Tying provisions are discussed in Chapter 6.

Massachusetts

In 2002, the OCC, at the request of the Massachusetts Bankers Association, applied the GLBA preemption principles to three provisions of the Massachusetts Consumer Protection Act and found that they were preempted by these provisions. These three sections of that Act prohibited:

- non-licensed personnel from referring prospective customers to a licensed insurance agent or broker except upon an inquiry initiated by the customer (Referral Prohibition);
- non-licensed bank personnel from receiving any additional compensation for making a referral, even if the compensation is not conditioned upon the sale of insurance (Referral Fee Prohibition); and
- banks from telling loan applicants that insurance products are available through the bank until the application is approved and, in the case of a loan secured by a mortgage on real property, until after the customer has accepted the bank's written commitment to extend credit (Waiting Period Restriction).

In the ensuing months, the Massachusetts Commissioners of Insurance and Banking sought relief in the First Circuit Court of Appeals under section 304 of GLBA, which provided for expedited dispute resolution in conflicts between state insurance regulators and federal agencies.[67] The court dismissed the petition for lack of jurisdiction holding that there was no regulatory conflict as required by section 304.[68]

Subsequently, the Massachusetts Bankers Association and several of its members filed a complaint in Federal District Court against the Commissioners challenging their enforcement of the three laws discussed above and an additional provision, the "separation restriction," which required the physical separation of insurance and banking

---

67. Codified at 12 USC 6714(a), which provides: In the case of a regulatory conflict between a State insurance regulator and a Federal regulator regarding insurance issues, including whether a State law, rule, regulation, order, or interpretation regarding any insurance sales or solicitation activity is properly treated as preempted under Federal law, the Federal or State regulator may seek expedited judicial review of such determination by the United States Court of Appeals for the circuit in which the State is located or in the United States Court of Appeals for the District of Columbia Circuit by filing a petition for review in such court.

68. Bowler v. Hawke, 320 F 3rd 59 (1st Cir. 2003).

activities. In 2005, the court held in favor of the plaintiffs with respect to the four laws that were challenged.[69]

Conclusion

The creation of financial holding companies (FHCs) by GLBA in 1999 was a major breach in the barriers between banking and commerce that were erected for bank holding companies in 1970, as well as the end of the ability of future unitary S&L holding companies to engage in unrestricted activities that their predecessors had always enjoyed (and continue to enjoy on a grandfathered basis).

The creation of FHCs was driven by competitive considerations, but the breakthrough was not sudden. Bills similar to GLBA had been under active consideration in Congress for several years preceding its enactment. In hindsight, it seems clear that the unfettered activities of unitary S&LHCs, which had always been strongly opposed by the Board as a threat to the financial safety net, among other reasons, were in increasing jeopardy as their savings association subsidiaries became increasingly "bank like" during the previous two decades.

The BHC structure and related laws are drafted so as to permit institutions of any charter—state or federal, stock or mutual, bank or savings institution—to organize an FHC or, in the case of savings associations, to form a holding company that is able to engage in all activities permissible for an FHC. National and state banks, as noted in Chapter 7, also have the option of engaging in most FHC activities in a financial subsidiary if they wish to so.

---

69. Massachusetts Bankers Association, Inc. et al. v. Bowler, et al., 392 F Supp 2d 24 (D. Mass., Jan. 19, 2005).

CHAPTER **6**

Four Policies Applicable to All Institutions

Introduction

Banks and savings associations are currently subject to several federal laws that did not apply to them when the laws were originally enacted. This chapter covers four of these laws that were originally enacted to cover national banks, Federal Reserve System (FRS) member banks, or "banks" in general, that Congress has extended, depending on the statute, to state nonmember banks and, in all cases, to federal and state savings associations.

These four statutes are:

- The transactions with affiliate sections of the Federal Reserve Act
- The insider loan provisions of the Federal Reserve Act
- Tying restriction in the Bank Holding Company Amendments of 1970
- The most favored lender provisions of the National Banking Act of 1864

This chapter discusses these statutes and the actions Congress took to extend them to institutions other than those to which they originally applied.

Transactions with Affiliates

Sections 23A and 23B of the Federal Reserve Act (FRA)[1] impose quantitative and qualitative restrictions on transactions between banks and their affiliates. The Federal Reserve Board (Board) has described these sections as follows:

> Sections 23A and 23B of the Federal Reserve Act are important statutory provisions designed to protect against a depository institution suffering losses in transactions with affiliates. They also limit the ability of a depository institution to transfer to its affiliates the subsidy arising from the institution's access to the Federal safety net.[2]

Section 23A, which was enacted in 1933, originally applied to banks that were members of the Federal Reserve System (member banks). It now applies, along with section 23B, which was enacted in 1987, to federally insured nonmember banks and savings associations.[3]

Until 2002, the Board had not adopted regulation implanting these sections' adopted regulations. Until then, institutions seeking interpretive guidance on compliance with these sections relied on Board interpretations and informal staff guidance.

These sections assumed increasing importance with the enactment of the Gramm Leach Bliley Act (Act, or GLBA).[4] The Act not only expanded the scope of activities in which banks and their subsidiaries could engage with affiliates, but also because the Act required the Board to adopt regulations under section 23A relating to derivative transactions and intraday credit extensions.

In response to these developments, the Board adopted final rules implementing these sections,[5] captioned as Regulation W (Reg W),[6] and final rules repealing most of its interpretive rulings,[7] most of which are incorporated into Reg W.

---

1. 12 USC 371c and 371c-1, respectively.
2. Federal Reserve Board, "Transactions Between Member Banks and Their Affiliates," Final rule, 67 FR 76559 (Dec. 12, 2002), p. 76560.
3. Section 8(j) of the Federal Deposit Insurance Act (1828(j)) and section 11(a) of the Home Owner's Loan Act (12 USC 1468(a)), respectively.
4. Pub. Law 106-102 Nov. 12 , 1999, 113 Stat. 1338.
5. Cited in footnote 2.
6. 12 CFR Part 223.
7. "Transactions Between Member Banks and Their Affiliates" [Miscellaneous Interpretations], Final rule. 67 FR 76620 (Dec. 12, 2002).

Chapter 6: Four Policies Applicable to Al

Application of Regulations

The Board points out that even though Reg W ap banks, nonmember banks and savings associations, covered by sections 23A and 23B, also must comply with the rule as if they were member banks.[8] Savings associations are subject to additional restrictions relating to transactions with affiliates, which are discussed below.

Scope of This Discussion

This section discusses the basic provisions of sections 23A and 23B as they apply to transactions with affiliates other than subsidiaries. GLBA amended these sections to cover certain transactions with subsidiaries—primarily financial subsidiaries of banks. These transactions are covered in Chapter 7, which deals with the general subject of subsidiaries of banks and savings associations.

Basic Provisions of Section 23A

Section 23A limits the amount of a member bank's "covered transactions" with a single affiliate to 10% of the bank's capital stock and surplus,[9] and limits such transactions with all affiliates to 20% of this amount.

Affiliates

Section 23A defines "affiliates" of member banks to include the following:

- a company that controls the bank (parent company);
- companies that are under common control by the bank's parent company or certain other entities;
- a company a majority of whose directors or general partners comprise a majority of the persons holding similar positions at the bank or the bank's parent company;

---

8. Transactions Between Member Banks, *op. cit.,* p. 76561.
9. Capital stock and surplus is a bank's tier 1 and tier 2 regulatory capital plus the allowance for loan and lease losses (ALLL) not used in tier 2 plus any investment in a financial subsidiary that is counted as a covered transaction and is required to be deducted from regulatory capital.

- a company, including a real estate investment trust, that is sponsored and advised by the bank on a contractual basis;
- an investment company as defined in section 2(a)(20) of the Investment Company Act of 1940[10] for which the bank or any of its affiliates serves as investment adviser or other investment company in which the bank and its affiliates control more than 5% of the voting securities or equity capital of the fund;
- a depository institution that is a subsidiary of the bank;
- a partnership in which the bank or affiliate, or any officer, director, or employee thereof, serves as a general partner;
- any subsidiary of the companies described above; and
- any company including a subsidiary of a member bank that the Fed determines to be an affiliate by regulation or order.

Subsidiaries

A company that is a subsidiary of a member bank is not an "affiliate" unless it is:

- a depository institution;
- directly controlled by one or more affiliates of the bank (other than a depository institution affiliate) or by a shareholder or group of shareholders that control the member bank;
- an employee stock option plan organized for the benefit of employees, shareholders, and others related to the bank; or
- a financial subsidiary (these subsidiaries are discussed in Chapter 7).

Other entities excluded from the definition of "affiliate" include certain companies acquired from the exercise of rights arising out of a bona fide debt previously contracted and companies engaged solely in:

- holding the premises of the member bank;
- the safe deposit box business; and
- holding U.S. and certain U.S.-guaranteed securities.

---

10. 15 USC 80a-(2)(a)(20).

Covered Transactions

Transactions subject to the 10% and 20% quantitative limits under section 23A include:

- extensions of credit to, or purchases of assets from, an affiliate, including loans to a third party that benefit an affiliate (see discussion of attribution rules below);
- purchase of, or investment in, a security of an affiliate;
- the acceptance of a security issued by an affiliate as collateral for an extension of credit to any person or company;
- the issuance of a guarantee, acceptance, or letter of credit on behalf of an affiliate, and the confirmation of a letter of credit issued by the affiliate; and
- cross-affiliate netting arrangements.[11]

Control

A company or shareholder controls another company if that company or shareholder, directly or indirectly, or acting through one or more other persons:

- owns, controls, or has power to vote 25% or more of any class of voting securities of the other company;
- controls in any manner the election of a majority of the directors of the other company; or
- is found by the Fed, after notice and opportunity for hearing, to exercise a controlling influence over the management or policies of the other company.

Attribution Rule

Under section 23A, a loan made to a third party for the benefit of an affiliate is regarded as a loan to the affiliate for purposes of section 23A. A loan by the bank to a third party used to purchase an item from an

---

11. A cross-affiliate netting arrangement is an arrangement between a member bank, one or more affiliates, and one or more nonaffiliates of the member bank, in which a nonaffiliate can deduct any obligation of the affiliate to the member bank when settling the nonaffiliate's own obligation to the member bank, and when a member bank is permitted or required to add any amount owed by the affiliate to the nonaffiliate when settling the member bank's obligations to the nonaffiliate.

affiliate of the bank, or from a company, such as an automobile dealership, that is controlled by persons who also control the bank is deemed to be a loan to the affiliate.

There are several exceptions to the attribution rule including a provision that general purpose credit cards, such as Visa and MasterCard, issued by a member bank will be exempt from these attribution rules if less than 25% of the purchases with the card are from an affiliate of the bank. The preamble to the final rules points out that most banks issuing special purpose cards comply with section 23A by selling receivables to an affiliate at the end of each day.[12]

Qualitative Restrictions on Covered Transactions

Asset Quality

A member bank may not purchase a "low quality asset" from an affiliate unless, pursuant to an independent credit evaluation, the bank contracted to buy the asset before it was acquired by the affiliate. Low-quality assets include those that have been classified as "substandard" or lower in the affiliate's most recent examination, assets on which principal and interest payments are more than 30 days past due, and those that are on a nonaccrual basis.

Collateral Requirements

A member bank's extension of credit to, or guarantees issued on behalf of, an affiliate must be secured by a statutorily mandated amount of collateral. Collateral requirements range from 100% of the loan if the collateral consists of U.S. government obligations or securities of equivalent safety to 130% if the collateral is stock, leases, or other real or personal property.

Safety and Soundness

The bank must conduct all covered transactions, including transactions that are exempt from other requirements of section 23A, on a safe and sound basis.

---

12. Transactions Between Member Banks, *op. cit.*, discussion of general purpose credit cards, pp. 76577–79578.

Exemptions from the Provisions of Section 23A

Covered Transactions Exempt from the Quantitative Limits and the Collateral Requirements (Section 223.41)

The exemptions in this section and the following section closely track statutory exemptions in section 23A(d)(6) from the quantitative limits and certain other restrictions of section 23A. All of the transactions in these two sections, however, are subject to the requirements that all transactions with affiliates be conducted on a safe and sound basis. The transactions in this section are also subject to the prohibition on transactions involving low-quality assets, discussed above. These exempt transactions are:

- transactions with another depository institution if the member bank controls 80% or more of the voting securities of the institution or with an institution that controls 80% or more of the member bank;
- transactions between a member bank and a depository institution if the same company has 80% or more control of both institutions (the "sister bank" exemption);
- purchases of a loan by a member bank from an affiliate on a nonrecourse basis; and
- purchase of assets from an affiliate and other transactions in connection with certain internal corporate reorganizations.

Covered Transactions Exempt from the Quantitative Limits, the Collateral Requirements, and the Low-quality Assets Prohibition (Section 223.42)

These transactions include the following:

- *Marketable Securities.* Purchases from an affiliate of securities or other assets at or below their market value are exempt if the securities are listed on an exchange or whose market value is otherwise "readily identifiable and publicly available."
- *Securities with a "Ready Market."* Securities purchased from an affiliate that is a registered broker-dealer are exempt if the

securities conform to the SEC criteria for having a "ready market"[13] and the securities:
- are not issued by an affiliate;
- are not purchased within 30 days of an underwriting by an affiliate (except for certain U.S. and U.S.-guaranteed obligations);
- are eligible for purchase by state member banks;
- are not low quality; and
- meet other requirements including having its prices quoted on an unaffiliated electronic service that provides data from real-time financial networks.
- *Other Exemptions.* Other activities that are exempt from the above provisions of section 23A include:
  - making deposits in correspondent banks;
  - making a loan to, or issuing a guarantee on behalf of, an affiliate that is fully secured by U.S. obligations or a segregated, earmarked deposit account at the member bank;
  - purchasing an extension of credit from an affiliate on a non-recourse basis subject to certain limits including the following: the bank must make an independent evaluation of the borrower's creditworthiness before the loan is made, and may not purchase each year more than 50% of the loans originated by the affiliate;
  - repurchase agreements with an affiliate;
  - purchasing a security from a securities affiliate of the member bank if the member bank or the securities affiliate is acting exclusively as a riskless principal, and the security purchased is not issued, underwritten, or sold as principal (other than as riskless principal) by any affiliate of the member bank[14];
  - purchasing from an affiliate a loan originated by the member bank and sold to the affiliate subject to a repurchase agreement or with recourse; and

---

13. SEC Rule 240.153c3-1(c)(11)(i) defines a "ready market" as a "recognized securities market in which there exits independent bona fide offers to buy and sell so that a price reasonable related to the last sales price or current bona fide competitive bid and offer quotations can be determined for a particular security almost instantaneously and where payment will be received in settlement of a sale at such price."

14. For a definition of a "riskless principal" transaction, see footnote 64, Chapter 10.

- extensions of intraday credit to an affiliate if the member bank maintains policies and procedures reasonably designed to manage the credit exposure of these transactions, the transactions comply with the "arm's length" requirements of section 23B, and the bank ceases to treat the transaction as an extension of intraday credit at the end of the bank's business day in the U.S.

Basic Provisions of Section 23B

Definitions

For purposes of section 23B, the terms "subsidiary" and "affiliate" have the same meaning as in section 23A except the term "affiliate" does not include an insured depository institution.

"Market Terms" Requirement

Section 23B requires that certain transactions between a member bank and its affiliates be on "market terms," that is, on terms including credit standards that are prevailing at the time for comparable transactions, or in the absence of comparable transactions, on terms that in good faith would be offered to nonaffiliated companies.

Transactions Covered by Market Terms Requirement

The market terms requirement applies to two kinds of transactions listed below.

1. The following transactions are *not* "covered transactions" under section 23A:
   - sales of securities or other assets to an affiliate, including assets subject to an agreement to repurchase;
   - payments of money or furnishing services to an affiliate;
   - transactions in which an affiliate acts as an agent or broker or receives a fee for its services to the bank or to any other person; and
   - transactions with a third party if an affiliate has a financial interest in the third party or is a participant in the transaction.
2. All transactions that *are* "covered transactions" under section 23A, with certain exceptions, include the following:
   - making deposits in correspondent banks;

- making a loan to, or issuing a guarantee on behalf of, an affiliate that is fully secured by U.S. obligations or a segregated, earmarked deposit account at the member bank;
- purchasing "marketable securities" from an affiliate and purchasing loans from an affiliate subject to a repurchase agreement;
- transactions between banks in which one has 80% control of the other;
- transactions between sister banks; and
- purchasing loans on a nonrecourse basis from an affiliated depository institution.

Prohibited Asset Purchases

A member bank or its subsidiary may not purchase as fiduciary any securities (as defined in section 3(a)(10) of the Securities Exchange Act of 1934[15]) from an affiliate unless the purchase is permitted:

- under the instrument creating the fiduciary relationship,
- by court order, or
- by the law of the jurisdiction governing the fiduciary relationship.

Member banks either acting as principal or fiduciary, are also prohibited from purchasing or otherwise acquiring any security during the existence of any underwriting or selling syndicate, if a principal underwriter of that security is an affiliate of such bank, unless:

- the purchase was approved, before the securities were initially offered for sale to the public, by a majority of the directors of the bank; and
- the approval was based on a determination that the purchase is a sound investment for the bank irrespective of the fact that an affiliate of the bank is the principal underwriter.

Advertising Restrictions

A member bank or any subsidiary or affiliate of a member bank may not publish any advertisement or enter into any agreement stating or suggesting that the bank shall in any way be responsible for the obligations of its affiliates. This provision, however, does not prohibit a member bank from issuing a guarantee, acceptance, or letter of credit on

---

15. 15 USC 78c(a)(10).

behalf of an affiliate, confirming a letter of credit, or entering into a cross-affiliate netting arrangement, to the extent the transaction satisfies the quantitative limits and collateral requirements of section 23A.

Further Regulations

The Fed may prescribe regulations to administer and carry out the purposes of section 23B, including regulations to:

- exempt transactions or relationships from the requirements of section 23B; and
- exclude any subsidiary of a bank holding company from the definition of affiliate for purposes of the section, if such exemptions or exclusions are found to be in the public interest and consistent with the purposes of section 23B.

Application of Sections 23A and 23B to Savings Associations

As noted above, section 11(a) of HOLA applies sections 23A and 23B to transactions of savings associations with their affiliates as if the associations were member banks. In adopting this provision in 1989, Congress imposed additional limits on these transactions. In addition, the OTS has adopted interpretations of some provisions of section 11 that vary the application of these sections to savings associations.

Statutory Variations

Two of the restrictions in section 11 provide that savings associations:

- may only make loans to affiliates that are engaged in activities that are permitted for bank holding companies under section 4(c) of the Bank Holding Company Act[16] (BHC-permissible activities); and
- may not purchase or invest in any security of an affiliate that is not a subsidiary of the association.

These restrictions were adopted in part because at that time, there were virtually no limits on the kinds of companies with which savings associations could affiliate. They were consistent with other

---

16. 12 USC 1843(c). These include the traditional "section 4(c)(8) activities," referred to in Chapter 5.

restrictions placed on savings associations by the 1989 banking legislation, which embodied congressional concerns with the ongoing S&L crisis.[17]

Regulatory Implementation

Final regulations implementing section 11(a) were published by OTS on Oct. 7, 2003 (68 FR 57790). These rules clarify several technical and substantive reasons why there is not a perfect fit between the OTS rules and Reg W and provide several interpretations of section 11 as it applies to transactions of savings associations.

Attribution Rules

- *Third Party Attribution Rule.* Based on its interpretation of section 11, OTS has taken the position that the attribution rule in section 23A does not apply to loans to third parties for the benefit of affiliates engaged in non-BHC permissible activities. The agency says section 11 does not specify a similar third party attribution requirement for the loan prohibition and that it has declined to infer such a requirement. The OTS, however, will act to prevent loans that are an attempt to circumvent the loan prohibition by one or more sham transactions and will require the loan to be divested or will otherwise terminate the transaction.
- *Attribution of Activities among Affiliates.* The final rules provide that activities of a subsidiary of an affiliate will not be attributed to the affiliate. This means that loans by an association to an affiliate engaged in BHC permissible activities will not be prohibited because the activities of a subsidiary of the affiliate is engaged in non-permissible activities. As in the above case, OTS will penalize sham transactions.
- *Attribution of Transactions.* OTS rules do not require an association, when measuring its total amount of covered transactions with a particular affiliate, to include all such transactions with subsidiaries of that affiliate. Transactions with these subsidiaries are counted under the 10% limit on transactions with a single affiliate, and will count as well toward the 20% ceiling on transactions with all affiliates.

---

17. The "Financial Institutions Reform, Recovery and Enforcement Act of 1989" (FIRREA), Pub. Law 101-73, Aug. 9, 1989, 103 Stat. 183.

Other Interpretations

Among the other interpretations and clarifications made by OTS in its final implementing regulations are the following:

- *Reverse Repurchase Agreements.* Based on a legal analysis of these transactions, OTS concluded that these transactions are not loans for purposes of section 11 and therefore are not prohibited loans to affiliates engaged in non-BHC permissible activities.
- *"Savings Association."* This term includes federal and state savings associations, federal savings banks, and state-chartered savings banks that have elected to be treated as savings associations for holding company purposes under section 10(l) of HOLA.
- *Primary Federal Regulator.* The OTS clarifies that in its rules, references to the Board in Reg W as the "appropriate federal bank regulator" should be read as referring to the OTS with a few exceptions, including provisions in Reg W that authorize the Fed to adopt exemptions from sections 23A and 23B by regulation or order. This provision ensures that the OTS, rather than the Board, has the power to administer and enforce regulations on affiliate transactions by savings associations other than exemption determinations.

Subsidiaries as Affiliates

Under Reg W, bank subsidiaries, with certain exceptions, including financial subsidiaries of banks, are not affiliates. (GLBA did not authorize financial subsidiaries for savings associations.) The OTS final rule generally follows the provisions of Reg W on this point, providing that a savings association subsidiary—either an operating subsidiary or a service corporation—is not an affiliate unless it is:

- a depository institution;
- an employee stock option plan (ESOP) or similar organization;
- directly controlled by another affiliate (other than a depository institution affiliate) of the association, by shareholders that control the association, or is controlled by a group of shareholders that control the association; or
- any other subsidiary designated by the OTS as an affiliate for supervisory or safety and soundness purposes.

Subsidiaries That Are Not Affiliates. Operating subsidiaries and service corporations that are not affiliates of a savings association are treated as part of the association and their transactions with its affiliates are aggregated with those of the association.

OTS has made additional technical interpretations not covered here.[18] Otherwise, the principal provisions of Reg W apply as intended to savings associations as if they were member banks.

Exportation and Other Interest Rate Issues

Exportation of interest rates is the use by a bank of the favorable interest laws of its home state in certain transactions with out of state borrowers. This practice, which arises from national most favored lending (MFL) laws applicable to banks and savings associations, is essential to today's credit card industry. Under these MFL laws, institutions can take advantage of favorable home state usury rates and in transactions with customers in other states. They can also export home state rules on charges, such as late fees, that qualify as interest under state law.

The original MFL provision for national banks was enacted as section 30 of the National Banking Act of 1864[19] (1864 Act), and it is now found in section 85 of the National Bank Act (NBA).[20] In 1978, the U.S. Supreme Court in *Marquette Nat. Bank v. First of Omaha Corp.*, 439 U.S. 299 (1978), held that exportation of favorable home state usury rates by a national bank in Nebraska to customers in Minnesota was permissible under section 85 and did not violate the usury laws of Minnesota. In 1996, the Court, in *Smiley v. Citibank (South Dakota), N.A.* 517 U.S. 735 (1996), held that section 85 permitted national banks to export late fees on credit card balances.[21]

---

18. See 12CFR § 563.41.
19. June 3, 1984, ch. 106, 13 Stat. 100, section 30.
20. 12 USC 85.
21. Exportation of late fees by state banks had been upheld in 1992 in the First Circuit in Greenwood Trust Co. v. Massachusetts, 971 F. 2d 818, 829–831 (1st Cir. 1992), *cert. denied,* 506 U.S. 1052 (1993).

The *Marquette* opinion is based on an extensive discussion of the legislative history of the 1864 Act as it related to exportation. In a statement that might be the theme for the developments discussed in this section, the court said:

> Petitioners' final argument is that the "exportation" of interest rates, such as occurred in this case, will significantly impair the ability of States to enact effective usury laws. This impairment, however, *has always been implicit in the structure of the National Bank Act,* [emphasis added] since citizens of one State were free to visit a neighboring State to receive credit at foreign interest rates. . . . This impairment may in fact be accentuated by the ease with which interstate credit is available by mail through the use of modern credit cards.[22]

Within two years after *Marquette*, Congress amended the federal banking laws to extend the benefits of section 85 to state banks and savings associations.

Most Favored Lender Laws

National Banks

Section 30 was enacted in part to prevent states from discriminating against national banks by subjecting them to lower rates that state banks could charge. This section provides in part that national banks

> may take, receive, reserve, and charge on any loan or discount made, or upon any note, bill of exchange, or other evidences of debt, interest at the rate allowed by the laws of the State or Territory where the bank is located, and no more; *except that where, by the laws of any State, a different rate is limited for banks of issue, organized under State laws, the rate so limited shall be allowed for associations organized in any such State under the act.* And when no rate is fixed by the laws of the State or Territory, the bank may take, receive, reserve or charge a rate not exceeding 7 per centum . . . (emphasis added)

Section 30 was given its current interpretation as an MFL statute in *Tiffany v. National Bank of Missouri*, 85 U.S. 409 (1873), in which a national bank in Missouri had charged 9% on a loan when the rate allowed by "the laws of the state" was 10% and state banks were limited to 8%. The plaintiff claimed that section 30 limited the national

---

22. *Marquette*, 439 U.S. 299, 318.

bank to the state bank rate of 8%. The court rejected these interpretations saying that national banks

> were established for the purpose, in part, of providing a currency for the whole country, and in part to create a market for the loans of the General government. It could not have been intended, therefore, to expose them to the hazard of unfriendly legislation by the States, or to ruinous competition with State banks.
>
> * * * *
>
> The only mode of guarding against such contingencies was that which, we think, Congress adopted [in section 30]. It was to allow to National [banks] the rate allowed by the State to natural to state banks and savings associations, persons generally, and a higher rate, if State banks . . . were authorized to charge a higher rate.[23]

Section 85 of the NBA, which, as noted, is the current version of section 30, is similar to the original version and permits a national bank to charge interest on any loan at the rate that is the greater of the rate allowed by the state in which the bank is located or 1% above the discount rate on 90-day commercial paper in effect in the bank's Federal Reserve District. If a state has a different rate for banks chartered in that state, national banks "organized or existing in that state" may charge that rate.

Section 85 also provides that if "no rate is fixed by the laws of the State, Territory or District [where the bank is located]," the bank may charge the greater of 7% or 1% above the discount rate on 90-day commercial paper in effect in the bank's Federal Reserve District.

It is this section of the NBA that the Supreme Court interpreted in its 1978 *Marquette* decision as permitting national banks to export interest rates. At that time, there were no federal statutes applicable to other insured institutions relating to MFL and interest rate exportation. As noted below, these companion statutes were enacted two years later.

State Banks and Savings Associations

In a 1998 legal opinion, the FDIC observed that as interest rates rose in the late 1970s, "Congress recognized that section 85 of the NBA [as evidenced by Marquette] provided national banks with a distinct competitive advantage over state-chartered lending institutions

---

23. *Tiffany*, 85 U.S. 409, 413.

whose interest rates were constrained by state laws."[24] As a result, Congress, in 1980, added section 27 to the Federal Deposit Insurance Act (FDIA) and section 4(g) to the Home Owners' Loan Act (HOLA), which are discussed below. These measures were intended to give state banks and savings associations the same MFL benefits as section 85 gave national banks. "Section 27 was intended to give state-chartered banks the benefit of section 85 and purposely engrafted, at several points, language from the NBA."[25]

These comments are also applicable to section 4(g) of HOLA, since that section was adopted concurrently with section 27, as noted below.

Section 27 of the FDIA. This section applies to state commercial and savings banks, industrial loan companies, and other institutions whose primary federal regulator is the FDIC.[26] Section 27(a) provides in relevant part:

> In order to prevent discrimination against State-chartered depository institutions, including insured savings banks . . . with respect to interest rates, if the applicable rate prescribed in this subsection exceeds the rate such State bank . . . would be permitted to charge in the absence of this subsection, such State bank . . . may, notwithstanding any State constitution or statute which is hereby preempted for the purpose of this section . . . charge on any loan . . . interest at a rate of not more than [the Federal Reserve discount rate] or at the rate allowed by the laws of the State . . . where the bank is located, whichever may be greater. (emphasis added)

Federal Savings Associations. Section 4(g)(1) of the Home Owners' Loan Act (HOLA),[27] which applies to state and federal savings associations and federal savings banks, provides as follows:

> Notwithstanding any State law, a savings association may charge interest on any extension of credit at a rate of [the Federal reserve discount rate], or at the rate allowed by the laws of the state in which such savings association is located, whichever is greater.

---

24. FDIC, General Council's Opinion No. 10, *Interest Rate Charges Under Section 27 of the Federal Deposit Insurance Act,* 63 FR 19258 (April 17, 1998), p. 19258.

25. *Id.,* citing *Greenwood Trust* (see footnote 3), among other cases, p. 15258.

26. 12 U.S.C. 1831d(a) added by section 512 of the Depository Institutions Deregulation and Monetary Control Act (DIDMCA), Pub. Law 96-221, March 31, 1980, 94 Stat. 132.

27. 12 U.S.C. 1463(g)(1), added by section 513 of (DIDMCA), *op. cit.,* new section 533 of the National Housing Act (12 USC 1730g(a) and reenacted as 4(g) of HOLA by section 301 of FIRREA, Pub. Law 101-73, Aug. 9, 1989, 103 Stat. 183.

OCC. In February 1996, a few months before the Smiley decision was handed down, the OCC published final interpretive rulings on several subjects, including most favored lender issues.[28]

The OCC's definition of interest as used in 12 U.S.C. § 85 is set out at 12 CFR § 7.4001 and includes the following:

> (a) . . . late fees, [fees for returned checks], over limit fees, annual fees, cash advance fees, and membership fees. It does not ordinarily include appraisal fees, . . . fees for document preparation or notarization, or fees incurred to obtain credit reports.

The agency's policy on interest rates on intrastate transactions (which are exportable under *Marquette*), states:

> (b) A national bank located in a state may charge interest at the maximum rate permitted to any state-chartered or licensed lending institution by the law of that state. *If state law permits different interest charges on specified classes of loans, a national bank making such loans is subject only to the provisions of state law relating to that class of loans that are material to the determination of the permitted interest.* For example, a national bank may lawfully charge the highest rate permitted to be charged by a state-licensed small loan company, without being so licensed, but subject to state law limitations on the size of loans made by small loan companies. (emphasis added)

OTS. The OTS published its MFL interpretations in September 1998, which were substantially the same as those of the OCC:

> Given the similarities between section 4(g) of the HOLA and the national bank most favored lender provision, OTS believes that the term "interest" as it appears in section 4(g) and OTS's implementing regulation should be interpreted in a manner consistent with the OCC regulation and the Supreme Court's decision . . . Therefore, rather than perpetuate nonsubstantive differences in syntax that could create confusion, OTS has decided to conform new Sec. 560.110 to the OCC regulation.[29]

The OTS noted that this decision was consistent with congressional policy calling for greater uniformity in banking agency regulations.

FDIC. The FDIC addressed several MFL issues in General Counsels Opinion No. 10, "Interest Charges Under Section 27 of the Federal Deposit Insurance Act," which concluded that "the term 'interest,' for purposes of section 27 [of the FDIA], includes those charges

---

28. 61 FR 4849 (Feb. 9, 1996), Interpretive Rulings, Final rule.
29. 61 FR 50951 (Sept. 30, 1996) *Lending and Investment*, Final rule, at p. 50968.

that a national bank is authorized to charge as interest under section 85 of the National Bank Act . . ."[30]

Exportation of Interest Rates by Interstate Banks

Banks. The above discussions dealt primarily with exportation of interest rates to states by banks that do not have branches outside their home state. As banks began to branch across state lines after the enactment of the Riegle-Neal Interstate Banking and Branching Efficiency Act of 1994 (Riegle-Neal I)[31] and the Riegle-Neal Amendments Act of 1997, Pub. L. 105–24, 111 Stat. 238 (1997) (Riegle-Neal II),[32] questions were raised, according to the FDIC in a 1998 General Counsel's Opinion:

> regarding the appropriate state law for purposes of [exportation of interest rates] that should govern the interest charges on loans made to customers of a State bank that is chartered in one state (the bank's home state) but has a branch or branches in another state (the host state) (an "Interstate State Bank"). These questions have not previously been addressed by the Legal Division.[33]

The conclusions of the FDIC on this and related questions pertaining to the applicable MFL laws for interstate banks are in accord with an earlier interpretation of these issues by the OCC in Interpretive Letter # 822 issued on February 17, 1988.[34] The following discussion is based on these interpretations.

Example: Bank B, located in state A, has branches in states C and D and credit card customers throughout the country. Under the Bank's MFL authority in section 85 of the NBA and section 27 of the FDIA (MFL statutes), it is able to export interest at the rate allowed by the laws of the state where it is "located."

For purposes of the MFL statutes, B is "located" in its home state and in every state in which it has a branch.

A branch in state C may export the interest rates of state C on loans to customers in any other state, including customers in state B

---

30. 63 FR 19258 (April 17, 1998), at p. 15259.
31. Pub. L. 103-328, Sept. 29, 1994, 108 Stat. 2338.
32. Pub. L. 105–24, July 3, 1997, 111 Stat. 238.
33. General Counsel's Opinion No. 11, "Interest Charges By Interstate State Banks," 63 FR 27282 (May 18, 1998), at p. 27282.
34. OCC Interpretive Letter # 822, available at http://www.occ.treas.gov/interp/mar98/intmar98.htm.

bank's home state, if the loan is "made" at that branch. ...usion is based on the legislative history of Riegle-Neal I.[35] ...egislative history also provided guidance on the activities relating to a loan that determines where a loan is made. These activities are classified as "ministerial," or routine activities relating to making a loan, and "non-ministerial" activities, which are those essential to making a loan.[36] These activities are illustrated as follows:

- *Non-ministerial activities* (Essential): the decision to extend credit, the extension of credit itself, and the disbursal of the proceeds of the loan.
- *Ministerial activities* (Routine): include providing loan applications, assembling documents, providing a location for returning documents necessary for making a loan, providing loan account information, and receiving payments.

Savings Associations. The OTS did not participate in the development of the foregoing guidance because Riegle-Neal I and II do not apply to savings associations. Federal associations, however, as noted in Chapter 4, were able to branch interstate several years before Riegle-Neal I was enacted in 1994.

In a March 2002 publication, the OTS notes the fact that associations, under the MFL provisions of section 4(g) of HOLA, have the same powers to export interest rates as other institutions. As to interstate associations, the agency says that "at a minimum," federal associations are regarded as located where they have a branch, and "under certain conditions, may export the most favored lender rate from those states."[37]

Insider Loans

Sections 22(g) and 22(h) of the Federal Reserve Act (FRA)[38] impose restrictions on loans a member bank may make to the bank's direc-

---

35. *Id.*, p. 7, citing a statement by Sen. Roth (R-Del.) during Senate debate on Riegle-Neal I referring to "the widespread congressional understanding that, in the context of nationwide interstate branching, it is the office of the bank branch making the loan that determines which state law applies." (25140 Cong. Rec. S12789 (daily ed., Sept. 13, 1994)).
36. *Id.*, p. 8, citing 25140 Cong. Rec. S12789 (daily ed., Sept. 13, 1994).
37. "Powers of Federal Savings Associations," March 1, 2002.
38. 12 USC 375a and 375b, respectively.

tors, executive officers, and principal stockholders. These restrictions also apply, with certain exceptions, to persons who hold these insider positions in the bank's subsidiaries and affiliates. The Fed's insider loan rules are implemented by Regulation O (Reg O).[39]

As it did with the FRA's provisions on transactions with affiliates, Congress extended the FRA sections on insider loans to state nonmember banks and savings associations.

Since the FDIC and OTS have incorporated Reg O with a few technical modifications into their own regulations, the following summary of Reg O, unless otherwise specified, applies to state nonmember banks and savings associations as well as to member banks. Reg O also applies to credit card banks, industrial loan companies (ILCs), and certain other institutions that are excluded from the definition of "bank" under the Bank Holding Company Act (BHCA)[40] and to the companies that control these institutions.

Principal Provisions of Reg O

Insiders

- *Insiders* are defined as directors, executive officers, and principal shareholders. Reg O imposes limits not only on loans the bank may make to its own insiders but also, with some exceptions, on loans to persons who are insiders of the bank's subsidiaries, parent company, if any, and subsidiaries of the parent company.
- *Directors.* This term is given its normal meaning; Reg O provides that a person's status as a director is not dependent on the person receiving compensation for his or her service. Advisory directors who are unelected or who do not vote are not "directors" for purposes of Reg O.
- *Executive officers.* Executive officer of a company or bank are persons who participate or have authority to participate (other than in the capacity of a director) in major policymaking functions of the company or bank.
- *Principal shareholders.* These are persons other than banks (and any company that controls the bank) that own or control

---

39. 12 CFR Part 215.
40. 12 USC 1811, *et seq.* Credit card banks and ILCs are excluded from this definition by sec. 2(c)(2)(F) and (H), respectively, of the BHCA and are discussed in Chapter 5, and in the section on "Tying Arrangements" in this chapter.

the power to vote 10% or more of any class of voting shares of a bank or company.

Related Interests. Reg O covers loans to insiders and to their "related interests." These are businesses and other companies controlled by the insider and political or campaign committees that are controlled by an insider or that provide funds or services that benefit the insider.

Loan Limits

There are four sets of overlapping loan limits in Reg O:

- loans to all insiders that require prior approval;
- separate rules on loans to executive officers of the bank;
- a ceiling on the aggregate amount of loans a bank may have outstanding to all insiders at any one time; and
- a limit on the maximum amount of loans that may be outstanding to a single borrower.

Loans by Subsidiaries. Subsidiaries of banks are considered part of the bank itself under Reg O. As a result, loans by bank subsidiaries to the bank's insiders are counted as loans made by the bank for purposes of Reg O.

Loan Limits for Certain Insiders. Loans to insiders of the bank and its subsidiaries (except loans to executive officer of the bank) and their related interests, that require prior approval of the bank's board of directors, when combined with all other outstanding loans from the bank to that person, may not exceed either:

- the greater of $25,000 or 5% of the bank's unimpaired capital and unimpaired surplus;[41] or
- $500,000.

Prior board approval is not required if the loan is made pursuant to a line of credit approved by the board within 14 months of the loan.

Bank Executive Officer "Carve Out." Separate rules apply to loans to executive officers of the bank. These rules permit the following loans, subject to the bank's normal underwriting standards:

---

41. A member bank's unimpaired capital and unimpaired surplus equals the bank's Tier 1 and Tier 2 capital plus the balance of the bank's allowance for loan and lease losses not included in its Tier 2 capital for regulatory reporting purposes.

- Loans "in any amount" to executive officers for financing the purchase, construction, or rehabilitation of their principal residence, for education of their children, and loans secured by certain interests in securities or by a segregated account. The phrase "in any amount" in Reg O means that the loans can be for any amount up to the loans-to-one-borrower (LTOB) limit summarized below, so long as the loan is made on a non-preferential basis and the executive officer meets the bank's underwriting standards for the loan.
- Loans for "other purposes," which may not exceed at any one time the higher of 2.5% of the bank's unimpaired capital and unimpaired surplus or $25,000, but in no event more than $100,000.

Maximum LTOB. Reg O provides that the maximum loan that may be outstanding by a member bank to any one insider and his or her related interests is the loans-to-one-borrower (LTOB) limit that is applied to national banks by section 5200 of the Revised Statutes.[42] This limit is:

- 20% of the bank's unimpaired capital and surplus for loans not fully secured; plus
- an additional 10% of the bank's unimpaired capital and unimpaired surplus in the case of loans that are fully secured by readily marketable collateral

For state member banks chartered in a state that has a LTOB limit lower than that provided in section 5200, the lower rate will prevail. LTOB limits for state nonmember banks are determined by state law.

Exclusion of Directors and Officers. Loans to directors and executive officers of an affiliate are not subject to the above general loan limits if the director or executive officer is excluded by a provision in the bank's bylaws or resolution of its board of directors from participating in (and the director or officer in fact does not participate in) major policymaking functions of the bank. The affiliate must meet certain size requirements and must not control the bank.

---

42. 12 USC 84.

Aggregate Loan Limit

General Rule. Section 22(h) provides that the aggregate amount of loans outstanding to all insiders may not exceed the bank's unimpaired capital and unimpaired surplus.[43]

Exception. Member banks with deposits of less than $100 million that are well managed and well capitalized may have up to twice that amount if authorized by an annual resolution of the bank's board of directors, which must determine, among other things, that the higher limit is consistent with safe and sound banking practices.

Recordkeeping Requirements

Insiders of Member Banks. Reg O requires member banks to adopt recordkeeping methods that:

- identify, through an annual survey, all insiders of the bank; and
- maintain records of all extensions of credit to insiders of the bank itself, including the amount and terms of each such extension of credit.

Insiders of Affiliates. Reg O has also required member banks to identify all directors, officers, and principal shareholders of the bank and its affiliates and their related interests and to specify the amounts and terms of all credit extended to these insiders. By the time the Board considered adoption of amendments to Reg O in 1994, it was obvious that financial institution holding companies had become so large and widely dispersed that literal compliance with these requirements was not practical.

The Fed realized that large banking organizations with "hundreds of affiliates with thousands of officers and directors would have no practical way to know who they are or whether they have a loan with the bank"[44] and adopted an amendment to Reg O permitting banks to use one of the three following methods to make these reports:

- *Survey method.* Identifying each insider of the member bank's affiliates through an annual survey and keeping records of loans made to these insiders;

---

43. See footnote 1, above.
44. Staff memo presented Jan. 24, 1994 during meeting at which the Board adopted final regulations amending Reg O at 56 FR 8837 (Feb. 24, 1994).

Chapter 6: Four Policies Applicable to All Institutions

- *Borrower inquiry method.* Requiring as part of each extension of credit that the borrower indicate whether the borrower is an insider of an affiliate of the member bank, and maintaining records that identify the amount and terms of each extension of credit by the member bank to borrowers so identifying themselves; or
- *Alternative recordkeeping method.* As approved by the banks' principal federal regulator.

Other Reports

- *Reports by Executive Officers.* Executive officers of a member bank who become indebted to any other bank or banks in an amount that exceeds any of the "unlimited" or "other purpose" loan ceilings referenced above for executive officers must report this fact to the board of directors of his or her bank within 10 days after the indebtedness reaches that level.
- *Reports on Credit to Executive Officers.* Each bank is required to include in its quarterly Call Reports, or Thrift Financial Reports in the case of a savings association, all extensions of credit made by the bank to its executive officers since its last Report.
- *Disclosure of Credit from Member Banks to Executive Officers and Principal Shareholders.* Banks that receive a request from the public must disclose details of certain loans to executive officers, principal shareholders, and their related interests.

Extension of Insider Loan Rules to Other Institutions

The sections of the FDIA and HOLA cited below provide essentially, that sections 22(g) and 22(h) of the FRA shall apply to every insured nonmember bank or savings association, as the case may be, as if the bank of the association were a "member bank" as defined in the FRA.

- *FDIA.* These rules are applied to state nonmember banks by section 18(j) of the Federal Deposit Insurance Act (FDIA) (12 USC 1828(j)):
  - Section 22(h) of the FRA, which deals with loans to all insiders, executive officers, was applied to state nonmember banks in 1978 by section 108 of Pub. Law 95-630 (Nov. 10, 1978), 92 Stat. 3664.

Section 22(g), relating to loans to executive officers, was added to section18(j) by section 306(k) of FDICIA, Pub. Law 102-242, Dec. 19, 1991, 105 Stat. 2236.
- HOLA. Insider loan rules are applied to savings associations by section 11(b) of the Home Owner's Loan Act (HOLA) (12 USC 1468(b)).
  - Section 22(h) of the FRA was applied to savings associations by section 301 of FIRREA.
  - A cross reference to section 22(g) was added to section 11(b) of HOLA by section 306(i) of FDICIA.

Tying Arrangements

A typical tying arrangement is one in which a seller conditions the sale of a product or service on the buyer's purchase of another product or service from the seller.

The product offered by the seller is known as the "tying product"; the product the buyer is required to buy is the "tied product." An example would be a bank conditioning the approval of an auto loan or the granting of a lower rate on the loan if the customer opened a checking account at the bank.

These arrangements can result in federal antitrust law violations if the seller has a dominant market position in the tying product and can stifle competition even if falling short of antitrust violations. The anticompetitive potential of tying arrangements led Congress to impose restrictions on tying arrangements by banks by adopting in section 106 of the Bank Holding Company Act Amendments of 1970 (BHCA).[45] Tying restrictions are imposed on savings associations by section 5(q) of the Home Owners' Loan Act (HOLA), which was adopted in 1982.[46]

According to the Board:

> Section 106 was adopted in 1970 when Congress expanded the authority of the Board to approve proposals by bank holding companies to engage in nonbanking activities. Section 106 was based on congressional concern that banks' unique role in the economy, in particular their power to extend credit, would allow them to create a competitive advantage for

---

45. Pub Law 91-607, title I, § 106(b), Dec. 31, 1970, 84 Stat. 1766, (12 USC 1972). The Board's tying rules are published at 12 CFR 225.7.

46. 12 USC Sec. 1464(q), added by section 331 of the Garn-St Germain Depository Institutions Act of 1982, Pub Law 97-320, Oct. 15, 1982.

their affiliates in the new, nonbanking markets that they were being allowed to enter. Congress therefore imposed special limitations on tying by banks—restrictions beyond those imposed by the antitrust laws.[47]

Section 106

Section 106 provides in part that a bank may not extend, or vary the price of, credit, leases, property, or services, on the condition that the customer obtain some additional credit, property, or service from

- the bank, other than "traditional bank products," that is, a loan, discount, deposit, or trust service; or
- the bank's holding company or any other subsidiary of that holding company.

A bank is also prohibited from conditioning the availability of these products and services on the condition that the customer

- provide some additional credit, property, or service:
- to such bank, "other than those related to and usually provided in connection with a traditional product"; or
- to any other subsidiary of such bank holding company; or
- agree not to obtain some other credit, property, or service from a competitor of the bank, from the competitor's holding company, or from or any subsidiary of such bank holding company, "other than a condition or requirement that such bank shall reasonably impose in a credit transaction to assure the soundness of the credit."

Exemptive Authority

Section 106 authorizes the Board by regulation or order to permit such exceptions to these prohibitions that it finds are not contrary to the purposes of the Bank Holding Company Act.

The Board has used this exemptive authority several times since 1970, including the adoption of regulations in 1997[48] that made the following changes in the application of section 106:

- extending the traditional bank product exception that applies to tied products and services within the bank, to tied products

---

47. Federal Reserve, Amendments to Regulation Y, Final Rule, 62 FR 9289 (February 28, 1997), at 9312, (citing S. Rep. No. 1084, 91st Cong., 2d Sess. (1970)) (1997 Reg Y amendments).

48. *Id.*

and services of the bank's holding company, and to the holding company's other subsidiaries;
- extending the traditional bank product exception to include combined-balance discounts, which was later adopted as an amendment to Reg Y, and which are discussed below; and
- permitting banks to require a customer to provide the same additional credit, property, or service that are "related to and usually provided in connection with a traditional banking product" to an affiliate of the bank that the bank could require to be provided as part of a tying arrangement within the bank.

Application to "Excluded Entities"

Section 106 itself does not apply to credit card banks (CCBs), industrial loan companies (ILCs), and other entities that are excluded from the definition of "bank" in section 2(c)(2) of the BHCA (excluded entities). These entities are discussed in greater detail in Chapter 5.

When Congress excluded these entities from the activities limits (and certain other provisions) of the BHCA in 1987,[49] it made certain that they remained subject to the tying restrictions of section 106. This purpose was accomplished by CEBA's adoption of section 4(h)(1) of the BHCA,[50] which provides that:

- excluded entities are treated as "banks" for the purposes of section 106; and
- a company that controls an excluded entity is treated as a "bank holding company" for purposes of that section.

Reverse Tying

Section 4(h)(2) also imposes "reverse tying" restrictions on excluded entities by providing that for purposes of section 106:

- companies that control an excluded entity and any of that company's affiliates are treated as a "bank"; and
- the excluded entity is treated as if it were "a subsidiary of a bank holding company."[51]

---

49. Section 101(a) of the "Competitive Equality Banking Act of 1987" (CEBA), Pub. Law 100-86 (Aug. 10, 1987), 101 Stat. 552.

50. 12 USC 1843(h)(1), enacted by section 101(b) of CEBA, *op. cit.*

51. Similar regulatory reverse tying restrictions were applied to companies excluded from the definition of "bank holding company" in section 4(f) of the BHCA by virtue of their control of certain "nonbank banks" on the date of enactment of CEBA. These restrictions were repealed by the Board in 1997.

Chapter 6: Four Policies Applicable to All Institutions 187

The reverse tying provisions in section 4(h) reflected regulatory reverse tying restrictions that had been imposed on banks by the Board in 1971[52] as the result of concerns that tying arrangements initiated by bank affiliates might be just as anticompetitive as tying arrangements initiated by banks themselves. These regulations had been adopted at that time, according to the Board:

> [These reverse tying provisions were] adopted at the same time that the Board approved by regulation the first laundry list of nonbanking activities under section 4(c)(8) of the [BHCA], apparently as a prophylactic measure addressed at potential anti-competitive practices by companies engaging in nonbanking activities.[53]

The "Traditional Bank Product" Exception

At the time CEBA was enacted, neither the Board's 1971 reverse tying regulations, nor the reverse tying provisions of section 4(h) provided for the "traditional bank product" exception for tied products. This "omission" reflected that fact that, as noted above, Section 106 at that time provided this exception only for intra-bank transactions and not to tying arrangements by banks with their affiliates.

The 1997 Regulatory Amendments

In 1997, the Board adopted extensive amendments to the regulations implementing section 106.[54] Among these changes were the following:

- The 1971 regulatory reverse tying restrictions applicable to banks covered under the BHCA were repealed.
- The traditional bank product exception was extended to transactions by a bank in which a bank tied one of its products or services to a tie product of an affiliate (as noted above).
- Any exemptions afforded to banks generally would also be available to credit card banks, ILCs, and other excluded entities.

With respect to its repeal of the 1971 regulatory reverse tying regulations, the Board said

> [Since 1971], the Board has gained extensive experience with bank holding companies, their nonbank affiliates, and the markets in which they operate. Based on this experience, the Board has concluded that these nonbank companies do not possess the market power over credit or other

---

52. 36 FR 10777 (June 3, 1971).
53. 1997 Reg Y amendments, *op. cit.*, at 9312.
54. *Ibid.*

unique competitive advantages that Congress assumed that banks enjoyed in 1970. Accordingly, the Board has decided that applying the special bank anti-tying rules to such companies is no longer justified.[55]

The Federal Reserve pointed out that it used its exemptive authority to adopt several exceptions to the anti-trying restrictions on nonbanking affiliates and that any competitive problems that might arise in the future from these exceptions would be best addressed through the general antitrust laws.

Combined-Balance Discounts

In 1995, the Federal Reserve amended Reg Y to permit banking organizations to offer customers a discount on the cost of certain products if they maintained a minimum balance in one or more "eligible products" specified by the bank, including non-traditional products such as securities brokerage and insurance products.[56]

The agency said it adopted this "combined-balance discount" safe harbor because it would, among other things, "permit banks to market products more efficiently and compete more effectively with their nonbanking competitors who currently offer combined-balance discount arrangements [and] would permit banks to package these products and therefore attract and retain more customers."[57]

The combined-balance discount program must meet the following requirements:

- the bank involved in the program must offer deposits;
- all such deposits must be eligible products; and
- deposit balances must receive equal or greater weight than nondeposit product balances in calculating the required minimum balance.

The agency points out that "a bank could count toward the minimum balance 100% of demand deposits, 80% of certificates of deposit, 70% of mutual fund shares, and 60% of stock held in a brokerage account. So long as the percentages assigned to all deposits are higher than [or equal to] the percentages assigned to the non-deposits, the safe harbor would apply."[58]

---

55. 1997 Reg Y amendments, *op. cit.*, at 9312.
56. "Revisions Regarding Tying Restrictions (Combined-balance discounts)," Final rule 60 FR 20186 (April 25, 1995).
57. *Id.*, p. 20187.
58. *Id.*, p. 20188.

The purpose of these provisions is to prevent banks from using product weighting to require the purchase of certain higher-cost non-traditional products in order to qualify for the discount.

Eligible Products

The variety of eligible products that may be included in combined-balance discount programs is exemplified in a 2001 inquiry by Citibank (South Dakota), N.A. and its banking affiliates (collectively, "bank") describing a combined-balance discount program that the bank wished to offer its customers.[59]

The program would offer incentives to the bank's credit card, mortgage, or loan customers who maintained "a combined minimum balance in a package of products and services that included annuities, auto, homeowners, life, and/or long-term care insurance from insurance affiliates of Citibank. The incentives would include lower interest rates and/or other items, such as airline frequent flyer miles or contributions to accounts maintained by a customer with other Citibank affiliates."

On the question of product weighting, the bank had "indicated that in [its] combined-balance discount program, deposits, credit card balances, and insurance premiums would count equally, dollar for dollar, towards the minimum balance."

The bank requested confirmation that insurance products may be included among the eligible products in the program and if so, "asked for confirmation that the principal amount of annuity products may be counted towards the minimum balance, and that insurance premiums may be counted towards the minimum balance for non-annuity insurance products." The agency agreed that Citi's combined balances may include these items.

Savings Associations

Restrictions on tying arrangements by savings associations and their affiliates are substantially the same for savings associations as they are for banks. These restrictions, however, are imposed by different combinations of statutes and regulations than those impose on banks.

---

59. Board: Legal Interpretations—Clarification of anti-tying exemption in Regulation Y—May 16. All quotes in this discussion are from the Board document.

Direct Tying

The tying restrictions on savings associations, which are found in section 5(q) of the Home Owners' Loan Act (HOLA)[60] are basically the same as those in section 106 of the BHCA for transactions in which the tied product or service is a traditional bank product of the association. The traditional bank product exception for transactions in which the tied product or service is that of an affiliate—in this case, "any service corporation or affiliate[61] of such association"—is built into the statute.[62]

In addition, an association may condition providing a product or service on the customer's providing the association *as well as an affiliate* with additional credit, property, or service that are "related to or usually provided in connection with similar loans, discounts, deposits, or trust service."

Finally, savings associations are subject to exclusive dealing restrictions that are substantially the same as those for banks. An association may not provide a product or service on the condition that:

> the customer shall not obtain some other credit, property, or service from a competitor of such association, or from a competitor of any service corporation or affiliate of such association, other than a condition or requirement that such association shall reasonably impose in connection with credit transactions to assure the soundness of credit.[63]

OTS Exemptive Authority

In addition, the OTS was granted authority in 1996 to exempt transactions from the restrictions of section 5(q) in a new paragraph (6) as follows:

> (6) Exceptions.—The Director [of OTS] may, by regulation or order, permit such exceptions to the prohibitions of section 5(q) as the Director considers will not be contrary to the purposes of this subsection and which conform to exceptions granted by the Board of Governors of the Federal Reserve System pursuant to section [106].[64]

---

60. 12 USC 1464(q).
61. An "affiliate" of a savings association is defined in the OTS holding company regulations as "any person or company [that] controls, is controlled by, or under common control with, such savings association." (12 CFR §583.2).
62. Section 5(q)(1)(A).
63. Section 5(q)(1)(C).
64. Added by Section 2216(b) of the "Economic Growth and Regulatory Paperwork Reduction Act" (EGRPRA) Pub. L. 104-208, div. A, title II, Sept. 30, 1999, 110 Stat. 3009-394.

The OTS used this exemptive authority in 1996 to adopt regulations to permit savings associations to offer combined balance discounts to customers as a tied product on the same terms as banks.[65]

Reverse Tying

Unlike banks subject to section 106, savings association holding companies and their nonbank subsidiaries are subject to *statutory* reverse tying restrictions at section 10(n) of HOLA,[66] which provides as follows:

> TYING RESTRICTIONS.—A savings and loan holding company and any of its affiliates shall be subject to section 5(q) and regulations prescribed under such section, in connection with transactions involving the products or services of such company or affiliate and those of an affiliated savings association *as if such company or affiliate were a savings association.* (emphasis added).

The effect of section 10(n) is mitigated by the fact that savings associations, as noted above, may tie a product or service to a traditional bank product of an affiliate. Their affiliates therefore, being treated as if they were associations, can tie their products and services to traditional banking services at other affiliates, including the savings association subsidiary of the holding company. An association affiliate, for example, may tie brokerage service, a mortgage loan, or any other lawful product or service to the maintenance of a checking account or combined-balance discount accounts at the association.

Conclusion

Of the laws discussed in this chapter, only one, that relating to tying arrangements, applied to state nonmember banks when originally enacted and none applied to savings associations.

With two exceptions,[67] these laws were extended to state nonmember banks and savings associations between 1978 and 1991—

---

65. Amendments Implementing EGRPRA, interim Final rule, 61 FR 60179 (November 27, 1996), adding new §563.36 to the OTS regulations.
66. 12 USC Section 1467a(n), (section 1467a is the codification of the S&L Holding Company Act).
67. The Bank Holding Company Amendments of 1970, *op. cit.*, for tying arrangements and Pub. Law 89-485 (July 1, 1966) 80 Stat. 242, for section 23A.

the period during which the savings association, or "S&L," and banking crises discussed in Chapter 2 occurred.

This period also saw the amendment of the Federal Reserve Act to require these institutions, for the first time, to hold monetary reserves under section 19 of the Act.[68] These reserve requirements, which are implemented by the Board's Regulation D,[69] are one of the principal instruments used by the Board to execute monetary policy.

As noted in Chapter 5, the activities of unitary S&L holding companies were restricted in 1999 to those permissible for financial holding companies primarily because the activities of savings associations had become more "bank like." These associations had already become more "bank like" on the regulatory side as the rules discussed in this chapter were extended to them.

---

68. 12 USC 401.
69. 12 CFR Part 204.

CHAPTER 7

Subsidiaries

Introduction

Subsidiaries are entities that are wholly owned or controlled by a depository institution or entities in which an institution holds an interest. Some subsidiaries provide institutions with the opportunity to engage in activities that they cannot engage in directly, such as real estate acquisitions and development for savings associations. Others provide operational flexibility by providing institutions a choice of conducting activities in a subsidiary (sub) or in the bank itself.

As separate corporate entities, subsidiaries can protect the parent bank from legal liability and "can enhance the safety and soundness of conducting new activities by distinguishing the subsidiary's activities from those of the parent bank (as a legal matter) and allowing more focused management and monitoring of its operations."[1]

The FDIC says,

> "such separation insulates banks and the deposit insurance fund from undue risk and potential liability stemming from litigation. To protect against 'piercing the corporate veil' between the subsidiary and parent, thus mitigating litigation risks, the FDIC [for example] usually has required that the bank conduct real estate investment activities in a majority-owned subsidiary which is adequately capitalized; is physically separate and distinct in its operations from the operations of the bank; maintains separate accounting and other corporate records; observes corporate formalities such as holding separate board of directors' meetings. . . .[2]"

---

1. OCC Final rules "Policies and Procedures for Corporate Activities," 61 FR 60341, 60354 (Nov. 11, 1996).
2. FDIC proposed rules "Activities and Investments of Insured State Banks," 61 FR 43486, 43491 (Aug. 23, 1996).

There are several types of subsidiaries, which will be discussed below. In the pages that follow, we will look at the principal types of subsidiaries of financial institutions.

Principal Kinds of Financial Institution Subsidiaries

Operating Subsidiaries are corporations or similar entities that may engage in activities in which the bank may engage directly or in activities related to banking, including those in which the bank can conduct directly.

Statutory subsidiaries are companies in which banks are authorized to invest by law, such as bank service companies, small business development corporations, safe deposit companies, companies that hold the premises of the bank, and, for national banks and state member banks, Edge Act and agreement corporations.

"Section 24" subsidiaries are operating and other subsidiaries of state banks that may not engage in activities that are prohibited for subsidiaries of national banks, unless approved by the FDIC under section 24 of the Federal Deposit Insurance Act (FDIA).[3]

Financial subsidiaries are subs authorized by the Gramm Leach Bliley Act (Act or GLBA),[4] in which banks may provide most of the financial services not permissible for the bank itself, such as general securities underwriting, that are authorized for financial holding companies (FHCs). Authority for financial subsidiaries is provided as follows:

- *National banks*—Section 5136A of the Revised Statutes (section 5136A),[5] added by section 121(a) of GLBA.
- *State banks*—Section 46 of the Federal Deposit Insurance Act[6] (FDIA), added by section 121(d) of GLBA.
- *Savings associations*—Financial subs are not authorized for savings associations.

---

3. 12 USC 1831a.
4. Pub. Law 106-102, Nov. 12, 1999, 113 Stat. 1338.
5. 12 USC 24a.
6. 12 USC 1831w.

Bank service companies are sometimes called bank service corporations. These companies can be organized and controlled by one or more banks to perform services for banks and other depository institutions including credit unions.

Subsidiaries as affiliates occur only under certain circumstances. A subsidiary of a depository institution is generally not an "affiliate" of the institution for purposes of transactions with affiliate restrictions of sections 232A and 23B of the Federal Reserve Act[7] unless it is:

- a depository institution;
- a financial subsidiary;
- a company controlled by one or more affiliates of the bank (other than depository institutions);
- a company controlled by a shareholder or group of shareholders that control the bank;
- an employee stock option plan or similar organization for the benefit of employees of the bank or any of its affiliates; or
- any company determined to be an affiliate by the Federal Reserve Board (Board) or the institution's primary federal regulator.

Principal Subsidiaries of National Banks

Operating Subsidiaries

An operating subsidiary (op sub) of a national bank is a corporation, limited liability company (LLC), or similar entity controlled by the bank. Op subs do not include:

- financial subsidiaries or bank service companies;
- certain "statutory subsidiaries," which are summarized below; and
- subs acquired through foreclosure or to avoid a loss in connection with a debt previously contracted.

Permissible Activities

For purposes of these activities, op subs are regarded as a department, or an extension of the bank, and can therefore do virtually anything the bank itself is permitted to do.

---

7. 12 USC 371c and 371c-1.

Permissible activities include offering the following insurance products authorized by sections 302 and 303 of GLBA[8]

- providing principal insurance products (other than title insurance or certain annuities) that were authorized by OCC in writing as of Jan. 1, 1999, or that were being lawfully provided as principal as of that date and that have not been overturned by court; and
- providing title insurance as principal if the national bank or a subsidiary was lawfully underwriting such insurance before Nov. 12, 1999, and if certain other qualifications are met.

Applications and Notice

A national bank, with certain exceptions, must file an application and obtain prior approval before acquiring or establishing an operating subsidiary or performing a new activity in an existing operating subsidiary.

Banks that are well capitalized and well managed (as those terms are defined in the regulations) may take these actions if they notify the OCC within 10 days after starting the activity or acquiring the sub.

Permissible activities of operating subsidiaries that are eligible for this after-the-fact notice are set out in Figure 7.1 on page 197.

No Application or Notice Required

A national bank may acquire or establish an operating subsidiary without filing an application or providing notice to the OCC if the bank is adequately capitalized or well capitalized and the activities of the new sub are the same as those conducted by a prior op sub, continue to be legal for the sub, and are conducted under any conditions imposed by the OCC in approving the conduct of these activities for any prior operating subsidiary of the bank.

Bank Service Companies (BSCs)

These are corporations or LLCs authorized by the Bank Service Corporation Act (BSCA)[9] that can be organized and controlled by one or more banks to perform services for banks and other depository institutions including credit unions.

---

8. 15 USC 6712 and 6713.
9. 12 USC 1861 *et seq.*

Figure 7.1
Permissible Activities of Operating Subsidiaries of National Banks (12 CFR § 5.34)

- Holding and managing assets acquired by the parent bank;
- Providing services to or for the bank or its affiliates, including accounting, auditing, appraising, advertising, public relations, and financial advice;
- Making loans, and selling money orders, savings bonds, and travelers checks;
- Providing management consulting, operational advice, and services for other financial institutions;
- Providing data processing, data warehousing, and data transmission products, services, and related activities and facilities, including associated equipment and technology, for the bank or its affiliates;
- Acting as investment adviser, financial adviser or counselor to government agencies, businesses, or individuals, including advising registered investment companies and mortgage or real estate investment trusts, furnishing economic forecasts or other economic information, providing investment advice related to futures and options on futures;
- Providing tax planning and preparation services;
- Providing financial and transactional advice and assistance, including advice and assistance for customers in structuring, arranging, and executing mergers and acquisitions, divestitures, joint ventures, leveraged buyouts, swaps, foreign exchange, derivative transactions, coin and bullion, and capital restructurings;
- Underwriting and reinsuring credit related insurance to the extent permitted under section 302 of the GLBA (15 U.S.C. § 6712);
- Leasing of personal property and acting as an agent or adviser in leases for others;
- Providing securities brokerage and tax planning;
- Underwriting and dealing, including making a market, in bank permissible securities and purchasing and selling as principal, asset backed obligations;
- Acting as an insurance agent or broker, including title insurance to the extent permitted under section 303 of the GLBA (15 U.S.C. § 6713); conducting certain mortgage reinsurance activity;
- Providing real estate settlement, closing, escrow, and related services; and real estate appraisal services for the subsidiary, parent bank, or other financial institutions;
- Acting as a digital certification authority to the extent permitted by published OCC precedent, subject to the terms and conditions contained in that precedent; and
- Providing or selling public transportation tickets, event and attraction tickets, gift certificates, prepaid phone cards, promotional and advertising material, postage stamps, and Electronic Benefits Transfer (EBT) scrip.

Subject to the exceptions discussed below, the BSCA requires the banks that control the corporation (controlling banks) to be located in the same state, limits the performance of services to locations within the state at which the bank could perform the services, and limits the services to be performed to those permissible for the bank or banks involved, except taking deposits. Banks must apply to their primary federal regulator to acquire the company and to perform these services.

No application is required, however, for one or more controlling banks to acquire a service company to perform, for depository institutions only, certain clerical and accounting services, including the following:

- check and deposit sorting and posting;
- posting of interest and other credits and charges; and
- preparing and mailing checks, statements, and notices.

BSCs may also, with the approval of the Board, provide services that were permissible for bank holding companies under section 1843(c)(8) of the Bank Holding Act on November 11, 1999. (These activities are discussed in Chapter 5.)

Statutory Subsidiaries

National banks are permitted to invest in certain corporations by statute, including bank service companies, which are discussed above.[10] The corporations and their statutory authority also include:

- *Agricultural credit corporations (12 USC 24(7th))*—corporations organized to make loans to farmers and ranchers.
- *Bankers banks (12 USC 24(7th))*—a national or state bank engaged exclusively in providing services for other depository institutions and their officers, directors, and employees.
- *Safe deposit corporations (12 USC 24(7th))*—corporations organized under state law to conduct a safe deposit business.
- *State housing corporations (12 USC 24(7th))*—investments in any state housing corporation that is incorporated in the state in which the bank is located.

---

10. OCC, *Comptrollers Handbook,* "Related Organizations," August, 2004.

- *Small business investment companies (12 USC 682(b))*—venture capital firms licensed by the Small Business Administration to provide debt and equity financing for small businesses.
- *Edge Act and agreement corporations (12 USC 601–604(a), 611–631)*—Edge Act and agreement corporations are chartered by the Federal Reserve Board and state banking agencies, respectively, generally as subsidiaries of member banks, as a means of financing international business transactions, particularly exports. They may conduct deposit and loan businesses in other states other than their parent bank's home state, so long as the business is related to international transactions. They may also make certain foreign investments that member banks may not make.

Subsidiaries of State Banks

"Section 24" Subsidiaries

Section 24 of the FDIA, which was enacted in 1991,[11] provides that subsidiaries of state banks may not engage in activities that are not permissible for subsidiaries of national banks unless the FDIC finds that the activity would not pose a significant risk to the bank's deposit insurance fund, and the state bank meets and maintains "applicable capital standards" imposed by its primary federal regulator.

This provision, and similar restrictions on state savings associations, which are discussed below, followed a similar limit imposed on subsidiaries of state savings associations. These limits were reactions by Congress to the savings and loan crisis and banking crises of the 1980s to which "unrestrained" activities of subsidiaries of these institutions were perceived as contributing factors.

---

11. 12 USC 1831a, enacted by section 303(a) of Pub. Law 102-242 (Dec, 19, 1991), 105 Stat. 2236, the "Federal Deposit Insurance Improvement Act of 1991 (FDICIA)."

The FDIC has pre-approved several activities for majority-owned subsidiaries under section 24.[12] These include:

- activities permissible for a national bank, including retail brokerage and other securities activities that are approved for national banks under section 16 of the Glass-Steagall Act[13];
- engaging in grandfathered insurance underwriting if the bank or its subsidiary on November 21, 1991, was lawfully providing insurance as principal (see Chapter 5 for a discussion of insurance powers of banks and savings associations);
- acting as an insurance agency;
- grandfathered investments in common and preferred stock and shares of investment companies;
- acquiring and retaining adjustable rate and money market preferred stock and similar instruments;
- investments in bank stock;
- real estate investment, development, and leasing; and
- general securities underwriting and distribution that had been approved for the subsidiary before Nov. 12, 1999, the date of enactment of GLBA (by which this activity became a financial sub activity under section 46, which is discussed below).[14]

The FDIC says it has the most experience with applications from state banks to engage in real estate investment and securities underwriting.[15]

As noted below, state banks are permitted to organize financial subsidiaries to engage in many of the new financial activities authorized by GLBA in 1999 for financial holding companies. Several of these activities were permissible for subsidiaries prior to the enactment of GLBA and had been approved for these subsidiaries under section 24 since its enactment in 1991. The interrelationship between section 24 of the FDIA and section 46, which authorizes financial subsidiaries, is discussed below.

---

12. FDIC, "Activities of Insured State Banks and Insured Savings Associations," Final rule, 63 FR 66275 (December 1, 1998), pp. 66294–66295.

13. 12 USC 24(7th).

14. The U.S. Court of Appeals, in Investment Company Institute v. FDIC, 815 F.2d 1540 (D.C. Cir. 1987), upheld an FDIC opinion stating that section 21 of the Glass-Steagall Act, which bars banks from underwriting securities, did not apply to subsidiaries of state nonmember banks.

15. FDIC, Activities of State Banks, op. cit., p. 66276.

Financial Subsidiaries of National and State Banks

In addition to authorizing banks to provide new financial products in subsidiaries of financial holding companies (FHCs), GLBA also authorizes banks to provide most, but not all, of these activities in new "financial subsidiaries."

Financial subs were authorized in part to give banks a choice between conducting these new activities in subs as well as in holding company affiliates. The financial sub authority, according to the GLBA Senate Report, is intended to allow small, independent national banks and state banks to take advantage of financial modernization legislation "without being required to incur the added costs and burdens of forming a new bank holding company."[16] And, it may be added, without the acquiring the Board as a new regulator, in its role as Board as the principal federal regulator of the holding company.

Financial Subsidiaries of National Banks

Section 21(a) of GLBA[17] authorizes national banks to control or participate in the ownership of a financial sub, but only if the sub, with certain exceptions, engages exclusively in activities that are:

- defined in section 4(k)(4) of the Bank Holding Company Act as "financial in nature or incidental to a financial activity" and therefore permissible for financial holding companies (FHCs) or determined to be such by the Secretary of the Treasury after consulting with the Board; or
- permissible for the national bank to engage in directly.

Permissible FHC powers

Activities that are financial in nature or incidental to financial activities, and therefore permissible for FHCs and financial subs of national banks, include:

---

16. S. Rept. 106-44, p. 28. This provision also provided an alternative for smaller bank holding companies that preferred to conduct these activities in a subsidiary of the bank rather than having to expand their holding company structure.

17. Adding section 5136A to the Revised Statutes codified at 12 USC 24a.

- securities underwriting, dealing, distribution, and market-making and related activities (these new powers mirror those GLBA provided for FHCs by its repeal of section 20 of the Glass-Steagall Act);
- providing investment, economic, and financial advisory services, including advising registered investment companies;
- activities authorized for bank holding companies under section 4(c)(8) of the Bank Holding Company Act as of Nov. 11, 1999 (these are the "section 4(c)(8) powers" discussed in Chapter 5); and
- activities that the Board, in consultation with the Secretary of the Treasury, finds to be financial in nature or incidental to a financial activity.

"Designated Activities"

GLBA requires the Secretary of the Treasury to consult with the Board to determine the extent to which three activities listed in the Act (and discussed below) are financial in nature or incidental to a financial activity and therefore permissible for financial subs are noted in Chapter 5. The Act requires the Board to make the same determination with respect to financial holding companies after consultation with the Secretary. The three activities are:

- lending, exchanging, transferring, investing for others, or safeguarding financial assets other than money or securities;
- providing devices for transferring money or other financial assets; and
- arranging or facilitating financial transactions for the account of third parties.

In the preamble to the interim rule adopted on this subject in 2001,[18] the agencies say that while these categories include some activities that are already permitted for FHCs, national banks, and financial subs, such as providing safe deposit services, electronic funds transfer activities, credit and stored-value card activities, and securities brokerage activities, these listed statutory categories are intended to allow these companies to engage in additional activities and solicited comment on what these activities should be.

---

18. Joint interim rule and request for comment, 64 FR 257 (Jan. 3, 2001). These rules remain in effect, and, as of May 30, 2006, had not been amended.

Prohibited Activities

The following activities, which are permissible for FHCs, are prohibited for financial subs by section 5136A:

- real estate investment and development;
- "portfolio investments"—investments that are made in the ordinary course of business by insurance company affiliates that sometimes result in control of the company that is engaged in nonfinancial activities (see Chapter 5);
- merchant banking, except that this activity may be permitted after Nov. 11, 2004 (five years after enactment of GLBA) by regulations issued by the Secretary of the Treasury after consultation with the Fed; and
- insurance activities, with certain exceptions discussed below.

Permissible Insurance Activities for Financial Subs

Section 5136A provides that financial subs of national banks may provide insurance products in accordance with the following provisions:

- *General.* Insurance other than title insurance and certain annuities that were authorized by OCC for national banks to offer as principal or that national banks were in fact conducting as principal on Jan. 1, 1999, if these powers as principal have not been overturned by a court since then.
- *Title insurance.* Title insurance that the sub was conducting on Nov. 11, 1999, unless an affiliate of the bank that was not a subsidiary was providing title insurance as principal on that date.
- *"New" insurance products.* Any insurance product including title insurance first offered after Jan. 1, 1999, that a state insurance regulator determines is insurance and is not a bank product, such as a deposit account, loan, or a trust or fiduciary product.

Other Qualifications

GLBA imposes the following additional restrictions on the operation of a financial sub by a national bank:

- *Capital and management.* The national bank and each of its depository institution affiliates must be well managed and well capitalized.

- *Rating requirements.* A national bank that is one of the 100 largest insured banks must have at least one issue of outstanding debt that is rated in one of the three highest investment grades.
  - A bank that is one of the second 50 largest insured banks may also satisfy this requirement by either satisfying the requirement or meeting an alternate standard requiring the bank to have a current "long-term issuer credit rating"[19] from at least one national rating agency that is in the highest three ratings used by that agency.
  - These requirements do not apply if the financial subsidiary is providing financial services only as agent.
- *Asset limits.* The total consolidated assets of all financial subs may not exceed the lesser of 45% of the consolidated assets of the parent bank or $50 billion.
- *Capital deduction and financial statement requirements.* A national bank must deduct the aggregate amount of its outstanding equity investment, including retained earnings, in all financial subsidiaries from its total assets and tangible equity; may not consolidate the assets of the subsidiary with those of the bank; and must separately present financial information relating to these investments in published financial statements.
- *Safeguards for the bank.* A national bank that establishes a financial subsidiary must ensure that it has procedures:
  - for identifying and managing financial and operational risks within the bank and the subsidiary that protect the bank from these risks; and
  - to preserve the separate corporate identity and limited liability of the bank and its financial subsidiaries.

Financial Subsidiaries of State Banks

Section 46 of the FDIA provides that a state bank that is well capitalized and meets other requirements can control or hold an interest in a subsidiary that engages as principal in activities that would only be permissible for a national bank to engage in through a financial sub.

---

19. This is a written opinion issued by a national rating agency about the bank's willingness and ability to pay certain obligations on a timely basis.

Conditions for Operation of a Financial Subsidiary by a State Bank

To qualify to operate a financial subsidiary, a state bank must, among other things:

- be well capitalized, along with each of its depository institution affiliates, if any;
- have a CRA rating of at least "Satisfactory";
- comply with the GLBA amendments that apply the restrictions of sections 23A and 23B of the Federal Reserve Act to transactions with financial subsidiaries (these amendments are discussed below);
- comply with the policies required for national banks under the "safeguards for the bank" heading, above; and
- make the capital deduction and financial disclosures with respect to these investments as required for a national bank (which are referenced in the above discussion of financial subs of national banks).

Implementation of Section 46 and Interaction with Section 24

On Jan. 5, 2001 (66 FR 1018), the FDIC issued final rules implementing section 46.

The agency pointed out that section 46 applies only to activities "as principal," and that state nonmember banks, therefore, may continue to engage in agency activities permissible under state law without regard to that section.

Congressional consideration of section 46 raised questions about its effect on activities already approved for the "section 24 subsidiaries" discussed above and the ability of the FDIC to continue to approve applications under section 24 for activities that would be prohibited by section 46. Congress added two subsections to section 46 in response to these concerns.

As to the interaction with section 24 subsidiaries, which are discussed above, section 46(b) provides in part that

> an insured State bank may retain control of a subsidiary, or retain an interest in a subsidiary, that the State bank lawfully controlled or acquired before the date of the enactment of the Gramm-Leach-Bliley Act, and conduct through such subsidiary any activities lawfully conducted in such subsidiary as of such date.

Section 46(d)(1) also provides that

(1) Federal deposit insurance act: No provision of this section shall be construed as superseding the authority of the Federal Deposit Insurance Corporation to review subsidiary activities under section 24.

These provisions are reflected in the final regulations as follows:

1. Post-GLBA applications to engage in section 24 activities, such as general securities underwriting and dealing, that GLBA made permissible as "financial activities" for section 46 subsidiaries, will be processed under section 46. Banks so engaged in these activities under section 24 before GLBA was enacted will continue to be supervised under section 24.
2. Post-GLBA applications to engage in activities that had been approved under section 24, that are prohibited for financial subs under section 46, such as real estate investment and development, will continue to be processed under section 24.
3. When activities that are permissible under section 24 but not under section 46 are later determined to be financial in nature or incidental to financial activities by the Secretary of the Treasury after consulting with the Board and therefore permissible for a financial sub under section 46:
    a. applications to engage in those activities that were filed after the determination is made will be processed and supervised under section 46; and
    b. banks that were engaged in section 24 activities before such determination will continue to operate under section 24.

Application of Transactions with Affiliates (TWA)

Since 1982, with few exceptions, the restrictions on transactions by banks with their affiliates in sections 23A and 23B of the Federal Reserve Act (as discussed in Chapter 6) have not applied to transactions by a bank with its subsidiaries.

Section 121(b) of GLBA, however, seeking to "limit the exposure of a bank to a financial subsidiary to the amount of permissible exposure to an affiliate" amends section 23A to provide that for the purposes of that section and section 23B, a financial sub is deemed to be an affiliate and "shall not be deemed a subsidiary."

Exceptions

GLBA provided two exceptions to these restrictions as applied to financial subs:

- transactions with financial subs are not subject to the 10% of capital limit on transactions with a single affiliate (but remain subject to the 20% limit on all transactions); and
- investments in securities of affiliates do not include the affiliates' retained earnings.

Implementation by the Board of TWA Restrictions on Financial Subs

The application of TWA restrictions to financial subs is implemented in the Board's final version of Reg W[20] (as discussed in Chapter 6).

Exemptions

Reg W exempts the following subsidiaries and activities from TWA restrictions:

- *Subsidiaries of state banks that engage in activities that the parent bank may engage in directly (in effect, operating subs).* The Board says this exemption is consistent with the view that these subs are functional equivalents of bank departments and that it is unaware of any "material supervisory reason to create a disincentive for the bank to conduct [these activities in] a subsidiary if the bank has determined—for tax, liability, or other reasons—that the activity is most safely and efficiently conducted through a subsidiary."[21]
- *Activities that a subsidiary of a state bank was legally conducting before Dec. 12, 2002.* This is the publication date of the final Reg W rule. Excepted from this exemption are activities that section 46 requires state banks to conduct in a financial sub as principal.
- *Subsidiaries of a national bank or state bank that would be considered financial subsidiaries solely because they engage in insurance agency activities that are not permissible for the parent bank.* The Board adds that the federal banking agencies have

---

20. Federal Reserve Board, "Transactions Between Member Banks and Their Affiliates," Final rule, 67 FR 76559 (Dec. 12, 2002).
21. *Id.*, at p. 76563.

had significant experience in supervising insurance agency subsidiaries of banks, and such subsidiaries do not pose the kind of threat to bank safety and soundness that section 23A was designed to prevent.[22]

Implementation of Reg W by the FDIC— An Unresolved Issue

On March 17, 2004,[23] the FDIC proposed regulations dealing with the application of TWA restrictions to financial subs of state nonmember banks. In the preamble to the proposed regulations, the FDIC refers to the language in section 18(j)(1) of the FDIA[24] providing that TWA restrictions and related regulations issued by the Board apply to state nonmember banks "in the same manner and to the same extent as if they were member banks of the Federal Reserve System."

The agency says it has taken those requirements into consideration in drafting its own proposals but asserts that under this language, it, not the Board, has the power to interpret and enforce these TWA restrictions as they apply to state nonmember banks. The FDIC adds that, "nothing in the text of section 23A or section 23B or the legislative history of those sections indicates that the [Board] has the 'exclusive' rulemaking authority with respect to institutions other than member banks [footnote omitted]."[25]

As this book went to press in July 2006, the FDIC had not reissued these rules.

Subsidiaries of Savings Associations

Historically, savings associations have been able to engage in activities in service corporations that they could not conduct directly. Like banks, savings associations are also authorized to invest in operating subsidiaries and in certain statutory subsidiaries.[26] As noted above, they are not authorized to organize and acquire financial subsidiaries.

---

22. *Id.*, p. 76564.
23. FDIC, "Filing Procedures; Transactions With Affiliates," Notice of proposed rulemaking, 69 FR 12571 (March 17, 2004).
24. 12 USC 1828(j)(1).
25. FDIC, Filing Procedures, *op. cit.*, 12572.
26. OTS regulations on subordinate organizations of savings associations are found at 12 CFR 559.

Operating Subsidiaries

These subs may be organized in any state and may conduct any activity that the association may conduct after notifying the OTS of the creation of the subsidiary. The association must control 50% or more of the voting shares of the sub, and no other entity may exercise operating control.

Other rules relating to these subs include the following:

- An association may hold another insured association or bank as an op sub.
- An op sub may hold a lower-tier op sub or other entity that complies with OTS regulations applicable to service corporations, except those limiting the organization of service corporations to the state in which the parent association has its home office.
- Loans to one borrower (LTOB) limits do not apply to loans from the parent to the op sub, but the sub's loans to other entities are aggregated with other loans of the parent for purposes of determining the parent's compliance with LTOB limits.
- The assets of the op sub are aggregated with those of the parent for purposes of calculating the investment limits and capital of the parent.
- Unless the op sub itself is an affiliate of the parent,[27] transactions of the op sub with affiliates of the parent are aggregated with those of the parent for determining its compliance with transactions with affiliates regulations.

Service Corporations of Federal Associations

Federal associations may invest up to 3% of its assets in one or more service corporations as long as the excess investment over 2% serves primarily community, inner city, or community development needs.

Other characteristics and requirements include the following:

- Service corporations are corporations chartered under state law, but OTS will consider applications to organize a first-tier

---

27. As described in the above section on transactions with affiliates, an operating subsidiary is generally not an affiliate, unless it is a depository institution; is directly controlled by another affiliate of the association; is controlled by a shareholder or shareholders that control the association; or is an employee stock option plan, trust, or similar organization, or determined to be an affiliate by the Federal Reserve Board or the OS.

- service corporation as an LLC or a limited partnership on a case-by-case basis.
- Service corporation ownership is limited to associations that have their home office in the state in which the corporation is chartered.
- There is no minimum percentage of ownership that the association is required to hold, and there is no requirement that the association control the service corporation.
- The investments of service corporations are not aggregated with those of the parent.
- Service corporations may invest in lower-tier entities that engage solely in activities permissible for the parent service corporation.
- Generally, an association that controls, or has a minority interest in, certain subsidiaries that are engaged as principal in activities not permissible for a national bank, must deduct its entire debt and equity investment in calculating its core capital under 12 CFR 567.5(a)(2)(iv).[28]
- LTOB limits do not apply to loans between the parent and the corporation, but loans by a service corporation to entities other than the association or entities it controls are aggregated with the loans of the association for LTOB purposes.
- Loans to a service corporation controlled by the association and to their lower-tier subs may be made from any of the association's investment or loan category in which there is remaining capacity, including the service corporation authority itself or the association's commercial lending authority.
- Service corporations are generally not affiliates for purposes of transactions with affiliates limits, with certain exceptions noted for op subs (and as discussed above in footnote 27).

For subordinate organizations that are not controlled by the parent, OTS regulations impose:

- a limit of 15% of the association's total capital on loans to any one subordinate organization; and

---

28. Subs for which this deduction is not required includes those engaged solely in mortgage banking, subs that are themselves insured depository institutions, and subs of certain federal associations that converted from a state savings bank charter before October 15, 1982.

- a 50% of total capital aggregate limit on loans to all subordinate organizations that are not GAAP-consolidated subsidiaries.

To determine compliance with these "15/50" limits, the association's loans to the subordinate organization must be aggregated with loans made by any subs it controls to the subordinate organization. (The OTS Regional Director may modify these limits on a case-by-case basis for safety and soundness reasons.)

Permissible Activities

Service corporations of federal associations may engage in activities listed at 12 CFR 559.4. In addition to any activity that all federal savings associations may conduct directly, except taking deposits, these permissible activities include:

- *Finance-related activities.* Accounting or internal audit; advertising and marketing research; data processing and data storage facilities operation; personnel benefit program development and administration; software development and systems integration; and operation, leasing, ownership, and establishment of remote service units.
- *Credit-related activities.* Acquiring and leasing personal property; appraising; operating a collection agency, check or credit card guaranty and verification; and acting as escrow agent or trustee.
- *Consumer services.* Financial advice or consulting; income tax return preparation; postal services; stored value instrument sales; welfare benefit distribution; and check printing and related services; and
- *Real estate related services.* Acquiring real estate for development, construction, resale or leasing to others for construction, acquiring improved real estate or manufactured homes to be held for rental or resale, acquiring improved real estate for remodeling, renovating, or demolishing and redevelopment; real estate management; and real estate brokerage for property owned by a savings association that controls or has an ownership interest in the service corporation.
- *Securities Brokerage, Insurance, and Related Services.* Retail brokerage services; investment advice, insurance brokerage or agency for liability, casualty, automobile, life, health, accident, or title insurance; and issuing notes, bonds, debentures, or other obligations or securities.

- *Investments.* Tax-exempt bonds used to finance residential real estate; property; tax-exempt obligations of public housing agencies used to finance housing projects with rental assistance subsidies; and investment in small business investment companies licensed by the U.S. Small Business Administration to invest in small businesses engaged exclusively in activities permissible for service corporations of federal associations.
- *Community Development and Charitable Activities.* Investments in community development projects that benefit low- and moderate-income borrowers; low-income housing tax credit projects and entities authorized by statute to promote community, inner city, and community development.

Service Corporations of State Savings Associations

In 1989, Congress granted the FDIC authority to operate two sets of controls over activities of savings association subsidiaries. The first is a notice requirement applicable to all savings associations. The second is an approval process for proposed activities of subsidiaries of state savings associations that is similar to the 1991 "section 24 subsidiary" procedures for state banks, which are discussed above.

The Notice Procedure

Section 18(m) of the FDIA[29] requires all federal and state savings associations to notify the FDIC 30 days in advance of acquiring or establishing a subsidiary or engaging in new activities through a subsidiary.

If either the FDIC or the OTS find that the activities of the subsidiary endangers the safety and soundness of the association or are in violation of sound banking principles, the agency may bring an enforcement action to require the association to divest control of the subsidiary. The OTS is granted the authority to take further enforcement action if necessary. This section does not apply to a federal association that was chartered as a savings bank under state law prior to October 15, 1982.

---

29. 12 USC 1828(m), implemented by 12 CFR 362, Subpart D.

Chapter 7: Subsidiaries

The Approval Procedure

Section 28(c) of the FDIA[30] states that a service corporation of a state-chartered savings association, subject to certain exceptions, may not directly acquire or retain any equity investment of a type or in an amount that is not permissible for a federal savings association.

Exceptions include investments in one or more service corporations if the FDIC has determined that no significant risk to the deposit insurance fund is posed by:

- the amount that the association proposes to acquire or retain or the activities in which the service corporation proposes to engage; and
- the savings association is and continues to be in compliance with fully phased-in regulatory capital standards.

Consent Obtained Through Application

Consent for activities for which an application is required will be granted if the FDIC determines that the activity poses no significant risk to the affected deposit insurance fund. These activities may include, but are not limited to, acquiring and retaining equity securities of a company engaged in the public sale, distribution, or underwriting of securities.

Pre-approved Activities

The following activities may be conducted by the service corporation of a state association or by a company controlled by the service corporation without filing an application with the FDIC:

- activities permissible for a federal savings association;
- acting as an insurance agency;

and, subject to certain investment limits:

- engaging directly or acquiring a company that acquires and retains adjustable-rate and money market preferred stock;
- ownership of shares in a company that engages in activities permissible for a state association an activity permissible for an insured state savings association; and

---

30. 12 USC 1831e(a), implemented by 12 CFR 362.12.

- activities which are not conducted "as principal," such as acting as an agent for a customer, acting in a brokerage, custodial, advisory, or administrative capacity, or acting as trustee, or in any substantially similar capacity.

Investment and Transaction Limits

The FDIC may apply limits on investments and transactions of a state association whose service corporation is engaging in activities that are not permissible for a service corporation of a federal savings association.

Among these discretionary restrictions is a limit of 20% of the association's tier 1 capital for investments in service corporation that is engaging in the following activities:

- the acceptance by the association of securities issued by the subsidiary as collateral for an extension of credit to any person or company; and
- any extensions of credit by the association to any third party for the purpose of making a direct investment in the subsidiary, making any investment in which the subsidiary has an interest, or which is used for the benefit of, or transferred to, the subsidiary.

Capital Requirements

If specifically required by this part or by FDIC order, state savings associations that wish to conduct principal activities through a service corporation that are not permissible for a service corporation of a federal savings association must:

- be well capitalized after deducting from its capital any investment in the service corporation, both equity and debt; and
- use such regulatory capital amount for the purposes of the insured state savings association's assessment risk classification under Part 327 of the FDIC regulations (relating to deposit insurance assessments as they existed prior to the reorganization of the insurance funds, as described in Chapter 2).

Conclusion

The ability of bank subsidiaries to engage in most of the activities permitted for a financial holding company (FHC) is the result of a compromise reached between the Treasury Department and the Federal Reserve Board while GLBA was pending in Congress.

The Board, in its role as guardian of the safety net, believed, among other things, that a holding company affiliation would provide greater protection from financial problems of a financial services company than would a parent-subsidiary relationship. On this point, the Department maintained that there were ample supervisory and regulatory safeguards in the banking laws to insulate banks from a subsidiary's financial problems. (It seems obvious in any case, that the GLBA provision extending section 23A coverage to financial subsidiaries would have had a significant role in the resolution of the dispute.)

The result of the compromise was a "win-win" solution that permits banks to engage in these activities (except for merchant banking and portfolio investments, which must be conducted in an FHC) in either a financial subsidiary or in an FHC, as best suits their business plan. This choice is particularly valuable for banks that do not want to organize a holding company as a prerequisite to engaging in these activities.

CHAPTER **8**

Corporate Governance Rules

Introduction

Corporate governance rules applicable to banks and savings associations reflect legal principles that have developed over the years under common law and state corporations laws. Federally chartered institutions, as noted below, may, consistent with minimum agency requirements as to charters and bylaws, adopt the governance procedures of at least two states, depending on their location and whether they are in a holding company.

The governance of state institutions, consistent with the dual banking system, is derived from laws of the state in which they are chartered.

Holding companies, with the exception of S&L mutual holding companies, and certain other non-corporate entities, are predominantly state-chartered corporations operating under the general corporate laws of the state in which they are chartered.

Federally Chartered Institutions

The similarity of federal governance rules relating to directors of federally chartered institutions to general corporate governance standards—and to each other—is illustrated in Figure 8.1.

Figure 8.1
Banking Laws Relating to Directors of National Banks, Federal Savings Associations, and Mutual S&L Holding Companies [1]

	National Banks	Federal Stock & Mutual Savings Associations	Mutual S&L Holding Companies[2]
Term	term "may not exceed three years"	1 to 3 years	same
Staggered	optional	same	same
Number	at least 5—no more than 25 [3]	no less than 5 or more than 15 unless a higher or lower number is approved by OTS	same
Quorum	"a quorum of the board of directors is at least a majority of the entire board then in office"	"A majority of the number of directors shall constitute a quorum for the transaction of business at any meeting of the board of directors."	same
Action of a Quorum	[4]	The act of a majority of the directors present at any meeting at which there is a quorum shall be the act of the board.	same
Age limit on service of directors	[4]	"A Federal association may provide a bylaw on age limitation, which "must comply with all Federal laws, rules and regulations."	same

1 These governance provisions are found in the following provisions of 12 CFR: national banks, Part 7, Subpart B; federal stock associations; Part 552; federal mutual associations: Part 544; and mutual S&L holding companies: Part 575.
2 Section. 575.9 of the OTS regulations(relating to mutual S&L holding companies) provides that § 544.5 relating to bylaws of federal mutual associations shall be applicable to mutual holding companies "as if mutual holding companies were federal mutual savings associations."
3 A national bank may increase the size of its board to more than 25 members after notifying OCC and giving reasons for the increase.
4 No specific reference in Part 7 or in the "Charters" Booklet (Jan., 2005) of the Comptroller's Licensing Manual, but likely available under "choice of law" regulations discussed below.

"Choice of Law" Provisions for Federal Institutions

National banks and federal stock associations, after conforming to the charter, bylaws, and safety and soundness regulations of the OCC and OTS, respectively, may designate in its bylaws that it has adopted the corporate governance procedures of one of the following sets of laws:[1]

- the law of the state in which the main office of the bank is located;
- the law of the state in which its holding company, if any, is incorporated;
- the Delaware General Corporation Law; or
- the Model Business Corporation Act.[2]

Directors' Qualifications and Duties

Qualifications

National Banks

The qualifications for directors of national banks are set out at 12 USC 72. The basic requirements are that a director must be a U.S. citizen throughout his or her term of service and must hold a minimum of $1,000 of stock of the bank at par value or market value or the equivalent in the parent company that controls the bank.

At least a majority of the directors must have resided in the state or territory or district in which the bank is located or within 100 miles of its location for at least one year before their election as director.

The Comptroller may waive the citizenship and residency requirements for a number of directors that is less than a majority of the board.

De Novo Federal Associations

A majority of the directors of a *de novo* federal stock or mutual association must be "representative" of the state in which the savings association is located—meaning generally that the director must

---

1. These regulations for national banks and federal stock associations are found at 12 CFR §§ 7.2000(b) and 552.5(b)(3), respectively.
2. The Model Act is developed by the Committee on Corporate Law, Section of Business Law of the American Bar Association with support from the American Bar Foundation.

reside, work, or maintain a place of business in the state in which the association is located.

The board must be "diversified and composed of individuals with varied business and professional experience," and, unless the new association is wholly owned by a holding company, only a third of the directors may be in closely related businesses. In addition:

> The background of each director must reflect a history of responsibility and personal integrity, and must show a level of competence and experience sufficient to demonstrate that such individual has the ability to direct the policies of the association in a safe and sound manner.[3]

Directors' Duties

Directors of bank and S&L holding companies are subject to the common law fiduciary duties of care and loyalty and variants on these duties that have included the duties of diligence, good faith, and candor. These duties are embodied in the business judgment rule, a common law principle designed to protect directors from liability for "bad decisions" if the decisions were made in accordance with these duties. This rule is codified in various forms in the general corporation laws of all 50 states. Its principles also have been adopted by the federal banking agencies in the publications cited in Figure 8.3.

These basic duties can be summarized as follows:

- *Care*—was a board decision made after careful consideration of all of the relevant facts and risks that could have reasonably been known to the directors?
- *Loyalty*—was the decision by each director free of preferential treatment, self-dealing or conflicts of interest?
- *Candor*—did directors with a personal or financial interest in a transaction before the board discloses fully their interest in the transaction?
- *Arm's length transaction*—If the transaction was approved, was it approved on an "arm's length" basis after full disclosure, consistent with the duties of care and good faith, and in compliance with applicable regulations?
- *Good faith*—was the decision in the best interest of the corporation or institution?

---

3. All quotes are from 12 CFR 543.3(d).

- *Diligence*—has a director devoted sufficient time to become familiar with the bank's conditions, the risks it faces, and the economic and regulatory environment in which it operates?

According to the OCC, the responsibilities of national bank directors include:

- being aware of the bank's operating environment;
- hiring and retaining competent management;
- maintaining an appropriate board structure;
- monitoring bank operations;
- remaining independent;
- overseeing business performance; and
- serving community credit needs.

Notice of Change of Director or Senior Executive Officer

Section 32 of the Federal Deposit Insurance Act[4] requires the federal banking agencies to adopt regulations requiring institutions they supervise and their holding companies to give their supervisory agency 30 days' notice, under certain circumstances, of their intention to appoint a person to its board of directors or employ a senior executive.[5] The notice requirement does not apply to a director who is elected.

The notice must be provided if the institution or holding company is in a "troubled condition." This condition means that an institution has a CAMELS rating of 4 or 5, or that an institution or a holding company is subject to a capital directive, a cease and desist order, a consent order, a formal written agreement or a prompt corrective action directive relating to safety and soundness. It also means that an S&L holding company has a rating of "unsatisfactory" and a bank holding company has a rating of 4 or 5 under the Bank Holding Company Rating System.

---

4. 12 USC 1831i, added by section 914(a) of FIRREA, Pub. Law 101-73, Aug. 9, 1989, 103 Stat. 183.

5. Agency regulations are found in the following provisions of 12 CFR: OCC: § 5.51; Board: Part 225, Subpart H; FDIC: Part 303, Subpart F; OTS: Part 563, Subpart H.

The proposed appointment or employment will be disapproved if the agency finds that the competence, experience, character, or integrity of the person in question reveals that the proposed action would not be in the best interests of the institution, its depositors, the holding company, or the public.

Director and Other Interlocks

Restraints on interlocks of directors and other officials between competing corporations have been imposed at least since the enactment of the Clayton Antitrust Act in 1914.[6] These prohibitions are based on the assumption that such interlocks are inherently anticompetitive.

Laws prohibiting certain interlocks among depository institutions and their holding companies were imposed in 1978 by the "Depository Institutions Management Interlocks Act."[7]

The Interlocks Act restricts the ability of a person to serve as a director, officer, or other "management official" of a "depository organization" (a bank, savings association, or holding company), and to serve at the same time as a management official of an unaffiliated depository organization, depending on the size and location of the two organizations.

For purposes of the Act, a holding company is a bank or S&L holding company. Diversified S&L holding companies are subject to different interlock rules in certain instances, which are discussed below.[8]

A "depository organization," or "organization," means a depository institution, or a bank or S&L holding company.

---

6. Oct. 15, 1914, ch. 323, § 8, 38 Stat. 732.

7. Pub. L. 95–630, title II, § 202, Nov. 10, 1978, 92 Stat. 3672 (12 USC 3201, et seq.). Agency interlock regulations are found at the following parts of 12 CFR: OCC: Part 26; Board: Part 212; FDIC: Part 348; OTS: Part 563f.

8. A diversified S&L holding company is one in which the savings association subsidiary and certain activities in which it is engaged comprise less than 50% of the company's consolidated net worth at the close of the company's most recent fiscal year and the company's consolidated net income for that fiscal year. 12 USC 1467a(a)(1)(F).

A "management official" is a director, trustee, senior executive officer, or branch manager; but does not include a person:

- whose management functions relate exclusively to the business of retail merchandising or manufacturing;
- whose management functions relate principally to a foreign commercial bank's business outside the United States; or
- described in the provisos of section 202(4) of the Interlocks Act[9] (referring to an officer of a state-chartered savings bank, cooperative bank, or trust company that neither makes real estate mortgage loans nor accepts savings).

The Act prohibits interlocks between depository organizations on the basis of one of three following tests:

- *Community test.* A management official of a depository organization may not serve at the same time as a management official of an unaffiliated depository organization if both organizations or their bank, savings association, or other depository institution affiliate thereof, have offices in the same or adjacent community. A "community" is a city, town, or village, and contiguous or adjacent cities, towns, or villages.
- *"RMSA" test.* An RMSA is a "relevant metropolitan statistical area" as defined by the Office of Management and Budget. A management official of a depository organization may not serve as a management official of an unaffiliated organization if both organizations (or their depository institution affiliates) have offices in the same RMSA unless each organization has assets of less than $20 million.
- *Size test.* A management official of a depository organization or affiliate with assets of more than $2.5 billion (or any affiliate of such an organization) may not serve as a management official of an unaffiliated depository organization with total assets of $1.5 billion (or any affiliate of such an organization), irrespective of the location of the organizations.[10]

---

9. 12 USC 3201(4).
10. The agencies will adjust these thresholds, as necessary, based on the year-to-year change in the average of the Consumer Price Index for the Urban Wage Earners and Clerical Workers, not seasonally adjusted, with rounding to the nearest $100 million.

The measurement of the assets of diversified S&LHCs for purposes of the Interlocks Act includes only the assets of the savings association subsidiary.

Exemptions

Statutory Exemption

These include interlocks involving institutions that are in danger of closing or that have been placed in liquidation, conservatorship, or receivership.

Also included are interlocks involving a director of a diversified S&L holding company, who may also serve as a director of an unaffiliated depository organization subject to the approval of each organization's primary federal regulator.

General Exemption

The agencies may exempt an interlock between two organizations that is otherwise restricted by their location or size if they find that the interlock would not result in a monopoly or substantial lessening of competition and would not present safety and soundness concerns. Permissible exemptions under this authority include interlocks involving organizations that serve low- and moderate-income areas and those that are owned by a minority group or by women.

Small Market Share Exemption

The agencies may grant an exemption for an interlock between two organizations if the assets that the organizations hold in the aggregate in each community or RMSA in which they are located is 20% or less of the total assets held by all depository institution organizations in that community or RMSA.

Changes in Circumstance

The legal status of interlocks can change with certain changes in circumstance, including changes in the size of a depository organization, opening a new branch, mergers, and changes in geographic boundaries. A management official whose service in an interlock becomes prohibited as a result of one or more of these changes must either terminate the prohibited service within 15 months or apply for a general exception. (These exemptions are discussed above.)

Conclusion

Bank directors are subject to the same common law standards that directors of other corporations are, but it seems fair to say that bank directors have to cope with a greater volume of information than most corporate directors. They are responsible for over seeing the bank's implementation of an increasing number of agency guidance and policy statements.

The increasing costs of compliance with this regulatory overload is disproportionately high for smaller institutions and is a serious concern to bank regulators. This overload is caused in part by the increasing complexity of the basic banking business itself, but also an increasing amount of the compliance issues ranging from money laundering to fair credit reporting.

In 2004, FDIC Vice Chairman John Reich, who was then in charge of an interagency task reduction of regulatory burden said that "since 1989, 801 new rules, regulations, and amendments to existing rules have been imposed on the industry, on top of what already existed prior to that time. That amounts to an average of more than 50 new rules, regulations, or amendments every year."[11] A list of basic regulations applicable to banks and savings association in the format used by the Federal Reserve Board is set out in Figure 8.2.

Directors do not have to review every regulation or policy statement at every meeting of course, but boards are responsible for managing their agenda so that key issues are reviewed on a regular basis. Virtually all regulatory and compliance issues can be referred to a board committee for preliminary analysis and drafting of recommended courses of action, if required and an effective board committee structure is even more important than it has been.

---

11. Remarks of FDIC Vice Chairman John Reich before the Exchequer Club of Washington, D.C., Nov. 17, 2004. Mr. Reich became Director of OTS on Aug. 9, 2005.

Figure 8.2
Federal Reserve Board

Reg A	12 CFR Part 201	Extensions of Credit by Federal Reserve Banks
Reg B	12 CFR Part 202	Equal Credit Opportunity Act
Reg C	12 CFR Part 203	Home Mortgage Disclosure
Reg D	12 CFR Part 204	Reserve Requirements of Depository Institutions
Reg E	12 CFR Part 205	Electronic Funds Transfers
Reg F	12 CFR Part 206	Limitations on Interbank Liabilities
Reg G	12 CFR Part 207	Disclosure and Reporting of CRA-Related Agreements
Reg H	12 CFR Part 208[12]	Membership of State Banking Institutions in the Federal Reserve System
Reg I	12 CFR Part 209	Issue and Cancellation of Federal Reserve Bank Capital Stock
Reg J	12 CFR Part 210	Collection of Checks and Other Items by Federal Reserve Banks and Funds Transfers through Fedwire
Reg K	12 CFR Part 211	International Banking Operations
Reg L	12 CFR Part 212	Management Official Interlocks
Reg M	12 CFR Part 213	Consumer Leasing
Reg N	12 CFR Part 214	Relations with Foreign Banks and Bankers
Reg O	12 CFR Part 215	Loans to Executive Officers, Directors, and Principal Shareholders of Member Banks
Reg P	12 CFR Part 216	Privacy of Consumer Financial Information
Reg Q	12 CFR Part 217	Prohibition against the Payment of Interest on Demand Deposits
Reg R	12 CFR Part 218	[Repealed]
Reg S	12 CFR Part 222	Reimbursement for Providing Financial Records; Recordkeeping Requirements for Certain Financial Records
Reg T	12 CFR Part 223	Credit by Brokers and Dealers
Reg U	12 CFR Part 224	Credit by Banks and Persons Other Than Brokers or Dealers for the Purpose of Purchasing or Carrying Margin Stock
Reg V	12 CFR Part 222	Fair Credit Reporting

(Continued)

---

[12]. These are regulations issued by the Board in its capacity as primary federal regulator of state member banks.

Figure 8.2—*Continued*
Federal Reserve Board

Reg W	12 CFR Part 223	Transactions between Member Banks and Their Affiliates
Reg X	12 CFR Part 224	Borrowers of Securities Credit
Reg Y	12 CFR Part 225	Bank Holding Companies and Change in Bank Control
Reg Z	12 CFR Part 226	Truth in Lending
Reg AA	12 CFR Part 227	Unfair or Deceptive Acts or Practices
Reg BB	12 CFR Part 228	Community Reinvestment (CRA)
Reg CC	12 CFR Part 229	Availability of Funds and Collection of Checks
Reg DD	12 CFR Part 230	Truth in Savings
Reg EE	12 CFR Part 231	Netting Eligibility for Financial Institution
Reg FF	12 CFR Part 232	Obtaining and Using Medical Information in Connection with Credit

Figure 8.3
Agency Guidance on Director's Duties

OCC	"The Director's Book" <http://www.occ.treas.gov/director.pdf>
	"Pocket Guide to Detecting Red Flags in Board Reports" <http://www.occ.treas.gov/rf_pock.pdf>
FDIC	"Pocket Guide for Directors" <http://www.fdic.gov/regulations/resources/directors/#Institution>
OTS	"Oversight by the Board of Directors," Regulatory Bulletin (RB) 37-5, Nov. 30, 2004. <http://www.ots,treas/docs/7/74813.pdf>
	"Directors Guide to Management Reports," Oct., 1999. <http://www.ots,treas/docs/4/48091.pdf>
	"Directors Responsibilities–Guide," Oct., 1999. <http://www.ots,treas/docs/4/48090.pdf>

CHAPTER **9**

Audits, Audit Committees, and Financial Reporting

Introduction

Banks, savings associations, and their holding companies (banking organizations) are subject to three sets of federal rules that apply to the preparation and auditing of their financial statements. These rules apply as follows:

- Banking organizations whose securities are registered with the SEC under the Securities Exchange Act of 1934 (Exchange Act)[1] are subject to the audit and reporting provisions of that Act and the other federal securities laws, as amended by the Sarbanes-Oxley Act of 2002 (SOX),[2] and to the auditing standards of the Public Company Accounting Oversight Board (PCAOB or Board) created by SOX.
- Individual banks and savings associations—both public and nonpublic—with assets of $500 million or more are subject to annual reporting and audit rules administered by the FDIC and the other banking agencies under the FDIC Improvement Act of 1991 (FDICIA)[3] and implementing regulations at 12 CFR Part 363. Public institutions that comply with Exchange Act rules are also in compliance with the FDIC's Part 363 rules. In

---

1. 12 USC 15 USC 78a, *et seq.*
2. Public Law 107-204, July 30, 2002, 116 Stat. 745.
3. The "FDIC Improvement Act of 1991," Public Law 102-242, Dec. 19, 1991, 105 Stat. 2236.

many cases, as discussed below, the obligations of individual institutions under both the SEC and FDIC rules can be met by the institution's holding company.
- Certain nonpublic banking institutions with assets of less than $500 million are required by banking agency rules to obtain an independent audit of their financial statements. The agencies encourage other institutions in this category to secure an audit on a voluntary basis, depending on their size and complexity of operations.

Final congressional action on auditing requirements in FDICIA and the SOX was triggered by two crises. FDICIA was a response to the S&L and banking crises of the 1980s; SOX was a response to the collapse of Enron, Global Crossing LLP, and others in 2001.

The Sarbanes-Oxley and FDIC Improvement Acts were preceded by more than 30 years of studies, hearings, agency rulemaking, and new standards by public and private groups to improve the reliability of audits and financial reports of public companies. Three prominent study groups that were organized during this period were the Committee on Auditors' Responsibilities (Cohen Commission), organized by the American Institute of Certified Public Accountants (AICPA) in 1978; the National Commission of Fraudulent Financial Reporting (Treadway Commission), organized by the AICPA; and other accounting groups organized as the Committee of Sponsoring Organizations (COSO), in 1986.[4]

In 1998, the New York Stock Exchange (NYSE) and the National Association of Securities Dealers (NASD) sponsored the Blue Ribbon Committee on Improving the Effectiveness of Corporate Audit Committees (the Blue Ribbon Committee). In response to the report of this Committee, the NYSE and the NASD, among others, "revised their listing standards relating to audit committees, and [the SEC] adopted new rules requiring disclosure relating to the functioning, governance and independence of corporate audit committees."[5] (The Audit Committe Rules)

---

4. See "CPA Audit Quality," Report of the General Accounting Office, March 1989 (GAO/AFMD-89-38). COSO also included the American Accounting Association, the Financial Executives International, the Institute of Internal Auditors, and National Association of Accountants.

5. SEC, "Standards Relating to Listed Company Audit Committees," Final rule, 68 FR 18787 (April 16, 2003) (Referred to herein as the "Audit Committee Rule"), p. 18789 (footnotes omitted).

Chapter 9: Audits, Audit Committees, and Financial Reporting

Audit Procedures and Standards

Elements of an Audit

- *Audit*—an examination of the financial statements of an issuer by an independent public accounting firm in accordance with the rules of the Board or the Commission for the purpose of expressing an opinion on the fairness and accuracy of such statements.
- *Audit committee*—a committee established by the board of directors of an issuer to oversee the accounting and financial reporting processes of the issuer and audits of its financial statements. If an issuer does not have an audit committee, SOX provides that the entire board of directors will be regarded as the audit committee.
- *Audit report*—while the official definition of this term is more technical, the audit report, for purposes of this book, is the opinion at the end of an annual report of a publicly traded company by the accounting firm that audited its financial statements that these statements fairly present the financial position and financial results of the company in accordance with generally accepted accounting principles (GAAP).

Audit Standards

The PCAOB was created by title I of SOX to oversee and regulate accountants and accounting firms that audit public companies. The Board's responsibilities include:

- establishment of auditing and related attestation standards;
- registration of public accounting firms;
- issuance of quality control, independence, and ethics standards to be used by registered public accounting firms in the preparation and issuance of audit reports; and
- conducting inspections, investigations, and disciplinary proceedings of registered accounting firms; and enforcing compliance with the Act.

The SEC has authority to oversee the operations of the PCAOB, including but not limited to the authority to appoint or remove members of the PCAOB, to approve its budget and rules, and to entertain appeals of adverse PCAOB inspection reports and disciplinary actions.

The Importance of Independent Audits and Audit Committees

The reasons for the critical importance attributed by the capital markets, policymakers, and the public to accuracy of financial statements of public companies were outlined by the SEC in the preamble to its Audit Committe Rule.

The agency noted that accurate financial reports are the foundation of the effective functioning of capital markets. Financial reports are supposed to reflect economic reality. If investors cannot rely on financial reports as reflecting the true value of a company as a basis for making informed investment decisions, the markets will not work. The importance of independent audits in this process was stated by the SEC as follows:

> Effective oversight of the financial reporting process is fundamental to preserving the integrity of our markets. The board of directors, elected by and accountable to shareholders, is the focal point of the corporate governance system. The audit committee, composed of members of the board of directors, plays a critical role in providing oversight over and serving as a check and balance on a company's financial reporting system.
>
> The audit committee provides independent review and oversight of a company's financial reporting processes, internal controls, and independent auditors. *It provides a forum separate from management in which auditors and other interested parties can candidly discuss concerns.*[6] (emphasis added)

The next section of this chapter discusses the following three principal changes SOX made to audit procedures of public companies:

1. Directing the SEC to require stock exchanges to impose standards on listed companies relating to audits and audit committees.
2. Ensuring that outside auditors conduct their audit in conjunction with the company's audit committee independent of management by requiring the auditor to report directly to the committee and prohibiting the auditor from performing certain management consulting and other non-audit services for the company.

---

6. *Id.*, p. 18789.

3. Involving management in the audit by requiring it to discuss its responsibilities to develop and maintain controls to assure accurate financial reporting, to assess the effectiveness of these controls, and to these controls.

Application of the Sarbanes-Oxley Reporting and Auditing Rules to Listed Companies

The SOX imposes extensive corporate governance and financial reporting requirements on companies whose stock is publicly traded and other public companies. These companies are defined in the Act as "issuers,"[7] which are predominantly those, including banking organizations, that are subject to the registration and reporting requirements of the Exchange Act.

SEC and Exchange Rules for Audit Committees of Listed Companies

The Sarbanes-Oxley Act focused particular attention on audit committees of companies whose stock is publicly traded. The Act required the SEC to direct the national stock exchanges and national securities associations (exchanges)[8] to prohibit the listing of any

---

7. Section 2(a)(7) of the Act defines "issuer" as a company or other entity "the securities of which are registered under section 12 of the Exchange Act (15 U.S.C. 78l), or that is required to file reports under section 15(d) (15 U.S.C. 78o(d)), or that files or has filed a registration statement that has not become effective under the Securities Act of 1933 (15 U.S.C. 77a *et seq.*), and that it has not withdrawn."

8. A "national securities exchange" is one of nine exchanges currently registered as such under section 6 of the Exchange Act (15 U.S.C. 78f). These include the New York and American Stock Exchanges (NYSE), (AMEX), the Boston, Philadelphia, and Pacific Stock Exchanges, and the Chicago Board Options Exchange (CBOE).

A "national securities association" is an association of brokers and dealers registered as such under section 15A of the Exchange Act [15 U.S.C. 78o-3]. The National Association of Securities Dealers (NASD) is the only national securities association registered under this section. "The NASD partially owns and operates The Nasdaq Stock Market (Nasdaq) [, which has]" filed an application with the [SEC] to register as a national securities exchange. (68 FR 18788, 18789 footnotes 15–16.)

securities by any issuer that is not in compliance with specified standards relating to audit committee independence.[9]

Issuers were to be in compliance with exchange rules no later than Oct. 30, 2004. Final rules providing guidance to the exchanges were published by the SEC on April 16, 2003.[10] The first set of exchange rules approved by the SEC were those of the New York Stock Exchange (NYSE) and NASD, which were published on Nov. 12, 2003.[11]

SEC Audit Rule Standards for Audit Committees

Independence of Audit Committee Members. Each member of the audit committee must be an independent member of the board of directors of the listed issuer. To be "independent" for purposes of these provisions, a director must meet tests related to compensation, affiliation, and control.

Compensation. A director must not receive any direct or indirect consulting, advisory, or other compensatory fee from the issuer or any subsidiary thereof, other than in compensation for service as a member of the audit committee, the board of directors, or any other board committee.

This restriction covers "indirect acceptance of compensation" of a consulting advisory or compensatory fee by an audit committee member including acceptance of such compensation by a member of the audit committee's immediate family or, with certain exceptions, by an entity of which the member is a partner or executive officer that provides accounting, legal, and other listed services to the issuer or to an issuer's subsidiary.[12]

In the preamble to its Audit Committee Rule, the SEC points out that its regulations do not preclude the exchanges from adopting stricter rules relating to standards of independence both as to categories of family members affected and to business relationships.

Affiliation. An audit committee member may not be an "affiliated person" of the issuer or any of its subsidiaries apart from his or her capacity as a member of the board of the issuer. An "*affiliate* of, or a person *affiliated* with, a specified person," is defined in the Audit Rule

---

9. These provisions are in new 10A(m)(1) of the Exchange Act, (17 USC 78j-1(m)(1)), as added by section 301 of the Act.
10. Audit Committee Rule, *op. cit.*
11. SEC, Notices [SRO Rule Approvals], 68 FR 64154 (Nov. 12, 2003).
12. 17 CFR § 240.10A-(3)(e)(8).

Chapter 9: Audits, Audit Committees, and Financial Reporting 235

as "a person that directly, or indirectly through one or more intermediaries, controls, or is controlled by, or is under common control with, the person specified."[13] (emphasis in original)

SEC regulations provide that affiliates also include:

- an executive officer of an affiliate; and
- a director who is also an employee of an affiliate.[14]

"Control" includes the possession, direct or indirect, of the power to direct or cause the direction of the management and policies of a person, whether through the ownership of voting securities, by contract, or otherwise.[15]

Exemptions from the Independence Requirements

New issuers. Because of the likelihood that companies coming to market for the first time may face difficulty in recruiting directors that meet SOX's independence requirements, the SEC rules offer a partial exemption from these rules.

The rules provide an exception for non-investment company issuers that require at least one fully independent member at the time of an issuer's initial listing, a majority of independent members within 90 days, and a fully independent committee within one year.

The SEC adds that the difficulty of recruiting independent directors before an initial public offering, coupled with the uncertainty of whether the initial public offering will be completed, may discourage companies from accessing the public markets to grow their business and provide liquidity, as well as from achieving the other benefits of being a public company.[16]

Holding company subsidiaries and other affiliates. In its proposed regulations, the SEC addressed the definition of independence as it applied to entities, including banking organizations, that do business in a holding company structure. The agency determined that if an audit committee member of a parent company is otherwise independent, "merely serving" also on the board of a subsidiary should not be in violation of the rules so long as the director meets the other independence requirements for both boards.

---

13. 17 CFR § 240.10A-(3)(e)(1)(i).
14. 17 CFR § 240.10A-3(e)(1)(iii).
15. 17 CFR § 240.10A-(3)(e)(4).
16. 17 CRF § 240.10A-3(b)(1)(iv), Audit Committee Rule, *op. cit.*, p. 18794.

In response to critical comments from the banking and other industries that this exemption was too narrow and did not cover other affiliates, such as sister institutions under common control, and 50%-owned joint ventures, the SEC expanded the exemption to include all affiliates. The agency described its final action as follows:

> To address [the concerns of these commenters], we are expanding the exemption. Under the final rule, an audit committee member may sit on the board of directors of a listed issuer *and any affiliate* so long as, except for being a director on each such board of directors, the member otherwise meets the independence requirements for each such entity, including the receipt of only ordinary-course compensation for serving as a member of the board of directors, audit committee or any other board committee of each such entity.[17] (emphasis added)

Audit Committee's Responsibilities

SEC regulations provide that the basic responsibilities of audit committees impose the following requirements on audit committees of listed companies:

> the appointment, compensation, retention and oversight of the work of any registered public accounting firm engaged (including resolution of disagreements between management and the auditor regarding financial reporting) for the purpose of preparing or issuing an audit report or performing other audit, review or attest services for the listed issuer, and each such registered public accounting firm must report directly to the audit committee.[18]

In addition, the committees or listed companies are required to do the following:

- *Complaints.* Each audit committee must establish procedures for:
    - the receipt, retention, and treatment of complaints received by the listed issuer regarding accounting, internal accounting controls, or auditing matters; and
    - the confidential, anonymous submission by employees of the listed issuer of concerns regarding questionable accounting or auditing matters.
- *Advisers.* Audit committees must have the authority to engage independent counsel and other advisers, as it deems necessary to carry out its duties.

---

17. *Id.*, p. 18795
18. 17 CFR § 240.10A-3(b)(2).

- *Funding.* Each listed issuer must provide for appropriate funding, as determined by the audit committee to compensate:
  - the accounting firm engaged to audit the company's financial reports or to perform other audit services;
  - the independent counsel or other advisers authorized by the Act advisers employed by the audit committee; and
  - the committee for its administrative expenses.[19]

Disclosures by Non-Listed Public Companies

In addition to their application to listed companies, the SEC audit rules also apply to all public companies, including banking organizations whose securities are not listed on an exchange. The proxy statements these companies must file require them to disclose whether they have an audit committee and, if so, whether the members of that committee meet the independence requirements of a national stock exchange or association.[20] Failure to disclose would lead to a disapproval of the proxy statement.

SRO Audit and Governance Rules

The SEC began final approval of new SRO rules on audit committees and other governance provisions for listed companies in late 2003. On November 12, 2003,[21] the SEC published its approval of several proposed rule changes by the two exchanges, some, but not all, of which, related to the SOX audit committee independence standards.

The complete SRO rules are beyond the scope of this book, but the summaries of the following rules of the New York Stock Exchange (NYSE) and the Nasdaq Stock Market, Inc. (Nasdaq) may be of interest.

The rules of the two exchanges have several rules that are virtually identical, include the following:

- *Board composition.* Both exchanges require the boards of directors of listed companies to be comprised of a majority of independent directors.

---

19. 17 CFR § 240.10A-3(b)(3)–(5).
20. 12 CFR § 240.14a-101 Schedule 14A, Item 7(d)(3)(iv)(B).
21. SEC, Notices [SRO Rule Approvals], 68 FR 64154 (Nov. 12, 2003)

- *Meetings of independent directors.* The NYSE requires "non-management" directors and the Nasdaq requires "independent" directors to conduct regularly scheduled meetings in the absence of management or other non-independent directors.

Definition of "Independent"

The standards of the two exchanges relating to independent directors are similar and are summarized briefly below with text based on the exchanges rules and the SEC Federal Register document approving these rules.[22]

NYSE Governance Rules. No director may qualify as "independent" unless the board of directors of the listed company affirmatively determines that the director has no material relationship with the company (either directly or as a partner, shareholder, or officer of an organization that has a relationship with the company).

References to "company" in these rules include the company's parents and subsidiaries in a consolidated group.

The following directors are not independent:

1. a director who is an employee, or whose immediate family member is an executive officer, of the company until three years after the end of such employment;
2. a director who receives, or whose immediate family member receives, more than $100,000 per year in direct compensation from the listed company, except for certain permitted payments, until three years after he or she ceases to receive such compensation;
3. a director who is affiliated with or employed by, or whose immediate family member is affiliated with or employed in a professional capacity by, a present or former internal or external auditor of the company until three years after the end of the affiliation or the employment or auditing relationship;
4. a director who is employed, or whose immediate family member is employed, as an executive officer of another company where any of the listed company's recent executives serve on that company's compensation committee until three years after the end of such service or the employment relationship; and

---

22. These comments are based on Section 303A of the NYSE Manual and Nasdaq Rules 4200 and 4350.

Chapter 9: Audits, Audit Committees, and Financial Reporting 239

5. a director who is an executive officer or an employee, or whose immediate family member is an executive officer, of a company that makes payments to, or receives payments from, the listed company for property or services in an amount which, in any single fiscal year, exceeds the greater of $1 million, or 2% of the other company's consolidated gross revenues until three years after the payments fall below that threshold.

Nasdaq Governance Rules. Under these rules, a director is not independent if he or she:

1. or any family member, at any time during the past three years was an employee or executive officer employed of the listed company or any of its parents or subsidiaries;
2. has a family member who accepted any payments from the company or any of its parents or subsidiaries greater than $60,000 during any period of 12 consecutive months;
3. is, or has a family member who is, a partner in, or an executive officer or controlling shareholder of, any organization that paid to, or received from the listed company for property or services in the current or any of the past three years, amounts in excess of the greater of 5% of the recipient's consolidated gross revenue, or $200,000, other than payments—
   - arising solely from investments in the company's securities, or
   - made under nondiscretionary charitable contribution matching programs;
4. is employed, or whose family member is employed, as an executive officer of another company where during the past three years, any executive officers of the listed company served on that company's compensation committee; and
5. is, or has a family member who is, currently a partner in the company's outside auditor, or was a partner or employee of the outside auditor who worked on the company's audit at any time during the past three years.

Audit committee. Each board must have an audit committee with at least three members composed entirely of directors who meet the independence in the SEC's "listed company" regulations, discussed above, and the additional independence requirements of the exchange on which the company is listed. Each member of these audit committees must meet financial literacy requirements and at least one committee member must have increased financial sophistication.

Nasdaq permits a director who does not meet its independence requirements to serve on the audit committee for up to two years if the board of directors of a listed company "under exceptional and limited circumstances" determines that the membership is in the best interests of the company, and if the director:

- meets the statutory definition of independence in section 301 of SOX[23]; and
- is not, or is not an family member of, an officer or employee of the company.

Other SRO Governance Rules

Nominating and Compensation Committees. The NYSE requires each issuer to have a nominating and a compensation committee that are composed entirely of independent directors. Each committee must have a written charter.

Nasdaq rules require that director nominees must be selected or recommended for the board's selection by a majority of the independent directors or by a nominating committee comprises of independent directors. Each Nasdaq issuer must certify that it has adopted a formal written charter for its nominating committee or a board resolution addressing the nominations process.

Nasdaq rules provide that compensation for the CEO and other executive officers be determined by either a majority of independent directors (with the CEO absent when his or her compensation is considered) or a nominating committee comprised solely of independent directors.

As in its rules for audit committees, Nasdaq permits a director who does not meet its independence requirements to serve on a listed company's nominating and compensation committees for up to two years if the board of directors of a listed company "under exceptional and limited circumstances" determines that the membership is in the best interests of the company, and if the director is

---

23. This section adds a new subsection (m)(3) to section 10A of the Securities Exchange Act providing that to be independent, an audit committee member must not, except in his or her capacity as "a member of the audit committee, the board of directors, or any other board committee—(i) accept any consulting, advisory, or other compensatory fee from the issuer; or (ii) be an affiliated person of the issuer or any subsidiary thereof."

not, or is not a family member of, an officer or employee of, the company. The director is not required to meet the independence standards in the SOX.

Variations for Closely Held Companies. The rules of both exchanges have exceptions to certain director independence rules for closely held, or "controlled" companies. These are defined as companies of which more than 50% of the voting power is held by an individual, a group, or another company.

The NYSE and Nasdaq rules provide that controlled companies are exempted from the requirement that their boards have a majority of independent directors, and that their nominating and compensation committees be composed entirely of independent directors. Independent directors of these companies would still be required to have regularly scheduled meetings at which only independent directors are present.

Auditor Independence—Standards Relating to Public Accounting Firms

The SOX's provisions relating to auditor independence are based on the principle that performance by outside auditors of consulting and other non-audit services for audit clients can compromise the objectivity of the audit. Members of the audit firm providing consulting services to the client may be reluctant to challenge management on critical accounting matters. These conflicts could lead to inaccurate, or, at worst, fraudulent audit reports. These independence provisions are set out in title II of the Act, which are implemented by the SEC in final rules published on February 5, 2003.[24]

Section 201 provides that an audit firm may not, subject to exceptions that may be approved by the Oversight Board on a case-by-case basis, perform the following non-audit services for an audit client:

- bookkeeping or other services related to the accounting records or financial statements of the audit client;
- financial information, systems design, and implementation;
- appraisal or evaluation services;
- actuarial services;

---

24. SEC, "Strengthening the Commission's Requirements Regarding Auditor Independence," Final rule. 68 FR 6005 (Feb. 5, 2003).

- internal audit;
- management functions or human resources;
- broker-dealer, investment advisor, or investment banking services;
- legal services; and
- any other service that the PCAOB determined by regulation is impermissible.

Other sections of title II impose the following requirements on accounting firms that provide external audit services for issuers:

- *Pre-Approval of Audit Services.* The performance of audit and permissible non-audit services, subject to certain de minimis exceptions, must be pre-approved by the audit committee.
- *Disclosures.* Issuers must disclose information to investors of information related to audit and non-audit services provided by, and fees paid to, the auditor of the issuer's financial statements.
- *Audit partner rotation.* Firms that audit financial reports of issuers must arrange for periodic changes of certain partners who are involved in an audit of a particular banking organization. Certain partners on an audit engagement team must be changed every five to seven years, depending on the partner's involvement in the audit. Certain small accounting firms may be exempted from this requirement.
- *Reports to the audit committee.* The auditor must report the following to the issuer's audit committee:
  - all critical accounting policies and practices used by the issuer,
  - all material alternative accounting treatments within GAAP that have been discussed with management, including the ramifications of the use of the alternative treatments and the treatment preferred by the accounting firm, and
  - other material written communications between the accounting firm and management of the issuer such as any management letter or schedule of "unadjusted differences."
- *Conflicts of interest.* A registered accounting firm may not perform an audit for an issuer if a person in a financial oversight role at the issuer (e.g., chief financial officer, controller) was employed by the auditing firm within the one-year period preceding the audit.
- *Managing the audit.* The audit committee of each issuer is responsible for the appointment, compensation, retention, and oversight of the firm that has been engaged to provide

Chapter 9: Audits, Audit Committees, and Financial Reporting 243

audit services for the issuer and the audit firm must report directly to the audit committee.

Management Statements and Auditor Reports on Internal Controls

Section 404 of SOX requires companies that file annual reports under the Exchange Act to include a report by management stating its responsibility for establishing and maintaining an adequate control structure and procedures for financial reporting, and an assessment by management of the effectiveness of these controls. Final regulations implementing Section 404 were published by the SEC on June 18, 2003.[25]

This section also requires the company's independent auditor to attest to, and report on, management's assessment in accordance with standards for attestation engagements adopted by the PCAOB. The SEC's approval of the Board's standards on attestation engagements, which was included in the Board's *Auditing Standard No. 2*, was published June 23, 2004.[26]

Definition of internal control. For several technical reasons having to do with the evolution of terminology in the accounting profession over the years, the SEC regulations adopt the term "internal control over financial reporting" in place of "internal control."

"Internal control over financial reporting" is defined in the final rules as a "process" developed by management and overseen by the board of directors, that is designed to provide "reasonable assurance" that the company's financial statements are reliable and prepared in accordance with GAAP. These controls must include policies and procedures that:

- apply to the maintenance of records that accurately reflect in reasonable detail the transactions and disposition of the assets of the issuer;

---

25. SEC, "Management's Report on Internal Control Over Financial Reporting and Certification of Disclosure in Exchange Act Periodic Reports," Final rule, 68 FR 36635 (June 18, 2003).

26. "Public Company Accounting Oversight Board; Order Approving Proposed Auditing Standard No. 2, An Audit of Internal Control Over Financial Reporting Performed in Conjunction With an Audit of Financial Statements ('Auditing Standard No. 2')," 69 FR 35083 (June 23, 2004).

- provide reasonable assurance that transactions are recorded as necessary to permit preparation of financial statements in accordance with GAAP, and that receipts and expenditures of the issuer are being made only in accordance with authorizations of management and directors of the registrant; and
- provide reasonable assurances that unauthorized transactions relating to the issuer's assets that would have a material effect on the issuer's financial statements will be detected in a timely manner.

Management's assessment. Management's assessment and report on the company's internal control over financial reporting must include the following:

- a statement of management's responsibility for establishing and maintaining adequate internal control over financial reporting for the company;
- a statement identifying the framework used by management to evaluate the effectiveness of the company's internal control over financial reporting;
- management's assessment of the effectiveness of the company's internal control over financial reporting as of the end of the company's most recent fiscal year, including a statement as to whether or not the company's internal control over financial reporting is effective;[27]
- the assessment must include disclosure of any material weaknesses in the company's internal control over financial reporting identified by management;
- management is not permitted to conclude that the company's internal control over financial reporting is effective if there are one or more material weaknesses in the company's internal control over financial reporting; and
- a statement that the outside auditor has issued an attestation report on management's assessment of the company's internal control over financial reporting.

---

27. The SEC points out that "Management must [positively] state whether or not the company's internal control over financial reporting is effective. A negative assurance statement indicating that nothing has come to management's attention to suggest that the company's internal control over financial reporting is not effective will not be acceptable." (SEC "Management's Report," 68 FR 36635, *op. cit.,* p. 36642, footnote 62).

In addition, in each quarterly financial report, management must evaluate any change in the company's internal control over financial reporting that occurred during a fiscal quarter that "has materially affected, or is reasonable likely to materially affect, the company's internal control over financial reporting."[28]

Auditor's attestation. Standard No. 2 sets out the requirements of the auditor's "attestation to, and report on, management's internal control report" requires the auditor to attest to, or evaluate, two items:

- First, the auditor must evaluate management's own assessment process, or methodology, to be satisfied that management has an appropriate basis for its conclusion about the company's internal controls.
- Second, the auditor must test and evaluate both the design and the operating effectiveness of internal controls themselves to be satisfied that management's conclusion is fairly stated.

Auditor's report. The auditor's report on internal control over financial reporting expresses two opinions:

- First, an opinion on whether management's assessment of the effectiveness of internal control over financial reporting as of the end of the most recent fiscal year is fairly stated.
- Second, an opinion on whether the company has maintained effective internal control over financial reporting as of that date.

Management's Certification of Financial and Other Information in Quarterly and Annual Reports

Section 302 reports. Section 302(a) of the Sarbanes-Oxley Act directs the SEC to adopt rules that require an issuer's principal executive and financial officers each to certify the financial and other information contained in the issuer's quarterly and annual reports. Final rule and proposed rules with request for comments were published September 9, 2002.[29]

---

28. *Id.* p. 36644.
29. SEC, "Certification of Disclosure in Companies' Quarterly and Annual Reports, Management Investment Company Shareholder Reports and Designation of Certified Shareholder Reports as Exchange Act Periodic Reporting Forms," Final rule and proposed rule. 67 FR 57275 (September 9, 2002).

These rules provide that the signing officers must certify that:

- each signing officer has reviewed the statement;
- based the signing officer's knowledge, the report does not contain any untrue statement of a material fact or omit to state a material fact that would make the report misleading;
- based on the signing officer's knowledge, the financial statements fairly present the financial condition of the issuer;
- the signing officers:
  - are responsible for establishing and maintaining internal controls;
  - have designed such disclosure controls and procedures to ensure that material information is made known to them, particularly during the period in which the periodic report is being prepared;
  - have evaluated the effectiveness of the company's internal controls within 90 days of the report's filing;
  - have presented in the report their conclusions about the effectiveness of the disclosure controls and procedures based on the required evaluation as of that date;
- the signing officers have disclosed to the issuer's auditors and to the audit committee of the board of directors:
  - all significant deficiencies in the design or operation of internal controls that could adversely affect the issuer's ability to record, process, summarize, and report financial data and have identified for the issuer's auditors any material weaknesses in internal controls; and
  - any fraud, whether or not material, that involves management or other employees who have a significant role in the issuer's internal controls; and
- the signing officers have indicated in the report whether there have been significant changes in the issuer's internal controls or in other factors that could significantly affect internal controls subsequent to their evaluation.

Section 906 reports. Section 906 of the Act imposes a second certification requirement on issuers' CEOs and chief financial officers. This section, which adds a new provision to the federal criminal statutes,[30] requires these officials to make the following certifications in writing relating to the company's annual report:

---

30. New section 1350 to title 18, U. S. Code, *Crimes and Criminal Procedure.*

- the report fully complies with the reporting requirements of sections 13(a) or 15(d) of the Exchange Act; and
- the information contained in the report fairly presents, in all material respects, the financial condition and results of operations of the issuer.

Certification filing. The SEC rules require a company to file the section 302 and 906 certifications as an exhibit to the periodic reports to which they relate. This requirement is designed to standardize filing procedures and to enhance the ability of investors and the staffs of the SEC and Department of Justice to review these certifications by making them available though through the SEC's Electronic Data Gathering, Analysis, and Retrieval ("EDGAR") system.

Banks and Saving Associations. The SEC reminds bankers that "certification requirement of section 302 of the Act also applies to principal executive officers and principal financial officers of banks and savings associations that file periodic reports under the Exchange Act." These reports also apply to bank and S&L holding companies that are issuers. As pointed out in Chapter 10, the SOX amended section 12(i) of the Exchange Act to make it clear that the federal banking agencies have the authority to administer and enforce various provisions of the Act, including the certification required by section 302.[31]

FDIC Audit and Reporting Rules for Banks and Savings Associations with Assets of $500 Million or More

As noted at the beginning of this chapter, banks and savings associations—both public and nonpublic—with assets of $500 million or more (covered institutions) have been subject since 1991 to audit and reporting standards similar to those in the Sarbanes-Oxley Act.

These standards were adopted by the FDIC Improvement Act of 1991 (FDICIA) as section 36 to the Federal Deposit Insurance Act (FDIA).[32] Section 36 requires covered institutions to file audited financial and other reports each year with the FDIC and their primary federal regulator, create an audit committee of independent

---

31. SEC, "Certification of Disclosure," *op. cit.*, 67 FR 77275 (Sept. 9, 2002), p. 57278.
32. 12 USC 1831m.

directors if they have assets of $1 billion or more, and to take other actions to ensure accurate financial reports. The FDIC regulations implementing section 36 are set out at 12 CFR Part 363 and are referred to herein as "Part 363 rules."

The FDIC has defined "financial reporting" ' to include financial statements prepared in accordance with generally accepted accounting principles (GAAP) and those prepared for regulatory reporting purposes.[33]

Basic Provisions of Part 363

Part 363 requires all covered insured depository institutions to file each year:

- *An audited financial statement.* This statement must be prepared in accordance with generally accepted accounting principles, and is required to be audited by an independent public accountant.
- *A management report.* This report, as of the end of the institution's most recent fiscal year, which must be signed by its chief executive officer and chief accounting or chief financial officer that contains:
    - A statement of management's responsibilities for preparing the institution's annual financial statements, for establishing and maintaining an adequate internal control structure and procedures for financial reporting and for complying with laws and regulations relating to safety and soundness which are designated by the FDIC and the institution's primary federal regulator;
    - An assessment by management of the institution's compliance with these laws and regulations during the fiscal year; and
- *Internal control assessments by management and external auditors.* For an institution with total assets of $1 billion or more at the beginning of its fiscal year, management must submit an assessment of the effectiveness of the institution's internal control structures. The institution's independent public accountant is required to examine, attest to, and report sepa-

---

33. FIL-86-94, Dec. 23, 1994. The regulatory reports are the annual Call Reports and Thrift Financial Reports filed by banks and savings associations. These reports are discussed in Chapter 11.

rately on management's assertions about the institution's internal control structure and procedures for financial reporting. The attestation must be made in accordance with generally accepted standards for attestation engagements.[34]

These are called "internal control assessments" by management and external auditors.

Audit committees

Each covered institution with assets of more than $1 billion must establish an audit committee composed of outside directors who are independent of management of the institution. Institutions with assets of $500 million or more and less than $1 billion may have an audit committee composed of a majority of outside directors. The primary federal regulator of these institutions may make exceptions to this requirement in cases in which the institution has experienced hardship in recruiting qualified directors.

Audit committees of institutions with total assets of more than $3 billion must include members with banking or related financial management expertise, have access to its own outside counsel, and not include any large customers of the institution.

If the institution is a subsidiary of a holding company and relies on the audit committee of the holding company to comply with this rule, the holding company audit committee may not include any members who are large customers of the subsidiary institution.

Holding Company Reports

The annual financial and other reports of covered institutions that are subsidiaries of a holding company may be satisfied by the holding company as follows:

- *Financial statements.* The requirement that covered institutions submit audited financial statements can be satisfied for

---

34. The assets threshold for these internal control assessments by management and attestations by external auditors was raised from $500 million to $1 billion for nonpublic institutions: FDIC, "Independent Audits and Reporting Requirements," Final rule, 70 FR 71232 (Nov. 28, 2005). This change was adopted in response to numerous statements from banks and industry groups that these control assessments, which were burdensome for smaller nonpublic institutions, particularly since many auditors in these audits were erroneously applying more detailed standards that were intended by SOX to apply to public institutions.

an insured depository institution that is a subsidiary of a holding company by audited financial statements of the consolidated holding company.
- *Management reports.* The management report and auditor's attestation report can be satisfied for a covered institution that is a subsidiary of a holding company if comparable reports are provided at the holding company level and the insured institution has:
  - total assets of less than $5 billion; or
  - total assets of $5 billion or more and a composite CAMELS rating of 1 or 2.

Effects of the Sarbanes-Oxley Act on Public and Nonpublic Banks

In March 2003, the FDIC issued initial guidance[35] on the effect of the Sarbanes-Oxley Act on FDIC-supervised banks. The guidance dealt with the application of the Act to:

- banks that are public companies;
- covered nonpublic banks (those with assets of $500 million or more); and
- noncovered nonpublic banks (those with less than $500 million in assets).

Banks that are public companies. These are banks whose securities are registered with their primary federal regulator under section 12 of the Exchange Act (as discussed in Chapter 10) or that are subsidiaries of holding companies that are public companies. The banks with securities registered with the FDIC are subject to SEC regulations incorporated by reference by the FDIC at 12 CFR Part 335. The holding companies are subject to SEC rules developed under the Act.

Covered nonpublic banks. These institutions are covered by FDIC regulations in 12 CFR Part 363 and by the SEC auditor independence rules. While these banks are not normally subject to the federal securities laws, they are brought under the SEC's rules on independent auditors by a provision in Appendix A to Part 363, "Guidelines and Interpretations." Guideline 14 in Appendix A, which addresses the

---

35. FIL-17-2003, March 6, 2003.

Chapter 9: Audits, Audit Committees, and Financial Reporting 251

qualifications of the independent public accountant that Part 363, states that:

> The independent public accountant also should be in compliance with the AICPA's Code of Professional Conduct and meet the independence requirements and interpretations of the SEC and its staff.

If a covered institution satisfies the annual independent audit requirement by relying on the audit of its parent holding company, the holding company's external auditor should meet the SEC's independence requirements.

These rules, which are summarized in greater detail above, relate to:

- restrictions on non-audit services permissible for the auditor's firm;
- requirements that the bank's audit committee pre-approve all audit and non-audit services provided to the company by the auditor of its financial statements;
- avoidance of conflicts of interest on the part of the auditor;
- periodic rotation of audit partners.

Nonpublic Institutions with Assets of Less Than $500 Million

The FDIC guidance says that while these institutions are not subject to SOX rules, they are encouraged to adopt SOX policies relating to audit committees, auditor independence, and other provisions that are appropriate to their size, risk profile, and complexity of operations.

Regulations of other agencies can also impose independent audit and other requirements. The OTS, for example, requires an independent audit for safety and soundness purposes, for savings associations (including those with assets of less than $500 million) that receive a composite CAMELS rating of 3, 4, or 5. The auditor must, among other things, "[meet] the independence requirements and interpretations of the Securities and Exchange Commission and its staff. . . ."[36]

---

36. 12 CFR §562.4(b) & (d)(3)(ii).

Conclusion

The special role that banking plays in the economy is evidenced by the fact that all but the smallest banks and savings associations—both stock and mutual institutions—have been subject to independent audit and audit committee requirements since 1991 that are substantially the same as those imposed on public companies in 2002 by the Sarbanes-Oxley Act (SOX).

SOX, however, imposes additional requirements relating to reports by an auditor to the company's audit committee. As noted in the chapter, auditors, in their reports to audit committees of issuers, must include a report on all alternative accounting treatments within GAAP that were discussed with management, the ramifications of these alternatives, and the accounting treatment preferred by the auditor.

This provision was designed to prevent collusion between management and auditors to present fraudulent audit reports to the board. It should also allow a board of directors of banks and savings associations to make more informed decisions on accounting and auditing issues.

CHAPTER **10**

Securities Activities of Banks

Introduction

This chapter deals with two aspects of the federal securities laws as they apply to banks, savings associations, and their holding companies (financial organizations). The first is the application of these laws to institutions as issuers of securities. The second touches on a few of the securities-related activities conducted by individual institutions.

Two federal statutes that apply to all issuers of nonexempt securities are the Securities Act of 1933 (Securities Act)[1] and the Securities Exchange Act of 1934 (Exchange Act)[2]. The Securities Act can be thought of as the "gateway" through which securities must pass before they can be sold to the public. The Exchange Act imposes registration and reporting requirements on securities that are traded on a stock exchange and securities of issuers that meet certain tests relating to asset size and number of shareholders.

Financial Institutions as Issuers of Stock

The Securities Act

The two basic objectives of the Securities Act, according to the SEC, are

- to require issuers of securities to provide full disclosure of all material financial and other information about the issuer to

---

1. 15 USC 77a, *et seq.*
2. 15 USC 78a, *et seq.*

enable investors to make informed judgments about whether to purchase a company's securities; and
- prohibit deceit, misrepresentation, and other fraud relating to securities.

While the SEC requires that the information provided be accurate, it does not guarantee the accuracy of these filings and does not express an opinion as to the merits of investment in the issue. Investors who purchase securities and suffer losses have recovery rights if they can prove that there was incomplete or inaccurate disclosure of material information.

Application of the Securities Act to Financial Institution

Bank and S&L holding companies that are issuers are subject to the federal securities law like other corporate issuers of stock and must register their securities directly with the SEC under the Securities Act unless the securities or the transaction is exempt from registration.

Securities issued by individual banks and savings associations are exempt from registration under the Act under sections 3(a)(2) and 3(a)(5),[3] respectively. Securities offerings of national banks and savings associations, however, are subject to regulations, forms, and procedures adopted by the OCC and OTS that closely parallel those issued by the SEC. Issues of securities by state banks are governed by state law. All financial organizations and other issuers, including those that are exempt from registration are subject to the Securities Act's antifraud provisions, which are referenced below.

General Provisions

The Securities Act prohibits any person, organization, or company from selling a security in interstate commerce unless a registration statement relating to the security has been declared effective by the SEC or unless the issuer or the security is exempt from registration under one or more provisions of the Act. Section 5(a) of the Act provides that:

> (a) Unless a registration statement is in effect as to a security, it shall be unlawful for any person, directly or indirectly:

---

3. 15 USC 77c(a)(2) & (a)(5).

(1) to make use of any means or instruments of transportation or communication in interstate commerce or of the mails to sell such security through the use or medium of any prospectus or otherwise; or (2) to carry or cause to be carried through the mails or in interstate commerce, by any means or instruments of transportation, any such security for the purpose of sale or for delivery after sale.

Registration

The Commission has adopted a number of forms for registering securities offerings under the Securities Act. These forms generally contain a prospectus, which includes narrative disclosure regarding the issuer and the terms of the offering, as well as independently audited financial statements. The Commission's basic registration statement is Form S-1. Other forms have been developed to meet the special needs of issuers and offerings. Form S-3, for example, was adopted to provide a simplified format for reporting companies widely known and followed by the investing public.

These registration forms are relatively short, but they cross-reference items of information listed in two documents that are repositories for most of the information that registrants are required for Securities Act filings and other filings. These documents are:

- Regulation S-K (17 CFR Part 229), which provides standard instructions for Securities Act and Exchange Act filings; and
- Regulation S-X (17 CFR Part 210), which provides the form and content of, and requirements for, financial statements, Securities Act and Exchange Act filings (including proxy and information statements under the Exchange Act), as well as filings under the Investment Company Act and the Investment Advisers Act (and other securities laws not covered here).

Application to Bank Holding Companies

Regulation S-X has separate Articles for certain categories of companies, including Article 5 for commercial companies, Article 6 for insurance companies, and Article 9 for bank holding companies.

Registration of Small Businesses

The Commission has adopted Forms SB-1 and SB-2 for small business issuers. These forms are used, respectively, for securities issues of up to $10 million and issues of any amount. One advantage of these forms is that "all of [their] disclosure requirements are in Regulation S-B (17 CFR Part 228) a set of rules written in simple, non-legalistic terminology." These forms also permit the company to:

- provide audited financial statements, prepared according to generally accepted accounting principles, for two fiscal years. In contrast, Form S-1 requires the issuer to provide audited financial statements, prepared according to more detailed SEC regulations, for three fiscal years; and
- include less extensive narrative disclosure than Form S-1 requires, particularly in the description of your business, and executive compensation.[4]

Definition of Small Business (Section. 228.10(a)(1))

A small business issuer is a company that:

- has revenues of less than $25 million;
- is a U.S. or Canadian issuer;
- is not an investment company;
- if a majority owned subsidiary, the parent corporation is also a small business issuer;
- has a public float (the aggregate market value of the issuer's outstanding voting and non-voting common equity held by nonaffiliates) of less than $25 million.

Required Information

As noted above, Securities Act registration forms require varying amounts of information depending on whether the registrant uses Form S-1 or one of the special forms developed by the Commission. Information required to be in both the prospectus and registration statement in Form S-1, for example includes the following:

- offering price of the securities, underwriters' discounts and commissions, and net proceeds to the issuer;
- risk factors related to the company, such as lack of operating history or nature of the business;

---

4. *Q&A: Small Business and the SEC,* Securities and Exchange Commission (May 1999).

- nature of any contingent interests that counsel and experts named in the registration statement have in connection with the offering and any relationship, such as director or officer, that these persons may have with the registrant or its affiliates; and use of the proceeds from the sale of the securities; and factors used in determining the offering price of the securities

Other information required to be in the registration statement but not in the prospectus include: descriptions of the issuer's business, properties, and competition; material transactions between the company and its officers and directors; material legal proceedings involving the company or its officers and directors; financial statements meeting the requirements of Regulation S-X.

Processing the Registration Statement

The Commission's Division of Corporation Finance uses nonpublic criteria to determine whether it will review the registration statement. If the statement is reviewed, the Division generally will provide comments on the registration statement to the issuer within 30 days of filing, to which the issuer responds in an amendment to the registration statement.

When the Division staff has no further comments on the statement it will declare the registration statement effective upon the request of the issuer. Even though registration statements become public immediately upon filing, an issuer cannot sell the securities covered by the registration statement until this effectiveness declaration has been made.

Exempt Securities and Exempt Transactions under the Securities Act

Sections 3 and 4 of the Securities Act provide, respectively, for exemption from registration of securities and for exemption of securities transactions.

Securities that are exempt from registration generally can be resold without restriction just as most securities that have been issued pursuant to an effective registration. Resale of securities purchased in an exempt transaction, however, must either be registered or be subject to an exemption from registration.

Securities Excluded from Registration

In addition to securities of banks and savings associations, several other kinds of securities are excluded from the provisions of the Act primarily because they are either subject to supervision by other agencies or are not regarded as posing the kinds of risk to investors that the Act is designed to protect.

These exclusions include securities issued by the federal government, state and local governments, certain nonprofit organizations, and the following:

- interests in common trust funds or similar funds that are excluded from the definition of the term "investment company" as defined in Section 3(c)(3) of the Investment Company Act of 1940[5] (section 3(a)(2));
- interests in collective trust funds maintained by a bank that are issued in connection with tax-qualified stock bonus, pension, or profit-sharing plans (section 3(a)(2) (common and collective trust funds are discussed below);
- insurance or endowment policies or annuity contracts issued by banks or insurance companies (section. 3(a)(8));
- intrastate offerings (section 3(a)(11));
- equity securities issued by a company or organization in connection with becoming a bank or savings association holding company by acquiring a bank or a savings association if certain conditions are met, including the following:
  - the acquisition occurs solely as part of a reorganization in which security holders receive exchange their shares of a bank or savings association for shares of a newly formed holding company;
  - the security holders receive, *after the reorganization,* substantially the same proportional share interests in the holding company as they held in the bank or savings association;
  - the rights and interests of security holders in the holding company are substantially the same as those in the bank or savings association prior to the transaction; and

---

5. 15 USC 80a-3(c)(3).

- the holding company has substantially the same assets and liabilities, on a consolidated basis, as the bank or savings association had prior to the transaction (Sec. 3(a)(12)).

Exempt Securities under Section 3(b)

This section authorizes the Commission to exempt any class of securities it finds that such exemption is not necessary in the public interest and for the protection of investors by reason of the small amount involved or the limited character of the public offering. No issue of securities exempted under this section that is offered to the public may exceed $5,000,000.

Exemptions under this section include:

- a "conditional small issues exemption" of up to $5 million for qualifying issuers under SEC Regulation A.[6]
- issues of up to $1 million and $5 million respectively, under Rules 505 and 506 of SEC Regulation D.[7]

Regulations A and D are designed to provide small issuers with the ability to raise capital without all of the formalities involved in a regular filing under the Securities Act.

Exempt Transactions under Section 4

Certain securities transactions are exempt from registration under section 4[8] of the Securities Act include the following:

- private placements, which are referred to in the statute as "transactions by an issuer not involving any public offering" (section 4(2));
- brokers' transactions executed upon customers' orders on any exchange or in the over-the-counter market but not the solicitation of such orders;
- qualified issues of mortgage-backed securities involving mortgages originated by banks and savings associations;
- transactions involving offers or sales by an issuer solely to one or more "accredited investors," (essentially sophisticated,

---

6. 17 CFR §§ 230.251–263.
7. 17 CFR §§ 230.501–508.
8. 15 USC 77d.

knowledgeable, and high-net-worth investors) as defined in section 2(15), and Rule 215,[9] including a bank or savings association acting in its individual or fiduciary capacity; and any employee benefit plan within the meaning of the Employee Retirement Income Security Act of 1974[10] for which a bank, savings association, insurance company, or registered investment adviser is a plan fiduciary (section 4(6)) (the maximum amount of the issue is tied to the limit in section 3(b), which is $5 million).

Other Regulatory Modifications

Shelf Registration

SEC Rule 415[11] permits securities, in many cases, to be offered on a delayed or continuous basis. This procedure permits registrants, for example, to wait for favorable interest rates before bringing debt instruments or mortgage-backed securities to market or to hold stock for sale as needed in connection with an employee stock option plan. This procedure is also used by companies contemplating acquisition of other companies and by closed-end management investment companies.

Qualified Institutional Investors

Rule 144A[12] provides a nonexclusive safe harbor from the registration requirements of the Securities Act for sales of qualified privately placed securities to and among institutional investors that meet the criteria for "qualified institutional buyer" ("QIB").

QIBs include banks and savings associations that own or invest at least $100 million in securities of nonaffiliated issuers and have a net worth of at least $25 million. These transactions must be for their own account or for the accounts of other qualified institutional investors.

---

9. 17 CFR § 230.215.
10. Pub. Law 93-406, Sept. 2, 1974, 88 Stat. 840.
11. 17 CFR § 230.415. This rule is issued under the Commission's authority to adopt regulations as necessary for carrying out the purposes of the Act, including the authority in section 19(a) of the Securities Act (15 USC 77s(a)).
12. 17 CFR § 230.144A.

Sales to and among "qualified institutional buyers, which include banks and savings associations acing for their own account or for the accounts of other qualified institutional investors that owns or invests at least $100 million in securities of nonaffiliated issuers and have a net worth of at least $25 million (Rule 144A—17 CFR 144A).

Antifraud Provisions

Section 17 of the Act[13] and related provisions impose civil and criminal penalties for insider trading, manipulation of stock prices, and other fraudulent activities relating to the issuance and sale of securities. These penalties apply to registered, unregistered, and exempt offerings, including those under Regulations A and D, intrastate offerings, transactions with accredited investors, Rule 144A transactions, and offerings of individual banks and savings associations.

Revisions to Securities Offering Rules

On August 3, 2005,[14] the SEC published extensive amendments to its rules on registration and other procedures under the Securities Act to be effective December 1, 2005. The new rules continue the efforts of the agency to increase the integration of the registration requirements between the Securities Act and the Exchange Act that began at least as early as 1966.[15]

These changes directly affect bank and S&L holding companies and the registration rules of the OCC and OTS, which are discussed below, that are cross-referenced to corresponding SEC rules. Among these changes are those that:

- simplify shelf registration under Rule 415;
- reduce the cost of using Form S-1 for many issuers by increasing the amount of information already on file with the Com-

---

13. 15 USC 77q.
14. "Securities Offering Reform," Final rule (70 FR 44721).
15. The agency quotes the late Milton H. Cohen, author of a six-volume study of SEC regulations, who suggested that if the Securities and the Exchange Acts had been enacted in reverse order or as one Act, we would likely have had a coordinated disclosure system involving "continuous disclosures covering issuers of actively traded securities" with the question of special disclosures involving public offerings being "faced in this setting." (*Id.*, p. 44724, footnote 20, quoting "Truth in Securities Revisited," 79 HARV. L. REV. 1340 (1966)).

mission and other information that can be cross-referenced in the Form; and
- simplify filing procedures for "well-known seasoned issuers," a new category of issuer, whose activities are "presumptively the most widely followed in the marketplace."[16]

Application of the Securities Act to Financial Institutions

Securities issues by banks and savings associations, as noted above, are exempt from registration under the Securities Act.

The OCC and OTS, however, have developed regulations on this subject for securities issues of national banks and state and federal savings associations that incorporate the registrations, forms, review procedures, and most exemptions under the Securities Act. Securities issues of state banks are governed by state law. Agency regulations exempting banks and associations from securities registration, which reflect SEC rules, are shown in Figure 10.1.

OCC

OCC rules for registration of securities issues by individual national banks are found at 12 CFR Part 16. Section 16.3(a) prohibits the offer or sale of securities by a national bank unless:

1. A registration statement for the security. . . . .has been filed with and declared effective by the OCC pursuant to this part, and the offer or sale is accompanied or preceded by a prospectus that has been filed with and declared effective by the OCC as a part of that registration statement; or
2. An exemption is available under [these regulations].

In 1994, the OCC revised its securities registration rules to conform them more closely to those under the Securities Act.[17] In the preamble to these amendments, the agency discussed its reasons (which are equally applicable to the OTS) for incorporating the rules and regulations of the Securities Act:

---

16. *Id.*, p. 44726 (footnote omitted).
17. 59 FR 54789 (Nov. 2, 1994).

Figure 10.1
Agency Regulations Providing Registration Exemptions for Bank Securities

Specific Regulatory	OCC 12 CFR Part 16:	OTS 12 CFR Part 563g:
Exemptions		
Regulation A	§16.8	not in Part 563g
Regulation D	§16.7	§ 563g.4(d)
Private placements	§16.5(b)	§§ 563g.3(d)) & 563.4(a)
Qualified institutional buyers, Rule 144A	§16.5(e)	*
Accredited investors -	§16.2(a)	§ 563g.1(a)(1)
Shelf registration	not in Part 16	§ 563g.16

* OTS has approved a Rule 144A transaction by a savings bank. ". . . the OTS' intent is to pursue a scheme of securities regulation that is . . . generally consistent with the SEC's securities registration and reporting scheme." Opinion of the Chief Counsel P-2003-8, Nov. 17, 2003.

By conforming its securities disclosure rules to those of the SEC, the OCC believes it can reduce significantly unnecessary regulatory burden.

Banks, bank counsel, and investors are familiar with SEC disclosure requirements. In addition to being well-known in the marketplace, the interpretation of SEC disclosure requirements is well established and benefits from a significant body of precedent.

Moreover, because the OCC rules will now actually reference the SEC rules, rather than parallel or copy them, the OCC rules will automatically remain current.

OTS Rules

Securities issued by federal and state savings associations are subject to regulations published in 12 CFR Part 563g. Section 563g.2(a) provides as follows:

(a) *General.* No savings association shall offer or sell, directly or indirectly, any security issued by it unless:
  (1) The offer or sale is accompanied or preceded by an offering circular which includes the information required by this part and which has been filed and declared effective pursuant to this part; or
  (2) An exemption is available under this part.

The Exchange Act

Registration

Most issuers are required to file reports with the SEC under one of two subsections of section 12 of the Exchange Act:

- section 12(b)[18] for issuers whose stock is to be traded on a national exchange or the Nasdaq (the issuer must apply to the exchange with a copy to the Commission); or
- section 12(g)[19] for other issuer issuers except that an issuer is exempt from registration of "any class of equity securities pursuant to section (g)(1) if on the last day of its most recent fiscal year, the issuer had total assets not exceeding $10 million . . ."[20]

The basic form for these registration statements is Form F-10, which requires detailed information about the registrant including the same information from Regulation S-K as required by Securities Act Form S-1.

This information becomes publicly available when filed. As in Securities Act filings, qualifying small businesses may choose to use small business forms and Regulation S-B for Exchange Act registration.

Termination of Regulation

Registration of any class of securities under Section 12(g) will "terminate" within 90 days of an issuer's certification to the SEC that the class is held by less than 300 persons or by less that 500 persons if the issuer had assets of less than $10 million on the last day of its three most recent fiscal years.[21]

Reporting

The Exchange Act also requires most issuers to file one of two essentially identical reports depending on whether they register and the status of the registration.

Upon approval of their Securities Act registration, issuers must begin filing reports with the Commission under section 15(d) of the

---

18. 15 USC 78l(b).
19. 15 USC 78l(g).
20. Rule 12g-1 (17 CFR 240.12g-1).
21. Rule 12g-4 (17 CFR 240.12g-4).

Exchange Act. Issuers that file under section 12 must begin filing reports under section 13 of that Act when their section 12 registration is complete and stop filing reports under section 15(d).

Companies registered under section 12 must file reports containing "such information and documents . . . as the Commission shall require to keep reasonably current the information and documents required to be included in or filed with an application or registration statement filed [under section 12]"[22] These reports also require filing of annual and quarterly financial reports (Forms 10-K and 10-Q, respectively) and Form 8-K reports, which provide information on changes in control, changes of auditors, and certain resignations of directors.

Issuers that are not required to file under section 12(g) may do so voluntarily. Those who choose not to file under that section must continue filing under section 15(d).

Their obligation to file under this section is suspended for any class of securities upon their certification to the Commission that the class is held of record:

- by fewer than 300 persons, or
- by fewer that 500 persons if the issuer has assets of less that $10 million.

Issuers may not take advantage of the "300 person" suspension for filing 15(d) reports during the fiscal year in which its registration was approved under the Securities Act and may not take advantage of the "500 person" suspension until the end of the second fiscal year after the year in which their registration was approved under the Securities Act.[23]

Application of the Exchange Act to Individual Institutions

Individual banks and savings associations are subject to the same registration and reporting requirements under the Exchange Act as other securities issuers except that the administration and enforcement of registration and reporting requirements under sections 12

---

22. 15 USC 78m(a).
23. Rule 12h-3. (17 CFR 240.12h-3).

and 13 (but not 15(d)) and certain other sections provisions of the Act are delegated by section 12(i) of the Act[24] to these institutions' primary federal regulator.

Section 12(i) requires the banking agencies, within 60 days of the issuance of rules by the SEC under these sections of the Exchange Act, which are listed below, to either adopt equivalent regulations for institutions that would otherwise be subject to registration and reporting requirements of the Exchange Act or publish detailed reasons why they believe such action is not on the public interest and necessary for the protection of investors.

It should be noted that while the banking agencies have extensive enforcement powers to deal with fraudulent activities of officers, directors, and employees and others affiliated with an institution, these persons are also subject to the antifraud provisions of the Exchange Act, which imposes both civil and criminal penalties on persons found to have engaged in insider trading or other fraudulent activities.[25]

Section 3 of the Sarbanes-Oxley Act[26] (Sarbanes-Oxley), added a new section 10A to the Exchange Act and amended section 12(i) to add eight of its own sections (separately codified in 15 USC 7201 et seq.) to those that are delegated to the banking agencies.

Administration and enforcement of the following sections of the Exchange Act are delegated to the federal banking agencies by section 12(i), as shown below in Figure 10.2

Agency Rules under 12(i)

Each of the four federal banking agencies has regulations that implement the authority delegated by section 12(i), which are set out in Figure 10.3

Number of Registered Institution

There are only a small number of institutions that are subject to these 12(i) rules, primarily because most are a part of a bank holding company, including "shell" holding companies whose principal asset is the bank or savings association subsidiary.

---

24. 15 USC 78l(i).
25. Section 10 (15 USC 78j).
26. Public Law 107-204, July 30, 2002, 116 Stat. 745.

Figure 10.2
Administration of Exchange Act Sections

Exchange Act Section	Subject (All at 15 USC):
10A(m)	78j-1 (m) Audit Requirements (added by sec. 3(b)(4) of the Sarbanes-Oxley Act)
12	78l Registration
13	78m Reports
14(a), (c), (d)& (f)	78n (a), (c), (d) & (f), proxies
16	78p Officers and principal shareholder
Sarbanes-Oxley Sections	
302	7241 Corporate responsibility for financial reports
303	7242 Improper influence on conduct of audits
304	7243 Forfeiture of certain bonuses and profits
306	7244 Insider trading during pension blackouts
401(b)	7261 Pro forma financial information
404	7262 Management assessment of internal controls
406	7264 Code of ethics for senior financial officers
407	7265 Disclosure of audit committee financial report

Figure 10.3
Section 12(i) Reporting for Institutions Subject to Registration under Sections 12(b) and 12(g) of the Securities Exchange Act of 1934

Institution	Federal Agency	Regulations
National banks	OCC	Sec. 12 reporting - 12 CFR Part 11 Sec. 15(d) reporting - 12 CFR Part 16
State member banks	Federal Reserve Board	12 CFR 208.36–incorporates 12(i) sections by reference. Banks with less than $150 million in assets and no foreign offices may elect to submit Call Report for Form 10-Q report with certain modifications.
State nonmember banks	FDIC	12 CFR Part 335–both replicates and incorporates SEC rules on Exchange Act registration and reporting.
Federal and state savings associations	OTS	12 CFR Part 563d

As of December 31, 2002, there were approximately 25 national banks that had a class of securities registered under section 12 of the Exchange Act and 20 banks filing reports under reporting under 12 CFR § 16.20, which implements section the Exchange Act's section 15(d) reporting requirements.[27] There were 19 state member banks registered with the Federal Reserve Board as of June 30, 2002.[28]

Coverage of Financial Institutions under the Investment Company Act of 1940 and the Investment Advisers Act of 1940

Investment companies are corporations or other entities that are defined in the Investment Company Act of 1940[29] as, among other things, ". . . issuers that hold themselves out as being engaged primarily . . . in the business of investing reinvesting, or trading in securities in, holding, or trading, securities . . ."[30]

The Act regulates the organization of these companies, but the SEC does not approve or evaluate the company's investment decisions. The most familiar examples of investment companies are mutual funds, which engage primarily in investing, reinvesting, and trading in securities, and whose own securities are offered to the investing public.

Banks and savings associations are excluded from the definition of "investment company" under by section 3(c)(3) of the Act,[31] which provides in relevant part as follows:

> (c) . . . none of the following persons is an investment company. . . .
> (3) Any bank . . . any savings and loan association, building and loan association, cooperative bank. . . .

The Investment Adviser Act of 1940[32] defines an adviser as a person who is in the business of providing advice on the value of, and the advisability of investing in, securities, or who "for compensation

---

27. OCC, "Reporting and Disclosure Requirements for National Banks under the [Exchange Act]," Final rule, 68 FR 68489 (Dec. 9, 2003) at pps. 68490 (footnote 14) and 68491.
28. FRB, "Reporting and Disclosure Requirements for State Member Banks [Under the Exchange Act," Interim Final rule, 67 FR 5738 (Sept. 13, 2002) at p. 57940.
29. Aug. 22, 1940, ch. 686, Title I, 54 Stat. 789, 15 USC 80a-1, *et seq.*
30. 15 USC 80a-3(a)(1).
31. 15 USC 80a-3(c)(3).
32. Aug. 22, 1940, ch, 686, title II, 54 Stat. 847, 15 USC 80b-1, *et seq.*

and as part of a regular business, issues or promulgates analyses or reports concerning securities."[33]

The SEC points out that, with certain exceptions, companies, and sole practitioners who are compensated for advising others about securities investments must register with the SEC and comply with regulations that implement the Act. Generally, advisers with at least $26 million of assets under management or who advise a registered investment company must register.

If investment advice is performed by a separate department or division of a bank, only the department or division, rather than the entire bank, must register.[34]

There is no exclusion in the Advisors Act, but as this book went to press, the SEC had proposed a limited exemption for savings associations under the Advisers Act.[35] The proposed rule "would except thrift institutions from the Advisers Act to the extent their investment advice is provided in their capacity as trustee, executor, administrator, or guardian for trusts, estates . . . and other [fiduciary] accounts . . . and [so long as] they do not, except in connection with the ordinary advertising of their services as [fiduciaries] . . . hold themselves out generally to the public as providing investment advisory services."[36]

Banks as Underwriters and Dealers: The Glass-Steagall Act

The Glass-Steagall Act is the commonly used term for four sections of the Banking Act of 1933[37] that were enacted to prevent banks from engaging in securities underwriting, distribution, and related activities either directly or through affiliates—practices considered by many to have been a major contributor to the stock market crash of 1929 and the depression that followed.

---

33. 15 USC 80b-2(a)(11).
34. 15 USC 80b-2(a)(11)(A).
35. 69 FR 25777 (May 7, 2004).
36. *Id.*, p. 25781.
37. June 16, 1933, ch. 89, section 21, 48 Stat. 189. These sections are named for Sen. Carter Glass (D-Va.) and Rep. Henry Steagall (D-Ala.) who were the sponsors of the bill in Senate and House, respectively. In some analyses, the 1933 Act itself, and certain other legislation they co-sponsored, are sometimes referred to as the "Glass-Steagall Act."

The Act presently consists of two sections that impose restrictions on the securities activities of banks but not on their affiliates or subsidiaries. These sections also restrict banking activities of securities firms. These two sections, which are commonly referred to by their section numbering the number of their section in the 1933 Banking Act, are:

- *Section. 16*[38]—which is section 24(7) of the National Bank Act—defines securities activities that are permissible for national banks;
- *Section. 21*[39]—which is codified at 12 USC 378—imposes limits on banking activities of securities firms, and, as discussed below, has a proviso to the effect that nothing in the section prohibits banks and other financial institutions from engaging in securities activities permissible for national banks.

The GLBA repealed the following two sections of the Glass-Steagall Act in 1999:

- *Section. 20*—formerly codified at 12 USC 377—which prohibited affiliations between member banks and firms "engaged principally" in underwriting, issuing, public sale, or distribution of securities. As discussed previously in Chapter 5, banks may now engage in these securities activities through financial holding company affiliates and through financial subsidiaries of the bank.
- *Section. 32*—formerly codified at 12 USC 78—which prohibited officer, director, and employee interlocks between firms principally engaged in underwriting or other listed activities and member banks.

Securities Activities of National Banks

Underwriting and dealing. Section 16 of the Glass-Steagall Act, with certain exceptions, prohibits national banks from underwriting the sale of "any issue of securities or stock." Exceptions include underwriting and dealing in "investment securities" (debt instruments) of

---

38. 12 USC 24(seventh).
39. 12 USC 378.

the U.S. and general obligations of state and local governments or agencies of state and local governments, including municipal revenue bonds that qualify as "exempt facility bonds" under section 147(b)(1) of the Internal Revenue Code. Securities activities permitted by section 16 are often referred to as "bank eligible" or "bank permissible" securities activities.

Brokerage activities. Section 16 also provides that national banks may engage in retail brokerage activities by executing purchases and sales of securities "solely upon the order, and for the account of, customers."

Limits on Securities Activities of All Depository Institutions

Section 21(a)(1) of the Glass-Steagall Act is designed to keep banks and securities firms out of each other's business. It prohibits any person or organization "engaged in the business of issuing, underwriting, selling, or distributing, at wholesale or retail, or through syndicate participation, stocks, bonds, debentures, notes, or other securities" from offering checking or savings accounts or other deposit accounts that are withdrawable at the request of the depositor.

A proviso clarifies that this language is not intended to conflict with the bank permissible activities of section 16:

> [These provisions] shall not prohibit national banks or State banks or trust companies *(whether or not members of the Federal Reserve System)* or other financial institutions or private bankers from dealing in, underwriting. purchasing, and selling investment securities, or issuing securities, to the extent permitted to national banking associations by the provisions of section 24 of this title. (emphasis added)

"This title" is title 12 of the U.S. Code and "section 24" is 12 USC 24, the seventh paragraph of which is section 16 of the Glass-Steagall Act.

This provision as it affects state banks is backed up by language in the Federal Reserve Act.[40]

---

40. The 20th paragraph of section 9 of the Federal Reserve Act (12 USC 335) which was enacted by section 5(c) of the 1933 Banking Act, provides that state member banks "shall be subject to the same limitations and conditions with respect to the purchasing, selling, underwriting, and holding of investment securities and stock [that apply to] national banks under [section 16]."

Federal Savings Associations

There is no statutory equivalent to section 16 for federal savings federal associations. These associations can engage in securities brokerage activities through service corporation subsidiaries. OTS regulations provide that a service corporation that meets certain requirements "may execute securities transactions on an agency or riskless principal basis solely upon the order of and for the account of customers, and may provide standardized and individualized investment advice to individuals or entities. . . ."[41]

Banks Acting as Brokers and Dealers

Individuals and businesses that engage in securities activities as brokers and dealers, as defined in the Exchange Act, must register as such under Section 15 of the Act.[42]

A "broker" is defined in section 3(a)(4)[43] of the Exchange Act as a person who is in the business of effecting securities transactions for the accounts of others. A "dealer" is defined in section 3(a)(5)[44] as any person engaged in the business of buying and selling securities for such person's own account through a broker or otherwise. Excluded are persons who buy or sell securities for their own account either individually or in a fiduciary capacity, but not as a part of a regular business.

Historically, banks were excluded from the definition of the definition of "broker" and "dealer" in the Exchange Act. This exemption was repealed in 1999 by the title II of the Gramm-Leach-Bliley Act (GLBA).[45] Savings associations were subject to the broker-dealer provisions of the Exchange Act prior to GLBA and remain covered by these provisions.

One rationale for the repeal of this exemption for banks was that if the barriers between banks and securities activities were to be lowered, as they were in GLBA, investors effecting securities transactions with banks should have the same protections afforded by the securi-

---

41. 12 CFR.§ 545.74
42. 15 USC 78o.
43. 15 USC 78c(a)(4).
44. 15 USC 78c(a)(5).
45. Public Law 106-102 (Nov. 12, 1999).

ties laws they have when effecting these transactions with registered broker-dealers.

Exceptions and Safe Harbors

In repealing the blanket broker-dealer exemption for banks, GLBA provided twelve exceptions, or "safe harbors," describing securities activities in which banks may continue to engage without registering as a broker-dealer. These exceptions are designed to strike a balance between bank activities that "should be subject to securities regulation" from those that "are connected to traditional banking activities."[46]

GLBA did not extend these safe harbor protections to savings associations and savings banks[47] (savings institutions). The SEC, however, in its first set of regulations implementing these broker-dealer provisions, published on May 18, 2001 (2001 interim final rules).[48] Among the rules adopted was Rule 15a-9, which extends these safe harbors to savings institutions as follows:

> savings associations and savings banks are exempt from the definitions of the terms "broker" and "dealer" under Sections 3(a)(4) and 3(a)(5) of the Act . . . based solely on the savings association's or savings bank's status as a broker or dealer on the same terms and under the same conditions that banks are excepted or exempted.[49]

Principal Statutory Safe Harbors

Of the 12 safe harbors in GLBA, three apply to the definition of both "broker" and "dealer," eight apply to brokerage activity only, and one applies to acting as a dealer.

---

46. H. Rept. 106-74, Part 3, p. 114 (the House Report on GLBA).

47. The reference to "savings banks" means federal savings banks and FDIC-supervised state savings banks.

48. SEC "Definition of Terms in and Specific Exemptions for Banks, Savings Associations, and Savings Banks Under Sections 3(a)(4) and 3(a)(5) of the Securities Exchange Act of 1934," Interim final rule, May 18, 2001 (67 FR 27759) *(2001 broker rules)* (2001 interim final rules).

49. A technical exception provides that savings institutions that are municipal securities dealers must register with the SEC. GLBA provides that banks dealing in these securities must register as such with their primary federal bank regulator. Since GLBA did not provide a statutory safe harbor for savings associations for this activity, these institutions must register with the SEC as other nonbank municipal securities dealers are required to do. See Exchange Act section 3(a)(34) (15 USC 78c(a)(34).

Safe Harbors Applicable to Both Broker and Dealer Activities[50]

- Trust and fiduciary activities;
- Permissible securities transactions"—including acting as brokers and dealers with respect to securities exempted under the Securities Act, commercial paper, and certain securities, including bankers acceptances, qualified Canadian government bonds, and Brady Bonds;
- "Identified banking products," which are defined as:
  - Checking, savings, and other deposit accounts;
  - Banker's acceptances;
  - Letters of credit issued and loans made by a bank;
  - Debit card accounts;
  - Certain participations in loans that the bank or an affiliate, other than a broker-dealer, owns, funds, or participates in, that are sold to qualified investors[51] and certain other persons; and
  - Certain swap agreements other than those sold to a person that is not a qualified investor.

Safe Harbors Applicable to Activities as a Broker

- Arrangements with third party brokers to sell securities on or off the bank's premises "under specified conditions";
- Transactions to effect certain securities transactions in employee benefit plans, dividend reinvestment plans, and issuer plans:
- Certain transactions for the accounts of affiliates;
- Sweep accounts into no-load money market funds;
- Certain private securities offerings;
- Certain safekeeping and custody services;
- Municipal securities brokerage; and
- A "de minimis" exception permitting banks to engage in 500 securities transactions per calendar year other than the above transactions without having to register as a broker.

---

50. These provisions are in sections 3(a)(4)(B)(ii)(iii) &(ix) and 3(a)(5)(C)(i),(ii) &(iv) of the Exchange Act as amended by GLBA, (78c(a)(4)(B)(ii)(iii) &(ix) & 78c(a)(5)(C)(i),(ii) &(iv)).

51. As defined in section 3(a)(54)(A) of the Act (17 USC 78c(a)(54)) as amended by GLBA. These investors include investment companies, banks, small business investment companies, state sponsored employee benefit plans, institutional trusts, market intermediaries, and natural persons, corporations or partnerships that own and invest on a discretionary basis more than $25,000,000.

Safe harbor applicable to activities as a dealer—underwriting and sale of certain asset-backed securities to qualified investors.[52]

Regulatory Implementation

The Interim Final Rules

In order to provide immediate responses to questions by banks, including questions about the GLBA "safe harbors," the SEC, on May 18, 2001, published the 2001interim final rules referenced above.

A "Two-Track" Approach

After issuing these interim rules, analyzing comments, and consulting with representatives of the banking industry, bank regulators, and other interested parties, the SEC divided the implementation process into two tracks in order to address "broker" and "dealer" issues separately and to provide additional time for consultations with the banking industry and the bank regulators. As a result, the 2001 interim final regulations were rewritten and republished as two separate proposals, one dealing with the definition of "broker" and the second covering the definition of "dealer," as described below.[53]

Proposed and Final Dealer Rules: November 5, 2002 (67 FR 67496)

The proposed dealer rules were published on November 5, 2002.[54] The SEC adopted final dealer rules on February 24, 2003,[55] to be effective March 26, 2003, with a compliance date of September 30, 2003. The final dealer rule is discussed further below.

---

52. Sec. 3(a)(5)(C)(iii).

53. A few sections **in the 2001 interim final rules** were not repealed and are still in effect, including Rule 15a-9, which extends the **statutory safe harbors in** GLBA *safe harbors* to savings associations.

54. SEC, "Definition of Terms in and Specific Exemptions for Banks, Savings Associations, and Savings Banks Under Sections 3(a)(4) and 3(a)(5) of the Securities Exchange Act of 1934," Proposed rule, 67 FR 67495 (Nov. 5, 2002).

55. SEC, "Definition of Terms in and Specific Exemptions for Banks, Savings Associations, and Savings Banks Under Sections 3(a)(4) and 3(a)(5) of the Securities Exchange Act of 1934," Final rule, 68 FR 8685 (Feb. 24, 2003). Is this the final dealer rule?

Proposed Broker Rules

The SEC published its proposed regulations relating to the definition of "broker" on June 30, 2004 (Reg B proposal).[56] This proposal changed the rule numbers of the brokerage exceptions in the interim final rules and re-codifies them in a new Regulation B, as Rules 710 through 781 in 17 CFR Part 242.

Several postponements of the effective date of the coverage of banks as "brokers" and "dealers" were necessary during these proceedings. The most recent SEC action, as this book went to press, postponed the effective date of the new definition of "broker" until September 30, 2006,[57] and an additional postponement seemed likely.

The banking industry and the SEC were still at an impasse on many of the issues discussed below relating to the implementation of GLBA's provisions on the definition of "broker" as it applies to banks and savings associations and many in the industry expected the SEC to issue a new proposal on the subject.

Implementation Issues

The implementation of GLBA's broker-dealer provisions proved to be more difficult than expected. One of the reasons was that functional regulation requires the Commission to break down securities transactions conducted by banks into two sets of components, which are:

- activities that should be within the exceptions because they are either traditional "banking" activities or "securities" activities that have become an integral part of bank securities services and do not pose undue risks to bank customers under the securities laws; and
- "securities" activities that should properly be subject to regulation under the securities laws.

Two of the most troublesome issues the Reg B proposal are the statutory provisions on compensation under two of the GLBA safe harbors:

- third party broker arrangements, and
- securities transactions in connection with trust activities.

---

56. SEC, "Regulation B," Proposed rule, 69 FR 39681 (June 30, 2004). *(2004 Broker Rules).*
57. SEC release No. 34-52405 (Sept. 9, 2005).

Referral

In third party brokerage arrangements, a bank or savings institution contracts with a registered broker-dealer to provide brokerage services both on and off the premises of the institution. Section 3(a)(4)(B)(i)(IV) of the Exchange Act provides that bank employees may receive compensation for referring customers to the broker so long as this compensation "is a nominal one-time cash fee of a fixed dollar amount and the payment of the fee is not conditioned on whether the referral results in a transaction."

A common theme in these provisions is to limit an employee's or a bank's ability to receive "incentive compensation or similar compensation that could foster a salesman's stake in promoting securities transactions."[58]

The purpose of the referral provision is twofold:

- to ensure that, irrespective of the amount of the reward, the conduct that is rewarded is a bona fide referral and not an attempt to sell brokerage services; and
- to avoid setting the reward so high as to "lead to unregistered bank employees being given an incentive not just to make referrals, but actually to sell securities brokerage services to bank customers."[59]

Trust Services

Securities transactions in connection with providing trust services are an exception in section 3(a)(4)(B)(ii) of the Exchange Act but only if the institution is "chiefly compensated" for these services:

> The cost incurred by the bank in connection with executing securities transactions for [customers] or any combination of such fees.[60]

In the trust provisions, of the 2004 Broker Rules, the statutory limits are designed to ensure the "that bank trustees and fiduciaries conducting securities activities outside the protection of the securities laws are compensated as traditional trustees and fiduciaries."[61]

---

58. 2001 Broker Rules, *op. cit.*, p. 27773, quoting House Report on GLBA (106-74. Part 3), p. 164.
59. 2004 Proposed Reg B, *Broker Rules, op. cit.*, p. 39688.
60. 2001 Interim final rules, *Broker Rules, op. cit.*, p. 27767.
61. 2004 Proposed Reg B, *Broker Rules, op. cit.*, p. 39693.

Principal Provisions of Proposed Regulation B

Additional Safe Harbors in Proposed Reg B

In addition to implementing the statutory broker safe harbors, proposed Reg B would grant new exemptions from the "broker" definition for banks. Some, but not all of these new exemptions would also apply to savings institutions, as discussed below. These proposed new exemptions are designed to further preserve established bank securities activities "where consistent with investor protection."

Safe Harbors in Proposed Reg B That Would Include Savings Institution

In addition to implementing the statutory broker safe harbors, proposed Reg B would grant new exemptions from the "broker" definition for banks. Some, but not all of these new exemptions would also apply to savings institutions. Among these provisions in Reg B are those that would:

- clarify definitions used in third party brokerage arrangements such as "nominal one-time cash fee of a fixed dollar amount";
- provide a "line-of-business" compensation test that would permit banks to bypass the account-by-account test in the trust and fiduciary activities exception;
- provide an exemption from broker-dealer registration requirements for banks and savings associations with less than $500 million if the size of its parent holding company, if any, is less that $1 billion for the two prior calendar years; and
- exempt savings associations and savings banks from the definition of "broker" and "dealer" in the Exchange Act, as currently provided in Rule 15a-9, referenced above.

Safe Harbors in Proposed Regulation B That Would Not Be Extended to Savings Institutions

These proposals include exemptions from the definition of "broker" and "dealer" for banks that:

- accept orders to effect transactions involving securities in certain custody accounts for customers whose accounts were opened before July 30, 2004 and for "qualified investors"[62];
- effect transactions in securities of open-end investment companies in accounts for plans that are qualified under the Internal Revenue Code for certain employee benefit plans;
- effect certain securities transactions as agent of a riskless principal under the SEC's Regulation S,[63] which includes provisions on sales of securities outside the U.S.

The SEC said that it did not have sufficient information on whether savings institutions actually engage in these activities and solicited detailed comments on the subject.

The Final Dealer Rules

The final dealer regulations adopted the following rules under the Exchange Act for banks and savings institutions:

Riskless Principal Transactions—Rule 3a5-1

The de minimis safe harbor exception in section 3(a)(4)(B)(xi) of the Act permits banks to engage in up to 500 securities transactions—other than other "safe harbor" transactions—per calendar year without having to register as a broker. These transactions would include those in which a bank (as broker or agent) executes customers' orders for purchases and sales of securities (as permitted by section 16 of the Glass-Steagall Act).

The banking agencies regard riskless principal transactions as agency activities that would fall within the de minimis broker exception.[64] The SEC, however, regards riskless principal transactions

---

62. As defined in section 3(a)(54)(A)of the Act (17 USC 78c(a)(54)), added by section 207 of GLBA. These investors include investment companies, banks, small business investment companies, state sponsored employee benefit plans, institutional trusts, market intermediaries, and natural persons, corporations or partnerships that own and invest on a discretionary basis more than $25,000,000.

63. 17 CFR 230.901-903.

64. Subsection (b) of this Rule provides as follows: "(b) For purposes of this section, the term riskless principal transaction means a transaction in which, after having received an order to buy from a customer, the bank purchased the security from another person to offset a contemporaneous sale to such customer or, after having received an order to sell from a customer, the bank sold the security to another person to offset a contemporaneous purchase from such customer."

as *dealer* activities (buying and selling for one's own account) requiring registration under the securities laws unless an exception exists. The GLBA de minimis exception is applicable only to *broker* activities.

In order to provide some accommodation for banks engaged in this activity, Rule 3a5-1 extends the de minimis exception to include riskless principal transactions, which, when combined with broker transactions, may not exceed 500 per calendar year. Riskless principal transactions, even those involving two separate counterparties will count as only on transaction under this annual limit.

Asset-Backed Transactions—Rule 3b-18

This rule clarifies and expands certain definitions in Section 3(a)(5)(C)(iii), the GLBA safe harbor that applies only to dealers. Definitions affected by this rule include: "syndicate," "originated," and "affiliate." Commenters said several of the definitions in the proposal were not consistent with banks' business practices.

Temporary Exemption for Banks and Savings Institutions from Liability under Section 29—Rule 15a-8

Section 29 of the Exchange Act[65] provides that contracts that violate any provision of the Act are void. This final rule provides that contracts entered into by banks and savings associations before January 1, 2003 will not be void because any bank that is a party to the contract should have been registered as a *broker* or *dealer*. Banks and savings institutions are further protected from failure to register as a dealer on contracts entered into before March 31, 2005.

Securities Lending Transactions—Rule 15a-11

This provision makes it clear that a bank is exempt from the definitions of both "broker" and "dealer" to the extent that, as a conduit lender, or as an agent, it engages in or effects securities lending transactions, and services for "qualified investors" or certain employee benefit plans.

Commenters said this exemption as proposed relating to safekeeping and custody activities was too narrow.

---

65. 15 USC 78cc.

Common Trust Funds

Purpose

Common trust funds are mutual funds created by banks and savings associations for investment of assets held in trust accounts. These funds provide trust customers with the same benefits of diversification of investment, reduced risk, and lower costs that are associated with mutual funds in the wider market.

Registration Issues

Historically, interests in these funds issued by banks have been exempt from registration as securities under the Securities Act and the funds themselves were exempt from registration as investment companies (mutual funds) under the Investment Company Act. These exemptions were based in part on the assumption that interests in these funds were distinguished from ordinary investment securities by the fiduciary obligations imposed on banks by state trust laws.

Common trust funds issued by savings associations, however, were not exempt and were registered by associations under these two acts. This discrepancy was addressed in 1999 by GLBA, as noted below. In 1999, GLBA amended these Acts to grant the same exemption from registration that apply to banks.

"Collective trust funds" are a variation of common trust funds that consist of interests in tax qualified employee benefit plans, including individual retirement plans, self-employment retirement accounts ("Keogh" or "HR 10" plans), stock bonus, and profit sharing plans.

Glass-Steagall Issues

The fiduciary nature of common trust funds also shielded them from the application of sections 16 and 21 of the Glass-Steagall Act: the funds were not regarded as posing the kinds of risks with respect to "investment securities" that the Glass-Steagall Act was designed to prohibit.

ICI v. Camp

In 1971, the Supreme Court, in *Investment Company Institute (ICI) v. Camp*,[66] had an opportunity to discuss the "outer limits" of the Glass-Steagall safe harbor for collective funds created by banks. The case involved a challenge by the ICI to a fund created by First National City Bank of New York (National City), which pooled funds in individual "managing agency" accounts into a collective investment fund. In managing agency accounts, the customer, as the name implies, had an agency, rather than a fiduciary, relationship with the bank.

The Court found no problem with the pooling of assets per se but objected to the legal relationship between the bank and the purchaser of shares in these managing agency accounts:

> For at least a generation. . . . there has been no reason to doubt that a national bank can, consistently with the banking laws, commingle trust funds on the one hand, and act as managing agent on the other. No provision of banking law suggests that it is improper for a national bank to pool trust assets, or act as a managing agent for individual customer, or to purchase stock for the account of its customers. But the union of these powers gives birth to an investment fund whose activities are of a different character.[67]

The Court enumerated several "hazards" that would be posed by a commingled investment fund that would not be present in a fiduciary relationship. These potential hazards, which would stem from the promotional pressures on the bank to meet or surpass the performance of nonbank investment funds, could lead the bank to such actions as unsound loans to companies in which the fund had invested; making loans to be used for buying shares in the fund and diverting resources from its commercial banking operation to the promotion of the fund.

Management of fiduciary accounts, "unlike the operation of an investment fund, do not give rise to a promotional or salesman's stake in a particular investment; . . . they do not entail a threat to public confidence in the bank itself; and they do not impair the bank's ability to give disinterested service as a fiduciary or managing agent [in a non-collective account]."[68]

---

66. 401 U.S. 617 (1971).
67. *Id.*, at 622, n. 8.
68. *Id.*, at 638.

On the basis if its analysis, the court concluded "that the operation of an investment fund of the kind approved by the Comptroller involves a bank in the underwriting, issuing, selling, and distributing of securities in violation of 16 and 21 of the Glass-Steagall Act."[69]

ICI v. Conover

The *Conover* case,[70] decided in 1986, involved a challenge by the ICI on Glass-Steagall grounds of a collective trust fund for IRA investments created by Citibank and approved by the Comptroller in 1982. ICI cited *Camp* as the basis of its assertion that the Citibank trust violated the Glass-Steagall Act. The Court affirmed the District Court's approval of the Comptroller's motion for summary judgment.

The opinion points out that, according the *Camp* opinion,

> it was the *combination* of the bank's commingling of trust assets *and* its acting as managing agent (rather than trustee) that spawned Glass-Steagall concerns. Here, by contrast, Citibank is seeking to exercise only one of the two powers which *Camp* held could not be joined: the power to commingle trust funds. The existence of the trust relationship is sufficient by itself, to take this case out of Camp's express teaching.[71] (Emphases in original.)

Camp did not hold, as contended by ICI, that the term "security" includes any interest in a fund consisting of pooled assets. While the Glass-Steagall Act does not define "security," it is clear that Congress did not intend to adopt such a broad standard. "If the term 'security' were indeed interpreted as broadly as the Institute suggests, then any ownership interest in a bank's common trust fund would constitute a security, and all commingling of trust funds by national banks would be effectively prohibited.[72]

The risks in the Citibank fund were substantially less than those in the *Camp* fund, including the fact the funds were not transferable and could not be purchased on margin. In addition, because of the restraints on IRA funds, contributions were limited to small amounts, $2,000 per year, and sudden demand for large amount of redemptions

---

69. *Id.*, at 639. An unusual aspect of the case was that the Comptroller's approval of National City's application was not accompanied by an analysis of the legal basis for his interpretation of sections 16 and 21 in approving the application. The Court was therefore not able to accord the Comptroller the traditional deference that is given to an agency's interpretation of the laws it administers.

70. Investment Company Institute v. Conover, 790 F2d 925, (D.C. Cir.), cert. denied, 497 U.S. 939 (1986).

71. *Id.*, at 930.

72. *Id.*, at 931.

were not likely because of the tax penalties for early withdrawal of IRA funds.

The fact that the fund was characterized as providing an "investment opportunity" had no bearing on the fact that it also provides "*bona fide* fiduciary services. "The two terms are not mutually exclusive . . . very few bank customers would be satisfied with the services of a bank's trust department if the bank did no more than safekeep their funds."[73]

Two other 1986 Circuit Court cases also upheld the Comptroller's ruling on collective IRA funds.[74]

In addition to Glass-Steagall concerns, some collective trust funds, as discussed below, are subject to registration under the Securities and Investment Company Acts.

OCC and OTS Regulations for "Collective Investment Funds"

OCC regulations on pooled trust accounts are found at 12 CFR § 9.18, Common Investment Funds (CIFs).[75] These funds are defined in section 9.18(a) as follows:

- (a)(1)—funds "maintained by the bank . . . exclusively for the collective investment and reinvestment of money contributed to the fund by the bank . . . in its capacity as trustee, executor, administrator, or guardian, or custodian under a uniform gifts to minors act."
- (a)(2)—funds "consisting solely of assets of retirement, pension, profit sharing, stock bonus or other trusts that are exempt from Federal income tax."

OCC guidance on these funds refers to them as "A1" and "A2" funds corresponding to the above definitions in section 9.18(a).[76]

The OTS regulations are set out at 12 CFR § 550.26 and provide that savings associations may invest funds of a fiduciary account "in a manner consistent with applicable law," including CIFs in accor-

---

73. *Id.*, at 937.
74. ICI v. Clarke, 793 F2d 220 (9th Cir.), *cert. denied*, 479 U.S. 939 (1986), and ICI v. Clarke, 789 F2d 175 (2nd Cir.), *cert. denied*, 479 U.S. 940 (1986).
75. In 12 CFR Part 9, "Fiduciary Activities of National Banks."
76. "Collective Investment Funds," Comptroller's Handbook, October, 2005.

dance with the OCC regulations at 12 CFR § 9.18. The OTS rules also provide that "bank" and "national bank" as used in § 9.18 shall be deemed to include a federal savings association.[77]

Registration Requirements

According to the OCC Handbook on "Collective Investment Funds," CIFs are not required to register their securities under the Securities Act or their fund under the Investment Company Act if they qualify for the specific exemptions under the Securities Act and exclusions under the Investment Company Act. A1 funds will qualify for these exemptions "if each of the underlying relationships is created 'for a bona fide fiduciary purpose' rather than as 'vehicles for general investment by the public.' "[78]

The securities in CIFs that accept IRAs must be registered under the Securities Act and the fund registered as investment companies under the Investment Company Act. CIFs that accept Keogh (HR 10) plans must also register under these Acts. The OCC points out that SEC Rule 180[79] provides a narrow "sophisticated investor" exception from Securities Act registration for CIFs that accept Keogh plans. Exempt employers include law and accounting firms that meet certain qualifications.[80] Banks might be well advised to consult with experienced securities counsel in these cases.

The provisions of the Securities and Investment Company Acts, as amended by GLBA that exclude certain interests in common and collective trust fund from the definitions of "securities" and "investment companies," respectively, are set out in the next section.

Exclusions—Securities and Investment Company Acts

GLBA, as noted above, adopted amendments to the Securities and other Acts to end the disparity between savings associations and banks with respect to registration of common trust funds.

---

77. See also "Introduction to Common and Collective Funds," OTS Trust and Asset Management Handbook, Section 880.
78. Pp 5–6.
79. 17 CFR § 240.180.
80. OCC Handbook, *op. cit.*, pps 61–62.

Exclusion as "Investment Companies"

GLBA amended sections 2(a)(5) and 3(c)(3) of the Investment Company Act to:

- include savings associations within the definition of bank, and
- exclude banks and savings associations from the definition of "investment company."

GLBA also amended that Act to exclude common or similar trust funds maintained by banks and savings associations from the definition of "investment company" if the fund is employed by the bank solely as an aid to the administration of trusts, estates, and other accounts created for a fiduciary purpose, and so long as:

- the funds are not advertised or offered for sale to the general public except in connection with the bank's ordinary advertising of fiduciary services; and
- the fees and fees expenses of the funds are consonant with fiduciary principles in applicable federal and state trust laws.

Section 3(c)(11) of the Act excludes from the definition of "investment companies" certain collective trusts, including employee's stock bonus, pension, or profit-sharing trusts that are qualified employee benefit plans under the Internal Revenue Code. As noted above, banks seeking exclusion under this section of collective funds consisting of IRAs and Keogh plans should consult with counsel since the grounds for exclusion are extremely narrow.

Exclusion as "Securities"

GLBA amended section 3(a)(2) of the Securities Act to exempt from registration any common trust fund or similar funds that are excluded as investment companies under the Investment Company Act.

Section 3(a)(12)(A) of the Exchange Act was also amended to include interests in any common trust fund that is exempt under the Investment Company Act as an exempt securities under that Act.

Securities Registration and Reporting under State Laws

State regulation of securities offerings, which began in Kansas in 1911, was preserved by Congress in the Securities Act of 1933. This dual system, which resulted in duplication of filings and added expenses for many issuers, was substantially altered in 1996 by the National Securities Markets Improvement Act of 1996 ("NSMIA").[81]

NSMIA amended Section 18 of the Securities Act[82] to preempt state "blue-sky" registration and review of specified "covered" securities and offerings. Offerings of these covered securities are primarily subject to federal regulation. Offerings of securities that are not covered securities continue to be subject to the dual system of federal-state regulation, including registration and review.

Covered Securities

These securities, defined in section 18(b) of the Act, include:

- "nationally traded securities"—these are securities listed or authorized for listing, on the New York Stock Exchange or American Stock Exchange, listed on the National Market System of the Nasdaq Stock Market, or listed, or authorized for listing (as determined by Rule 146), in Tier I of the Pacific Exchange, Tier I of the Philadelphia Stock Exchange, and on the Chicago Board Options Exchange;
- the Pacific Exchange, Tier I of the Philadelphia Stock Exchange, and on the Chicago Board Options Exchange;
- securities that are equal in seniority or senior to nationally traded securities—these include debt securities and preferred stock that are senior to these listed securities but do not include asset-backed and mortgage-backed securities;

---

81. The discussion in this section is based in the 1997 SEC publication: "Report on the Uniformity of State Regulatory Requirements for Offerings of Securities That Are Not 'Covered Securities' " Pursuant to Section 102(b) of [NSMIA], Public Law 104-290 (October 11, 1996).
82. 15 SC 77r.

- securities that are sold in transactions that are exempt from registration under sections 4(2) [private placements] and 4(4) [brokers' execution of customer's orders] of the Securities Act;
- securities of companies that report under sections 13 or 15(d) of the Exchange Act that are sold in exempt transactions under section 4(1) of the Securities Act [transactions by any person other than an issuer, underwriter, or dealer] or section 4(3) [certain transactions by dealers acting as underwriters];
- securities that are sold in a transaction that is exempt from registration under section 3(a) of the Securities Act, *other than* securities that are exempt under section 3(a)(4) [certain tax exempt religious, educational, charitable organizations] or 3(a)(11) [intrastate offerings] and certain municipal securities in the state in which the issuer of such security is located;
- securities issued by an investment company registered under the Investment Company Act of 1940; and
- securities that are offered or sold to "qualified purchasers," as defined by the Commission.

Rights Retained by States under Section 18

State securities agencies retain the authority under section 18 to conduct the following activities respect to covered securities:

- conduct of investigations and bringing enforcement actions relating to covered securities with respect to fraud or unlawful conduct by a broker or dealer;
- requiring the filing of any document filed by the issuer with the Commission plus annual or periodic reports of the value of securities sold or offered to persons located in the state; and
- collection of filing or registration fees relating to securities transactions with respect to filings (except for those relating to listed securities) and to suspend the offer and sale of securities within a state as a result of the failure to submit a required filing or fee.

Securities That Are Not "Covered Securities"

Securities that are not preempted by section 18 of the Securities Act include the following:

- securities traded on the Nasdaq SmallCap system or quoted on the NASD OTC Bulletin Board system;
- securities listed on regional exchanges;

- various debt securities of non-listed issuers, including asset-backed and mortgage-backed securities;
- securities issued in private placements under section 4(2) of the Securities Act that do not meet the requirements of Rule 506 under Regulation D;
- securities issued in Rule 504 and 505 offerings under Regulation D; and
- securities issued under Regulation A.

Exemptions under State Laws

The study reports that 41 states have adopted or substantially adopted with modifications the Uniform Securities Act of 1956 (the "Uniform Act"), which provides for exemption from registration of both exempt securities and exempt transactions.

Examples of exempt securities under the Uniform Act include:

- securities issued by banks or savings institutions;
- securities listed or approved for listing on the New York Stock Exchange (the "NYSE"), the American Stock Exchange (the "AMEX"), or the Midwest Stock Exchange;
- securities issued by an organization formed for religious, charitable, or other purposes, if certain conditions are met; and
- an investment contract issued in connection with an employee benefit plan if notice is provided to the state securities commission.

Examples of transactional exemptions under the Uniform Act include:

- an offer or sale of a security to specified purchasers, including banks, savings institutions, and institutional buyers;
- any transaction pursuant to an offer to not more than 10 persons in the state during any 12-month period, if certain conditions are met; and
- any transaction pursuant to an offer to existing security holders of the issuer, if certain conditions are met, including advance notice to the state securities commission.

The study summarizes further progress that the state had made at the time of its publication (1997) under the auspices of the North American Securities Administrators Association toward achieving uniformity in the regulation of securities offerings.

Conclusion

The controversy between the banking agencies and the SEC on the broker rules that is discussed in this chapter can be illustrated by the phrase "salesman's stake." It appears in *ICI v. Camp*, which was brought under the Glass-Steagall Act, as well as in the SEC's 2001 interim final broker rules, which construes provisions in the Exchange Act.

This phrase reflects the principle that different kinds of disclosures are required by a person whose compensation is based on the volume of sales of a product than are required when a person is offering a service for a fee. This issue is at the heart of the many restrictions proposed by the SEC in Regulation B.

The resolution of the salesman's stake issue in *Camp* and the subsequent Glass-Steagall Act cases discussed in the chapter was relatively simple in that the court was considering the legality of a single, innovative product.

GLBA, by contrast, carves out over 20 activities, some with detailed variations, most of which are summarized in the chapter, in which banks may engage without registration as a broker dealer. It is, therefore, not surprising that the broker issue has proven difficult to resolve.

CHAPTER **11**

Capital

Congress and the banking agencies place a high priority on the maintenance of adequate levels of regulatory capital by banks and savings associations. Institutions that slip below minimum capital requirements are subject to increasingly severe statutory restrictions, including higher deposit insurance premiums and limitations on branching.

The Federal Reserve Board's examination manual illustrates this priority:

> The primary function of capital is to support the bank's operations, act as a cushion to absorb unanticipated losses and declines in asset values that could otherwise cause the bank to fail, and provide protection to uninsured depositors and debt holders in the case of liquidation.[1]

The Fed adds that capital adequacy—the "C" in a bank's composite CAMELS rating—is the component of that rating "that triggers the most regulatory action" from the agencies. (CAMELS ratings are discussed in Chapter 3.)

Background

What Is Capital?

One accounting text defines *capital* as "the residual interest in assets of an entity after deducting its liabilities."[2] Another defines capital as

---

1. *Commercial Bank Examination Manual*, Federal Reserve Board, Section 3020.1, p. 1.
2. *GAAP 2002*, John Wiley & Sons, p. 733.

assets that have no offsetting liability on the bank's balance sheet; that is, capital is money that the bank does not owe anyone. If an entity is liquidated, capital is "what's left after all of its assets have been sold and its creditors paid." For going concerns, capital, much like a personal savings account, allows the business to absorb losses without becoming insolvent.

GAAP Capital Standards for Public Companies

Companies that register securities under the federal securities laws, including bank and savings and loan holding companies and institutions that register independently, are required to file financial reports with the SEC that are presented in accordance with generally accepted accounting principles (GAAP).[3] These are principles that have been developed over several decades by the private sector and the SEC to ensure the fair and efficient functioning of capital markets.

GAAP is designed to provide a workable, transparent, and accurate representation of the economic condition of public companies. It is also designed to provide comparable statements of financial results across the entire spectrum of domestic capital markets so that investors, creditors, and other parties can make meaningful comparisons of earnings, assets, stockholders' equity, and other financial data of individual companies.

The most authoritative accounting principles are those developed by the Financial Accounting Standards Board (FASB), a private organization established in 1974. FASB pronouncements are formally recognized as GAAP by the SEC.

Regulatory Capital for Depository Institutions

The SEC's priority in enforcing the securities laws is ensuring complete and accurate disclosures by registrants. The agency's rules do not impose minimum capital requirements on registered companies.

Insured depository institutions, however, *are* required by banking agency rules to hold minimum levels of *regulatory* capital.

---

3. Section 19(b)(1) of the Securities Act of 1933 (12 USC 77a, *et seq.*), section 77s(b)(1); section 13(b)(2) of the Securities Exchange Act of 1934 (12 USC 78a, *et seq.*), section 78m(b)(2).

Regulatory Capital versus GAAP Capital

Insured depository institutions and their holding companies are required to file quarterly reports of financial results with their primary federal regulator. Financial data in these reports is filed in accordance with GAAP, and the balance sheets in these reports reflect the institution's GAAP capital, or stockholders' equity.

Regulatory capital standards for banks and savings associations are based on GAAP as modified to meet supervisory requirements. Bank holding companies with assets of $150 million or more are subject to similar standards.[4]

The Federal Reserve describes the different purposes of GAAP capital and regulatory capital as follows:

> Although GAAP informs the definition of regulatory capital, the Board is not bound to use GAAP accounting concepts in its definition of [regulatory capital components] because regulatory capital requirements, *are regulatory constructs designed to ensure the safety and soundness of banking organizations* not accounting designations established to ensure the transparency of financial statements. In this regard, the definition of [certain regulatory capital components] since the Board adopted its risk-based capital rule in 1989 has differed from GAAP equity in a number of ways. The Board has determined that these differences are consistent with its responsibility for ensuring the soundness of the capital bases of banking organizations under its supervision. These differences are not differences between regulatory reporting and GAAP accounting requirements, but rather are differences only between the definition of equity for purposes of GAAP and the definition of [regulatory capital] for purposes of the Board's regulatory capital requirements for banking organizations.[5] (emphasis added)

These regulatory capital requirements, as noted below, require institutions to hold specified amounts of capital as a percentage of assets that are weighted according to the risks they pose to the institution.

Source of Current Regulatory Capital Standards

Current regulatory capital standards have evolved from principles developed by the Committee on Banking Regulations and Supervisory Practices (Supervisory Committee) of the Bank for International

---

4. S&L holding companies file quarterly reports with OTS but are not subject to formal regulatory capital requirements.
5. Risk-Based Capital Standards: Trust Preferred Securities and the Definition of Capital, Final rule, 70 FR 11827, 11828 (March 10, 2005).

Settlements (BIS) in Basel, Switzerland. The committee is comprised of representatives of the central banks of the Group of Ten (G-10) countries,[6] who meet on a regular basis in Basel. Founded in 1930, the BIS "is an international organization [that] fosters cooperation among central banks and other agencies in pursuit of monetary and financial stability. Its banking services are provided exclusively to central banks and international organizations."[7]

The oil crisis of the 1970s and later developments prompted the Bank to focus its attention on the issue of regulatory supervision of internationally active banks. International risk-based capital standards were endorsed in 1988 by the Governors of the central banks of the G-10 countries and are referred to as the Basel Capital Accord, or "Basel I."

Former Federal Reserve Board Vice Chairman Roger W. Ferguson, Jr. notes that the Supervisory Committee "has no formal authority":

> Rather, it works to develop broad supervisory standards and promote best practices in the expectation that each country will implement the standards in ways most appropriate to its circumstances. Agreements are developed by consensus, but decisions about which parts of the agreements to implement and how to implement them are left to each nation's regulatory authorities.[8]

One of the purposes of the Basel I Accord was the development of uniform capital measures for large internationally active banks in order to enhance the soundness of the international banking system, among other things, and to reduce competitive inequalities among these banks that result from differences in international capital standards.

In practice, Basel I, which has been adopted in various versions in over 100 countries, "has been applied beyond the largest institutions to cover most banking organizations worldwide."[9]

As the size and complexity of large banking organizations increased after 1988, bank regulators realized that more sophisticated

---

6. These countries are Belgium, Canada, France, Germany, Italy, Japan, Luxembourg, the Netherlands, Spain, Sweden, Switzerland, the U.K., and the U.S.

7. BIS website: http://www.bis.org/.

8. *Capital Standards for Banks: The Evolving Basel Accord*, FEDERAL RESERVE BULLETIN, Sept., 2003, p. 396. This article is based on testimony by Vice Chairman Ferguson on June 18 and 19, 2003 before the Senate Committee on Banking, Housing and Urban Affairs and the House Committee on Financial Services, respectively.

9. Ferguson, *op. cit.*, p. 401.

capital standards were needed. As a result, the Basel Committee began work on a second round of international capital standards, known as "Basel II." A proposed Basel II Framework was approved for comment by the BIS on April 29, 2003. When implemented, Basel II will only apply to the largest banking organizations in the U.S. and other organizations that volunteer to be governed by its standards. Basel I, including any modifications that may be made to it in the future, will continue to apply to all other institutions. The proposed Framework and the activities of the U.S. bank regulators with respect to it are discussed at the end of this chapter.

Capital Standards for Banks and Savings Associations

Structure of Regulatory Capital

The Basel I standards are based on the following two capital ratios:

- *The risk-based capital ratio.* This ratio is designed to reflect the credit risks posed to an institution by various categories of assets in its portfolio and is expressed in terms of capital required against a percentage of "risk-weighted assets," that is, total assets after their face amounts have been adjusted to reflect their credit risk.

  Current capital regulations require an institution to hold minimum regulatory capital equal to 8% of its risk-weighted assets. At least 50% of this amount must consist of "Tier 1" capital components with the reminder held in "Tier 2" capital, as explained below.

  Under this system, lesser amounts of capital are required to be held against lower-risk assets. Bank assets are divided into four risk-weighted categories of zero, 20, 50, and 100%. The minimum amount of capital required for assets in each category is determined by multiplying the amount of the assets in each category by their risk weight and then by 8%.

  For example, the capital required to be held against a $1000 loan in the 50% risk-weight category would be $40 ($1,000 × .5 = $500 × .08 = $40). Figure 11.1 provides additional examples.

Figure 11.1
Risk-Based Capital Ratios

Calculation of minimum regulatory capital requirements for ABC Bank, which has total assets of $11,000 divided among the four risk-weight categories as noted in column A.

A Assets	B Risk Weight Category	C Asset as Risk Weighted	D Minimum Capital Ratio	E Minimum Capital Requirement
$ 3,000 ×	100% =	$3,000 ×	.08 =	$240
5,000 ×	50% =	2,500 ×	.08 =	200
2,000 ×	20% =	400 ×	.08 =	32
1,000 ×	zero % =	0 ×	.08 =	0
$11,000		$5,900 ×	.08 =	$472

Total assets (Column A):	$11,000	
Total risk-weighted assets (Column C):	$5,900	
Minimum capital required under risk-based ratio (Column E):	$472	($5,900 × .08)
Minimum Tier 1 capital required	$236	($5,900 × .04)

Leverage ratio (minimum Tier 1 capital to total assets):

Required Tier 1 capital at leverage ratios of 3% and 4%			**Minimum Tier 2 capital (total capital of $472 minus required tier 1 capital)**
at 3%:	$330 ($11,000 × .03)	$142	($472 – 330)
at 4%:	440 (11,000 × .04)	32	(472 – 440)

The regulators make it clear that institutions are expected to maintain capital in excess of the 8% minimum requirement, and the ability of institutions to engage in many activities is dependent on their being "well capitalized," which requires total regulatory capital of 10% or more, Tier 1 capital of 6% or more and a leverage ratio of 5% or more. (Supervisory capital categories are discussed below under Prompt Corrective Action.)

- *Leverage ratio.* This ratio requires institutions to hold a minimum amount of Tier 1 capital as a percentage of *total assets*. This ratio is 3% for institutions with a CAMELS rating of 1 that are not experiencing or anticipating significant growth and 4% or more for others, depending on their financial condition and risk profile as determined by the institution's primary federal regulator.

The leverage ratio is designed, among other things, to curb excessive leveraging of capital, thereby preventing institutions from reducing their risk-based capital to dangerously low levels by investing in assets that require little or no capital to be held against them. The ratio is also designed to provide a relatively high capital level to compensate for the fact that the Basel I standards do not include a component for interest rate risk, market risk, and other risks faced by depository institutions.

Calculation of Regulatory Capital

Regulatory capital is GAAP capital (assets minus liabilities) that has been modified to meet supervisory requirements. This modification is accomplished by subtracting assets that are not useful, or are unreliable, for supervisory purposes, and adding non-GAAP assets that regulators regard as being available to absorb losses.

Regulatory capital is divided into two categories, Tier 1 (Core) capital and Tier 2 (Supplemental) capital. Tier 1 capital is comprised of assets that are the most stable and reliable forms of capital, such as common stock and retained earnings. Tier 2 capital is made up of capital items that do not qualify as Tier 1, including assets that are more volatile or less liquid than Tier 1 assets. These assets include certain subordinated debt, loan loss reserves, and certain "cumulative preferred stock," which is preferred stock on which dividends that have not been paid accumulate and must be paid before the stock can be liquidated. Additional information on components of Tier 1 and Tier 2 capital are found in Figure 11.3 at the end of the chapter.

The calculation of an institution's regulatory capital can be seen as a process of "conversion" of its GAAP capital to regulatory capital. This conversion procedure is the same for both institutions.

Risk Weight Categories

The Basel Accord recognizes the obvious fact that that some assets pose greater credit risks to banks and savings associations than do others. Consumer and residential mortgage loans, for example, pose more credit risk to an institution than U.S. government bonds, and more capital is required to back these loans than government bonds.

The risk-based system divides assets into five risk-weight categories with varying degrees of risk. These risk-weight categories and typical assets within each category are as follows:

- *Zero percent category:* Cash; gold bullion; obligations of the U.S. Treasury; obligations of central governments of countries that are members of the Organization for Economic Cooperation and Development (OECD countries); deposit reserves and other balances at Federal Reserve Banks; and securities issued by, and other direct claims on, the U.S. government or its agencies, or the central government of an OECD country.[10]
- *20 percent category:*
  - Includes securities of Government Sponsored Enterprises (GSEs)[11] and general obligation claims on, or portions of claims guaranteed by the full faith and credit of states or other political subdivisions of the U.S. or other OECD countries.
  - This category also includes certain privately issued mortgage-backed securities, e.g., collateralized mortgage obligations (CMOs) and real estate mortgage investment conduits (REMICs), if the underlying pool is comprised solely of mortgage-related securities issued by Ginnie Mae, Fannie Mae, and Freddy Mac, and claims on, or guaranteed by, official multilateral lending institutions or regional development institutions in which the U.S. government is a shareholder or contributing member.[12]

---

10. OECD countries are: Australia, Austria, Belgium, Canada, Denmark, Czech Republic, Finland, France, Germany, Greece, Hungary, Iceland, Ireland, Italy, Japan, Korea, Luxembourg, Mexico, Netherlands, New Zealand, Norway, Poland, Portugal, Slovak Republic, Spain, Sweden, Switzerland, Turkey, the U.K., and the U.S.

11. These agencies were originally established or chartered by the federal government to serve public purposes specified by the U.S. Congress, whose obligations are not explicitly guaranteed by the full faith and credit of the U.S. government. These agencies include the Federal Home Loan Mortgage Corporation (Freddie Mac), the Federal National Mortgage Association (Fannie Mae, the Government National Mortgage Association (Ginnie Mae), the Farm Credit System, the Federal Home Loan Bank (FHLB) System, and the Student Loan Marketing Association (SLMA). GSE claims include capital stock in an FHL Bank that is held by banks and savings associations as a condition of membership in the FHLB System.

12. These include the International Bank for Reconstruction and Development (World Bank), the Inter-American Development Bank, the Asian Development Bank, the African Development Bank, the European Investments Bank, the International Monetary Fund and the Bank for International Settlements (BIS).

- *50 percent category:*
  - First mortgages on 1- to 4-family residential properties, either owner-occupied or rented, and on multifamily residential properties that meet certain criteria; loans to builders with substantial project equity for construction of 1- to 4-family homes that have been presold to buyers who have firm mortgage commitments.
  - Privately issued mortgage-backed securities, i.e., those that do not carry the guarantee of a government or government-sponsored agency, if they meet other underwriting criteria.
  - Revenue bonds of states or other political subdivisions of the U.S. and other OECD countries; and the credit equivalent amount of certain derivative contracts that do not qualify for inclusion in a lower risk category.
- *100 percent category:*
  - Most assets not included in the above categories are assigned to this category, which includes commercial, consumer, and residential property loans that do not qualify for a lower risk weight. Federal Reserve documents say the bulk of the assets typically found in a loan portfolio would be assigned to the 100% category.[13]
  - Certain claims on non-OECD banks and central governments; investments in fixed assets, premises, and other real estate owned; common and preferred stock of corporations, including stock acquired for debts previously contracted; all stripped mortgage-backed securities and similar instruments.
  - Industrial-development bonds and similar obligations issued under the auspices of states or political subdivisions of the U.S. and other OECD countries.

Off-balance-sheet Assets

Regulatory capital is required to be held against off-balance-sheet transactions. These assets include loan commitments, letters of credit, sales with recourse and repurchase agreements, and other obligations that are contingent on future events or actions of another party.

In most cases, the capital requirements of off-balance-sheet items are calculated in two steps. First, the face amount of the item is

---

13. Regulation H (12 CFR Part 208), Appendix A.

multiplied by one of four credit-conversion factors, or percentages, which are designed to "reflect the risk characteristics of the activity in terms of an on-balance-sheet equivalent." This credit equivalent is then assigned to its proper on-balance-sheet risk weight category for a determination of the amount of capital it requires.[14]

Example: Performance letters of credit have a conversion factor of 50%. Loans for construction of a personal residence that are subject to a legally binding sales contract and meet certain other requirements are in the 50% risk-weight category.

The capital amount for a performance letter of credit with a face amount of $100,000 on a loan of $100,000 for completion of construction of an individual's residence would be calculated as follows:

- Balance sheet equivalent: $50,000 ($100,000 × 50% conversion factor)
- Risk weighted amount: $25,000 ($50,000 balance sheet equivalent × 50% risk weight factor)
- Required capital: $ 2,000 ($25,000 × .08 capital rate)

Conversion Factors

Following are examples of items in each of the five off-balance-sheet conversion factor categories:

- *Zero percent:* Unused portions of certain commitments with an original maturity of one year or less or which are cancelable at any time, provided a separate credit decision is made before each drawing under the facility. Unused portions of lines of credit on retail credit cards and related plans are considered short-term commitments if the institution has the unconditional right to cancel the line of credit at any time.
- *10 percent:* Unused portions of eligible asset-backed commercial paper liquidity facilities with an original maturity of one year or less.
- *20 percent:* Short-term, self-liquidating, trade-related contingencies that arise from the movement of goods. These contingencies include commercial letters of credit and other documentary letters of credit collateralized by the underlying shipments. Trade-related contingencies, such as short-term, self-liquidating

---

14. A schedule of credit conversion factors for off-balance-sheet items is set out at 12 CFR Part 3, Appendix A, Table 2.

instruments, including commercial letters of credit used to finance the movement of goods and collateralized by the underlying shipment.
- *50 percent:* Transaction-related contingencies, including performance bonds, bid bonds, warranties, and performance-based standby letters of credit related to a particular transaction; unused portions of certain commercial and consumer credit commitments, including home equity lines of credit, overdraft protection, and revolving credit, with an original maturity exceeding one year.
- *100 percent:* Risk participations purchased in bankers' acceptances; forward agreements and other contingent obligations with legally binding agreements to purchase assets at a specified future date; loans by a bank of its own securities and certain loans of a customer's securities as agent of the customer with the customer indemnified against loss.

Tier 3 Capital—Market Risk

In 1995, the Basel Supervisory Committee amended Basel I to add a market risk measure to the regulatory capital of banks engaged in substantial trading activities.

The Federal Reserve, OCC, and FDIC amended their risk-based capital standards in 1996 to incorporate a "Tier 3" capital measure for market risk for banks and bank holding companies whose trading activity equals 10% or more of its total assets or equals $1 billion or more.[15]

An institution subject to the final rule must hold capital to support its exposure to general market risk arising from fluctuations in interest rates, equity prices, foreign exchange rates, and commodity prices and its exposure to specific risk associated with certain debt and equity positions.

Capital also must be held against specific risks, which refers to changes in the market value of specific positions resulting, for example, from insolvency or other adverse changes in the financial condition of counterparties or issuers of a particular instrument. These risks include potential losses caused by mismatches in maturities of

---

15. *Risk-Based Capital Standards: Market Risk,* Joint Final rule, 61 FR 47357 (September 6, 1996).

assets and liabilities, the timing of their repricing, and shifts in indexes used in interest rate swaps and other transactions.

These banks must measure their market risk "using their internal value-at-risk (VaR) measurement model and, subject to parameters in the market risk rule, hold sufficient levels of capital to cover the exposure."[16]

Tier 3 capital generally "consists of short-term subordinated debt subject to certain criteria, including a lock-in provision that prevents the issuer from repaying the debt even at maturity if the issuer's risk-based capital ratio [would be] less than 8.0% following the payment."[17]

The regulations include a formula for integrating Tier 3 capital into the bank's Tier 1 and Tier 2 holdings.

Other Capital Elements

The agencies' regulatory capital standards deal with several other aspects of capital that are not covered here. These include securitizations and sales with recourse, direct credit substitutes, and residual interests.

Regulatory Capital for Holding Companies

Bank Holding Companies

Bank holding companies (BHCs) that are publicly held must register their securities with the SEC and report their financial results in accordance with GAAP, as discussed in Chapter 10. In addition, *all* BHCs with assets of $150 million or more are required to meet regulatory capital standards, which differ in certain respects from the regulatory standards applied to individual banks. These companies report their quarterly financial data in Bank Holding Company Performance Reports (BHCPRs) Form FR Y-6.

Following are some of the principal differences in regulatory capital standards for BHCs.

---

16. Federal Reserve Board, *Commercial Bank Examination Manual*, section 3020.1, p. 7. For further information on VaR and related issues, see Risk Glossary, http://www.riskglossary.com, which provides links to additional information, and Michael Gordy, *A risk-factor model foundation for risk-based bank capital rules*, Journal of Financial Intermediation, July, 2003, p. 119.

17. Joint Final rule, *op. cit.*, p. 47359.

Cumulative Preferred Stock and Trust Preferred Securities

Up to 25% of BHC Tier 1 capital can be comprised of qualifying *cumulative* perpetual preferred stock and related surplus that is issued directly by the BHC or which consists of minority interests in consolidated subsidiaries.

In 1996, the Federal Reserve expanded the definition of cumulative preferred stock to include trust preferred securities (TPS), which could count as capital within this 25% Tier 1 sublimit. These instruments, which are issued by a special purpose entity (SPE) created by the BHC, qualified under GAAP at that time as minority interests in a consolidated subsidiary and therefore as regulatory capital. TPS are discussed in greater detail below.

In 2003, FASB issued two Financial Interpretations, FIN 46, and a revision, FIN 46R, that, in effect, prevented BHCs from treating SPEs that issue trust preferred securities as consolidated entities on their balance sheets. This "deconsolidation" requirement prevented TPS from being counted as minority interests in a consolidated subsidiary—thereby preventing TPS from being counted as regulatory capital under then-applicable Federal Reserve rules.

TPS and Restricted Core Capital Elements

In March 2005,[18] the Federal Reserve issued final regulations that, among other things, provided that TPS could continue to be counted as regulatory capital in limited amounts, despite the FASB Interpretations.[19] The new rule combined these securities with other cumulative preferred stock in a capital sublimit—called "restricted core capital elements"—that is, restricted to 25% of the following core capital elements:

- qualifying common stockholders' equity and noncumulative perpetual preferred stock,
- qualifying minority interest in the equity accounts of consolidated subsidiaries, and
- qualifying trust preferred securities.

---

18. Federal Reserve Board, *Risk-Based Capital Standards: Trust Preferred Securities and the Definition of Capital,* Final rule, 70 FR 11827 (March 10, 2005).

19. It is in the preamble to this final rule that the Federal Reserve made the statement on the different purposes served by GAAP and regulatory capital rules, which is quoted above.

Amounts of qualifying cumulative perpetual preferred stock and qualifying trust preferred securities in excess of this limit may be included in Tier 2 capital.

The 2005 final rules provide that after March 31, 2009, additional components will be added to "restricted core capital elements," which will then consist of the following:

- qualifying cumulative preferred stock (including related surplus);
- minority interest related to qualifying cumulative preferred stock issued by a consolidated U.S. depository institution or foreign bank subsidiary (Class B minority interest);
- minority interest related to common shareholders equity or perpetual preferred stock issued by a consolidated subsidiary that is neither a U.S. depository institution nor a foreign bank (Class C minority interest); and
- qualifying trust preferred securities.

These interests are limited to 25% of the sum of all core capital elements, including these restricted core capital elements themselves, minus goodwill and any associated deferred tax liabilities.

Internationally active BHCs after March 31, 2009 "would be subject to a further limitation. In particular, the amount of restricted core capital elements (other than qualifying mandatory convertible preferred securities discussed below) that an internationally active BHC may include in Tier 1 capital must not exceed 15% of the sum of core capital elements (including restricted core capital elements), net of goodwill less any associated deferred tax liability."[20]

The Federal Reserve says until March 31, 2009, a BHC with restricted core capital elements in excess of these limits must consult with the agency to develop a plan for ensuring that it is not unduly relying on these elements in its capital base and, where appropriate, for reducing this reliance to ensure that the BHC meets these limits by that date.

Characteristics of Trust Preferred Securities

The Federal Reserve describes TPS and a typical TPS offering as follows:

---

20. *Ibid.*, p. 11830.

- TPS are undated cumulative preferred securities issued by a special purpose entity (SPE), usually a trust created by the BHC. The proceeds of the TPS are transferred to the BHC.
- The BHC owns all of the common stock of the SPE.
- The only asset of the SPE is a deeply subordinated note issued by the BHC that is senior only to the BHC's common and preferred stock.
- The note has terms that are generally the same as the TPS, except the note has a fixed maturity of 30 years.
- Dividends on the TPS can be deferred for 20 quarters.
- The failure of the BHC to pay the cumulative dividend owed to investors after the 20-quarter deferral causes an event of default and acceleration. This gives the investors the right to take over the subordinated note issued by the BHC and causes the note to become immediately due and payable.
- The Federal Reserve points out that "A key advantage of trust preferred securities to BHCs is that for tax purposes the dividends paid on trust preferred securities, unlike those paid on directly issued preferred stock, are a tax deductible interest expense. The Internal Revenue Service ignores the trust and focuses on the interest payments on the underlying subordinated note."[21]

Trust Preferred Securities as Capital

The Federal Reserve gives several reasons why it considers TPS capital for regulatory purposes, including "two key features . . . their long lives, approaching economic perpetuity, and their dividend deferral rights (deferral for 20 consecutive quarters) approaching economically indefinite deferral—are features that provide substantial capital support." Additional reasons include the following:

- While TPS are not equity capital and cannot forestall a BHC insolvency, they are able to absorb losses more widely than most other minority interests available to the BHC because the cash flow available from a deferred dividend payment can be deployed anywhere in the BHC's consolidated organization.
- TPS are widely traded, transparent, and well understood by the markets.

---

21. *Ibid.*, p. 11828.

- The favorable tax treatment of dividends lowers BHCs' cost of capital, and the inability to use this kind of funding would place an international BHC at a competitive disadvantage.
- Eliminating the ability to include trust preferred securities in Tier 1 capital would put BHCs at a disadvantage to domestic and foreign competitors. The agency noted that foreign competitors had issued as much as $125 billion of similar tax-efficient Tier 1 capital instruments.[22]

BHCs that are "internationally active" will be limited to 15% of certain Tier 1 capital elements.

Small BHC Policy Statement

This policy generally exempts small BHCs (those with consolidated assets of less than $150 million) from the Federal Reserve's risk-based capital and leverage capital guidelines. Instead, small BHCs generally apply the risk-based capital and leverage capital guidelines on a bank-only basis and must only meet a debt-to-equity ratio at the parent BHC level. As this book went to press in July 2006, the agency said it expected to issue supervisory guidance on this matter in the near future.[23]

Financial Holding Companies (FHCs)

FHCs are bank holding companies that have elected to engage in one or more of the new financial services activities authorized by the 1999 Gramm Leach Bliley Act (GLBA).[24] These new services include insurance and securities activities that were formerly prohibited under the Bank Holding Company Act (BHCA).

Congress made it clear in GLBA that while the Federal Reserve would be a kind of "umbrella agency" with respect to nonbank subsidiaries of both BHCs and FHCs to protect the safety of the holding company, the holding company's depository institution subsidiaries, and its securities, insurance, and other financial subsidiaries would continue to be regulated by their primary regulator as if the subsidiary were not in the holding company.

---

22. *Ibid.*, p. 11830.
23. *Ibid.*, p. 11834.
24. Pub. Law 106-102 (Nov. 12, 1999).

This principle of functional regulation extends to issues of capital adequacy. Section 5(c) of the BHCA (12 USC 1843(c)), as amended by GLBA, provides that the Federal Reserve may not, by regulation or otherwise, impose capital standards on a functionally regulated subsidiary of a BHC or FHC that is not a depository institution if the subsidiary meets the capital requirements of its primary, or "functional" regulator, which includes state insurance regulators for insurance companies, for example, and the SEC and state securities agencies for securities firms.

While acknowledging that it does not have the authority to issue separate capital requirements for an FHC (or BHC) subsidiary that is in compliance with the capital rules of its functional regulator, the agency made it clear that it will keep a sharp eye on risk profiles and capital levels of FHCs:

> The Federal Reserve will rely, to the fullest extent possible, on reports that an FHC or its subsidiaries are required to file with federal or state authorities (or self-regulatory organizations) or on reports that are prepared by [these] authorities.
>
> * * *
>
> The Federal Reserve is responsible for assessing consolidated capital for FHCs with the ultimate objective of protecting the insured depository institution subsidiaries from the effects of disruption in the nonbank portions of the organization.
>
> * * *
>
> As [bank holding companies], FHCs are subject to the Federal Reserve's holding company capital guidelines, which set forth minimum capital ratios that serve as tripwires for additional supervisory scrutiny and corrective action. The [agency] will review these requirements as they apply to FHCs and may, if warranted, adapt the manner in which they apply to FHCs that engage in a broad range of financial activities.[25]

S&L Holding Companies (S&LHCs)

The 1998 Basel Accord does not apply to S&LHCs, and, historically, these companies have not been subject to other formal quantitative regulatory capital standards. They are, however, required to file quarterly financial reports with the OTS on Form H-(b)11.

This lack of quantitative standards means examiners must determine the company's capital adequacy on a case-by-case basis. The

---

25. Federal Reserve *Bank Holding Company Supervision Manual,* sections. 3900.0.4.2.2 and 3900.0.4.2.3.

OTS requires examiners to conduct a "capital sufficiency/risk analysis," which includes measurement of the company's credit, market, funding, liquidity, and operational risks and evaluation of the company's internal risk management systems.

In evaluating capital on a cases-by-case basis, examiners must consider the following:

- *Debt levels*—including debt-to-equity ratios.
- *Capital quality and availability*—over-reliance on particular kinds of assets, such as deferred tax credits, intangible assets, and off-balance-sheet assets; the company's ability to raise capital if needed, access to capital markets, and capital-to-asset ratios.
- *Dividends*—including the ability of earnings to support the level of dividend payments.

Another set of conditions examiners must evaluate is the company's capital management and oversight. These conditions include:

- quality of management and risk management systems;
- stability, level, and direction of earnings;
- the effect of direct or indirect impact of inter-company transactions; and
- transactions with insiders (including loans, asset purchases and service contracts).

Examiners are required to rate a company's capital adequacy on a descending scale of "1" to "3." A "3" rating, for example, means that the company does not have sufficient capital to serve as a buffer for its own activities and those of its subsidiaries.[26]

Prompt Corrective Action

In 1991, the banking agencies were granted the power to impose increasingly severe sanctions on institutions whose capital levels fall below that of "well-capitalized," as defined in agency regulations. This authority, conferred by the FDIC Improvement Act of 1991

---

26. OTS, *Holding Company Handbook*, sec. 300.

(FDICIA),[27] creates four other levels of capital adequacy ranging from "adequately capitalized" to "critically undercapitalized."

These capital categories are defined in FDIC regulations[28] as follows:

- *Well capitalized*—the institution:
  - has total risk-based capital ratio of 10.0% or greater;
  - has Tier 1 risk-based capital ratio of 6.0% or greater;
  - has a leverage ratio of 5.0% or greater; and
  - is not subject to any written agreement, order, capital directive, or prompt corrective action directive requiring it to meet and maintain a specific capital level for any capital measure.
- *Adequately capitalized*—the institution:
  - has total risk-based capital ratio of 8.0% or greater;
  - has Tier 1 risk-based capital ratio of 4.0% or greater;
  - has a leverage ratio of 4.0% or greater; or
  - has a leverage ratio of 3.0% or greater if it has a CAMELS rating of 1; and
  - does not meet the definition of a well-capitalized bank.
- *Undercapitalized*—the institution has:
  - total risk-based capital ratio that is less than 8.0%;
  - Tier 1 risk-based capital ratio that is less than 4.0%; or
  - a leverage ratio that is less than 4.0%; or
  - a leverage ratio that is less than 3.0% if the bank is rated "1" under the CAMELS rating system in the most recent examination of the bank and is not experiencing or anticipating significant growth.
- *Significantly undercapitalized*—the institution has a:
  - total risk-based capital ratio that is less than 6.0%; or
  - Tier 1 risk-based capital ratio that is less than 3.0%; or
  - leverage ratio that is less than 3.0%.
- *Critically undercapitalized*—the institution has:
  - a ratio of tangible equity to total assets that is equal to or less than 2%. (Tangible equity is Tier 1 capital plus cumulative perpetual preferred stock (including related surplus), minus all intangible assets except mortgage servicing assets to the extent approved by the institution's primary federal regulator.

---

27. Public Law 102-242, Dec. 19, 1991, which added section 38 (12 USC 1831o) to the Federal Deposit Insurance Act (FDIA).

28. 12 CFR Part 35.

Restrictions

- *Well and adequately capitalized institutions:* May not pay dividends, with certain exceptions, or management fees if such payments would cause the institution to become undercapitalized.
- *Deposit insurance premiums:* Institutions that are less than well capitalized are subject to higher deposit insurance premiums than those that are well capitalized. (See Chapter 2).
- *Undercapitalized institutions:* The banking agencies must take the following actions against institutions that become undercapitalized:
  - restrict payment of capital distributions and management fees;
  - require the institution to develop a capital restoration plan;
  - monitor the condition of the institution and its capital plan;
  - restrict asset growth; and
  - require prior approval of new activities, including acquisitions, branching, and new lines of business.
- *Significantly undercapitalized institutions:* Institutions that reach this level of capitalization are subject to the above restrictions applicable to undercapitalized institutions. In addition, the institution may not pay bonuses to, or grant raises to, senior executive officers, until a capital restoration plan has been submitted and unless approved by the appropriate agency.

The Act provides that the agencies "shall take" the following actions unless they determine that such actions would not be effective:

- require the institution to be acquired by a depository institution holding company, or to combine with another insured depository institution, if one or more grounds exist for appointing a conservator or receiver for the institution;
- restrict transactions with affiliates; and
- restrict future interest rates paid on deposits to those prevailing in the institution's market area.

The agencies may also impose the following restrictions on institutions that become significantly under capitalized:

- restrict asset growth;
- require the institution or any of its subsidiaries to alter, reduce, or terminate any activity that the agency determines poses excessive risk to the institution;

- improve management by requiring one or more of the following:
  - ordering the election of new directors;
  - ordering the dismissal of directors or senior executive officers[29]; or
  - requiring the institution to employ qualified senior executive officers (who, if the agency so specifies, shall be subject to approval by the agency);
- prohibit deposits from correspondent banks, including renewals and rollovers of prior deposits;
- prohibit a bank holding company from making any capital distribution to a subsidiary institution without the prior approval of the Federal Reserve Board;
- require the institution to divest subsidiaries that are deemed to pose a significant risk to the institution;
- require the parent of the institution to:
  - divest a nondepository affiliate if the "appropriate Federal banking agency for that company"[30] determines that the affiliate posed a significant risk to the institution,
  - divest the institution itself if the appropriate Federal banking agency for that company determines that divestiture would improve the institution's financial condition and future prospects,
- require the institution to take any other action that the agency deems advisable.

Critically Undercapitalized Institutions

The appropriate banking agency is required to appoint a receiver for the institution within 90 days after it becomes critically undercapitalized. There are several exceptions to this requirement, including a case in which the agency and the FDIC finds that the institution has positive net worth, is viable, and is not expected to fail. The institution is also prohibited from making payments of principal and interest on its subordinated debt, except as permitted by the FDIC.

---

29. The Act provides that dismissal under this provision clause "shall not be construed to be a removal under section 1818 of this title" relating to agency enforcement powers under the banking laws.

30. The Board for bank holding companies and the OTS for S&L holding companies.

The FDIC is required "at a minimum" to prohibit the institution from doing any of the following without its prior written approval:

- entering into any material transaction other than in the usual course of business, including any investment, expansion, acquisition, sale of assets, or other similar action with respect to which the depository institution is required to provide notice to the appropriate banking agency;
- extending credit for any highly leveraged transaction;
- amending the institution's charter or bylaws, except to the extent necessary to carry out any other requirement of any law, regulation, or order;
- making any material change in accounting methods;
- engaging in any transaction that is a "covered transaction" under the transactions with affiliates rules of section 23A of the Federal Reserve Act[31] (see Chapter 7);
- paying excessive compensation or bonuses;
- paying interest on new or renewed liabilities at a rate that would increase the institution's weighted average cost of funds to a level significantly exceeding the prevailing rates of interest on insured deposits in the institution's normal market areas; and
- making any principal or interest payment on subordinated debt beginning 60 days after becoming critically undercapitalized.

Capital Restoration Plan

Institutions whose capital levels decline to undercapitalized or lower are required to submit a capital restoration plan to their regulator that must, among other things, specify the steps the institution will take to become adequately capitalized. The plan must include a guarantee executed by each company that controls the institution.[32] These companies must guarantee that the institution will comply with its capital plan until it is adequately capitalized for four consecutive calendar quarters. The Act provides, however, that the aggregate

---

31. 12 U.S.C. 371c.
32. The Fed says it will "consider on a case-by-case basis the appropriate type of guarantee for multi-tier holding companies, or . . . shell [holding] companies that have limited resources." (Federal Reserve Board, *Commercial Bank Examination Manual,* section 4133.1).

amount of liability for all companies that control a specific bank is limited to the lesser of 5% of the institution's total assets or the institution's capital shortfall.

Relation to Other Authority

The Act's provisions do not limit any authority of an appropriate banking agency or any state "to take action in addition to (but not in derogation of) that required under this section."

The FDIC regulations further state that nothing in the Act or its regulations "in any way limits the authority of the FDIC under any other provision of law to take supervisory actions to address unsafe or unsound practices, deficient capital levels, violations of law, unsafe or unsound conditions, or other practices."[33]

The Basel II Project

On June 26, 2004, the central bank governors and bank supervisors of the Group of Ten (G-10) countries endorsed the publication of a proposed amendment[34] to the 1998 Basel I capital standards that was drafted by the Basel Committee on Bank Supervision. This new document, known as the Revised Framework, or simply as Basel II, is designed to strengthen capital standards for large internationally active banks (large banks).

Reasons for Amendments to Basel I

Basel I, which has been adopted in more than 100 countries, "is widely viewed as having achieved its purpose of promoting financial stability and providing an equitable basis for competition among larger banks."[35] As larger banks grew in size, risk, and complexity, however, the Basel I standards became less useful as a measure of the capital adequacy of larger banks.

---

33. 12 CFR §325.101(d).
34. This document, *International Convergence of Capital Measurement and Capital Standards: A Revised Framework,* was approved by the Basel Committee on Bank Supervision on June 25, 2004.
35. Ferguson, *op. cit.* p. 396.

Many of these banks were developing new internal methodologies to measure the "real" economic risk underlying their increasingly complex activities, but these economic capital requirements bore little relationship to regulatory capital measured under the four risk categories of Basel I.

One of the results of the disparity between economic and regulatory capital standards is that banks could be regarded as well capitalized under regulatory capital rules while being undercapitalized on an economic basis. One of the dangers of this capital "arbitrage" is that:

> nominally high regulatory capital ratios can be used to mask the true level of insolvency probability. For example, consider the case where the bank's own risk analysis calls for a 15 percent internal economic capital assessment against its portfolio. If the bank actually holds 12 percent [regulatory] capital, it would, in all likelihood, be deemed to be "well-capitalized" in a regulatory sense, even though it might be undercapitalized in the economic sense.[36]

When this disparity was reversed and the economic risk of certain assets was less than regulatory capital requirements, banks, in order to avoid an artificially low return on capital, were induced to sell or securitize these assets to lower their regulatory capital requirements. Arbitrage in this situation often resulted in a more efficient allocation of assets and was not regarded as harmful by many regulators. The underlying concern, however, was that asset management should not be driven by artificial capital requirements.

Another problem with Basel I as a capital measure for large banks is that, until 1996, Basel I covered only credit risk and ignored other banking risks, such as market, operational, and interest rate risk. Market risk was added in 1996,[37] but there was a consensus among international bank regulators that if there were to be a convergence of capital standards for LCBOs across national boundaries (one of the goals of Basel I), international capital standards had to cover other risks.

---

36. Alan Greenspan, Chairman Federal Reserve Board, *The Role of Capital in Optimal Banking Supervision and Regulation,* Conference on Capital Regulation in the 21st Century, Federal Reserve Bank of New York, April 26, 1998.

37. Market risk was added as a component of Basel I in 1966 by the three banking agencies: *Risk-Based Capital Standards: Market Risk,* Joint Final rule, 61 FR 47357 (Sept. 6, 1996).

In addition, the measures of credit risk itself in Basel I was inadequate, as noted by Federal Reserve Chairman Alan Greenspan in 1998, because, among other things,

> The formal capital ratio requirements, because they do not flow from any particular insolvency probability standard, are, for the most part, arbitrary. All corporate loans, for example, are placed into a single 8 percent 'bucket'.[38]

In remarks a year later, the Chairman commented that:

> In recent years it has become clear that the largely arbitrary treatment of risks within [Basel I] has distorted risk-management practices and encouraged massive regulatory capital arbitrage. . . . That is, our rules have induced bank transactions that have the effect of reducing regulatory capital requirements more than they reduce a bank's risk position. Consequently, the fundamental credibility of regulatory capital standards as a tool for prudential oversight and prompt corrective action at the largest banking organizations has been seriously undermined.[39]

In addition to the above considerations, regulators were concerned about the systemic risk to the international financial system posed by the concentration of assets held by large banks and the increasing risk embedded in these assets. Federal Reserve Board Vice Chairman Ferguson testified in 2003 that the 20 largest U.S. LCBOs held 99% of the foreign assets and more than 65% of total assets held by U.S. banking organizations.[40]

The Basel II amendment revises the methodology for calculating credit risk and extends risk-based coverage to operational risk. Interest rate risk in the bank's loan portfolio is determined by bank supervisors on a case-by-case basis. In calculating capital, banks are given greater latitude to use their own internal rating systems to assess risk.

---

38. Before the Conference on Capital Regulation in the 21st Century, Federal Reserve Bank of New York, February 26, 1998.

39. *The evolution of bank supervision*, remarks of Chairman Greenspan before the American Bankers Association, Phoenix, Arizona, October 11, 1999.

40. *Capital Standards for Banks: The Evolving Basel Accord*, Federal Reserve *Bulletin*, Sept., 2003, based on testimony June 18 and 19, 2003 before the Senate Committee on Banking, Housing and Urban Affairs and House Committee on Financial Services, respectively.

In June, 2005, Federal Reserve Board Governor Susan Schmidt Bies summed up the major objectives of Basel II as including:

- creating a better link between minimum regulatory capital and risk;
- enhancing market discipline;
- supporting a level playing field in an increasingly integrated global financial system;
- establishing and maintaining a minimum capital cushion sufficient to foster financial stability in periods of adversity and uncertainty; and
- grounding risk measurement and management in actual data and formal quantitative techniques.

She said the last point is often overlooked and emphasized that,

> "[i]n a general sense, Basel II expands advanced risk-measurement and [risk]-management techniques from a set of tools used in an operating and control environment into the basis for making minimum regulatory capital more reflective of risk exposures. Since individual organizations employ various types of risk-management techniques, moving to Basel II as a minimum regulatory capital framework requires a certain degree of standardization so that risk measures can be reasonably compared across organizations and over time."[41] (emphasis added)

Next Steps

The Basel Committee suggested that provisions relating to credit and operating risks would be available for implementation by G-10 members at year end 2006, with the most technical approaches to risk measurement available for implementation Jan. 1, 2008. A one-year "parallel run" trial period to test Basel II standards would begin Jan. 1, 2006, and continue for two additional years for institutions using the advanced implementation approaches, which are discussed below (and which are the only approaches available to U.S. banking organizations) and one year for banks in other countries using the less advanced approaches. The G-10 representatives believed that regulators in nonmember countries should proceed at their own pace to implement these standards. As noted below, the transition

---

41. Remarks by Governor Susan Schmidt Bies, *Enhancing Risk Management under Basel II*, at the Risk USA 2005 Congress, Boston, Massachusetts, June 8, 2005.

period including a one-year parallel run has been rescheduled to start Jan. 1, 2008.

Implementation by U.S. Banking Agencies[42]

The U.S. bank regulators, who participated in the development of Basel II, have made it clear that while they remain committed to the principle of international capital standards, they will not adopt regulations implementing Basel II unless and until a) they have thoroughly analyzed its contents; b) incorporated any adjustments needed to address legitimate concerns of U.S. institutions; and c) are satisfied that the standards are consistent with safe and sound banking in this country.

The U.S. agencies had expected to issue a notice of proposed rulemaking (NPR) on the Revised Framework in mid-2005 with implementation proceeding in accordance with the G-10 schedule. The timing of the NPR, however, was delayed by the results of a study in which 26 institutions participated that was designed to be a "trial run" of the Basel II standards to show how they would affect minimum capital levels at U.S. banking institutions and for specific portfolios. (As noted at the end of this chapter, the Board released a draft notice of proposed rulemaking on March 30, 2006, which as of May, 2006 is being reviewed by the other three agencies.)

The preliminary results of this exercise, called the Fourth Quantitative Impact Study (QIS-4), showed that implementation of the Basel II framework by participants would have resulted in an average decrease in minimum required capital (MRC) of 15.5% from Basel I requirements and a median decrease in MRC of 26.3%. The study also showed a "significant dispersion of results across institutions and portfolio types," with regulatory capital changes ranging from an MRC increase of 55% for one institution to a decrease of 47% for

---

42. The discussion in this section is derived from statements of agency witnesses at hearings held May 11, 2005, before the Subcommittee on Financial Institutions and Consumer Credit and Subcommittee on Domestic and International Monetary Policy, Trade, and Technology of the House Committee on Financial Services on Basel II: Capital Changes in The U.S. Banking System and the Results of The Impact Study. Agency witnesses were Susan Schmidt Bies, Governor, Federal Reserve System; Thomas J. Curry Director, FDIC; Julie L. Williams, Acting Comptroller of the Currency; and Richard M. Riccobono, Acting Director, OTS.

another. Changes in capital requirements for specific portfolios varied from an average increase of 66% for credit card portfolios to an average decrease of 61.4% for residential mortgages.[43]

The agencies agree that it is highly unlikely that these results reflect differences in underlying risks at these institutions. They will conduct additional analysis to determine whether these figures result from one or more of the following:

- actual differences in risk in the portfolios of the participants;
- limitations in the structure of the QIS-4 study;
- variations in the participating institutions' internal rating systems;
- flaws in the Basel II framework that require adjustment.

On April 29, 2005, the agencies announced a delay in issuing a notice of proposed rulemaking (NPR) on the Revised Framework in order to better assess the results of the Study.[44]

In September 2005 the agencies issued a revised implementation schedule calling of an NPR during the first quarter of 2006 with the parallel run transition period to begin in January 2008.[45] The Release says the agencies will add prudential safeguards in the NPR to address concerns raised by the study.

The agencies released detailed summary findings of QIS-4 on February 24, 2006.[46] The release reiterated the agencies' intention to add prudential safeguards to the NPR and said that the experience gained during the parallel run "will provide both a better basis to assess the quantitative implications of and make adjustments to this framework, or make other changes to minimum risk-based regulatory capital requirements, as appropriate."

The parallel run would begin on January 1, 2008, during which institutions would calculate regulatory capital under both Basel I and Basel II standards. During the following three-year transition period, "institutions adopting the Basel II-based capital rules would be subject to a minimum three-year transition period during which the agencies would apply limits on the amount by which each institu-

---

43. *Basel II and the Potential Effect on Insured Institutions in the United States: Results of the Fourth Quantitative Impact Study,* CAPITAL AND ACCOUNTING NEWS, SUPERVISORY INSIGHTS, FDIC, Winter, 2005.
44. FDIC-PR-12-2005, April 29, 2005.
45. FDIC-PR-38-2005, Sept. 30, 2005.
46. FDIC-PR-20-2006, Feb. 24, 2006.

tion's risk-based capital could decline with the application of Basel II. These limits would be implemented through floors that are intended to be simpler in design and more conservative in effect than those set forth in Basel II." The schedule for the transitional period is shown in Figure 11.2 as follows:

Figure 11.2
Basel II Transition Period

Year	Transitional Arrangements
2008	Parallel Run
2009	95% floor
2010	90% floor
2011	85% floor

Application of Basel II to U.S. Banks

On April 29, 2003, the BSC approved for comment The New Basel Capital Accord (New Accord). On August 4, 2003, the U.S. banking agencies published two advance notices of proposed rule making (ANPRs) soliciting comments on draft supervisory guidance on the application of the proposed revisions in the New Accord to the risk-based capital standards in the U.S.

The first proposal (ANPR I) solicited comment on proposed rules that would implement Basel II.[47] The second (ANPR II) requested comment on draft supervisory guidance for implementing the advanced approaches to measuring credit risk and operational risk.[48]

Structure of the Revised Basel Framework

The efforts of the Basel Supervisory Committee to amend Basel I evolved into three interdependent components or "Pillars," which are:

- Pillar 1   Minimum capital requirements
- Pillar 2   Supervisory review process
- Pillar 3   Market discipline

---

47. *Risk-Based Capital Guidelines; Implementation of New Basel Capital Accord,* Advance notice of proposed rulemaking. 68 FR 45899 (August 4, 2003) (ANPR I).

48. Internal Ratings-Based Systems for Corporate Credit and Operational Risk Advanced Measurement Approaches for Regulatory Capital, Draft supervisory guidance with request for comment, 68 FR 45949 (August 4, 2003) (ANPR II).

Pillar 1—Minimum Capital Requirements

This component of Basel II preserves the existing minimum regulatory capital ratios of 8% of risk weighted assets, with eligible Tier 2 capital limited to 100% of Tier 1 capital.

Under the first pillar, a banking organization must calculate capital requirements for exposure to both credit risk and operational risk (and Tier 3 market risk for institutions with significant trading activity). Pillar 1, however, does not change the definition of assets that qualify as regulatory capital, or the methodology for determining capital charges for market risk. It does, however, change the way banks calculate risk weights for measuring credit risk and develops a methodology for calculating operational risk, which is a new risk component of Basel II.

ANPR II defines credit risk generally as the risk of loss arising from a contractual relationship between a creditor and a borrower. Operational risk is the risk of loss arising outside of a relationship between a creditor and a borrower.[49]

The Advanced Approaches

The New Accord provides three methodologies each for dealing with credit and operational risk. The first two are for smaller and medium-sized institutions. Since Basel II will only apply to the largest banking organizations in the U.S., the banking agencies propose to implement only the most advanced of the three alternatives for each risk category: the advanced internal-ratings based (A-IRB or IRB) approach for credit risk and the advanced measurement approach (AMA) for operational risk (collectively, the advanced approaches).

For purposes of implementing Basel II in the U.S., the banking agencies propose to apply the advanced approaches to three categorys of banks as described below:

- *Core banks*—banking organizations with total banking (and thrift) assets of $250 billion or more or with total on-balance-sheet foreign exposure of $10 billion or more. These organizations are subject to the mandatory application of Basel II, generally, and the advanced approaches in particular.
- *Opt-in banks*—banking organizations that are not subject to mandatory coverage by Basel II or the advance approaches,

---

49. *Id.*, p. 45983.

but that choose to adopt the advanced approaches on a voluntarily basis; and
- *General banks*—institutions that are not required to, and elect not to, be covered by Basel II.[50]

Nature of the Proposed Guidance

In the ANPRs, the agencies stress that the proposed guidance is designed to strike a balance between the opportunity for organizations to develop their own internal risk rating capabilities, subject to agency oversight to comply with overall agency guidance, and to ensure comparability of results among organizations subject to these standards. This procedure is in contrast to the application of the more formulaic measure of capital allocation involved in Basel I.

Some of the highlights of this guidance are summarized below.

Proposed Guidance for the IRB Approach

The supervisory guidance on advanced approaches in ANPR II applies to corporate credit, with guidance on retail and other credit risks to be issued at a later date. The guidance provides that the IRB approach "harnesses a bank's own risk rating and quantification capabilities" to "enhance the sensitivity of regulatory capital requirements to credit risk."

Banks will then have to modify their own credit risk management practices to provide an IRB framework that is acceptable to the agencies.[51] The ANPR II proposed guidance on credit risk includes the following:

> The accounting guidance for credit losses provides that creditors recognize credit losses when it is probable that they will be unable to collect all amounts due according to the contractual terms of a loan agreement. Credit losses may result from the creditor's own underwriting, processing, servicing or administrative activities along with the borrower's failure to pay according to the terms of the loan agreement.[52]

The key components of the IRB approach for corporate credits as outlined by the agencies in ANPR II are summarized below.

---

50. ANPR I, p. 45902.
51. ANPR II, p. 45950.
52. *Id.*, p. 45983.

Ratings Assignment

Institutions must develop a "two-dimensional" risk-rating system that ranks corporate borrowers by probability of default and estimates of the severity of loss on loans when a default occurs.

The analysis for estimating loss severity—called "loss given default" (LGD)—is one of the measures that the agencies are using in Basel II that is still in the early stages of development.[53] It is defined as the percentage of the estimated total loss on a loan that will not be recovered by the bank. The estimated total loss, or exposure, on default is called EAD (exposure at default).

There must be a high correlation—verified by back-testing and other validation procedures—between actual default frequencies and losses over given periods of time and default rates and losses predicted by an institution's internal estimates.

Quantification

The second component of an IRB system is quantification, which is the process of assigning numerical values to the four key components for internal ratings-based assessments of credit risk capital:

- possibility of default (PD);
- the expected loss given default (LGD);
- the expected exposure at default (EAD);
- and maturity (M).[54]

This process also can be described as the reduction of risk ratings to a number that is tied to capital requirements. Like the ratings system, the quantification process must be a disciplined one that produces values, not only for probability of default and LGD, but also for EAD. An effective quantitative procedure must be thoroughly documented, updated periodically, subjected to independent review, and validated frequently.[55]

Data Maintenance

An IRB system is no better than the accuracy and relevance of the data developed by the bank. ANPR II provides a checklist of standards that an advanced data management system must meet, which

---

53. ANPR II p. 45955.
54. *Id.*, p. 45958.
55. *Id.*, pps. 45958–48970.

cover validation techniques, calculation of capital ratios based on the risk of the underlying asset, data validation, managing data quality, and other aspects of data maintenance.[56]

Controls and Oversight

IRB institutions must create a system of internal controls with oversight procedures to ensure that the system is functioning effectively. Independence of the internal risk-rating process, which is tied directly to capital calculations, should be assured by such components as board and senior management oversight, internal audits, checks and balances, and transparency.

The agencies say that the draft guidance in ANPR II

> "reflects work performed by supervisors to evaluate and compare current practices at institutions with the concepts and requirements for an IRB framework. . . . Given that institutions are still in the early stages of developing qualifying IRB systems, it is expected that this guidance will evolve over time to more explicitly take into account new and improving practices."[57]

Proposed Guidance on the AMA Measures for Operational Risk

The draft guidance points out that

> "institutions using the AMA will have considerable flexibility to develop operational risk measurement systems appropriate to the nature of their activities, business environment, and internal controls. An institution's operational risk regulatory capital requirement will be calculated as the amount needed to cover its operational risk at a level of confidence determined by the supervisors. . . ."[58]

Following are highlights of the AMA guidance.

Risk measurement. Banking organizations using AMA are expected to analyze the following risks:

- *Operational risk*—includes risk of loss resulting from inadequate or failed internal processes, people, and systems, or from external events.

---

56. *Id.*, pps. 45070–45087.
57. *Id.*, p. 45952.
58. *Ibid.*, p. 45978.

- *Operational risk loss*—the financial impact associated with an operational event that is recorded in the institution's financial statements, including all out-of-pocket expenses associated with an operational event, including the following:
  a. Internal fraud and external fraud;
  b. Employment practices and workplace safety—acts inconsistent with employment, health or safety laws or agreements, and loses from claims from personal injury and employment practices claims;
  c. Damage to physical assets from natural disasters or other events;
  d. Business disruption and computer or other system failures; and
  e. Failed transaction processing or process management, from relations with trade counterparties and vendors.
- *Business environment and internal control factor assessments*—the range of tools, including audit scores "that provide a meaningful assessment of the level and trends in operational risk across the institution."[59]
- *Quantification*—in order to come up with a "number" for capital representing operational risk, a banking organization "must have a comprehensive operational risk analytical framework that provides an estimate of the institution's operational risk exposure, which is the aggregate operational loss that it faces over a one-year period at a soundness standard consistent with a 99.9 per cent confidence level."

Management must document the rationale for all assumptions underpinning its chosen analytical framework, including the choice of inputs, distributional assumptions, and the weighting across qualitative and quantitative elements. The final minimum regulatory capital number will be 8% of total risk-weighted assets.[60]

Pillar 2—Supervisory Review Process

The Revised Framework says the supervisory review process is designed to ensure that banks have adequate capital and to encourage them to improve their risk measurement techniques.

---

59. ANPR II, p. 45978.
60. *Ibid.*, p. 45979.

Pillar 2 also provides risk management guidance on risks not covered in Pillar 1, including interest rate risk in the bank's loan portfolio, market risk, and liquidity risk, as well as guidance on the basics of credit risk (including credit concentration and stress testing) and operational risk.[61]

The Supervisory Committee hopes that the interaction between management responsibility for setting adequate capital targets and the supervisory review process will foster an "active dialogue between banks and supervisors such that when deficiencies are discovered prompt and decisive action can be taken to reduce risk or restore capital."[62]

The U.S. banking agencies say in effect that the supervisory principles of Pillar 2 are already in effect in this country. These agencies have the power to require an institution to hold additional capital and, if necessary, can subject institutions to penalties under prompt corrective action if capital falls below regulatory minimums. Consequently:

> [g]iven these long-standing elements of the U.S. supervisory framework, the Agencies are not proposing to introduce specific requirements or guidelines to implement Pillar 2. Instead, existing guidance, rules, and regulations would continue to be enforced and supplemented as necessary as part of this proposed new regulatory capital framework.[63]

Chairman Greenspan suggested that as large banks, motivated by market discipline, develop more accurate internal risk models, and as supervisors become more confident in the accuracy of these models, the less detailed agency examinations are likely to be. Some transaction testing will remain, but in best-case situations, he believes that the basic thrust of examinations will "shift from largely duplicating many activities already conducted in the bank to providing constructive feedback that the bank can use to enhance further the quality of its risk-management systems."[64]

Pillar 3—Market Discipline

Market discipline is regarded as essential to the achievement of two major goals of Basel II: correlation of regulatory capital standards

---

61. Revised Framework, ¶ 719, p. 158.
62. *Ibid.*, ¶ 722, p. 158.
63. ANPR I, p. 45905.
64. Greenspan, Phoenix, *op. cit.*

with underlying economic risks and the convergence of international capital standards. Pillar 3 is designed to impose this discipline by requiring large banking organizations to make extensive public disclosures about their risk assessments and risk management.

Under Pillar 3, market participants, including investors, customers, counterparties and credit rating agencies,[65] would not only have information on the economic risks underlying an institution's activities but would also be able to make their own assessment of how effective the institution's risk exposures were identified and measured. They could then reach their own conclusion about how well the institution is capitalized.

Role of Market Participants

Chairman Greenspan pointed out that the market's judgment of an institution governs its ability to access capital funds and the price it pays for those funds.[66] "The risks to which banking organizations are exposed and the techniques that they use to identify, measure, monitor, and control those risks are important factors that market participants consider in their assessment of an institution."[67]

Regulators expect that Pillar 3 disclosures will improve correlations between capital estimates and underlying risks, thereby resulting in large banks paying the "market" price for capital. This, in turn, should have the effect of reducing existing differences in capital standards among the G-10 and other countries, which place some banks at a competitive disadvantage in international markets.

Regulators add that market participants, who include investors, counterparties, and credit rating agencies, play useful roles "by requiring banks to hold more capital than implied by minimum regulatory capital requirements, or sometimes their own economic capital models, and by demanding additional disclosures about how risks are being managed."[68]

---

65. The five current credit rating agencies, which are known as "nationally recognized statistical reporting agencies" (NRSROs) are: A. M. Best Company, Inc. (A.M. Best); Dominion Bond Rating Services Limited (DBRS); Fitch, Inc. (Fitch); Moody's Investors Service Inc. (Moody's); and Standard & Poor's Division of McGraw Hill Companies, Inc. (S&P).
66. Greenspan, Phoenix, *op. cit.*
67. ANPR I p. 45944.
68. Bies, Boston, *op. cit.*

Risk Identification and Measurement

The information covered by Pillar 3 disclosures in the proposed rules is detailed. Credit risk disclosures, for example, "would include breakdowns of the banking organization's exposures by type of credit exposure, geographic distribution, industry or counterparty type distribution, residual contractual maturity, amount and type of impaired and past due exposures."[69] Disclosures of securitization risks must describe "the organization's accounting policies for securitization activities. . . . impairments and losses, exposures retained or purchased broken down into risk weight bands and aggregate outstanding amounts of securitized revolving exposures."[70]

Risk Management

For each separate risk area, a banking organization would describe its risk management objectives and policies. Such disclosures would include an "explanation of the banking organization's strategies and processes; the structure and organization of the relevant risk management function; the scope and nature of risk reporting and/or measurement systems; and the policies for hedging and/or mitigating risk and strategies and processes for monitoring the continuing effectiveness of hedges/mitigants."[71]

Calculation of Capital Requirements

Capital adequacy disclosures would include a summary discussion of the banking organization's approach to assessing the adequacy of its capital to support current and future activities. These requirements include a breakdown of the capital requirements for credit, equity, market, and operational risks. Banking organizations would also be required to disclose their Tier 1 and total capital ratios for the consolidated group, as well as those of significant bank or thrift subsidiaries.[72]

Publication

Banking organizations would have some discretion in the "medium and location" of required disclosures and would not need to duplicate

---

69. ANPR I, p. 45944.
70. *Id.,* p. 45945.
71. *Id.,* p. 45944.
72. *Id.,* p. 54944.

information that has already been provided in securities and regulatory filings. One possibility under consideration is a requirement that the organizations provide a summary table on their websites showing where the information can be found.[73]

Compliance with Other Laws

The agencies point out that Pillar 3 disclosures relating to internal controls must comply with sections 302 and 404 of the Sarbanes-Oxley Act of 2002 (12 USC 7241 and 7262), which require:

> management . . . to certify to the effectiveness of internal controls over financial reporting and disclosure controls and procedures, and the banking organization's external auditor would have to attest to management's assertions with respect to internal controls over financial reporting. The scope of these reports would need to include all information included in regulatory reports and the disclosures outlined in this ANPR.[74]

Leverage Ratio and PCA

Agency witnesses at the House hearings cited above said that the U.S. version of Basel II, when adopted, will retain the current standards' leverage ratio and prompt corrective action (PCA) requirements.[75] While the agencies might legally have adopted Basel II without these provisions, this action would likely have been difficult politically.

Provisions of this kind are consistent with the Basel II Framework, which provides that participating nations are free to adopt higher or supplementary standards, such as leverage ratios, that are designed, among other things, to "constrain the extent to which an organization can fund itself with debt" and to "compensate for the uncertainties inherent in any capital rule."[76]

Revisions to Basel I

U.S. bank regulators are working to improve the risk sensitivity of Basel I standards without imposing the complexities of Basel II and

---

73. *Id.*, p. 45943.
74. *Id.*, p. 45944.
75. See sections 38(c)(1)(A) and (B)(ii) of the Federal Deposit Insurance Act (12 USC 1831o(c)(1)(A) & (B)(ii)). For a dissenting view on retention of the leverage ratio and PCA, see statement of Karen Shaw Petrou, Managing Partner, Federal Financial Analytics, Inc., House Hearings, *op. cit.*
76. *Framework, op. cit.*, p. 3, ¶ 9.

to narrow the anticipated differences in capital rates that some believe will place non-Basel II banks at a competitive disadvantage to those that adopt Basel II standards.

Some analysts have suggested that several factors well mitigate any disparity in capital standards between Basel II banks and non-Basel II banks.[77] These include the fact that virtually all institutions, irrespective of their minimum capital requirements, will strive to maintain sufficient capital to qualify as "well-capitalized" under PCA not only to achieve favorable market ratings but also to be able to secure the benefits, such as lower deposit insurance premiums and branching rights that this capital level confers.[78]

On October 20, 2005,[79] the agencies requested comments on a new version of Basel I, which is generally referred to as "Basel IA." The subjects of these comments include the following:

- increasing the number of risk weight categories;
- expanding the use of external credit ratings as an indicator of credit risk for externally rated exposures;
- using loan-to-value ratios, credit assessments, and other broad measures of credit risk for assigning risk-weights to residential mortgages;
- requiring that certain loans 90 days or more past due or in a non-accrual status be assigned to a higher risk weight category; and
- modifying the risk-based capital requirements for certain commercial and real estate loans.

Comments on the Basel IA request were due on January 18, 2006. As of July 2006, the agencies had taken no further action on this request.

---

77. See Ferguson, *op cit.*

78. To be "well capitalized," an institution must have total capital of 10% or more, Tier 1 capital of 6% or more and a Tier 1 leverage ratio of 5% or more. As of March 31, 2005, 99.3% of insured domestic institutions met this standard (FDIC, *Quarterly Banking Report,* First Quarter, 2005).

79. Joint advance notice of proposed rulemaking, Risk-Based Capital Guidelines; Capital Adequacy Guidelines; Capital Maintenance: Domestic Capital Modifications 70 FR 61068 (October 20, 2005).

GAO Study

On February 15, 2006, a bill was signed containing an amendment by Senator Richard Shelby (R, Ala.), Chairman of the Senate Committee on Banking, Housing and Urban Affairs, requiring the General Accountability Office (GAO), an arm of the U.S. Congress, to conduct a study of Basel II implementation.[80] The study, which is due February 15, 2007, is to cover among other things:

1. Whether Basel II would result in a reduction in capital requirements;
2. Whether Basel II could hinder enforcement of prompt corrective action laws and regulations;
3. The feasibility and appropriateness of Basel II's statistical models; and
4. The ability of the United States financial institution regulatory agencies to conduct the necessary oversight of capital and risk modeling by regulated financial institutions subject to Basel II.

As this book went to press in July 2006, it was not clear what the effect of the GAO study would be on the Basel II implementation timetable.

Basel II Implementation

On March 30, 2006, the Federal Reserve Board announced the release of notice of proposed rulemaking (NPR) that would implement the Basel II risk-based capital requirements for large, internationally active banking organizations. The FDIC, OCC, and OTS are reviewing the NPR and the notice will be published in the Federal Register after it has been approved by these agencies.

"Conversion" of GAAP Capital to Regulatory Capital

This conversion is shown in Figure 11.3, which is based on the information banks must provide in the Call Reports they file each quarter with their primary federal regulator. The official name of these reports is "Consolidated Reports for Condition and Income for a

---

80. Federal Deposit Insurance Reform Conforming Amendments Act of 2005, PL 109-173, Feb. 15, 2006, 119 Stat. 3601, section 6(e).

Bank with Domestic Offices Only—FFIEC [Form] 041."[81] The Call Report that banks are required to have filed as of June 30, 2006 has 20 Schedules covering 39 pages, including "Schedule RC-Balance Sheet," that is referenced below, where the calculations involving the conversion of GAAP equity capital to regulatory capital begins.

Figure 11.3
Calculation of Regulatory Capital for Banks
Conversion of GAAP CAPITAL to REGULATORY CAPITAL

The conversion of GAAP capital to regulatory capital begins with the identification of the bank's GAAP capital, which is found under "equity capital" in Schedule RC, the balance sheet in the bank's Call Report. Regulatory capital is calculated in accordance with Call Report Schedule RC-R. Following is an abbreviated version of how this calculation is made.

I. Determination of GAAP Capital
   START with TOTAL EQUITY (GAAP) Capital in the Call Report BALANCE SHEET :
   This is the sum of the equity capital line items listed below that make up "Total Equity Capital" on the Call Report Schedule RC- Balance Sheet. *Balance Sheet (Schedule RC)* (The following heading and line numbers 23–28 are from the actual Call Report Schedule RC):
   EQUITY CAPITAL
   23. Noncumulative perpetual preferred stock and related surplus. This is preferred stock with no maturity on which payment of dividends may be deferred indefinitely.
   24. Common stock.
   25. Surplus (excluding surplus related to preferred stock).
   26. a. Retained earnings.
       b. Accumulated other comprehensive income.
   27. Other equity capital components.
   28. TOTAL EQUITY CAPITAL (sum of lines 23 through 27).

II. Calculation of Tier 1 (Core) Capital
   A. ENTER the "Total Equity Capital" on the Balance Sheet on line 1, in Call Report Schedule RC-R (Regulatory Capital).
   This Schedule is used to calculate the conversion of GAAP Capital to Regulatory Capital.

(Continued)

---

81. Domestic banks with foreign offices file "Consolidated Reports for Condition and Income for a Bank with Domestic and Foreign Offices–FFIEC [Form] 031.

Figure 11.3—*Continued*
Calculation of Regulatory Capital for Banks

Conversion of GAAP CAPITAL to REGULATORY CAPITAL

   B. SUBTRACT the following items from "Total Equity (GAAP) Capital"; Items to be subtracted are components of GAAP capital that are not eligible to be used in calculating regulatory capital. They include, but are not limited to the following:
1. Net unrealized gains (or losses) on available-for-sale securities. This is a component of a bank's GAAP capital, that is not eligible for Tier 1 capital. Net gains on these portfolios, therefore, do not count as Tier 1 capital and should be subtracted from GAAP capital. Conversely, since GAAP capital would have been reduced by unrealized *losses* on these portfolios, these losses are added back to GAAP capital for purposes of calculating Tier 1 capital.

   A portion of any unrealized gain on *equity* securities in these portfolios, however, may be included in Tier 2 capital, as noted below.
2. Net unrealized losses on available-for-sale equity securities. After the add back of losses on available-for-sale securities in item 1, above, banks are then required to *deduct* any unrealized losses from *equity* securities in these portfolios from GAAP capital in calculating Tier 1 capital.
3. Nonqualifying perpetual preferred stock.
   a. Perpetual preferred stock on which unpaid dividends accumulate as an obligation of the bank (cumulative perpetual preferred stock) may not be included in Tier 1 capital.
   b. Nonperpetual preferred stock
   Portions of these assets are includable in Tier 2 capital, as noted below.
4. Disallowed goodwill and other disallowed intangible assets. Goodwill is an intangible asset that represents the excess of the purchase price over the fair market value of tangible and identifiable intangible assets acquired in business combinations accounted for under the purchase method of accounting. Goodwill acquired after April 12, 1989, is not eligible to be used in calculating regulatory capital.

   Other intangible assets that may arise from these business combinations include those accounted for under the purchase method and acquisitions of portions or segments of another institution's business, such as branch offices, mortgage servicing portfolios, credit card portfolios, core deposit intangibles (the added value to the bank of long term, stable deposits) favorable leaseholds, branch offices, patents, and trademarks.

Chapter 11: Capital

While most intangible assets are not recognized for regulatory capital purposes, an agency may approve inclusion of otherwise ineligible intangible assets, except goodwill, on a case-by-case basis.

Intangible assets, including mortgage servicing assets, that *are* recognized for regulatory capital calculations are discussed below. /a/

C. ADD to GAAP capital:

Qualifying minority interests in consolidated subsidiaries

This is stock held by minority stockholders in a bank-controlled subsidiary whose assets are consolidated with those of the bank. These interests are not recognized as equity capital under GAAP, but the agencies count them as regulatory capital "they represent equity that is freely available to absorb losses in operating subsidiaries whose assets are included in a bank's risk-weighted asset base."[82]

Agencies' note: "Although nonvoting common stock, noncumulative perpetual preferred stock, and minority interests in the equity capital accounts of consolidated subsidiaries are normally included in Tier 1 capital, voting common stockholders' equity generally will be expected to be the dominant form of Tier 1 capital. Thus, banks should avoid undue reliance on nonvoting equity, preferred stock and minority interests.[83]

D. The result of the above calculations equals the TIER 1 CAPITAL SUBTOTAL

This subtotal is important because the amount of certain GAAP capital assets that can be included in Tier 1 capital is limited to a percentage of this subtotal.

E. SUBTRACT from Tier 1 Subtotal:

1. *Disallowed servicing assets and purchased credit card relationships (PCCRs)* /a/

   The following intangible assets are recognized as GAAP capital assets and may be included in Tier 1 capital subject to certain deductions, which are discussed below.[84]

   - MSAs (mortgage servicing assets): contractual rights to service portfolios of mortgages that the bank has either purchased from another entity or retained on mortgages originated by the banks and sold.

(Continued)

---

82. *Commercial Bank Examination Manual*, Federal Reserve Board, section 3020.1, p. 10.1. The Federal Reserve (and the other banking agencies) caution banks against using these interests to introduce other securities, that is, certain investments in the subsidiary "that would not otherwise qualify as tier 1 capital."

83. 12 CFR Part 325, Appendix A, section I., A.

84. Joint Final Rule: OCC, FDIC, Federal Reserve and OTS: *Risk-Based Capital Guidelines; Capital Adequacy Guidelines, and Capital Maintenance: Servicing Assets;* Final Rule, 63 FR 42267, p. 42267 (Aug. 10, 1998).

Figure 11.3—*Continued*
Calculation of Regulatory Capital for Banks

Conversion of GAAP CAPITAL to REGULATORY CAPITAL

- NMSAs (non-mortgage servicing assets): servicing rights on loans other than mortgages, such as commercial loans, automobile loans, credit card receivables, unsecured installment loans, student loans, Small Business Administration loans, home equity loans, and commercial mortgages.
- PCCRs (purchased credit card relationships): credit card portfolios that a bank purchases from another entity, which allows the bank to develop business relationships with the cardholders.

2. *Disallowed deferred tax assets*

   Tax carryforwards are deductions or credits that cannot be used for tax purposes during a current reporting period, but can be carried forward to reduce taxable income or taxes payable in a future period or periods.

   The following item is **deducted** from Tier 1 capital: deferred tax assets, with certain exceptions, that are dependent upon future taxable income, that exceed the lesser of:

   a. The amount of deferred tax assets that the bank could reasonably expect to realize within one year of the quarter-end Call Report, based on its estimate of future taxable income for that year; or
   b. 10% of the Tier 1 capital subtotal.

   If the bank is a member of a consolidated group for tax purposes, however, "the amount of carryback potential that may be considered in calculating the amount of deferred tax assets that [the bank] may include in Tier 1 capital may not exceed the amount which the member could reasonably expect to have refunded by its parent.[85]"

F. Other DEDUCTIONS from Tier 1 Capital
   1. *Credit enhancing I/O strips.*
      General. Interest only (I/O) strips are the contractual right to receive cash flows from pools of mortgage and other loans that are comprised of the interest payments on these loans. I/O strips

---

85. The discussion of deferred tax assets is drawn from 12 CFR § 325.5(g). The quote is in subsection (g)(2)(A)(ii).

receivable are not deducted from GAAP capital, but the agencies will monitor banks' valuation of these interests. As with other assets, banks may be required to hold additional capital commensurate with increased risk resulting from excessive concentrations of I/O strips, valuation problems or from other concerns.

Credit-enhancing interest-only strips. This instrument is defined as an on-balance sheet asset that, in form or in substance:
(i) Represents the contractual right to receive some or all of the interest due on transferred assets; and (ii) Exposes the bank to credit risk directly or indirectly associated with the transferred assets that exceeds a pro rata share of the bank's claim on the assets, whether through subordination provisions or other credit enhancement techniques.[86]

Credit-enhancing interest-only strips, whether purchased or retained, that exceed 25% of the Tier 1 capital subtotal must be deducted from Tier 1 capital. Banks must value each credit-enhancing interest-only strip included in Tier 1 capital at least quarterly.

Banks may elect to deduct disallowed credit-enhancing I/O strips on a basis that is net of any associated deferred tax liability. These deferred tax liabilities cannot also be netted against deferred tax assets when determining the amount of deferred tax assets that are dependent upon future taxable income. App A section 2(c)(4):

2. *Nonfinancial equity investments /b/.*
Regulatory capital regulations of the OCC, Federal Reserve, and FDIC (but not the OTS) impose additional capital requirements for certain equity investments in nonfinancial companies.[87] These requirements, which were adopted in 2002, reflect the agencies' belief that investments in nonfinancial companies pose greater risk to banking organizations than investments in traditional bank and financial activities. These rules were prompted in part by the increased nonfinancial investment authority conferred on banking organizations by the Gramm Leach Bliley Act (GLBA).[88]

The sum of these items equals TOTAL TIER 1 CAPITAL

(Continued)

---

86. 12 CFR Part 3, Appendix A, section 4(a)(2).
87. 12 CFR Part 325, Appendix A, section II.B. 5(i)(6).
88. Pub. Law 106-102 (Nov. 12, 1999). This new investment authority is discussed in Chapter 5.

Figure 11.3—*Continued*
Calculation of Regulatory Capital for Banks

Conversion of GAAP CAPITAL to REGULATORY CAPITAL

Notes on Tier 1 Capital Components

/a/ **Eligibility of servicing assets and PCCRs as Tier 1 capital.** The amount of these assets that are eligible to be included in Tier 1 capital is calculated as follows:

Adjustment for capital calculation (adjusted value). The balance sheet assets for MSAs, PCCRs and NMSAs must each be reduced to an amount equal to the lesser of:

- 90% of their fair value of these assets, or
- 100% of their remaining unamortized book value calculated in accordance with instructions in the Call Report.

Valuation. The fair value of each of these assets must be estimated quarterly and must include adjustments for any significant changes in original valuation assumptions, including changes in prepayment estimates.

Tier 1 capital limitations. The maximum allowable amount of MSAs, PCCRs and NMSAs *in the aggregate* that's includable in Tier 1 capital is limited to an amount equal to the lesser of 100% of the Tier 1 subtotal or the "adjusted value" of these assets, that is referred to above.

Sublimits for NMSAs and PCCRs. The maximum allowable amount of the PCCRs and NMSAs that is includable in Tier 1 capital *within the above 100% limit* is restricted to the lesser of:

- 25% of the amount of the Tier 1 capital subtotal; or
- the total adjusted value of these assets.

Banks may elect to deduct disallowed servicing assets on a basis that is net of any associated deferred tax liability. Deferred tax liabilities netted in this manner cannot also be netted against deferred tax assets when determining the amount of deferred tax assets that are dependent upon future taxable income.

/b/ Nonfinancial Equity Investments. The higher charges for nonfinancial equity investments apply to investments made under the following authorities:

- Merchant banking investments in section 4(k)(4)(H) of the Bank Holding Company Act (BHCA) (12 USC 1843(k)(4)(H)), as amended by GLBA.
- The provisions of sections 4(c)(6)&(7) of the BHCA (12 USC 1843(c) & (c)(7)) that permit bank holding companies to invest in up to 5% of the shares of nonfinancial companies.
- Investments in Small Business Investment Companies under section 302(b) of the Small Business Investment Act of 1958 (15 U.S.C. 682(b)).
- Certain Investments held by state banks in nonfinancial companies under section 24 of the Federal Deposit Insurance Act (other than section 24(f)) (12 USC 1831(a)). Section 24 subsidiaries are discussed in Chapter 3.
- Holdings under the portfolio investment provisions of Reg K, International Banking Operations (12 CFR 211.1, *et. seq.*).

Deduction for Nonfinancial Equity Investments

Nonfinancial equity investments as a percentage of Tier I Subtotal	Deduction from Tier 1 Capital as a percentage of the adjusted carrying value of the investment
Less than 15%	8%
15 % or more, but less than 25%	12%
25 % or more	25%

III. Tier 2 (Supplemental) Capital

Tier 2 capital is the sum of the following components:

A. Term subordinated debt (excluding mandatory convertible debt securities) and intermediate-term preferred stock (original average maturity of five years or more) and any related surplus.
   These instruments are eligible to be included in Tier 2 capital in an amount equal to 50% of Tier 1 capital. /c/

B. Cumulative perpetual preferred stock, long-term preferred stock (original maturity of at least 20 years), and any related surplus. /d/

C. Auction rate perpetual preferred stock(and any related surplus). This is stock for which the dividend is reset periodically based, in whole or part, on the bank's current credit standing, regardless of whether the dividends are cumulative or noncumulative.

D. Allowance for loan and lease losses (ALLL).
   These are reserves the bank has set aside to absorb losses on loans and leases. ALLL is includable in Tier 2 capital up to a maximum of 1.25% of the bank's risk-weighted assets.

E. Unrealized gains on available for sale equity securities.
   Up to 45% of pretax net unrealized holding gains (that is, the excess, if any, of the fair value over historical cost) on available-for-sale equity securities with readily determinable fair values may be included in supplementary capital. /e/

F. Hybrid capital instruments.
   These include mandatory convertible debt securities. These are subordinated debt instruments that require the issuer to convert such instruments into common or perpetual preferred stock by a date at or before the maturity of the debt instruments. The maturity of these instruments must be 12 years or less and the instruments must also meet certain other criteria. /f/

G. Other elements of Tier 2 capital permitted by the bank's primary federal regulator.

The sum of these items equals TOTAL TIER 2 CAPITAL

(Continued)

Figure 11.3—*Continued*
Calculation of Regulatory Capital for Banks

Conversion of GAAP CAPITAL to REGULATORY CAPITAL

IV. TOTAL REGULATORY CAPITAL = Tier 1 + Tier 2 (Tier 2 may not exceed 100% of Tier 1 capital).

Notes on Tier 2 Capital Components

/c/ Term subordinated debt and intermediate-term preferred stock should generally have an original average maturity of at least five years to qualify as supplementary capital. In addition to other requirements, a term subordinated debt instrument must be unsecured and state expressly that it is subordinated in right of payment to the issuing bank's obligations to its depositors and to its general and secured creditors.

/d/ Cumulative perpetual preferred stock and long-term preferred stock qualify for inclusion in supplementary capital provided that the issuer must have the option to defer payment of dividends on these instruments. Given these conditions, and the perpetual or long-term nature of the instruments, there is no limit on the amount of these preferred stock instruments that may be included with Tier 2 capital.

/e/ An agency may exclude all or a portion of these unrealized gains from Tier 2 capital if it determines that the equity securities are not prudently valued. Unrealized gains or losses on other types of assets, such as bank premises and available-for-sale debt securities, are not included in supplementary capital, but an agency may take these unrealized gains (losses) into account as additional factors when assessing a bank's overall capital adequacy.

/f/ Hybrid capital instruments include instruments that have certain characteristics of both debt and equity. These instruments, among other things, should be unsecured, subordinated to the claims of depositors and general creditors, and fully paid-up. They should also provide an option for the issuer to defer principal and interest payments if the issuer does not report a profit in the most recent four quarters, and eliminates cash dividends on its common and preferred stock.

These instruments include mandatory convertible debt securities. These are subordinated debt instruments, which among other things require the issuer to exchange either common or perpetual preferred stock for such instruments by a date at or before the maturity of the instrument, which must be 12 years or less.

V. Deductions from Total Capital

Agency rules and Call Reports provide for adjustments to Tier 1 and total capital for investments in finance subsidiaries and other items. FDIC regulations, for example, provide as follows:

> The insured state nonmember bank will deduct the aggregate amount of its outstanding equity investment, including retained earnings, in all financial subsidiaries. . . . from the bank's total assets and tangible equity and deduct such investment from its total risk-based capital (this deduction shall be made equally from Tier 1 and Tier 2 capital).[89]

---

89. 12 CFR § 362.18(a)(3).

Figure 11.4
Calculation of Regulatory Capital for Savings Associations

The calculation of regulatory capital for savings associations is made in the same manner as it is for banks: GAAP capital is modified to meet supervisory requirements. The forms on which these calculations are made, which are in the institution's Thrift Financial Reports (TFRs), are essentially the same as the bank Call Report forms summarized in Table A.

In the TFR:
- The savings association's equity (GAAP) capital is found in Schedule SC—Consolidated Statement of Condition, line SC80 (Corresponds to Call Report Schedule RC-Balance Sheet).
- The "conversion" of GAAP capital to regulatory capital is made on Schedule CCR—Consolidated Capital Requirement (Corresponds to Call Report Schedule RC-R).

There are, however, a few differences between OTS regulatory capital rules and those applicable to banks. In a 2005 joint report to Congress, the four agencies described the few remaining differences in their capital rules:

Some of [these] remaining capital differences are statutorily mandated. Others were significant historically but now no longer affect in a measurable way, either individually or in the aggregate, institutions supervised by the federal banking agencies.[90]

Several of the differences between OTS capital rules and those of the other agencies are discussed below.

Tangible Capital. One statutorily mandated capital difference is found in section 5(t) of the Home Owners' Loan Act (12 USC 1464(t)), which requires savings associations to maintain a ratio of "tangible capital" to adjusted assets of at least 1.5%. The principal components of tangible capital are:
- Common stockholders' equity (including retained earnings);
- Noncumulative perpetual preferred stock and related earnings;

(Continued)

---

90. *Joint Report: Differences in Accounting and Capital Standards Among the Federal Banking Agencies; Report to Congressional Committees,* 70 FR 15379, 15380 (March 25, 2005).

Figure 11.4—*Continued*
Calculation of Regulatory Capital for Savings Associations

- Nonwithdrawable accounts and pledged deposits that would qualify as core capital for mutual savings associations (see below); and
  - Minority interests in the equity accounts of fully consolidated subsidiaries.
  - MINUS certain assets, including investments in certain subsidiaries, intangible assets, and servicing assets.

This standard, which was imposed by banking legislation in 1989, may no longer be material. In the report to Congress quoted above, the agencies say that, "Other subsequent statutory and regulatory changes, however, [including the provisions for prompt corrective action have] imposed higher capital standards rendering it unlikely, if not impossible, for the 1.5% tangible capital requirement to function as a meaningful regulatory trigger."[91]

Financial Subsidiaries. There are no provisions in OTS capital standards for deductions of investments in financial subsidiaries because savings associations, although able to engage in a broad range of activities through subsidiary organizations, are not authorized to organize the kind of financial subsidiaries that are authorized for banks (see Chapter 7).

Following are other differences described in the 2005 Report to Congress:

- In Tier 1 capital, mutual savings associations may hold pledged deposits and nonwithdrawable accounts to the extent that such accounts or deposits have no fixed maturity date, cannot be withdrawn at the option of the accountholder, and do not earn interest that carries over to subsequent periods.
- In Tier 2 capital the OCC, the Federal Reserve and the FDIC limit the amount of subordinated debt and intermediate-term preferred stock that may be treated as part of Tier 2 capital to 50% of Tier 1 capital. The OTS does not prescribe such a restriction.

The OTS also permits the inclusion in Tier 2 capital of remaining instruments that were authorized during the financial crisis of the 1980s: worth certificates, mutual capital certificates, and income capital certificates.

---

91. *Ibid.*, p. 15381.

Conclusion

Federal regulators are the first to acknowledge that there are many unresolved issues relating to the implementation of the Basel II Framework. This is not surprising given its complexity and is the reason for the adoption of the four-year transition period that is scheduled to begin January 1, 2008.

Basel IA, the proposed amendments to Basel I, would provide a much-needed update of these standards and is designed to provide capital rules that more accurately reflect the economic risk of activities of institutions that will not be covered by Basel II.

Meanwhile, Congress is keeping a wary eye on these proceedings, particularly with respect to any indications that Basel II may result in lower levels of minimum capital for Basel II organizations than for those remaining under Basel I (or Basel IA, as the case may be).

In any case, all interested parties—regulators, Congress, and the banking industry—will be able to observe and comment on Basel II in operation as the parallel run begins in 2008.

Index

A

Acquittal, of an IAP, 91
Acting in concert, definition, 144–45
Adequately capitalized institutions, 309
Administration Procedures Act, 85
Administrative law judge (ALJ), 90
Advanced internal-ratings based (A-IRB) (IRB) approach, 320, 321–23
Advanced measurement approach (AMA), 320, 323–24
Advance notices of proposed rule making (ANPR), 319
Advertising requirements, 168–69
Affiliates
   attribution of activities among, 170
   definition, 161–62
   insiders of, 182–83
   as subsidiaries, 171–72
   subsidiaries as, 195
   transactions with, 206–08
Affiliate transactions
   application of sections 23A and 23B to savings associations, 169–72
   definition of *affiliate*, 161–62
   exemptions from provisions of section 23A, 165–67
   under Federal Reserve Act, 11
   introduction, 160–61
   provisions of section 23A, 161–64
   provisions of section 23B, 167–69
   qualitative restrictions on, 164
Age laws, for acquisitions, 105, 113
Agency
   branching and, 113–14
   enforcement of orders of, 93

Aggregate loan limit, 182
Agreement corporations, 199
Agricultural credit corporations, 198
Alfred I. duPont Trust, 124–25
Allocation factors, dividends, 42
Alternative recordkeeping method, 183
American Institute of Certified Public Accountants (AICPA), 230
Anti-discrimination standard, 153
Antifraud provisions, Securities Act (1933), 261
Approval procedure, 213
Arm's length requirements, 167
Assessment ceiling, 40
Asset-backed transactions, 280
Asset purchases, prohibited, 168
Asset quality, 55, 164
Attribution rule, 163–64, 170
Audit committees
   importance of, 232–33
   introduction, 229–30
   NYSE and Nasdaq, 239–40
   SEC rules for, 233–37
   SRO rules, 237–41
Audits
   auditor reports on internal controls, 243–45
   FDIC rules, 247–51
   importance of, 232–33
   introduction, 229–30
   procedures and standards, 231–33
   public accounting firms, 241–43
   SRO audit and governance rules, 237–41

B

Bank Activities and Operations, 31
Bank charters, first issuance, 5
Bank eligible securities activities, 271
Bankers banks, 198
Bank examiners, 50
Bank executive officer "carve out", 180–81
Bank for International Settlements (BIS), 293–94
Bank Holding Act (1999), 198
Bank holding companies (BHCs)
   application of Securities Act to, 255
   BHCA and, 21–22
   examinations, 65–69
   interstate acquisitions by, 112–14
   regulatory capital for, 302
Bank Holding Company Act Amendments (1970), 184
Bank Holding Company Act (BHCA) (1956)
   enactment of, 21
   FHCs and, 306
   interstate banking and, 97, 104
   for regulation of BHCs, 123–26
   savings associations restrictions and, 169
   section 106, 185–89
Bank Holding Company Performance Reports (BHCPRs), 302
Banking Act (1933), 11, 14, 35, 122–26, 270
Banking agencies, implementation of Basel II by, 317–19
Banking laws. *See* Corporate governance rules
Bank Insurance Fund (BIF)
   federal deposit insurance and, 36
   institution's contribution to, 42
   merger with SAIF, 41, 46
   premium disparity and, 37–40
   savings association regulation and, 23
Bank Merger Act (BMA), 101, 104
Bank of the United States, 2
Bank permissible securities activities, 271
Banks
   application of Exchange Act to, 265–66
Basel II categories, 320–21
BHCA definition of, 131
   as brokers and dealers, 272–73

   capital standards for, 295–302
   definition of, 23–24
   resolution during 1980-1994 financial crisis, 79–81
   subset of, 23–24
   temporary exemption for, 280
   as underwriters and dealers, 269–70
Bank Secrecy Act/Anti-Money Laundering examinations, 54
Bank securities activities
   antifraud provisions, 261
   as brokers and dealers, 272–73
   common trust funds, 281–86
   coverage under 1940 Investment Company Act and 1940 Investment Advisers Act, 268–69
   exceptions and safe harbors, 273–75
   Exchange Act, 264–68
   final dealer rules, 279–81
   Glass-Steagall Act, also on 200, 202, 269–70
   history of, 11–12
   introduction, 253
   limits on, 271–72
   of national banks, 270–71
   OCC, 262–63
   proposed Regulation B, 278–79
   qualified institutional investors, 260–61
   regulatory implementation, 275–77
   revisions to securities offering rules, 261–62
   Securities Act (1933), 253–60, 262
   shelf registration, 260
   state regulation of, 287–89
Bank service companies (BSCs), 195, 196, 198
Banks Service Corporation Act (BSCA), 196
Bank subsidiaries, 171
Bank System, design of, 15
Barnett Bank of Marion County, N.A. v. Nelson, 29–30, 31, 150, 154
Barnett Standard, 152
Basel Capital Accord. *See* Basel I
Basel Committee, 295
Basel I
   explained, 64–65
   market risk, 301–02
   purpose of, 294

revisions to, 328–29
risk weight categories, 297–302
standards, 295–97
Basel IA, 329
Basel II project
   AMA measures for operational risk, 323–24
   application to U.S. banks, 319
   explained, 64–65
   GAO study, 330
   implementation by U.S. banking agencies, 317–19
   implementation of, 330–40
   IRB approach, 321–23
   parallel run, 316–17
   pillar 1—minimum capital requirements, 320–21
   pillar 2—supervisory review process, 324–25
   pillar 3—market discipline, 325–28
   reasons for, 313–16
   standards, 295
Beneficiaries, on POD accounts, 45
BHCA. *See* Bank Holding Company Act (BHCA) (1956)
BHCA Amendments (1970), 21–22, 125
Bies, Susan Schmidt, 316
BIF. *See* Bank Insurance Fund (BIF)
BIF-SAIF merger, 46
Blanket broker-dealer exemption, 273
Blanket preemption, 154
Blanket standard, 151, 152
Blue Ribbon Committee on Improving the Effectiveness of Corporate Audit Committees (the Blue Ribbon Committee), 230
Blue-sky registration, 287
Board. *See* Federal Reserve Board (Board)
Board of Governors of the Federal Reserve System, 10
Board resolution and commitment letter, 83
Boards of institutions, examiner meetings with, 72
Boards of trustee, for MSBs, 5
Borrower inquiry method, 183
Branches/branching
   activity conducted at, 109–10

closing, 114
definition of *branch*, 98, 115
interstate, for bankers, 103–12
interstate acquisitions by BHCs, 112–14
interstate activity before 1994, 102–03
introduction, 97–98
laws applicable to savings associations, 117–19
merger laws and, 98–102
non-branch facilities, 114–17
regulations, 99
retention policies, 111
of state banks, 100
Brokerage activities, national banks and, 271
Brokers, banks as, 272–73

C

Call Reports, 330–31
CAMELS composite rating, 50–51, 54–58
Capital
   background, 291–95
   Basel II project, 313–19
   capital restoration plan, 312–13
   as CORE component, 70
   defining, 291–92
   prompt corrective action, 308–13
   regulatory, for holding companies, 302–08
   standards for banks and savings associations, 295–302
   structure of revised Basel framework, 319–40
   TSPs as, 305–06
Capital adequacy, of CAMELS rating, 55
Capital directives, 88
Capital requirements, for branching, 99–100
Capital restoration plan, 312–13
Cease and desist (C&D) orders, 84–85
CEBA. *See* Competitive Equality Banking Act (CEBA) (1987)
Certification filing, 247
Chain banks, 121–22
Change in Bank Control Act, 142–46
Changes in circumstance, interlocks, 224–25
Charitable activities, 212

Chartered banks, 2
Chartering agencies, 26, 27
Checking accounts, interest on, 20
Choice of law provisions, 219
Civil money penalties (CMP), 84–87
Civil offenses, 86
Civil War, U.S. bonds to finance, 7
Clayton Antitrust Act (1914), 222
Closely held companies, 241
Closing meetings, of examiners, 71–72, 82
Cohen Commission, 230
Collateralized mortgage obligations (CMOs), 298
Collateral requirements, 164
Collective investment funds, regulations for, 284–85
Collective trust funds, 281
Combined-balance discounts, 188–89
Commercial banks/banking, 3, 12–14
Committee of Sponsoring Organizations (COSO), 230
Committee on Auditors' Responsibilities (Cohen Commission), 230
Committee on Banking Regulations and Supervisory Practices (Supervisory Committee), 293–94
Commodities Futures Trading Commission, 69
Common trust funds, 281–86
Community development, 212
Community Reinvestment Act (CRA), 52, 138
Community test, interlocks and, 223
Compensation committees, 240–41
Competitive Equality Banking Act (CEBA) (1987)
 definition of *bank*, 132
 ILCs and, 134–35
 unrestricted activities by S&LHCs and, 128
Compliance examinations, 50, 52
Composite ratings, 57–58, 70–71
Concentration limits, of interstate merger, 106
Conference of State Bank Supervisors (CSBS), 59
Conservator
 FDIC and OTS powers as, 78

FDIC as, 77, 78–79
 general grounds for appointment of, 76–77
 powers of, 77–79
Conservatorships, 73–79
Consolidated Reports for Condition and Income for a Bank with Domestic Offices Only—FFEIC [Form] 041, 330–31
Consumer services, 211
Control
 of another company, 163
 definition, 145
Controlled companies, 241
Conversions
 of GAAP capital to regulatory capital, 330–40
 mutual to stock, savings associations, 16–17
Conviction, of an IAP, 91
Cooperative agreements, 63
Cooperative banks, 6
Coordination of Expanded Supervisory Information Sharing and Special Examinations (Interagency Agreement) (2002), 64
Core banks, 320
Core capital, 297
CORE components, 70–71
Corporate governance rules
 agency guidance on director's duties, 227
 director and other interlocks, 222–25
 directors' qualifications and duties, 219–21
 federally chartered institutions, 217–19
 FRB regulations, 226–27
 introduction, 217
 notice of change of director/senior executive officer, 221–22
Covered institutions, required filings, 248–49
Covered nonpublic banks, 250–51
Covered securities, 287–88
Covered transactions
 exempt from section 23A, 165–67
 qualitative restrictions on, 164
 under section 23A, 161, 163, 167–68
CRA compliance, 107

Credit card banks, 133, 179
Credit-related activities, 211
Credit risk
  Basel I, 315
  disclosures, 327
Criminal violations, against an IAP, 91–92
Critically undercapitalized institutions, 309, 311–12
Cross-affiliate netting arrangements, 163
CSBS nationwide agreements, 61
Cumulative preferred stock, 297, 303
Currency
  Federal Reserve Bank Notes, 10
  history of, 3–4
  issuance, U.S. bond holdings and, 7
Currency Act (1863), 1

D

Dealers, banks as, 269–70, 272–73
Dealing, national banks and, 270–71
Debt securities, 287
Deconsolidation requirements, 303
Demand deposits, 8, 9
De novo branches, 98, 104–05
De novo federal associations, director qualifications, 219–20
De novo savings associations, 15
Department of Housing and Urban Development, 23
Deposit insurance
  basic coverage, 44–46
  for commercial banks, 12
  coverage, 43
  federal, before the Reform Act, 36–37
  "free ride" and other issues, 39–40, 41
  introduction, 35–36
  premium disparity, 37–39
  Reform Act provisions, 41–43
  for savings associations, 15–16
Deposit Insurance Fund, 46
Deposit Insurance Funds Act (Funds Act) (1996), 39
Deposit insurance premiums, 310
Depositor preference, 80
Depository Institution Management Interlocks Act (1978)
  restrictions imposed by, 222
  violation of, 90

Depository institutions
  definition, 23
  evolution of, 6
  regulatory capital for, 292–93
Depository Institutions Deregulation and Monetary Control Act (1980) (1980 Act), 20–21
Depository Institutions Deregulation Committee (DIDC), 20–21
Depository organization, definition under Interlocks Act, 222
Deposit production, mergers for, 106–07
Deposit production offices (DPOs), 115, 116, 117
Depression, 11
Designated activities
  of FHCs, 137
  financial subsidiaries of national banks, 202
Designated reserve ratio (DRR), 37, 40, 42
Direct deposit payout, 80
Directors
  agency guidance on duties of, 227
  banking laws for, 218
  definition, 179
  notice of change of, 221–22
  qualifications and duties, 219–21
  restraints on interlocks of, 222–25
Direct tying, 190
Disclosures, of risk assessments and management, 326–28
Discount window loans, 35
Discrete legal entities, 66
Dispute resolution, holding companies and, 153–54
Dividends, 42
Domestic branch, 99, 115
Douglas Amendment, 21, 97
DRR. *See* Designated reserve ratio (DRR)
Dual banking system, 2, 18
Due on sale clauses, 32

E

Earnings
  of CAMELS rating, 56
  as CORE component, 71
Edge Act, 199

Electronic Data Gathering, Analysis, and Retrieval (EDGAR) system, 247
Electronic operations, branches and, 118–19
Eligible products, in combined-balance discount programs, 189
Employee benefit plans, 43
Employee stock option plan (ESOP), 171
Enforcement
  additional powers of FDIC, 93–95
  of agency orders, 93
  criminal violations, 91–92
  formal actions, 84–88
  informal actions, 83
  introduction, 82–83
  judicial review, 92
  removal and prohibition orders, 88–90
Equal deference, 153
Essential activities, 178
Examinations
  compliance, 50, 52
  coordination of, of state institutions, 59–65
  of holding companies, 65–73
  objectives of, 49
  process, 50
  reliance standards for state agencies, 63
  safety and soundness, 13, 50, 51
  scoring, 50–51
  specialty, 50, 53–58
  types of, 50
Exchange Act. *See* Securities Exchange Act (1934)
Excluded entities, 186
Executive officers
  definition, 179
  reports by, 183
  reports on credit to, 183
Exempt facility bonds, 271
Exemptive authority
  of the Board, 185–86
  OTS, 190–91
Exempt securities, under Uniform Act, 289
Exit meetings, of examiners, 71–72, 82
Exportation, 172–73, 177–78
Exposure at default (EAD), 322

F
Failed institutions, 79–82
Failing institutions acquisition provisions, 102
Family trusts, 46
Farm Credit Administration, 92
Farm Credit Banks, 92
FDIA
  1991 amendments, 74–75
  administration, 35
  definitions, 24
  insider loan rules, 183–84
  section 10(d), 60–61, 63
  section 11(c), 75, 76, 77
  section 18(d), 100
  section 18(m), 212
  section 24(j), 107–09
  section 27, 175
  section 28(c), 213
  section 32, 221
  section 38(f), 75
  section 42, 114
  section 44, 103–04
  section 46, 154, 204–06
  section 8(e), 89, 92
FDIC
  additional enforcement powers of, 93–95
  administration of insurance program, 12
  audit and reporting rules, 247–51
  as bank regulator, 13
  capital categories, 309
  as conservator, 77, 78–79
  conservator powers, 78
  creation of, 11, 35
  funding of, 12
  goals of, 14
  implementation of Reg W by, 208
  MFL issues and, 176–77
  part 363, 248–49
  power or obligation of, 79
  as receiver, 78–79
  as receiver of national banks, 74
  resolution of banks by, 80–81
  special examinations - 2002, 64
  special examinations - 2005, 64–65
  state bank subsidiaries and, 200

Index

on subsidiaries, 193
Tier 3 capital measure for market risk, 301
FDIC Improvement Act (FDICIA) (1991)
annual reporting and audit rules, 229, 230
audit and reporting rules, 247
on conservatorships and receiverships, 74–75
PCA and, 308–09
premium disparity and, 37
Federal associations
conversion to stock charter, 17
definition, 24
service corporations of, 209–12
Federal deposit insurance
for commercial banks, 12–14
before the Reform Act, 36–37
for savings banks, 14–15
Federal Deposit Insurance Act (1950). *See* FDIA
Federal Deposit Insurance Corporation. *See* FDIC
Federal Deposit Insurance Reform Act (Reform Act) (2005), 35
Federal Financial Examinations Council (FFEIC), 59
Federal Home Loan Bank, 92
Federal Home Loan Bank Act (FHL Bank Act) (1932), 15
Federal Home Loan Bank Board (FHLBB), 15–16, 22–23, 32, 74, 127
Federal Housing Finance Board, 23, 92
Federal Land Banks, 92
Federal regulators, 25–27
Federal Reserve Act (FRA), 10, 35, 100, 178–79
Federal Reserve Bank Notes, 10
Federal Reserve Board (Board)
definitions, 144–45
FHCs and, 138–39
holding companies and, 121, 126
on importance of capital, 291
new composition ratings, 66–69
powers from 1933 Banking Act, 122–25
on purposes of capital, 293
regulations, 226–27

Tier 3 capital measure for market risk, 301
on TPSs, 304–05
Federal Reserve District Banks, 10
Federal Reserve System (FRS), 8–11, 122, 159
Federal Savings and Loan Insurance Corporation (FSLIC), 15, 22–23, 36–37, 47, 81
Federal savings associations
banking laws for directors of, 218
branching laws and, 117–18
charters, 18–19
interest rates and, 175
preemption, 31–32,
securities brokerage activities and, 272
Federal savings bank charters, for MSBs, 18–19
Federal statutory requirements, for coordination of examinations, 60
Ferguson, Roger W. Jr., 294, 315
FFEIC Information Technology (IT) Examination Handbook, 54
FHL Bank Act (1932), 15
FHLMC, 23
Fidelity Federal Savings Loan Assn. v. de la Cuesta, 32
Fiduciary accounts, management of, 282
50 percent category, 299
Final dealer rules, 275, 279–80
Finance-related activities, 211
Financial Accounting Standards Board (FASB), 292
Financial activities, by FHCs, 136
Financial crisis, 1980-1994, 79–82
Financial holding companies (FHCs)
explained, 136–40
functional regulators and, 63
permissible powers, 201–02
regulatory capital for, 306–07
subsidiaries and, 194
Financial institutions, application of Securities Act to, 254, 262
Financial Institutions Reform, Recovery and Enforcement Act (FIRREA) (1989), 22–23, 36–37
primary federal regulators and, 25

Financial Interpretations (FASB), 303
Financial panics, 8–9
Financial reporting
    FDIC definition, 248
    FDIC rules, 247–51
    introduction, 229–30
    management certification in quarterly and annual reports, 245–47
Financial Services Roundtable, 109
Financial statements, audited, 248
Financial subsidiaries
    definition, 194
    of national banks, 201–04
    of state banks, 204–06
FIRREA. *See* Financial Institutions Reform, Recovery, and Enforcement Act (FIRREA)
First National Bank in Plant City v. Dickinson, 116–17
First National Bank of Philadelphia, 2
First National City Bank of New York, 282
Follow-up examinations, 63
Formal agreement, enforcement, 84
Fourth Quantitative Impact Study (QIS-4), 317, 318
Free ride, 39–40, 41, 42
Functional regulators, 63, 127, 138, 307

G
GAAP capital
    conversion of, to regulatory capital, 330–40
    vs. regulatory capital, 293
    standards for public companies, 292
Garn-St Germain Act (1982), 21, 134
General Accountability Office (GOA), study of Basel II implementation, 330
General banks, 321
General exemption, interlocks, 224
Generally accepted accounting principles (GAAP). *See* GAAP capital
Glass-Steagall Act
    banks and savings associations securities, 11
    banks as underwriters and dealers, 269–70
    common trust fund issues, 281–84
    section 21(a)(1), 271–72

GLBA
    affiliate transactions and, 160
    amendments to the Securities and Investments Acts, 285–86
    BHCs and, 22, 126
    broker-dealer provisions, 272–73
    common trust funds and, 281
    exclusion as securities, 286
    exclusion on investment companies, 286
    financial subsidiaries and, 194
    implementation of broker-dealer provisions, 276
    in insurance activities of banks, 31
    on new financial services by FHCs, 306
    preemption issues and, 150
    on safe harbors, 273
    section 121(b), 206
    section 20, 270
    section 32, 270
    sections 302 and 303, 196
    state anti-affiliation laws, 151–52
Good faith discussions, 82
Government Sponsored Enterprises (GSEs), 298
Gramm Leach Bliley Act (GLBA) (1999). *See* GLBA
Greenspan, Alan, 315, 325, 326
Group banks, 122
Group of Ten (G-10), 313

H
Historical overview
    1836-1863, 3–4
    1930s, 11–16
    bank and S&L holding companies, 21–27
    national banks, 1–3
    preemption, 27–32
    savings institutions, 4–11
    subsequent developments, 16–21
HOLA. *See* Home Owners' Loan Act (HOLA) (1933)
Holding companies
    BHCs, 122–27
    Change in Bank Control Act, 142–46
    definition under Interlocks Act, 222
    dispute resolution, 153–54
    early developments, 121–22

examination of, 65–72
financial, 136–41
insurance activities of savings associations, 149
McCarran-Ferguson Act, 150–51
mutual, 141–42
NARAB, 155
nonbank, 131–35
other provisions, 154–55
post-GLBA developments, 156–58
post-GLBA insurance activities of national banks, 148–49
post-GLBA S&LHCs, 129–31
preemption of state laws, 151
pre-GLBA insurance activities of national banks, 146–47
regulatory capital for, 302–08
S&LHCs, 127–28
standards for preemption of state insurance laws, 149–50
state anti-affiliate laws, 151–52
state laws restricting insurance activities, 152–53
Holding company affiliate, 122
Holding company reports, 249–50
Home Loan Banks, 15
Home Owners' Loan Act (HOLA) (1933)
branching by federal savings associations, 117–18
dual system for savings associations, 15
federal savings associations, 74, 175
federal savings associations regulations, 32
insider loan rules, 184
mutual to stock conversions, 16
OTS as conservator, 78
savings associations, 169
savings associations regulations, 23
tying restrictions and, 184–85, 190, 191
Home states, 61, 104
Host states, 61, 104, 107–08, 111–12

I

IAPs. *See* Institution-affiliates parties (IAPs)
Incidental powers, 146–47
Independent examinations, 62
Independent, NYSE and Nasdaq definition of, 237
Indictment, of an IAP, 91
Industrial loan companies (ILCs), 131, 134–35, 179
Industrywide prohibition, 92
Inflation index, 43
Information Technology (IT), examinations, 54
Insider loans under FRA
aggregate loan limit, 182
definition of *insiders*, 179–80
extension of rules to other institutions, 183–84
introduction, 178–79
loan limits, 180–81
other reports, 183
recordkeeping requirements, 182–83
Insiders
of affiliates, 182–83
definition, 179–80
of member banks, 182
Institution-affiliates parties (IAPs), 82–83, 94–95
Insurance, definition, 148–49
Insurance activities
financial subsidiaries of national banks, 203
state laws restricting, 152–53
Insurance affiliates, portfolio investments by, 137
Insurance customer protections, 154–55
Insured depository institution, 142, 145
Insured deposit transfer (IDT) transaction, 80–81
Interagency Consumer Compliance Rating System, 52
Interest, on demand deposits, 20
Interest rates
exportation of, 172–73
exportation of, by interstate banks, 177–78
Garn-St Germain Act (1982), 20–21
on intrastate transactions, 176
Interim final rules, 275
Interlocks, 222–25
Interlocks Act. *See* Depository Institution Management Interlocks Act (1978)

Internal control assessments, 248–49
Internal controls, management statements and auditor reports on, 243–45
Internal Revenue Code, 128, 271, 286
Interstate acquisitions, of S&LHCs, 130
Interstate banking
  before 1994, 102–03
  acquisitions for BHCs, 112–14
  branching, 103–12
  exportation of interest rates by, 177–78
  limitations on, 105–07
  Riegle-Neal I's provisions, 103–04
Interstate Banking and Branching Supervisory Protocol (the Protocol) (1995), 61
Intraday credit, 167
Investment Advisers Act (1940), 268–69
Investment Company Act (1940), 162, 268–69, 281
Investment Company Institute (ICI) v. Camp, 282–83
Investment Company Institute (ICI) v. Conover, 283–84
Investments, 137, 212
IRB approach, 320, 321–23

J
Joint examinations, 62
Judicial review, 92

L
LCBOs, 314, 315
Leverage ratio, 296–97, 328
Limited liability company (LLC), 195
Liquidity, of CAMELS rating, 56
Living trusts, 46
Loan production office (LPO), 115, 116–17
Loans
  aggregate limit, 182
  to directors and officers, 181
  limits for certain insiders, 180
  by subsidiaries, 180
Loans-to-one-borrower (LTOB), 181, 209
Long-term trusts, 124
Loss given default (LGD), 322
Low-quality assets, 164

M
Management
  of CAMELS rating, 55–56
  certification of information in reports, 245–47
  examiner meetings with, 71–72
Management official, definition under Interlocks Act, 223
Management reports, 248
Managing agency accounts, 282
Marketable securities transactions, 165
Market discipline, under Basel II, 325–28
Market risk, 301–02
  Basel I and, 314
Market terms requirement, 167–68
Marquette Nat. Bank v. First of Omaha Corp., 172, 173
Marshall, Justice, 2–3
Martin, William McChesney Jr., 123, 125
Massachusetts Commissioners of Insurance and Banking, 157
Massachusetts Consumer Protection Act, 156, 157–58
Maturity (M), 322
Maximum LTOB, 181
McCarran Ferguson Act, 30, 150–51
McCulloch v. Maryland, 2
McFadden Act (1927)
  amendments, 110–12
  branches and, 97–100, 104
  branching restrictions of, 11
  definition of *branch*, 115
Member banks
  affiliates of, 161–62
  disclosure of credit from, 183
  insiders of, 182
  subsidiaries of, 162
Memorandum of understanding (MOU), 83
Merchant banking, 136–37, 203
Mergers
  Bank Merger Act, 101, 104
  basic transaction authority and, 104
  for deposit production, 106–07
  interstate, 104
  interstate banking and, 98–102
  under Riegle-Neal I, 101–02

Messenger services, 117
Mid-tier stock holding company, 141–42
Minimum capital requirements, under Basel II, 320–21
Minimum required capital (MRC), 317
Ministerial activities, 178
Model Cooperative Agreement, 63
Money laundering violations, 94
Money market deposit accounts, 21
Mortgage loans, due on sale clauses, 32
Mortgages, 298, 299
Most favored lending (MFL) laws, 172, 173–78
MSBs. *See* Mutual savings banks (MSBs)
    deposit insurance and, 14
Multi-bank holding companies, 123–24
    restrictions on, 21
Multiple S&LHCs, 128
Multi-state foreign banks, 63
Mutual funds, 281–86
Mutual holding companies (MHCs), 141–42
Mutual savings and loan holding companies, banking laws for directors of, 218
Mutual savings banks (MSBs)
    creation of, 4
    Federal charters for, 18–19
    mutual to stock conversions, 18
    state-chartered, 5
Mutual savings institutions, 16
    conversion to savings and loan type institutions, 16–17

N
NARAB, 155
Nasdaq Stock Market, Inc. (Nasdaq), 237
    governance rules, 239
National Association of Registered Agents and Brokers. *See* NARAB
National Association of Securities Dealers (NASD), 230, 234
National Association of State Insurance Commissioners (NAIC), 63
National Bank Act (1933), 74, 104, 172
National Bank Consolidation and Merger Act (1918), 101–02, 112

National Banking Act (1864), 2, 3, 6–8, 146–47, 172
National Bank Notes, 7
National banks
    banking laws for directors of, 218
    definition, 24
    deposit insurance and, 12
    director qualifications, 219
    financial subsidiaries of, 201–04
    history of, 1–3
    MFL laws and, 173–74
    post-GLBA insurance activities of, 148–49
    preemption, 29–31
    pre-GLBA insurance activities of, 146–47
    relocation of main office, 102–03
    restrictions from National Bank Act, 9
    securities activities, 11–12
    securities activities of, 270–71
    subsidiaries of, 195–99
    supervision of, 10
National Commission of Fraudulent Financial Reporting (Treadway Commission), 230
National Credit Union Administration (NCUA), 43, 92
National Housing Act (NHA), 23, 131
Nationally traded securities, 287
National Mentary Commission, 10
National Securities Markets Improvement Act (NSMIA) (1996), 287
Nationwide Cooperative Agreement (Cooperative Agreement) (1997), 61
Nationwide Cooperative Agreement for Multi-State Trust Institutions (1999), 63
Nationwide Federal/State Supervisory Agreement (Supervisory Agreement), 61, 62
Negotiable orders of withdrawal. *See* NOW accounts
New Accord. *See* New Basel Capital Accord (New Accord)
New Basel Capital Accord (New Accord), 319
New York Stock Exchange (NYSE), 230, 234, 237

governance rules, 238–39
1980 Act, 20–21
Nominating committees, 240–41
Nonbank activities, 126
Nonbank holding companies, 131–35
Nonbanking agencies, as regulators, 25–27
Non-branch facilities, 114–17
Non-covered securities, under Securities Act, 288–89
Non-FDIC supervised institutions, enforcement action against, 94–95
Non-ministerial activities, 178
North American Securities Administration Association, 289
Notice of proposed rulemaking (NPR), 109, 317, 318, 330
Notice procedure, 212
NOW accounts, 131–32
  for banks and savings institutions, 19–21

O

OCC
  changes to registration rules, 261–62
  creation of, 1–2
  definition of *acting in concert*, 145
  FRA and, 10
  on good faith discussions, 82
  Handbook on Collective Investment Funds, 285
  MFL laws and, 176
  preemption and, 29, 31, 149–50
  registration rules of securities issues, 262–63
  regulations for collective investment funds, 284–85
  responsibilities of national bank directors, 221
  Tier 3 capital measure for market risk, 301
Off-balance-sheet assets, 299–301
Office of the Comptroller of the Currency. *See* OCC
Office of Thrift Supervision (OTS), 18–19, 23, 121, 126
Olson, Mark W., 33
100 percent category, 299
Open bank assistance (OBA), 81

Operating subsidiaries
  definition, 194
  of national banks, 195–96, 197
  of savings associations, 209
Operational risk, 323–24
Opt-in banks, 320–21
Organization, definition under Interlocks Act, 222
Organizational structure, as CORE component, 70
Organization for Economic Cooperation and Development (OECD) countries, 298
OTS. *See* Office of Thrift Supervision (OTS)
  changes to registration rules, 261–62
  conservator powers, 78
  examiner meetings, 72
  exemptive authority, 190–91
  on federal branches, 118
  MFL laws and, 176
  notice procedure and, 212
  regulation of S&LHCs, 130
  regulations for collective investment funds, 284–85
  regulatory implementation, 170
  on S&LHCs, 69
  securities rules, 263
Ownership rights, in deposit accounts, 44
Oxford Provident Building Association (Philadelphia County), 5

P

Panics, financial, 8–9
Parallel run, of Basel II, 316–17, 318
Parent company, 122
Payable-on-death (POD) accounts, 45–46
PCOAB, 231
Permissible activities, of service corporations of federal associations, 211–12
Person, definition, 145
Philadelphia Savings Fund Society, 5
Pillars, of Basel II, 319–28
Plain vanilla accounts, 44
POD accounts, 45–46

Portfolio investments, 203
  by insurance affiliates, 137
Possibility of default (PD), 322
Post-GLBA activities, by S&LHCs, 129–30
Powell, Donald E., 40
Preemption, 27, 29–32
  state insurance law standards, 149–50
  of state laws, 151
Preferred stock, 287
Premium disparity, 37–39
Premiums, Reform Act, 41
Primary federal regulators (PFRs), 25, 26, 27, 126, 142, 171
Principal shareholders, definition, 179–80
Private clearinghouses, 4
Private deposit insurance, 9
Private placements, 288
Prohibited activities, financial subsidiaries of national banks, 203
Prohibited asset purchases, 168
Prompt Corrective Action (PCA), 74, 75
Prompt corrective action (PCA), 88, 99–100, 308–13, 328
Proposed broker rules, 276
Proposed Regulation B, 276, 278–79
Provident Institution for Savings (Boston), 5
Public accounting firms, auditor independence, 241–43
Public companies
  banks as, 250
  GAAP capital standards for, 292
Public Company Accounting Oversight Board (PCOAB), 229
Purchase and assumption (P&A) transactions, 80

Q

QTL tests, 128
Qualified beneficiaries, on POD accounts, 45
Qualified institutional buyer (QIB), 260
Qualified institutional investors, 260–61
Qualified thrift lender (QTL), 118, 128

R

Ratios, capital, 295–97
Ready market securities transactions, 165–66
Real Estate Lending and Appraisals, 31
Real estate mortgage investment conduits (REMICS), 298
Real estate related services, 211
Receiver
  FDIC as, 78–79
  general grounds for appointment of, 76–77
  powers and obligations of FDIC as, 79
  powers of, 77–79
Receivership estate, 77–78
Receiverships, 73–79
Recordkeeping requirements, under Reg O, 182–83
Rediscounting, 10
Referral Fee Prohibition, 157
Referral Prohibition, 157
Referrals, third-party brokerage arrangements and, 277
Reform Act
  basic provisions of, 41–43
  federal deposit insurance before, 36–37
  proposal of, 40
Registered institutions, under section 12(i), 266, 268
Registration issues, for trust funds, 281
Regulation B proposal, 276
Regulation O (Reg O), 179–84
Regulations, branching, 99
Regulation S-K, 255
Regulation S-X, 255
Regulation W (Reg W), 160, 161, 170, 207–08
Regulatory capital
  calculation of, 297
  conversion of GAAP capital to, 330–40
  for depository institutions, 292–93
  vs. GAAP capital, 293
  for holding companies, 302–08
  source of current standards, 293–95
  structure of, 295–97
Reich, John, 225
Relationship, as CORE component, 70

356 Index

Remote service units (RSUs), 115
Removal and prohibition orders, 88–90
Reserve ratio, 41–42
Resolution, of the institution, 73
Resolution Trust Corporation (RTC), resolution of savings associations by, 81
Responsible agency, 101
Restricted core capital elements, 303–04
Retirement accounts, 43
Reverse repurchase agreements, 171
Reverse tying, 186–87, 191
Revised Framework. *See* Basel II project
Revocable trusts, 45–46
RFI/C(D) rating, 66–69
Riegle-Neal Amendments Act (Riegle-Neal II) (1997), 107–08, 177
Riegle-Neal Interstate Branching and Banking Efficiency Act (Riegle-Neal I) (1994)
  CSBS and, 61
  exportation of interest rates and, 177
  interstate branching and, 98
  provisions relating to interstate transactions, 103–04
Risk
  Basel I and, 314–16
  under Basel II, 320–28
Risk-based capital ratios, 295–96
Risk categories, for S&LHCs, 70
Riskless principal transactions, 279–80
Risk management, 66–68
Risk weight categories, under Basel I, 297–302
Risk-weighted assets, 295
RMSA test, interlocks and, 223
Routine activities, 178
RSUs, 118–19
Runs on banks, 9

S

S&LHCs. *See* Savings and loan holding companies (S&LHCs)
S&L Holding Company Act (S&LHCA) (1959), 22, 69
Safe deposit corporations, 198
Safe harbors, 152, 273–75, 278–79

Safety and soundness directives, 87–88
Safety and soundness examinations, 13, 50, 51
Safety and soundness, of covered transactions, 164
Safety net, 35–36
SAIF. *See* Savings Association Insurance Fund (SAIF)
Sarbanes-Oxley Act (SOX) (2002)
  auditing and, 229, 230
  disclosures and, 328
  effects of, on public and nonpublic banks, 250–51
  for publicly traded companies, 233–37
  section 3, 266
  section 302(a), 245–46
  section 906, 246–47
Savings accounts, interest, 20
Savings and Loan Act Amendments (1967), 128
Savings and loan holding companies (S&LHCs)
  after GLBA, 129–31
  examinations, 69
  legislation, 127–28
  regulatory capital for, 307–08
S&L Holding Company Act and, 22
Savings Association Insurance Fund (SAIF), 23, 36, 37–42
Savings associations
  application of Exchange Act to, 265–66
  application of sections 23A and 23B to, 169–72
  branching laws applicable to, 117–19
  capital standards for, 295–302
  definition, 24
  Federal charters and deposit insurance for, 15–16
  history of, 5–6
  insurance activities of, 149
  MFL laws and, 174–78
  mutual to stock conversions, 16–17
  OTS definition, 171
  regulatory changes in, 23
  resolution during 1980-1994 financial crisis, 79, 81–82
  RTC resolution of, 81

securities activities, 11–12
  subsidiaries of, 208–14
  tying arrangements and, 189–91
Savings banks, Federal deposit insurance for, 14–15
Savings institutions
  creation of, 4
  Federal Reserve System, 8–11
  National Banking Act (1864), 6–8
  savings associations, 5–6
  state-chartered MSBs, 5
  temporary exemption for, 280
Scoring, examinations, 50–51
Secondary federal regulators, 25, 27
Section 23A/23B, of FRA, 160–72
Section 24 subsidiaries
  definition, 194
  of state banks, 199–200
Securities Act (1933)
  antifraud provisions, 261
  application of, to financial institutions, 262
  application to BHCs, 255
  application to financial institutions, 254, 262
  definition of *small business*, 256
  exempt securities under section 3(b), 259
  exempt transactions under section 4, 259–60
  general provisions, 254–55
  objectives, 253–54
  OCC, 262–63
  processing the registration statement, 257
  qualified institutional investors, 260–61
  registration, 255–56
  registration requirements and, 11–12
  requirements information, 256–57
  revisions to securities offering rules, 261–62
  securities excluded from registration, 258–59
  shelf registration, 260
Securities activities
  of banks. *See* Bank securities activities
  of national banks, 270–71

Securities and Exchange Commission (SEC)
  exchange rules for listed companies, 233–37
  final dealer rules, 275, 279–80
  functional regulators and, 127
  proposed broker rules, 276
  regulation by, 63
  on safe harbors, 273
Securities Exchange Act (1934)
  agency rules under section 12(i), 266–68
  application to individual institutions, 265–66
  audit and reporting rules, 229
  definition of *broker* and *dealer*, 272–73
  prohibited asset purchases and, 168
  registration, 264
  reporting, 264–65
  section 29, 280
  termination of regulation, 264
Securities lending transactions, 280
Securities market, financial panics and, 9
Securities offerings
  rule revisions, 261–62
  state regulation of, 287–89
Securities services, 211
Self-appointment, 75
Senate Banking Committee, 20, 123–25
Senior executive officer, notice of change of, 221–22
Sensitivity to market risk, of CAMELS rating, 56
Separation restrictions, 157–58
Service corporations
  of federal associations, 209–12
  of state savings associations, 212–14
Shelby, Richard, 330
Shelf registration, 260
Shell banks, 105, 113
Shortfalls, 9
Significantly undercapitalized institutions, 309, 310
Sister bank exemption, 165
Size test, interlocks and, 223
Small businesses, Securities Act and, 255–56

Index

Small business investment companies, 199
Small market share exemption, interlocks, 224
Smiley v. Citibank (South Dakota), N.A., 173
Sophisticated investor exception, 285
Special purpose entity (SPE), 303
Specialty examinations, 50, 53–58, 62
Spence Act, 22, 127
SRO, rules on audit committees and governance provisions, 237–41
Standard maximum deposit insurance amount (SMDIA), 43
State agencies, reliance standards for examinations, 63
State anti-affiliation laws, 151–52
State associations, definition, 24
State banking tax, 7–8
State banks
  definition, 24
  demand deposits and, 8
  deposit insurance and, 12
  financial subsidiaries of, 204–06
  MFL laws and, 174–78
  subsidiaries of, 199–200
State-chartered banks, 3
State-chartered MSBs, 5
State-Federal Working Group, 62
State housing corporations, 198
State institutions
  coordination of examinations of, 59–65
  receiverships and conservatorships, 77
State insurance laws, preemption, 30
State insurance system, 4
State law issues, interstate banking and, 107–10
State laws
  exemptions under, 289
  preemption of, 151
  restricting insurance activities, 152–53
  of securities offerings, 287–89
State member banks
  branching of, 100
  deposit insurance and, 12
  in the system, 10
State nonmember banks
  branching of, 100
  deposit insurance and, 12–13

State savings associations
  branching laws and, 119
  service corporations of, 212–14
Statutory exemption, interlocks, 224
Statutory subsidiaries
  definition, 194
  of national banks, 198–99
Stock charters, 16
Stock holding company (SHC), 141–42
Stock institutions, vs. savings associations, 6
Stock savings and loan associations, in 1950s, 17
Subsidiaries
  as affiliates, 171–72, 195
  financial, of national and state banks, 201–08
  introduction, 193–94
  loans by, 180
  of member banks, 162
  of national banks, 195–99
  of savings associations, 208–14
  of state banks, 199–200
  types of, 194–95
Suffolk Bank of Boston, 4
Supervisory agreements, 84
Supervisory Committee, 293–94
Supervisory review process, under Basel II, 324–25
Supplemental capital, 297
Survey method, 182

T

Temporary suspension orders, 90
Termination of insurance, 93–94
Third party attribution rule, 170
Thrift certificates, 134
Tier 1 capital, 297
Tier 2 capital, 297
Tier 3 capital, 301–02
Tiers, of CMPs, 86–87
Tiffany v. National Bank of Missouri, 173–74
Time deposits, 11
Title insurance, 148
Traditional bank product exception, 187
Transactional exemptions, under Uniform Act, 289

Index

Transactions, attribution of, 170
Transactions with affiliates (TWA), 206–08
Transitional credit, 42–43
Treadway Commission, 230
Treasury Department, 1
Treasury notes, replacement of, 10
Trust accounts, OCC and OTS on, 284–85
Trust activities, examinations, 53
Trust funds, 281–86
Trust preferred securities (TSPs), 303–06
Trusts, 5, 124–25
Trust services, securities transactions and, 277
20 percent category, 298
Two-track approach, 275
Tying arrangements
　direct tying, 190
　introduction, 184–85
　reverse tying, 186–87, 191
　savings associations, 189–91
　section 106, 185–89

U

Undercapitalized institutions, 309, 310
Underwriters, banks as, 269–70
Underwriting, national banks and, 270–71
Uniform Financial Institutions Rating System (UFIRS), 55
Uniform Interagency Trust Rating System (UITRS), 53
Uniform Securities Act (Uniform Act) (1956), 289
Unitary holding companies, 22
Unitary S&LHCs, 128
U.S. banks
　application of Basel II to, 319
　implementation of Basel II by, 317–19
U.S. bonds, required purchase by national banks, 6–7

V

Value-at-risk (VaR) measurement, 302
Voting permits, of BHCs, 122–23

W

Waiting Period Restriction, 157
Well and adequately capitalized institutions, 310
Well capitalized institutions, 309, 310
West Virginia Insurance Sales Consumer Protection Act, 156, 157–58
Wildcat banks, 3–4
Williams, Julie L., 50

Z

Zero basis point premium rate, 40
Zero percent category, 298

About the Author

Harding de C. Williams is a graduate of Middlebury College and the University of Michigan Law School. He is the author of *Directors and Trustees Handbook,* written in 1990 and updated quarterly through January 2003 and editor of three editions of *Bank Director's Manual,* both for the former National Council of Savings Institutions and its successor, America's Community Bankers.

He was Counsel for the Association of Financial Services Holding Companies and General Counsel for the former National Savings and Loan League. Before joining the National League, he was Washington Representative, Industrial Relations for the National Association of Manufacturers and Manager of the Washington Office of the Del Monte Corporation. A member of the District of Columbia Bar, Mr. Williams writes extensively on corporate governance, banking, and accounting issues.